BASIC

A Guide to
Structured Programming

BASIC

A Guide to
Structured Programming

Thomas A. Dwyer
Margot Critchfield
J. Michael Shore
University of Pittsburgh

Michael S. Kaufman

Houghton Mifflin Company   **Boston**
Dallas   Geneva, Illinois   Lawrenceville, New Jersey   Palo Alto

Kew Garden Hill

The photos in Figures 1.2 and 1.5 are courtesy of Radio Shack. All other photos, and the color photo for the cover, are by Margot Critchfield. The program that produced the cover art is described in Section 9.6 of this book.

Use of the AT&T logo is courtesy of AT&T Communications.

Use of the Commodore logo is by permission of Commodore Electronics, Limited.

Use of the Heathkit logo is courtesy of Heath, Inc.

Use of the IBM logo on pages 7, 9, 10, 16, 49, 51, 58, 135, 136, 152, 168, 209, 210, 223, 224, 230, 231, 233, 259, 264, 269 is by courtesy of International Business Machines Corporation.

Use of the Kaypro logo is courtesy of Kaypro Corporation.

Use of the Radio Shack logo is courtesy of Radio Shack, A Division of Tandy Corporation.

Use of the Zenith logo is courtesy of Zenith Electronics Corporation.

Printed in the U.S.A.

Library of Congress Catalog Card Number: 84-61356

ISBN: 0-395-35653-9

BCDEFGHIJ-SM-898765

11/27/2000

Contents

Preface

In 1980, a friend of ours adopted a 5 pound "shepherd-mix" puppy from the local animal shelter. He promptly named him BASIC, and then spent the months ahead explaining to people that the pup's name wasn't all that strange, especially when you knew that it was also the name of a computer programming language.

By 1984, two noticeable changes had taken place. BASIC weighed in at 90 pounds plus, and most people who were told his name smiled and said "Oh, yes—just like the computer programming language."

The level of people's awareness of the computer culture has increased even more dramatically in recent years. In particular, the number of persons who are familiar with the programming language BASIC now numbers in the millions, and it's growing at an astonishing rate. There may soon be as many people acquainted with BASIC programming as there are with the three R's.

The purpose of this book is to help students join this group, but in a rather special way. Our goal is to guide beginning programmers in mastering the art and science of *professional* BASIC programming, but without forsaking the informal aspect of BASIC that makes its use such a satisfying experience.

This goal presents some problems, of course. How does one reconcile the precision demanded by professionalism with the informality of BASIC, an informality deliberately built into the language so that computer programming might be accessible to beginners of all ages and backgrounds? This dilemma is akin to that faced by the flight instructor who knows that fledgling pilots will never become real professionals without discipline—and lots of it. But the same instructor knows that to try and communicate the hundreds of techniques that define that discipline during the first few hours of instruction is an exercise in futility. While learning to program may not be quite as traumatic an experience as learning to fly, the same kind of futility can easily be experienced by novice programmers who are given too many techniques too soon.

Our approach to resolving this dilemma has been to organize the content and style of the book in two parts. Part I (Chapters 1 through 4) introduces the fundamental features of BASIC in a relaxed, low-key manner. These opening chapters also contain numerous short but useful examples, written for the most part in minimal BASIC. While short examples do not permit meaningful discussion of the modern concept of structured programming, they allow one to quickly gain the experience that is vital to understanding the philosophy behind this (and other) techniques of professional programming.

Part II of the book (Chapters 5 through 12) is called "Professional BASIC." In addition to introducing the many advanced features of extended

BASIC, it emphasizes structured problem solving and structured program design. These ideas appear throughout the book, but formal discussions of the techniques involved are reserved for the later chapters. By this time the student will have had time to become comfortable with the many procedural details that seem so complicated at first, but that soon become second nature. The techniques of structured program design can then be introduced, not as isolated theory, but as powerful aids in the development of new programs that go beyond the limits traditionally associated with first courses.

In particular, Part II illustrates the use of structured design methodology in connection with programs related to statistical grade analysis and string manipulation (Chapter 6); modern searching and sorting techniques (Chapters 7 and 8); simulations, games, and graphics (Chapter 9); menu-driven software, data encryption, and word processing (Chapter 10); data processing and sequential file manipulation (Chapter 11); and random access files and database programs (Chapter 12). A series of colored headings is used in the margins of these chapters to show the connection between the structured design of specific examples and the general principles of design discussed in the text.

The principal dialect of BASIC used throughout the book is Microsoft Disk Extended BASIC, which is very similar to BASIC PLUS. Microsoft BASIC is available on all the Radio Shack TRS-80 and most Commodore microcomputers; the Apple II, IIe, IIc, and Macintosh; the IBM PC and PC Jr; and microcomputer systems that use either the CP/M or MS-DOS operating systems (for example, Tandy, Zenith, Heathkit, Monroe, DEC Rainbow, AT&T, Sanyo, and Kaypro). BASIC PLUS is used on the time-sharing systems supplied by the Digital Equipment Corporation (for example, the PDP-11 and VAX series) and on the DEC 350 personal computer. When the text discusses features that apply to a specific computer, the logo of that computer manufacturer (for instance, IBM, Tandy, or Apple) appears in color in the margin.

To help support the general discussions in the text, and the more than 150 program examples used to illustrate these discussions, the book contains numerous exercises and programming problems. Those designated as *Exercises* are paper-and-pencil explorations. Those called *Lab Exercises* serve as guides to doing work directly on a computer. In addition, each chapter ends with a comprehensive summary, followed by a collection of more demanding problems and projects.

Most of the projects are connected with writing programs that have real applications. The principal piece of advice we would offer anyone is to do as many of these projects as possible on either a home or school computer, allowing plenty of time to experiment. Also talk to others, and share ideas. Then experiment some more. You can't hurt anything, but if you persevere with this stratagem, you're in for a treat. Not only will things get easier, but they'll take on a fascination that will return your investment of time and energy many times over.

Acknowledgements

The authors wish to thank Sherrilyn Reiter, who typed much of the manuscript and special technical material in the appendices. We are grateful to the many reviewers whose valuable suggestions helped shape the book's content and pedagogical style. Particular thanks go to Martha Baxter of Mesa Community College, Louis A. DeAcetis of Bronx Community College, John J. DiElsi of Mercy College, Wesley Fasnacht of West Chester State College, June Fordham of Prince George's Community College, James Gips of Boston College, John B. Lane of Edinboro State College, C. Gardner Mallonee II of Essex Community College, Theodore V. Smith of Broward Community College, and Kenneth W. Veatch of San Antonio College.

T.A.D.

M.C.

J.M.S.

M.S.K.

About the Authors

Thomas Dwyer is Professor of Computer Science at the University of Pittsburgh. He is coauthor with Margot Critchfield of a dozen books on computing, including *CP/M and the Personal Computer, A Bit of IBM BASIC, A BIT of Applesoft BASIC,* and *Structured Program Design with TRS-80 BASIC.*

Margot Critchfield holds her Ph.D. from the University of Pittsburgh where she teaches computer programming.

J. Michael Shore teaches computing at the University of Pittsburgh and Taylor Allderdice High School.

Michael Kaufman is a graduate of the Harvard Law School and is presently practicing law in New York.

PART

I

Informal BASIC

## CHAPTER ONE

Getting Acquainted with a Computer

NEW TOPICS INTRODUCED IN CHAPTER 1

- *Digital computers*
- *Microcomputer systems*
- *Central processor/memory components*
- *Floppy disks*
- *Login procedures*
- *Modems*
- *Entering and running BASIC programs*

- *Personal computers*
- *Input/output components*
- *Mass-storage components*
- *Time-sharing systems*
- *Acoustic couplers*
- *BASIC interpreters and compilers*
- *Correcting errors in programs*

1.1 The Plan for Part I

A good starting place for any book on computing is to try to answer the question: What can a computer do? There are thousands of answers to this question, but in general they all boil down to this: A computer can do those things that can be explained to it in terms of instruction sets called *computer programs*.

Generally speaking, there are two kinds of computer programs. First, there are customized programs written by the person using the computer (or by a consultant the user has hired) to do something special—something of unique interest to that user. Second, there are "off-the-rack" or packaged programs of a more general nature. These are of greatest value to users whose needs match the capabilities built into the packages by their original designers.

Three examples of packaged programs will be shown later in this book. One is an electronic spreadsheet program, shown in Chapter 9. The second is a word-processing program, discussed in Chapter 10 (where you'll also be shown how to write your own simplified word-processing program). The third is a database-management program, illustrated in Chapter 12.

The primary purpose of this book, however, is to show you how to write your own customized programs, using a computer programming language called BASIC. It's something like showing a hi-fi enthusiast how to assemble a customized stereo system. Selecting and interfacing the components for such a system takes professional know-how, and not everyone will want (or be able) to go this route. But when you consider the level of insight, personalized control, and pride of accomplishment associated with the customized approach, this option has a lot more going for it than anyone might suspect.

The goal of Part I (the first four chapters of the book) is to help a beginner get started programming in BASIC with a minimum of fuss. For that reason, these chapters say very little about the theory of program design (that's coming in Part II). The idea is to get you acquainted with small, but real, programs that are geared to taking the mystery out of programming as soon as possible.

The best strategy for making this plan work will be to mix "off-line" preparation with "on-line" practice. The term *on-line* means working at the keyboard of a computer (or a terminal connected to a computer), entering and executing programs *interactively,* that is, in a manner that lets you immediately see the results of your work on the computer's display device.

To guide you in preparing for on-line work, the text is sprinkled with self-study sections called *Exercises.* For example, Exercise 2.1 is the first exercise of Chapter 2. It is based on material in the first part of Chapter 2, and it helps prepare for the actual computing work that follows.

Directions for on-line experimentation are given in the form of *Lab Exercises.* Each lab exercise is associated with a program that (like all the other programs in the book) has been given a unique file name. For example, Lab Exercise 2.1 (file name ARITH) is the first lab exercise in Chapter 2, and it guides you in working on-line with a program called ARITH. (The rules for inventing file names will be explained in Section 2.5.)

There is also a collection of programming projects at the end of each chapter. In general, these are best approached as a combination of off-line planning and on-line experimentation, repeated in a cycle that emphasizes both aspects of program design.

Off-line planning and documentation   On-line testing and experimentation

1.2 Types of Computers

The full name for the kind of computer we will study is "general-purpose digital computer." From now on we'll refer to such machines simply as *computers,* which is what everybody does anyway. Although at one time there was considerable attention given to nondigital computers, called *analog* machines (including slide rules), today just about all computing activity is done on digital machines. (The reason why the word digital is used will be seen in Section 6.2.)

Digital computers come in many sizes and shapes, but there are two general types you are most likely to encounter: microcomputers and time-sharing computers.

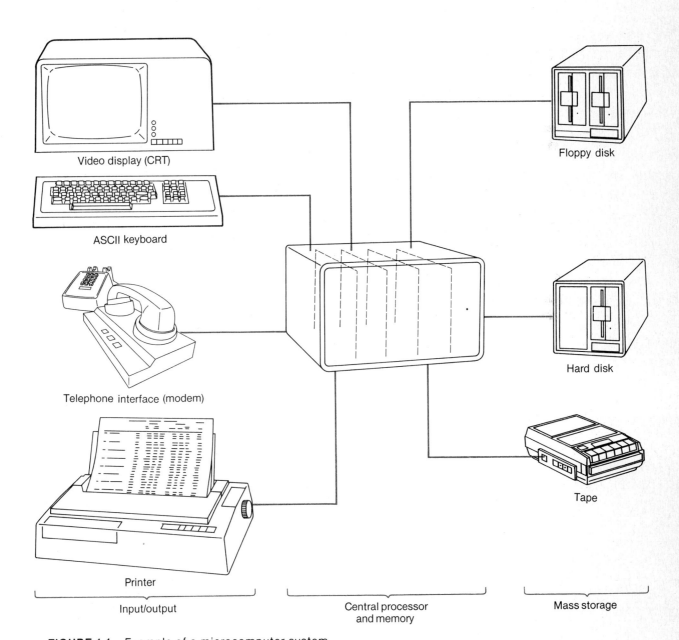

Video display (CRT)

ASCII keyboard

Telephone interface (modem)

Printer

Floppy disk

Hard disk

Tape

Input/output

Central processor and memory

Mass storage

FIGURE 1.1   Example of a microcomputer system

Microcomputer Systems

Microcomputers (also known as personal computers) first appeared in the early 1970s. Today they are used by literally millions of people. A better term for micro (or personal) computer is *microcomputer system*. It is called a system because it consists of several parts, or *components,* that work together. As Figure 1.1 shows, there can be quite a number of these components, but they can all be grouped into three categories: *input/output* components, *central-processor/ memory* components, and *mass storage* components.

The input/output (also called I/O) components allow the user to communicate with the machine. For input, you usually use a keyboard to "talk" to the computer, typing in the programs (sets of instructions) that tell the computer what you want it to do. In this book, you will learn how to express such instructions as statements in a language called BASIC (*Beginner's All-purpose Symbolic Instruction Code*). BASIC instructions are stored in the computer's memory, along with any *data* (numbers or alphabetical symbols) that the program is to work on. The central processing unit (CPU) of the machine then manipulates this data* according to the program's instructions. The results of this processing are displayed on an output device—usually a video display or a printer.

Section 1.3 will show photographs of several microcomputer systems. They can all be called *microcomputer* systems, since the central processing unit of each uses a *microprocessor chip.* This is a thin slice of silicon on which thousands of circuits are engraved, placing all the power of general-purpose computing within low-cost desk-top units. You'll also notice that the microcomputer systems shown in these photos have *floppy disks* for mass storage. Floppy disks are circular pieces of magnetically coated plastic on which both programs and data can be stored for future use. We will have more to say about disks in Section 2.5 and Chapter 11.

Time-Sharing Computer Systems

The second type of computer that you may use is a machine large enough to require a room all to itself. The machine may be close at hand, or it may be miles away. Such machines can be controlled by several users, each one working at a separate terminal. (The word *terminal* refers to a combination of a keyboard input device and a video or printer-like output device.) However, the terminals are hardly ever in the same room as the computer. This is no problem, since two-way communication with a computer can take place over long cables or telephone lines. The setup looks something like that shown on page 7.

With such an arrangement, many people can be given the illusion that they are simultaneously communicating with the central computer. The process that makes this possible is called *time sharing.*

How does time sharing work? The computer carries out its operations at such tremendous speed that it can give you enough computing time to keep you busy in a fraction of a minute. The rest of that minute can go to the other users (*user* means anyone working at an on-line terminal). The situation is something like that of a stockbroker taking telephone orders from several customers at the same time. If the stockbroker could switch back and forth from one telephone to

---

Data is the plural of *datum.* However, through usage, the word data has become accepted as being both singular *and* plural: *this data* and *these data* can both be used. This is one of the many changes that computers have brought to the English language.

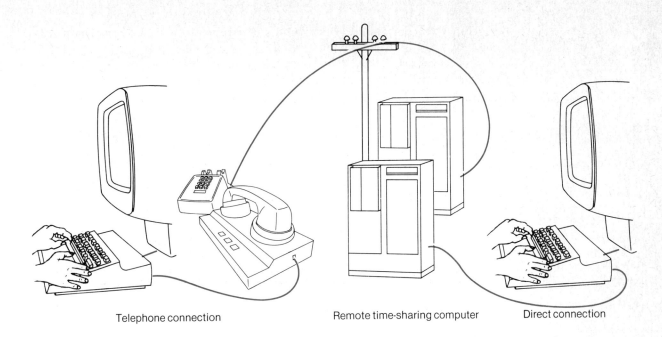

Telephone connection   Remote time-sharing computer   Direct connection

another fast enough, each customer would think that he or she was getting the stockbroker's full attention. The computer *is* that fast; you think it's talking only to you.

To make things clearer, let's consider the two types of computer systems separately. You need read only the section that deals with the type of computer you have (Section 1.3 for microcomputers, Section 1.4 for time-sharing computers).

1.3   Using a Microcomputer: Procedures for the TRS-80, Apple, and IBM Micros

Radio Shack

APPLE

IBM

Getting a microcomputer ready for BASIC programming is usually a simple procedure. It consists of two steps.

1. Turn on the power to all components in the system.
2. Load a special program called the BASIC interpreter.

Step 1 can be made even easier by having all the components plugged into a switched multiple-outlet box (110-volt ac). Then, if you leave the power switches for all the components in their ON position, you can turn the entire system on or off with the switch on the outlet box. (Some manufacturers may advise against this. If so, follow their recommendations.)

The exact procedure for step 2 depends on whether you are using a computer system with floppy disks or not. If you are, then a BASIC *system* disk—a disk that contains the BASIC interpreter—must be inserted into the computer's primary disk drive. On some systems, if you insert the system disk and close the drive door before turning the power on, step 2 will take place automatically after step 1. If you *don't* use disks, BASIC is usually stored in a part of the computer called ROM (*Read Only Memory*). In this case, it's not necessary to take any special action in step 2. In all cases, be sure to read the manual for your specific system before you do any of this.

Figures 1.2, 1.3, and 1.4 show the procedures for three popular microcomputer systems. Figure 1.5 shows a more advanced microcomputer system.

Radio Shack

FIGURE 1.2   The Radio Shack TRS-80 Model 4P. After turning the power on and inserting the system disk in the leftmost drive, you load BASIC by pressing the reset button, then typing the date and time. You then type BASIC and press ⟨enter⟩ three times, at which point you're ready to enter a BASIC program.

APPLE

FIGURE 1.3   The procedure for starting an Apple II, IIc, or IIe computer varies. On some models, BASIC is stored in ROM (Read Only Memory); you start it by pressing the ⟨control⟩ and B keys simultaneously. Other models of the Apple store BASIC on disk. Read your manual to see how to handle this. In either case, if you see the symbol], you're all set to use Applesoft BASIC. If you see the symbol ⟩, then type FP (floating point) followed by ⟨return⟩. You should then see the] symbol.

FIGURE 1.4 You start the IBM PC by placing the system disk in drive A on the left, and then turning the power on. When you see a startup message on the screen, press the ⟨enter⟩ key (marked ↵) twice (or give the date and time). When you see the prompt "A⟩", type BASICA ⟨enter⟩. Now you're ready to enter BASIC programs. The same procedure applies to the Tandy 2000 computer shown in Figure 1.5, since it is really a "superset" of the IBM.

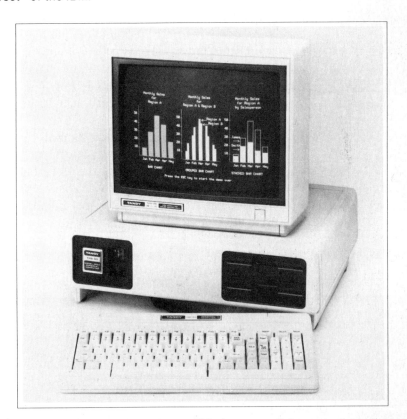

FIGURE 1.5 The Tandy 2000 computer. This is a powerful personal computer with a very fast CPU, large-capacity disk storage, and high-resolution color graphics. It uses the MS-DOS operating system and a very advanced version of Microsoft BASIC, both of which include all the IBM PC features as subsets. Thus all the sections in this book marked with the IBM logo indicate features that are also included in the Tandy 2000.

The Great RETURN versus ↵ versus ENTER Debate

APPLE

IBM

Radio Shack

All computer keyboards have a key on the right-hand side that acts something like the carriage-return key on a typewriter. In fact, many manufacturers (including Apple) label this key RETURN or CAR RET. On the IBM PC it is labeled with the symbol ↵ , to indicate that you get both a new line *and* a return to the left. On the TRS-80 (and several other) machines, the same key is labeled ENTER. We will show this key as ⟨enter⟩ when we want to remind you that it should be pressed. However, you'll also find books that call it ⟨ret⟩, CR, ®, or something else. After awhile, you'll get used to pressing this key at the end of most lines, so we won't even mention it for most of the book.

1.4   Getting Ready to Communicate with a Time-Sharing Computer

You might want to glance enviously at the instructions for the microcomputer users. They had a rather simple explanation of how to get the computer ready. Time-sharing users have more things to consider, although the process is much easier to do than to read about. The *exact* steps you should follow depend on the particular time-sharing system that you are using. The best way to learn is to have someone show you. However, the instructions that follow should help in a general way.

The first thing you have to do is call up your computer. In many places there is a direct connection from terminal to computer, so about all you do is turn on the terminal and press one or two keys. In other cases, you must use a small box called an *acoustic coupler* with a telephone. To use a coupler, you turn it on, then dial the telephone number of the computer. The computer should answer with a high-pitched whistle. Then you place the telephone handset into the coupler, as shown in Figure 1.6.

Another device used to connect terminals to telephones, but without removing the handset, is called the **direct-connect modem.** MODEM is an acronym for "modulator-demodulator," where the word modulate refers to the process of converting digital signals to tones that are acceptable to the telephone switching network. Both acoustic couplers and direct-connect modems use modulation and demodulation techniques.

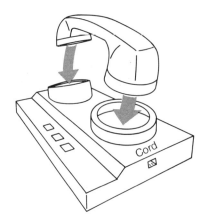

FIGURE 1.6   Receiver and coupler

With either direct or acoustic coupler connections, the next step is to log into the computer system.

Logging in is the process of identifying yourself to the computer. This is necessary because many people are using the computer, and it has to know who you are in order to keep track of the work you do.

We'll show an example of logging in on one particular time-sharing system. After studying this example, you should write down the procedure for the system you are using, since it may be a little different from our example. Also note that some systems do not require a login command for directly wired terminals. Figure 1.7 gives a final checklist to guide you in the login process. (It also illustrates the idea of a *flowchart,* which we'll return to in Chapter 3.)

```
PITT DEC-1099/B 701A.14 19:08:39 TTY64 system 1237/1240/1278
Please LOGIN or ATTACH

.SET TTY SYS A
```

The user typed all the messages after "." and ">". Here the user asks for computer A instead of B.

```
PITT DEC-1099/A 701A.14 19:08:49 TTY64 system 1217/1239/1339
Please LOGIN or ATTACH

.LOGIN 113052/121641
JOB 65 PITT DEC-1099/A 701A.14 TTY64 Wed 21-Mar-84 1909
Password:
Last login: 21-Mar-84 1543
Usage ratio: 0.43   Units used: 0.0   Pages printed: 0
```

The user's password was entered here, but not "echoed" by the computer.

```
.R BASIC
```

The user now asks that a BASIC interpreter be run.

```
READY, FOR HELP TYPE HELP.
>10 FOR K=1 TO 9
>20 PRINT K;" TIMES 9 =";K*9
>30 NEXT K
>40 END
>RUN
```

This BASIC interpreter will print out a 2-page list of key words and explanation if you type HELP <enter>.

This is a BASIC program typed in by the user.

```
NONAME          19:10          21-MAR-84
```

All programs, even one with no name, are given a name on this system.

```
1   TIMES 9 = 9
2   TIMES 9 = 18
3   TIMES 9 = 27
4   TIMES 9 = 36
5   TIMES 9 = 45
6   TIMES 9 = 54
7   TIMES 9 = 63
8   TIMES 9 = 72
9   TIMES 9 = 81
```

This is the output of the program.

```
TIME:  0.05 SECS.
>SAVE NINES
>BYE
```

The BASIC command BYE can often be used to log out. This system then tells you something about the record it has kept of this session.

```
Job 65 [113052,121641] off TTY64 at 1911 21-Mar-84 Connect=3 Min
Disk R+W=110+17  Tape IO=0  Blocks saved USRA:5
CPU 0:00  Core HWM=6P  Units=0.0103 ($0.44)
```

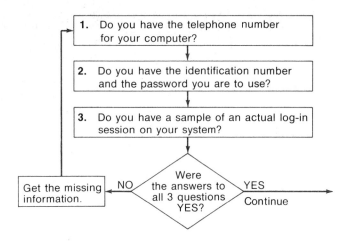

FIGURE 1.7   Final checklist for time-sharing users

Notes for Users of Other Time-sharing Systems

Note 1   When logging in, the user is usually the first one to type. On some time-sharing systems, the computer types a short message (like the date) as soon as you connect the telephone. Then it's your turn.

Note 2   On some systems, the computer is ready to accept programs written in BASIC right after login. On systems that offer other languages in addition to BASIC, you'll have to type the word BASIC (or something similar) during some part of the login procedure to tell it which language you are going to use.

Note 3   Some time-sharing systems ask you the question New or Old? right after login. This means that the computer wants to know whether you are going to work on an old program that is stored in its memory, or write a new one. Your instructor will tell you how to handle this.

1.5   The BASIC Language

Now that you have the computer's attention, what do you say to it? The conversation that you carry on with a computer through a terminal can't be in ordinary English (or any other natural language). Instructions to a computer have to be written in a special *programming* language.

A number of such programming languages have been developed for "conversational" computing. The most popular of these, and by far the best one for any beginner, is called **BASIC** (*B*eginner's *A*ll-purpose *S*ymbolic *I*nstruction *C*ode).

Computers don't actually "understand" BASIC. They translate BASIC into machine code, a sequence of binary digits that's not easily understood by human beings. The translation is usually done by a special program called a

TABLE 1.1 English Sentences and their BASIC Translations

English Sentences	BASIC Statements
Instructions to Robot: Please memorize the following instructions. *Do not execute them until you are told to.*	
1. The chalkboard behind you has several squares drawn on it. Write the letter X next to one of these. Then write the number 9 *inside* this square.	1 LET X=9
2. Now write the letter Y next to another square. Then write the number 12 inside the square.	2 LET Y=12
3. There is a piece of paper on your desk. On the first line, print PROBLEM 1.	3 PRINT "PROBLEM 1"
4. On the next line of this paper, print the *sum* of the number written next to X and the number written next to Y.	4 PRINT X+Y
5. On the next line of the paper, print PROBLEM 2.	5 PRINT "PROBLEM 2"
6. On the next line of the paper, print the *product* of the number written next to X and the number written next to Y.	6 PRINT X*Y (Note that a * means "multiply" in BASIC.)
7. This is the end of your instructions. Stand by.	7 END
Now execute the preceding instructions. Begin.	RUN

BASIC *interpreter.** You don't have to know anything about the interpreter, since it is used automatically any time you RUN a BASIC program.

Sentences written in BASIC are called *statements.* Table 1.1 compares some BASIC statements with English sentences that we might use to instruct a robot. To give you an idea of how the computer interprets BASIC, imagine that you have recorded your instructions to the robot on tape, and that the instructions are translated (interpreted) one by one as the tape is played back.

Notice how few words BASIC uses, compared with English. BASIC also requires that you give your instructions in very small steps—one statement at a time.

▶ *Note:* The statements in this example were numbered 1, 2, 3, ..., 7, since this is the sequence in which they are to be executed. Most programmers would probably have numbered them 10, 20, 30, ..., 70 in order to leave room for insertion of future statements.

We won't say any more about BASIC for now. If you didn't follow all of the preceding discussion, don't worry. We'll go through everything again step by step in Chapter 2. The important thing for now is to get *on-line,* so that you can get a feel for how these ideas work on a real computer.

---

*Another type of translator program that is sometimes used is called a *compiler.* Interpreters translate one statement at a time, and thus have the advantage of allowing quick changes in the program. Compilers must always translate the entire program as a unit. Unlike interpreters, they translate statements just once, so compiled programs usually run faster than interpreted programs. On the other hand, if there's an error, the entire program must be recompiled.

1.6   Putting It All Together

Figure 1.8 is a summary of how the things we have discussed so far go together during an on-line session. There are four major steps in any on-line session.

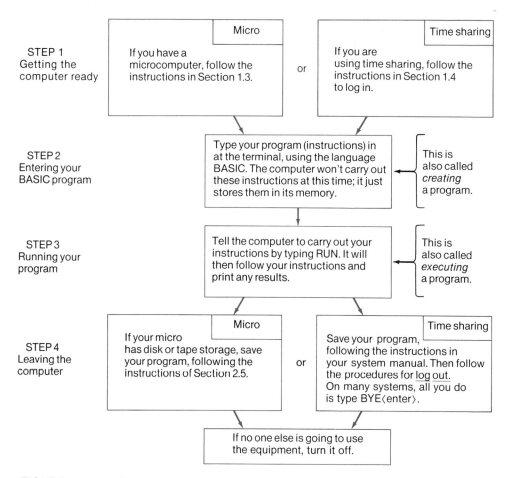

FIGURE 1.8   The four steps in an on-line session, for micro and time-sharing systems

1.7   You're On!

The time has come for you to try out these ideas at a real computer terminal, even though you have not yet learned to write your own programs in BASIC. Simply follow the directions given in steps 1, 2, 3, and 4. You can't hurt anything, so don't be afraid to make mistakes. (The examples in Sections 1.8 and 1.9 illustrate some of the things that may happen.)

Step 1   Get the computer ready by following the directions in Section 1.3 if you have a micro or Section 1.4 if you use time-sharing.

Step 2 Type in your BASIC program. Use the example from Section 1.5 (the robot example).

If you are in the middle of a line and make a typing error, press the RETURN key. The computer may then print ??? or a message saying it found an error. Just ignore the message, and type the *entire* line over again.

► *Note:* Some computer systems have additional features for correcting errors, such as use of the EDIT command, or certain special keys like backspace (◄——). Find out what these are on your system from your instructor or from the instruction manual that came with your system.

For step 2, here's what you type:

```
1 LET X=9            <enter>    <enter> means "press the
2 LET Y=12           <enter>    RETURN key"—also called
3 PRINT "PROBLEM 1"  <enter>    the ENTER key.
4 PRINT X+Y          <enter>
5 PRINT "PROBLEM 2"  <enter>
6 PRINT X*Y          <enter>
7 END                <enter>
```

If you make mistakes and would like to be sure that you have corrected everything, just type:

```
LIST <enter>
```

The computer will type back all the BASIC statements that it has stored in its memory. If you see something you don't like in one of the statements (for example, statement 3), just type it over. The *last* version of statement 3 you type is what counts—all other versions are erased.

Even though you may have put in a "revised" statement 3 *after* statement 7, the computer will put statement 3 back in order. To check this, just type LIST again.

Step 3 Now you're ready to see the computer *execute* (carry out) your instructions. Simply type:

```
RUN <enter>
```

You can type RUN as often as you like. If you get tired of seeing the same answers, you can change some of the statements in your program. For example, you might type:

```
1 LET X=99 <enter>⎫     This changes statements 1 and 2
2 LET Y=49 <enter>⎬◄—   only; statements 3, 4, 5, 6, and 7 are
RUN        <enter>      still in the computer.
```

What do you think will happen?

► *Note:* If you wish to *delete* (get rid of) some statements, just type the line numbers, followed by a carriage RETURN.

► *Example:* If you type

```
3 <enter>
4 <enter>
```

statements 3 and 4 will be erased from your program (forever).

Step 4   Leave the computer. If you are the last to use it for the time being, follow Step 4 of Section 1.6.

1.8   Example of a Perfect Session

Let's first show what happens when someone follows the preceding directions without making a single mistake (which seldom happens!).

► *Note:* The next two examples are shown as a session on the IBM personal computer. The wording of error messages and the manner of correcting errors may differ on other systems. Check with your instructor and/or computer reference manual for further information.

Here's our perfect session (notice that this student has made the messages in statements 3 and 5 a little more precise). From now on, we won't show pressing the RETURN or ENTER key. You must do this after every line you type.

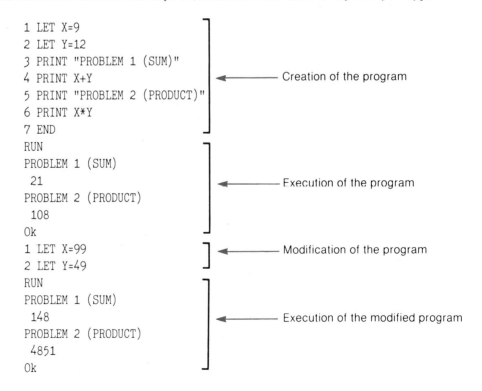

```
1 LET X=9
2 LET Y=12
3 PRINT "PROBLEM 1 (SUM)"
4 PRINT X+Y                    ◄────────── Creation of the program
5 PRINT "PROBLEM 2 (PRODUCT)"
6 PRINT X*Y
7 END
RUN
PROBLEM 1 (SUM)
 21
PROBLEM 2 (PRODUCT)            ◄────────── Execution of the program
 108
Ok
1 LET X=99                     ◄────────── Modification of the program
2 LET Y=49
RUN
PROBLEM 1 (SUM)
 148
PROBLEM 2 (PRODUCT)            ◄────────── Execution of the modified program
 4851
Ok
```

1.9 Example of a Normal Session (the Kind with Typing Mistakes)

Here's a more realistic example of what a first-time programmer might do (and see) when trying the preceding example on-line.

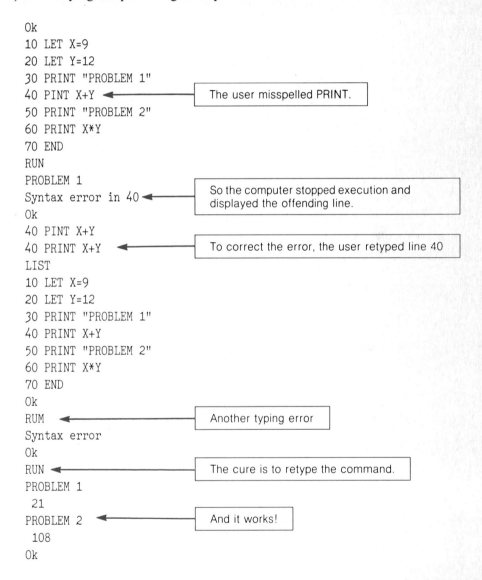

```
Ok
10 LET X=9
20 LET Y=12
30 PRINT "PROBLEM 1"
40 PINT X+Y          ◄——  The user misspelled PRINT.
50 PRINT "PROBLEM 2"
60 PRINT X*Y
70 END
RUN
PROBLEM 1
Syntax error in 40  ◄——  So the computer stopped execution and
Ok                         displayed the offending line.
40 PINT X+Y
40 PRINT X+Y        ◄——  To correct the error, the user retyped line 40
LIST
10 LET X=9
20 LET Y=12
30 PRINT "PROBLEM 1"
40 PRINT X+Y
50 PRINT "PROBLEM 2"
60 PRINT X*Y
70 END
Ok
RUM                 ◄——  Another typing error
Syntax error
Ok
RUN                 ◄——  The cure is to retype the command.
PROBLEM 1
 21
PROBLEM 2           ◄——  And it works!
 108
Ok
```

► *Note:* On most microcomputers, errors are not detected until the program is run. The program stops as soon as it finds the first error, and tells you the line number. You then correct the offending line by retyping it (including its line number). After this, you try another run, repeating the correction process for each error that the computer reports.

One last suggestion: It is a good idea to save your first successful program as a guide for your next on-line session.

1.10 Summary of Chapter 1

- Computer programs are sets of instructions that describe the procedure you wish the machine to follow.

- Programs may be purchased, or you can write them yourself, using a programming language. This book aims to help you learn to write programs using the programming language called BASIC.

- Procedures for starting to use BASIC vary with each system, and are best learned in actual practice, using local manuals as guides.

- All computers, large and small, have components that fall into three broad categories: (1) input-output (I/O) components, (2) central processor and memory components, (3) mass storage components.

- BASIC programs and data are communicated to the computer via input devices (usually a keyboard), and are stored in memory.

- The central processing unit (CPU) follows the program's instructions, manipulates the data, and may store the results in memory.

- Results are communicated to the programmer via output devices (usually a printer or display screen).

- Programs and data may be saved for later use on cassette tapes, floppy disks, or hard disks.

- Computers translate BASIC instructions into machine code. The program that does the translation is called a BASIC interpreter or compiler.

- Errors in BASIC statements may be corrected in several ways.

   A backspace or delete key is found on most keyboards. This allows you to erase by backing up within a line before you press the ⟨enter⟩ key (or ⟨return⟩ key).

   Retyping a numbered program line causes that line to be immediately replaced in memory.

   Typing a new line with a line number ⟨ln⟩* between two existing lines causes that line to be inserted in the program at that point.

   Typing a line number followed by ⟨enter⟩ erases any previous line with that number.

   Many computers have additional typing and editing aids.

- After a BASIC program has been entered in memory, it is made to execute with the RUN command. The BASIC program in memory may be displayed on the output device with the command LIST. On some systems, the program can be displayed on a printer with the command LLIST.

---

*The special notations used in this and other chapter summaries (for example, ⟨ln⟩) are explained at the beginning of Appendix B.

1.11 Problems and Programming Projects

The rest of this book will be devoted to the art of programming in the BASIC language. At the end of each chapter there is usually a section called Problems and Programming Projects, related to the material contained in the chapter. There is no such section in Chapter 1. However, if you want to run another program or two for practice, here are two to try. You can find out what they do by typing them into your computer and then typing RUN.

```
NEW
Ok


4 REM-----------------------
6 REM        COMPUTER
8 REM-----------------------
10 PRINT "THIS IS A COMPUTER"
20 FOR K=1 TO 4
30   PRINT "NOTHING CAN GO"
40   FOR J=1 TO 3
50     PRINT "WRONG"
60   NEXT J
70 NEXT K
80 END


RUN


NEW
Ok


4 REM-------------------------------
6 REM              PEOPLE
8 REM-------------------------------
10 LET Y=1970
20 LET P=200
30 PRINT "YEAR","MILLIONS OF PEOPLE"
40 PRINT Y,P
50 LET Y=Y+5
60 LET P=1.2*P
70 IF Y<2075 THEN 40
80 END


RUN
```

► *Remember:* You are not expected to understand how these programs work (you will by the end of Part II). The programs are given here to let you try out your computer system and become more familiar with using a terminal. You'll also find that the experience will help you understand things a great deal better when you return to reading.

FIGURE 1.9   The Apple computer is one of the most popular machines in current use. The photo shows a cluster of Apple IIe computers at the Touchstone Computer Learning Center in Pittsburgh. The Apple II, II Plus, IIe, and IIc all support the programming language called Applesoft BASIC. This is a special adaptation of the Microsoft BASIC used in this book. Variations between Applesoft and Microsoft BASIC are discussed in sections of the book marked with the boxed APPLE symbol seen here in the margin. Additional information about Applesoft BASIC can be found on pages 29 and 172, and in Appendix C.

APPLE

## CHAPTER TWO

The Elements
of BASIC Programming

NEW TOPICS INTRODUCED IN CHAPTER 2

- *Key words*
- *Statements*
- *Commands*
- *REM*
- *PRINT*
- *END*
- *Operators*
- *Use of parentheses*
- *Use of commas and semicolons*

- *RUN*
- *NEW*
- *LIST*
- *LET*
- *Assignment statements*
- *Arithmetic expressions*
- *INPUT*
- *Exponential notation*
- *Storing programs on disk and tape; DOS*

2.1 The Basic Vocabulary of BASIC; Using Remarks

Once you know how to manage an on-line session with your computer, you can turn your attention to learning how to write programs for it in BASIC. Chapters 2 and 3 will show you how to get started by concentrating on the use of a dozen *key words* in the BASIC language. Even with this small a vocabulary, it will be possible to write several interesting programs. (Chapters 4 and 5 will extend this vocabulary to include another dozen or so key words, while Chapters 6–12 will bring the total to more than 50.)

Most of the sections in these chapters will show you how to use key words to make BASIC *statements*. Once you have learned how to put a few statements together, you'll have a program. It's as simple as that: You use key words to make statements, and statements to make programs.

The key words you will learn in Chapter 2 are:

```
REM           LET
PRINT         INPUT
END
```

The key words you will learn in Chapter 3 are:

```
GOTO          FOR ... TO ... (STEP)
IF ... THEN   NEXT
STOP
```

In addition to these key words, you will also use the three *commands* that you have already met:

LIST
RUN
NEW

What is the difference between a key word and a command? A key word is never used *alone.* It's always *part* of a BASIC statement that has some other components—things like a statement number, a math expression, or even a message in English.

For example, here's a short BASIC program with five statements followed by a command.

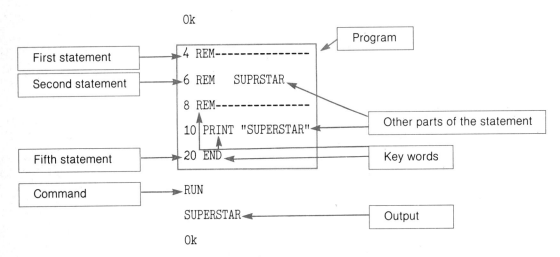

The statements are instructions to the computer. The computer stores these instructions in its "memory," but it doesn't *execute* them (carry them out) until you say so. You do this by typing the command RUN. Then the computer executes all your instructions. Any results that it prints out after you tell it to RUN are called OUTPUT.

▶ *Note:* The Ok shown just above our program was printed by the computer to indicate that it was ready to accept a BASIC program. Most computers also print a message *after* you run a program to indicate that the output is complete. (Examples: END, DONE, RAN, and so on.) Our system types the second Ok shown in the printout.

Statements 4, 6, and 8 use the key word REM, which means "remark" or "comment." It is used to document programs, making them easier to read and understand. The computer actually ignores REM statements (they're for people). Microsoft BASIC allows a shorthand for REM: the single quote ('). This will be illustrated in Section 3.3, and in most of the programs of Part II. Programs written in BASIC-PLUS may use the exclamation point (!) as an abbreviation for REM.

▶ *Note:* Another use of REM (or ' or !) is to put "empty" lines in a program. This makes the program easier to read. For an example, see the program MELODY in Lab Exercise 5.12.

2.2   BASIC Statements Using the Key Words REM, PRINT, and END

Let's look at the outline of a BASIC program that uses only three key words: REM, PRINT, and END.

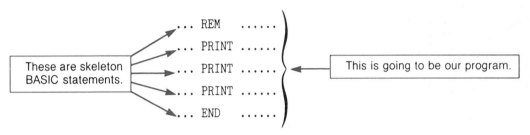

The dots mean that something is missing and must be inserted in these positions before we have real BASIC statements.

Here's an example that shows how these skeleton statements can be fleshed out to make a full-fledged program. We'll call it DEMO.

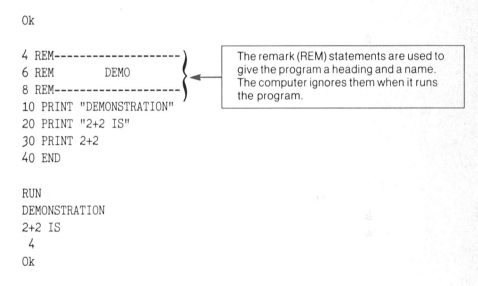

```
Ok

4 REM--------------------
6 REM        DEMO
8 REM--------------------
10 PRINT "DEMONSTRATION"
20 PRINT "2+2 IS"
30 PRINT 2+2
40 END

RUN
DEMONSTRATION
2+2 IS
 4
Ok
```

The first thing you should notice is that every BASIC statement starts with a *line number*. This can be any whole number from 1 to some maximum value (65529 in Microsoft BASIC). Note that you do not use commas in writing large numbers. The line numbers serve as a guide to the computer in running the program, telling it in what *order* to carry out your instructions. As long as you specify the order you want correctly, you can use any line numbers you want. Many programmers use 10, 20, 30, and so forth. This leaves room for later inserting statements you didn't realize were needed.

The most important key word in the program DEMO is PRINT. We will look at this in detail shortly. But first let's take care of the key word END (used in line 40).

The END statement means just what you would expect: The computer should *end* execution at this point. In most versions of BASIC, you don't need an END statement if it's the last one in the program. The program will end simply because "there is no more." However, it is also possible to use END in the middle of a program. We'll show examples of how this works in Chapter 3.

Statements Using the Key Word PRINT

The key word PRINT is usually followed by what are called *items*. One kind of item that can follow PRINT is shown in statement 10 of our example, DEMO.

Line number

`10 PRINT "DEMONSTRATION"`

Key word

> One of the items you can put *after* PRINT is any message you want, provided it's placed between quotation marks.

When you say RUN, the computer will obediently print back whatever was typed between the quotation marks. However, there is *one* thing you can't have inside the quotation marks: You can't have another quotation mark. If you say, for example,

```
10 PRINT "THAT'S A "HOT" ISSUE"
```

to a computer, it will probably not print what you want. It may not accept the statement at all, or it may simply print an error message.

To get around this limitation, you can use single quotation marks, as shown in line 10 of the following program.

```
Ok

4 REM-------------------------
6 REM           HOT
8 REM-------------------------
10 PRINT "THAT'S A 'HOT' ISSUE"
20 END

RUN
THAT'S A 'HOT' ISSUE
Ok
```

What else can you put after PRINT? Look at line 30 of DEMO. In this statement we *didn't* use quotes:

```
30 PRINT 2+2
```

When you run the program, the computer will print 4 for line 30. In other words, if you don't use quotation marks, the computer will *calculate* what's there, and then print the answer.

> ► *Moral:* If you don't use quotation marks, you had better have a number or a numerical expression that can be calculated using arithmetic. (Later on, you'll also see that such expressions can include both numbers and variables.)

By now you have probably noticed the four most common symbols that computers use for doing arithmetic:

+   means add

−   means subtract

*   means multiply (don't use ×)

/   means divide (you're not allowed to use ÷)

These symbols are also called *operators*. There is one other operator computers use:

↑ means exponentiate

(Some computers use ** or ^ instead of ↑.) Don't let that word "exponentiate" worry you. Most of the time it simply means *repeated multiplication*. (There's also a more sophisticated use, as you will see later in Section 11.1.) For now, think of 3 ↑ 4 as shorthand for 3*3*3*3. In other words, 3 ↑ 4 means "take the product of *four* threes." Watch:

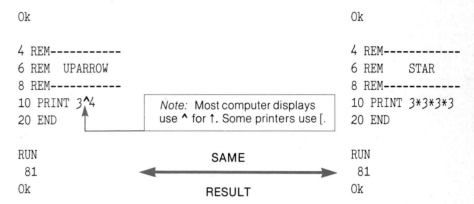

```
Ok                                              Ok

4 REM-----------                                4 REM------------
6 REM   UPARROW                                 6 REM      STAR
8 REM-----------                                8 REM------------
10 PRINT 3^4          Note: Most computer displays   10 PRINT 3*3*3*3
20 END                use ^ for ↑. Some printers use [.  20 END

RUN                        SAME                  RUN
 81                  ◄─────────────────►          81
Ok                        RESULT                 Ok
```

EXERCISE

Most of the *Exercises* in this book are short problems that you can work out by hand, using pencil and paper. *Lab Exercises,* on the other hand, usually present programming problems that are meant to be run on the computer.

2.1   Write down the output you think a computer would produce after it got the signal to run the following program. [This is called *simulating* a computer run. It's good practice, and can come in handy when you are trying to find a *bug* (error) in a program.] Check your answers with those printed upside down.

```
Ok


4 REM--------------
6 REM    OPERATOR                               Ok
8 REM--------------                             19
10 PRINT 8+4                                    23
20 PRINT 8-4                                     1
30 PRINT 8*4                                    3.1
40 PRINT 8/4                                     27
50 PRINT 80/40                                    4
60 PRINT .5*8                                     2
70 PRINT 3^3                                      2
80 PRINT 10.8-7.7                                32
90 PRINT 3+4-6                                    4
100 PRINT 5*4+3                                  12
110 PRINT 4+3*5                                 RUN
120 END
```

Using Parentheses in BASIC Statements; Precedence of Operators

Don't be surprised if you were puzzled by statements 100 and 110 in the program OPERATOR. There is really no way to predict what

```
100 PRINT 5*4+3     or     110 PRINT 4+3*5
```

will do unless you know that computer scientists have agreed that, in a given problem, multiplication should be done before addition. Thus, in line 110, the computer will *first* calculate that 3*5 is 15, and *then* add 4 to get the answer, 19.

But suppose that's not what you want. In that case, you can use parentheses. For example, suppose you type

```
110 PRINT (4+3)*5
```

Then the computer first calculates what is inside the parentheses. This means that it *first* finds that 4 + 3 is 7, and *then* multiplies this 7 by 5 to get 35 as its result.

▶ *Practical rule:* When you ask the computer to calculate answers to arithmetic problems, group things together the way you want them by means of parentheses. Be sure that every left parenthesis has a matching right parenthesis. If you don't use parentheses, the operations will be done using the *precedence* of exponentiation first, multiplication and division second, addition and subtraction third.

Formal Precedence Rules for Using Arithmetic Operators

1. If there are no parentheses, the computer performs operations by going from left to right *three* times. The first time, it carries out all exponentiation operations (↑ or **). The second time, it carries out * and / operations, in order from left to right. The third time, it carries out + and − operations in order from left to right.

▶ *Example:* 3 + 5*2↑3 − 4/2*3   becomes 3 + 5*8 − 4/2*3
                                 then 3 + 40 − 6
                                 then 37

2. If there are parentheses, the computer looks for the first *right* parenthesis, backs up to the matching left parenthesis, and then applies rule (1) to convert everything inside this *inner* pair of parentheses to a single number. It then throws these parentheses away, and repeats the process. If you use several pairs of parentheses, the computer works from the inside out.

▶ *Example:* ((3 + 5)*3)/4   becomes (8*3)/4
                             then   6

EXERCISE

2.2   Copy and complete the following.

a. 4 + 9 = _____?_____

b. (4 + 9) = _____?_____

c. $(4 + 9)*2 = $ _____?_____

d. $4 + (9*2) = $ _____?_____

e. $(4 + (9*2))*3 = $ _____?_____

f. $(4 + (9*2))*(3 + 1) = $ _____?_____

g. $.5*((8 + (9*2))*(3 + 1)) = $ _____?_____

↑

Note: To the computer, .5 is the same as 0.5.

When in doubt, use parentheses. They can't do any harm—and they may make the difference between a right and a wrong answer.

Here are two more computer programs using PRINT. Simulate running each of these by writing down the output you expect the computer to produce.

EXERCISES

2.3 Simulate running the following program.

```
4 REM----------------------------
6 REM            AGENTS
8 REM----------------------------
10 PRINT 42+44
20 PRINT "AND"
30 PRINT 3*33
40 PRINT "ARE TWO SECRET AGENTS."
50 END
```

2.4 Simulate running the following program.

```
4 REM--------------------------------
6 REM                USA
8 REM--------------------------------
10 PRINT "WHAT HAPPENED IN THE YEAR"
20 PRINT 1000+776
30 PRINT "OR"
40 PRINT (5*200)+(2*450)+(9*5)
50 PRINT "OR"
60 PRINT ((5*(5*16)/4)*5*(2^2))+1
70 END
```

Using Commas with PRINT Statements

Let's see what else can be done with the PRINT statement. For one thing, we can do several calculations on one line. Here is an example.

▶ Note: The following discussion applies to computer terminals or video displays that have 80 columns across.

```
Ok

4 REM----------------------
6 REM         COMMAS
8 REM----------------------
10 PRINT 9^1,9^2,9^3,9^4,9^5
20 END

RUN
 9             81           729          6561         59049
Ok
```

Line 10 calculated the answers to five problems and printed them *on the same line*. Notice what the comma does. When you use commas in a PRINT statement, most computers space the answers into five areas called *print zones,* as follows. (The TRS-80 and Apple use 16 spaces per zone).

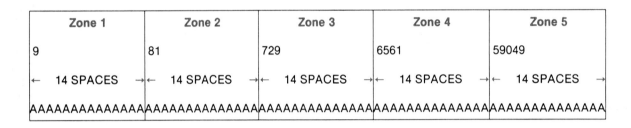

Zone 1	Zone 2	Zone 3	Zone 4	Zone 5
9	81	729	6561	59049
← 14 SPACES →	← 14 SPACES →	← 14 SPACES →	← 14 SPACES →	← 14 SPACES →
AAAAAAAAAAAAAA	AAAAAAAAAAAAAA	AAAAAAAAAAAAAA	AAAAAAAAAAAAAA	AAAAAAAAAAAAAA

If there are more than five items in the PRINT statement, the output will usually be continued on the next line.

```
Ok

4 REM------------------------------
6 REM            COMMAS2
8 REM------------------------------
10 PRINT 3,3*2,3*3,3*4,3*5,3*6,3*7
20 END

RUN
 3             6            9            12           15
 18            21
Ok
```

Using Semicolons with PRINT Statements

Another mark of punctuation used in PRINT statements is the *semicolon*. What the semicolon does varies somewhat from computer to computer. But it is always true that the semicolon leaves *less space between answers* than the comma.

On most systems, using the semicolon puts the answers as close together as possible. However, it leaves two spaces between numbers. It leaves a trailing blank after each number, and it leaves a space before each number, just in case there might be a negative sign.

To see the difference between what a comma does and what a semicolon does, look at the following example. (Your computer may do things slightly differently.)

```
Ok

4 REM------------------          ┌──────────────────────────────────┐
6 REM            SMICOLON ◄────── │ Note that we abbreviated the file name from │
8 REM------------------          │ SEMICOLON TO SMICOLON (8 letters).          │
10 PRINT 97,3+4,9*8,1/8,"FOOT"    │ Section 2.5 will explain why.               │
20 PRINT 97;3+4;9*8;1/8;"FOOT"    └──────────────────────────────────┘
30 END               ┌────────────────────────────┐
                     │ Some systems, such as the Apple, │
RUN                  │ may need a space here.           │
 97          7          72          .125 FOOT
 97  7  72  .125 FOOT
Ok
```

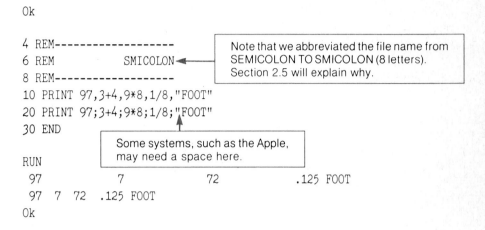

► *Quick Summary:* If you want output spread out, use a comma. If you want output close together, use a semicolon. Of course, you use the comma and semicolon only when you want more than one item on the same line.

Note to Apple II Users

There are two extended versions of BASIC available on the Apple II. The first is called Applesoft BASIC. As the name implies, it is an adaptation of Microsoft BASIC for the Apple II computer. Applesoft BASIC includes most of the features discussed in this book. However, as you'll find out later, it does not have the IF ... THEN ... ELSE, WHILE ... WEND, and PRINT USING statements. Also, it handles disk files differently (see Appendix C).

For this section, the main thing to note is that Applesoft BASIC treats the semicolon differently in PRINT statements. It does *not* put leading or trailing spaces around numbers. Thus

```
PRINT "ANS IS";4        produces      ANS IS4
```

as output. To fix this, type a space after IS, as follows:

```
PRINT "ANS IS ";4
```

The fact that many Apple II systems are limited to 40 columns must also be taken into account. In general, the best way to control the output spacing of numbers in Applesoft BASIC is (1) to use the TAB(X) function (which we'll discuss in Section 4.4), or (2) to squeeze in your own spaces. For example,

```
PRINT "ROW A ";X;" ";Y
```

Another difference Applesoft BASIC users soon discover is that Applesoft won't preserve spaces typed at the beginning of a statement to improve its readability (as shown, for example, in line 50 of Lab Exercise 2.3). If you want to *insist* on indented statements in Applesoft BASIC, you can use colons instead of spaces (for example, 100 :::PRINT K). Also, when you LIST (see next page) an

Applesoft BASIC program, you'll find that some extra spaces have been inserted at various places. This doesn't hurt anything; it just looks different.

A second, more powerful version of Microsoft BASIC is available on Apple II systems fitted with the CP/M card. This version is called MBASIC or GBASIC. It includes all the features discussed in this book, including the file statements of Chapters 11 and 12.

Using a Semicolon at the End of a PRINT Statement

The usual way the PRINT statement works in BASIC is to send one line of information to the screen or paper of the computer's output device, and then start a new line. Technically, we can say that PRINT statements always finish up by sending *carriage return* (CR) and *line feed* (LF) codes to the terminal to produce a new line. For example, the following program prints "SUM IS," sends (CR) (LF), prints 127, and sends (CR) (LF) again. Finally, it prints * DONE *, and sends a final (CR)(LF) pair.

```
10 PRINT "SUM IS>>>"
20 PRINT 42 + 85
30 PRINT "* DONE *"
RUN
SUM IS>>>
  127          New line from 10
* DONE *
```

New line from 20

However, if we put a semicolon at the end of a PRINT statement—say line 10—then the normal (CR) (LF) code will not be sent.

```
10 PRINT "SUM IS>>>";
20 PRINT 42 + 85
30 PRINT "* DONE *"
RUN
SUM IS>>> 127      No new line from 10
* DONE *
```

New line from 20

Using this technique, one can use the semicolon to force the output from several PRINT statements to appear on the same line. We'll return to this idea in later sections, and show several applications where it is of value.

The following lab exercises will enable you to try some of the preceding ideas on a computer. Before going on-line, you probably should review the information about correcting typing errors in Sections 1.6 and 1.9.

LAB EXERCISE 2.1   File Name: ARITH

Run the following program on your computer.

```
Ok

4 REM----------------------------------------------
6 REM                      ARITH
8 REM----------------------------------------------
10 PRINT "147 + 38 =";147+38
```

```
20 PRINT 5280*5;"FEET IN 5 MILES"
30 PRINT "THERE ARE";26*26*26;"THREE-LETTER CODE NAMES."
40 PRINT "COMPARISON OF 22/7 AND 355/113:";22/7,355/113
50 END
```

► *Warning:* Before you do the next on-line program, notice that it has line numbers past 50. If you had typed it in right after ARITH, the computer would have tried to put the two programs together, with statements 10 to 50 followed by statements 100 to 150.

If you were then to type RUN, the computer would start execution at line 10. As a result, it wouldn't look past the END statement in line 50. So, even though you were trying to run ARITH2, you would just get ARITH again.

To avoid this difficulty, you must get rid of the old program before you type in the new one. You do this by typing NEW and pressing RETURN. To check that there is no program there, type LIST. The computer will let you know in some way that there is no program in memory.

```
NEW
LIST ◄————  There was nothing to LIST.
Ok
```

► *Moral:* Use the NEW command before typing in a new program. Double-check that the computer's memory has been cleared by typing LIST.

LAB EXERCISE 2.2   File Name: ARITH2

Run the following program. Experiment with changes in it.

```
Ok

4 REM--------------------------------------------------
6 REM                       ARITH2
8 REM--------------------------------------------------
100 PRINT "HAT SIZES IN DECIMAL FORM"
110 PRINT 6+5/8;6+3/4;6+7/8;7;7+1/8;7+1/4;7+3/8
120 PRINT "DRILL SIZES"
130 PRINT 1/32;1/16;3/32;1/8;5/32;3/16;7/32;1/4
140 PRINT "MONEY AFTER DOUBLING $1 FOR 15 DAYS = $";2^15
150 END
```

Sneak Preview

By now you are probably discouraged by the amount of typing you have to do to get a little output. The trouble is that you can't write very interesting programs if the only key words you know are PRINT and END. Here's an exercise in which we've used two extra key words (FOR and NEXT, which we'll discuss in detail later) to get around this limitation. You aren't expected to understand what these key words do at this time. Just type them in as shown, with the idea of seeing how they work by experiment.

LAB EXERCISE 2.3   File Name: MULTABLE _____

Enter and run the following program.

```
Ok

4 REM---------------------------------------------
6 REM                    MULTABLE
8 REM---------------------------------------------
10 PRINT "MULTIPLICATION TABLES FOR 10, 11, AND 12"
20 PRINT "--------------------------------------"
30 PRINT
40 FOR X=1 TO 12
50   PRINT X;"*10=";X*10,X;"*11=";X*11,X;"*12=";X*12
60 NEXT X
70 END
```

▶ *Note:* PRINT with nothing after it produces what is called a *line feed*. This means that the paper "feeds" up one extra line. Thus the effect of line 30 here is to put a blank line in the output, making it look neater.

Review of Section 2.2

■ Different forms of the PRINT statement look like the following.

```
123 PRINT 45
50  PRINT 900/450
36  PRINT "HELLO THERE"
900 PRINT 10, 10*2, 10*3, 5^7*3, ((16+32)/8)*123
20  PRINT 3+1; "SCORE AND"; 4+3; "YEARS AGO"
```

If more than one item is used after PRINT (as in lines 900 and 20 here), the following punctuation marks are used to separate the output.

1. A *comma* causes the output to fall into zones of 14, 15, or 16 spaces:

```
10 PRINT "2","3","4"
2          3          4
```

The "2", "3", and "4" are characters, so no space is left for a sign.

```
10 PRINT 2,3,4
```

The "2", "3", and "4" are characters, so no space is left for a sign.

$\uparrow^2 \qquad\qquad \uparrow^3 \qquad\qquad \uparrow^4$

Notice that a space is left in front of each number for a sign (except on the Apple).

| APPLE |

2. A *semicolon* prints the output items close together, leaving a space before and after numbers (except on the Apple).

```
10 PRINT "2";"3";"4"
234
10 PRINT 2;3;4
 2  3  4
```

■ RUN is a command that tells the computer to execute the statements of the program currently in its memory

■ NEW is a command that *erases* the previous program from the computer's memory.

■ LIST is a command that causes the computer to type out all the BASIC statements it has in its memory. It can specify a range of line numbers, as follows:

LIST	(all lines)
LIST-900	(all lines to 900)
LIST 100-	(all lines from 100 to end)
LIST 200–500	(all lines from 200 to 500)

2.3   Statements Using the Key Word LET

It is election time, and the votes for the three leading candidates have just been tallied. Flamboyant has 8497 votes, Handsome has 7231 votes, and Moderate topped the group with 9821 votes. Here's how the workers at election headquarters have "stored" this information on the chalkboard in the back room.

```
F    8497

H    7231

M    9821
```

Note that there are three spaces or *locations* on the board, called F, H, and M. We can think of F, H, and M as *labels* pasted on the board. Next to each of these labels is written the number of votes "stored" in the chalkboard memory. These numbers can, of course, be erased at any time, and new numbers can be put in each location.

Now let's use this picture to get a feel for what goes on in computer memories. We can also "store" numbers in the memory of a computer. In order to know where these numbers are being kept, we must also use labels to serve as addresses for the memory locations.

The LET statement in BASIC does both these things at once.

1. It gives a label called a *variable name* to the memory location.

2. It stores a number in this memory location.

For example, the statement

```
10 LET F=8497
```

gives the variable name (label) F to a location in the computer's memory.

It also stores the number 8497 in the memory location having that label. The number 8497 is called the *contents* of the memory location F. Since the LET statement allows the program to assign a value to a memory location, it is also called an *assignment statement*.

▶ *Note:* Most versions of BASIC allow you to omit the word LET when writing assignment statements. Thus you can write

```
10 LET F=8497     as     10 F=8497
```

Labels are sometimes compared to the names on mailboxes. The *label* on a mailbox is very different from the *contents* of the box. A mailbox may have the *label* Smith, but its contents can be anything from a letter to a sample bar of soap. That is why the label Smith may also be called a *variable.* The material put into the Smith mailbox can *vary:* one day a postcard, the next day a catalog.

In a similar way, the labels used for memory locations in a computer are called *variables.* In minimal BASIC, the variable names are usually made up of one or two characters, the first character being a letter. Examples are X, A, J, M, B, C4, FL, JM, and X8. However, in most extended versions of BASIC, longer names may be used for variables. Thus names like SUM23, MORTGAGE, and ACCOUNTS are all legitimate. Check your BASIC manual to see what the rules are for your system. Also see the Review at the end of this section.

The actual memories of computers don't look like chalkboards or mailboxes, of course. They are actually constructed of electronic circuits that can store information in the form of binary "on/off" signals. However, a person who wants to program a computer in BASIC doesn't have to know about the electronic construction of memories. From a programmer's point of view, a "chalkboard" picture like the following is better.

This picture suggests that we can *erase* the number next to a label and put in a new number. This is exactly what computers do in their electronic memories. If we put a new number in the same location as an old number, the first number is erased.

If a BASIC program says

```
10 LET A=4
```

we may imagine that the computer's memory looks like this.

If the BASIC program now says

    20 LET A=12

here is what the memory looks like.

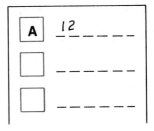

The 4 is gone (forever), and a 12 is now in its place.

For this reason, the portion of a computer's memory used by a programmer is said to have the property of *destructive read in*. That is, when we "read in" the 12, we destroy the 4. Conversely, memories have *nondestructive readout*. When you read data from memory, you get a copy of it; the original is *not* destroyed.

An important difference between a computer and a chalkboard is that the computer can do arithmetic on the numbers on the right side of a LET statement *before* storing the answer in its memory. For example, in the statement

    10 LET A=5*5

the computer first calculates 5*5 and *then* stores the answer (25) in location A. The statement

    30 LET A=6*6

stores 36 in location A, wiping out the 25.

```
NEW
Ok

4 REM------------
6 REM     LET
8 REM------------
10 LET A=5*5
20 PRINT "A =";A
30 LET A=6*6
40 PRINT "A =";A
50 END

RUN
A = 25
A = 36
Ok
```

► *Suggestion:* It helps if you read LET statements from right to left. In the statement

    10 LET A=5*5

the computer first calculates the expression on the right-hand side (using special arithmetic circuits). It then stores the answer in memory location A.

As noted earlier, the word LET is actually optional in most modern versions of BASIC. Thus

```
10 LET A=5*5    and    10 A=5*5
```

mean exactly the same thing. We'll continue to use LET in most of Part I, but will discontinue its use in Part II.

Now let's apply all this discussion by writing a program to give us the total votes in the election (the one with candidates Flamboyant, Handsome, and Moderate). We'll also have our program print out the *percentage* of the votes that each candidate received. You may recall that such a percentage is found as follows:

$$\text{Percentage of votes received by a candidate} = \left(\frac{\text{number of votes candidate received}}{\text{total number of votes}}\right)*100$$

This formula is used in lines 60, 70, and 80 of the following program.

```
NEW
Ok

4 REM-------------------------------------------------
6 REM    VOTE (PRINTS PERCENTAGES IN ELECTION)
8 REM-------------------------------------------------
10 LET F=8497
20 LET H=7231
30 LET M=9821
40 LET T=F+H+M
50 PRINT "TOTAL NO. OF VOTES CAST IS";T
60 PRINT "% FOR FLAMBOYANT =";(F/T)*100;"%"
70 PRINT "% FOR HANDSOME =";(H/T)*100;"%"
80 PRINT "% FOR MODERATE =";(M/T)*100;"%"
90 END

RUN
TOTAL NO. OF VOTES CAST IS 25549
% FOR FLAMBOYANT = 33.2577 %
% FOR HANDSOME = 28.3025 %
% FOR MODERATE = 38.4399 %
Ok
```

Notice that 33.2577 + 28.3025 + 38.4399 = 100.0001 instead of exactly 100. This is because the computer *rounded off* its answers. Round-off error isn't serious in this example (only .0001%), but it can sometimes cause trouble if the programmer lets it pile up too much.

Summary of What Can Be Used in a LET Statement

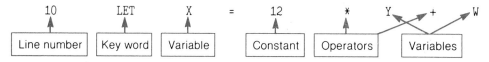

1. X, Y, and W are called *variables,* since different numbers can be stored in the locations they represent. The number 12 is called a constant because it doesn't change.

2. You're allowed to use only *one* variable on the left side of the equals sign (=) in a LET statement, but as many as you want on the right side. Constants can be used only on the right side. The combination of variables, operators, and constants used on the right side is called an *arithmetic expression.*

More Examples of LET Statements

Let's look at some LET statements in action. On the left is a BASIC program. On the right, there's a "picture" of what happens inside the computer.

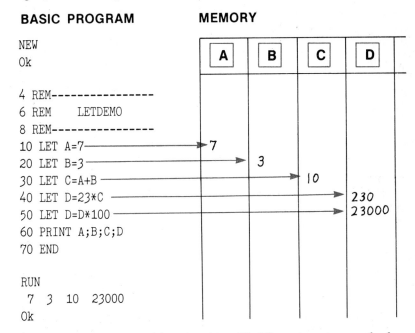

```
BASIC PROGRAM                MEMORY

NEW
Ok                           A    B    C    D


4 REM---------------
6 REM     LETDEMO
8 REM---------------
10 LET A=7                   7
20 LET B=3                        3
30 LET C=A+B                           10
40 LET D=23*C                               230
50 LET D=D*100                              23000
60 PRINT A;B;C;D
70 END

RUN
 7  3  10  23000
Ok
```

Notice what happened in statement 50. The computer worked on the *right* side of the statement first, calculating D*100, when the D location still had 230 in it from the previous step. *Then* it took the answer (23000) and put it back in location D. This means that the 230 was *erased,* and *replaced* by 23000.

More about Variable Names

So far, our examples have used *single letters* for variable names. That limits us to only 26 names. But, as noted earlier, longer names can also be used. Up to 40 letters and/or characters are allowed in Microsoft and IBM BASIC. TRS-80 and Applesoft BASIC also allow longer names, but they recognize only the first two characters. Thus they consider BANK45 and BATAVG to be the same. A summary of the exact rules for choosing names in Microsoft and IBM BASIC is given at the end of this section.

When choosing variable names, or when working with other parts of computer programs, be careful to distinguish between the letter O and the numeral zero (0). Some terminals print zero as Ø, while others simply give it a narrower shape. Also watch out for the difference between the number 1, the capital I, and the lower-case L. Here's an example to use in checking the way your printer produces these characters:

```
10 PRINT "Old Illya is #10"
```

EXERCISES

2.5 Check your computer manual and determine which of the following variable names are allowed. (If you don't have a manual, how can you find out?)

AMY	B	C8	C23	XY	2D	LET	W8	W13
W2	END	09	SUM88	J + 9	IOU	F − 2	3	X3.1

2.6 Simulate a run of the following program. Copy and fill in the chart at the right, showing the contents of memory, as you proceed.

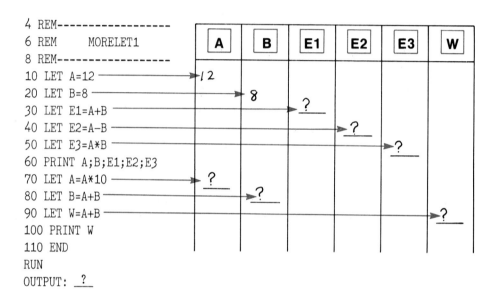

```
NEW
Ok

4 REM------------------
6 REM      MORELET1
8 REM------------------
10 LET A=12
20 LET B=8
30 LET E1=A+B
40 LET E2=A-B
50 LET E3=A*B
60 PRINT A;B;E1;E2;E3
70 LET A=A*10
80 LET B=A+B
90 LET W=A+B
100 PRINT W
110 END
RUN
OUTPUT: __?__
```

2.7 Simulate a run of the following program. Make a chart like that for Exercise 2.6, and fill in the memory locations as you proceed.

```
NEW
Ok

4 REM------------------
6 REM      MORELET2
8 REM------------------
10 LET A=3*4
20 LET B=10*A
30 LET C=B/4+6
40 PRINT A;B;C
50 LET A=B+C
60 PRINT A
70 END
```

2.8 Rewrite the preceding programs in abbreviated form. [*Hint:* The final END statement is optional, and you can omit LET when you are writing assignment statements. You can also use arithmetic expressions in PRINT statements, provided that all the variables used have already been assigned correct values.]

2.9 In the following "program," all the statements contain errors. Find each error and rewrite the lines in a form that makes sense. (It is impossible to guess what the original programmer had in mind, so there is no one "right" way to correct each line.)

```
10 LET A-2=4
20 PRIN 4
30 LET 4=C
40 PRINT*C,A
50 LET C/3=6
60 LET A=C+
70 PRINT AC=4
80 LET D=4×A
90 PRINT THE ANSWER IS D
100 THE END
```

LAB EXERCISE 2.4   **File Name: RAT1**

You are the program director of a national TV network, ABS (Acme Broadcasting System). And it's that time of year again: The rating reports are in. This means that you have to make your annual appearance before the board of directors with a list showing what percentage of the audience ABS had for each of the prime hours (7 P.M. to 11 P.M.).

For each time slot, you must provide the total number of viewers, the number of viewers watching ABS, and then the percentage of viewers watching ABS. Your meeting with the board is in just half an hour, and your list of percentages still isn't ready. Can the computer help? Let's find out.

Here's a partial picture of the computer output you'd like. The number of viewers came from the ratings survey report.

TIME SLOT	TOTAL VIEWERS	VIEWERS OF ABS	% WATCHING ABS
1	31546	8876	
2	36530	9604	
3	47867	16390	
4	35483	6379	
Ok			

Write a program, using a series of LET and PRINT statements, that will generate a complete chart. The formula you need for the last column in the chart is:

$$\text{Percent watching ABS} = \left(\frac{\text{No. of viewers of ABS}}{\text{Total no. of viewers}} \right) * 100$$

Your program should first print headings. Then for the first time slot, here's what you might do:

```
LET N=1
LET A=the total number of viewers
LET B=the number of viewers watching ABS
LET C=(B/A)*100
```

Then print N, A, B, C. Now repeat the process for N = 2, and so on. Of course, you'll have to write statements in correct BASIC, with line numbers, and sticking exactly to the rules you've seen so far. When you've done this and are pretty sure your program is correct, take it to the computer and run it.

LAB EXERCISE 2.5   File Name: RATSTUDY _____

In order to make this program more interesting, we're going to sneak in the FOR and NEXT statements again *without explanation* (the explanation is coming in Chapter 3). We'll use them to write a program that shows how the percentage ratings of ABS in time slot 1 would change for *each extra* thousand viewers added until ABS had 30,876 people watching their shows. For this Lab Exercise, study and run RATSTUDY and see if you can figure out how it works. (If you can't, all will be revealed in Section 3.4.)

```
NEW
Ok

4 REM-------------------------------------------------------
6 REM            RATSTUDY (FOR-NEXT IN A 'LET' PROGRAM)
8 REM-------------------------------------------------------
10 PRINT "RATING STUDY FOR TIME SLOT 1"
20 PRINT "TOTAL VIEWERS-VIEWERS OF ABS-% WATCHING ABS"
30 LET A=31546
40 LET B=8876
50 FOR X=1 TO 21
60   PRINT A,B,(B/A)*100;"%"
70   LET B=B+1000
80 NEXT X
90 END

RUN
```

Review of Section 2.3

■ The LET statement is called an assignment statement because it is used to *assign a value to a variable.* The value is stored in the computer's memory in a location that has a label, or *address,* that is given by the variable's name. For example:

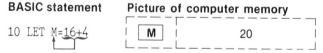

BASIC statement   **Picture of computer memory**

10 LET M=16+4 | M | 20

The value 20 is stored in the computer's memory in a location that has the address, or label, of M. The computer calculates the right-hand side of the BASIC statement first, then stores the result in the location named on the left-hand side of the equals sign.

■ The word LET is optional, so the above may also be written as

10 M=16+4

■ Names of variables can be single letters (A, B, C, . . ., X, Y, Z), or single letters followed by single digits (such as A1, B7, W0, X3). In most versions of BASIC, they can also be composed of two letters (such as EN, BK, MM).

■ In some versions of extended BASIC, names of variables can be up to 40 alphanumeric characters. In TRS-80 and Applesoft BASIC, only the first two characters are recognized. The first character *must* be a letter, while the remaining characters can be letters, numbers, or certain special symbols. However, reserved words (such as function names or key words) may *never* be used for variable names.

2.4   The INPUT Statement

In Lab Exercise 2.4, (the television-viewers program), you had to use several LET statements. You may have had something like this:

```
LET N=time slot number
LET A=total viewers
LET B=viewers of ABS
LET C=(B/A)*100 (percentage of viewers watching ABS)
PRINT N, A, B, C
```

This meant that you had to write a set of similar statements for each time slot. Well, that's not very efficient programming.

Let's see if there's a better way. We'll keep A, B, and C as variables meaning the same things as before. First, let's write the essential statements:

```
30 LET C=(B/A)*100    This calculation is needed to get a percent.
40 PRINT A,B,C;"%"     We have to print the answers to get output.
```

Of course, this program would not work, because it has no values assigned to A and B. To give A and B values, we'll use a new kind of BASIC statement—the INPUT statement.

This can be done by adding the following two statements at the beginning of our program:

```
10 INPUT A
20 INPUT B
```

Here is what a few runs would look like.

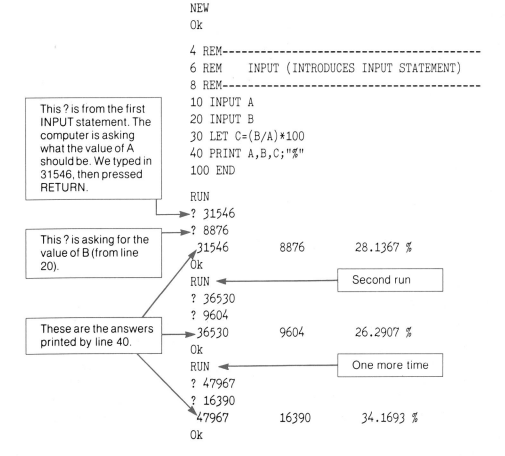

```
NEW
Ok

4 REM----------------------------------------
6 REM     INPUT (INTRODUCES INPUT STATEMENT)
8 REM----------------------------------------
10 INPUT A
20 INPUT B
30 LET C=(B/A)*100
40 PRINT A,B,C;"%"
100 END

RUN
? 31546
? 8876
 31546          8876           28.1367 %
Ok
RUN
? 36530
? 9604
 36530          9604           26.2907 %
Ok
RUN
? 47967
? 16390
 47967          16390          34.1693 %
Ok
```

This ? is from the first INPUT statement. The computer is asking what the value of A should be. We typed in 31546, then pressed RETURN.

This ? is asking for the value of B (from line 20).

These are the answers printed by line 40.

Second run

One more time

Let's summarize the effect of the statements

```
10 INPUT A
20 INPUT B
```

When the computer executes the program and gets to statement 10, it does two things:

1. It prints a ?

2. It then waits for you to type in a number for A, followed by a carriage return

In (2), you are said to be "inputting" a value for A. In a similar manner, 20 INPUT B allows you to input* a value for B.

Now that we have the basic idea, let's spruce up our program a bit. First, *you* know what A, B, and C stand for, and the network president knows what they stand for, but not everyone does. So let's put in a few PRINT statements to clear this up. Let's also show the numbers for the time slots. In other words, let's clarify the input requests shown by question marks with some *prompting messages,* as follows.

```
NEW
Ok


4 REM------------------------------------------------------------
6 REM      RAT2 (DEMONSTRATES INPUT AND PRINT COMBINED)
8 REM------------------------------------------------------------
10 PRINT "TYPE IN THE TIME SLOT NUMBER:"
20 INPUT N
30 PRINT "INPUT THE TOTAL NUMBER OF VIEWERS:"
40 INPUT A
50 PRINT "TYPE IN THE NUMBER OF ABS VIEWERS:"
60 INPUT B
70 LET C=(B/A)*100
80 PRINT "TIME SLOT NO.","TOTAL VIEWERS-VIEWERS OF ABS";
90 PRINT "-% WATCHING ABS"
100 PRINT N,A,B,C;"%"
110 END


RUN
TYPE IN THE TIME SLOT NUMBER:
? 1
INPUT THE TOTAL NUMBER OF VIEWERS:
? 31546
TYPE IN THE NUMBER OF ABS VIEWERS:
? 8876
TIME SLOT NO. TOTAL VIEWERS-VIEWERS OF ABS-% WATCHING ABS
 1              31546         8876          28.1367 %
Ok
```

---

*Programmers often use the words input and output as verbs, a fact that you may wish to add to your list of English-language changes being wrought by the computer age.

The prompting message before each ? makes it clear what is to be typed in by the program's user. Although not strictly needed for the program to work, such messages are good practice, and should always be included.

► *Note:* Because of the semicolon at the end of line 80, the computer prints the output from lines 80 and 90 on the same line. Also note that a new run is needed for each new time slot.

LAB EXERCISE 2.6   **File Name: RAT2**

Run the preceding program, using the data for time slots 2, 3, and 4 given in the program RAT1.

Additional Uses of INPUT

Let's take a look at another program that uses the INPUT statement. Suppose that you'd like to calculate how many hours a person has slept in his or her lifetime. Assume that everyone sleeps about one-third of the time (8 hours out of 24). Also assume that a year is 365 days (ignore leap years). Here's a program you might use, with a sample run.

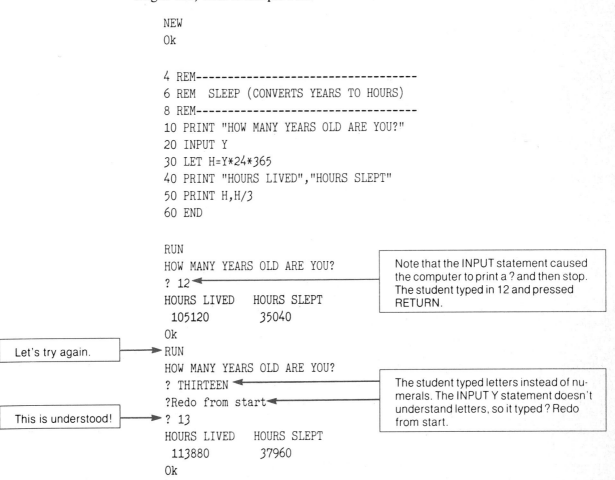

```
NEW
Ok


4 REM------------------------------------
6 REM  SLEEP (CONVERTS YEARS TO HOURS)
8 REM------------------------------------
10 PRINT "HOW MANY YEARS OLD ARE YOU?"
20 INPUT Y
30 LET H=Y*24*365
40 PRINT "HOURS LIVED","HOURS SLEPT"
50 PRINT H,H/3
60 END


RUN
HOW MANY YEARS OLD ARE YOU?
? 12
HOURS LIVED      HOURS SLEPT
 105120            35040
Ok
RUN
HOW MANY YEARS OLD ARE YOU?
? THIRTEEN
?Redo from start
? 13
HOURS LIVED      HOURS SLEPT
 113880            37960
Ok
```

Note that the INPUT statement caused the computer to print a ? and then stop. The student typed in 12 and pressed RETURN.

Let's try again.

The student typed letters instead of numerals. The INPUT Y statement doesn't understand letters, so it typed ? Redo from start.

This is understood!

(continued)

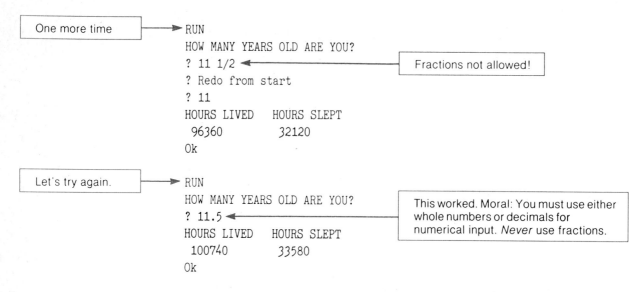

One more time
```
RUN
HOW MANY YEARS OLD ARE YOU?
? 11 1/2  ◄──────── Fractions not allowed!
? Redo from start
? 11
HOURS LIVED    HOURS SLEPT
 96360          32120
Ok
```

Let's try again.
```
RUN
HOW MANY YEARS OLD ARE YOU?
? 11.5  ◄──── This worked. Moral: You must use either
HOURS LIVED    HOURS SLEPT   whole numbers or decimals for
 100740         33580        numerical input. *Never* use fractions.
Ok
```

▶ *Special trick:* To put the input ? at the end of the question being asked, end the PRINT statement that comes just ahead of the INPUT statement with a semicolon (;), as shown here.

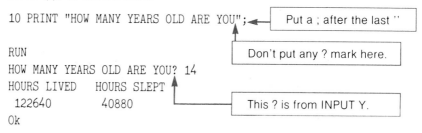

```
10 PRINT "HOW MANY YEARS OLD ARE YOU";  ◄── Put a ; after the last "

RUN
HOW MANY YEARS OLD ARE YOU? 14   ◄── Don't put any ? mark here.
HOURS LIVED    HOURS SLEPT
 122640         40880   ◄── This ? is from INPUT Y.
Ok
```

LAB EXERCISE 2.7   File Name: SLEEP

Run the preceding program for Y = 10, 20, 30, 40, 50, 60. Compare the results for 10 and 30 and for 20 and 60. What do you discover? Try the program for a variety of ages, including ages like 12.75 (which means 12¾ years or 12 years and 9 months).

LAB EXERCISE 2.8   File Name: RETIRE

Run the following program for a variety of values of Y.

```
NEW
Ok


4 REM------------------------------------
6 REM    RETIRE (SUBTRACTS FROM 65)
8 REM------------------------------------
10 PRINT "HOW MANY YEARS OLD ARE YOU?"
20 INPUT Y
30 PRINT "YOU CAN RETIRE IN";65-Y;"YEARS."
40 END

RUN
```

Some versions of BASIC may require spaces here

INPUT with Several Variables

We can use an INPUT statement for several variables. To see how this works, study the following printout.

```
NEW
Ok
4 REM-------------------------------------------------------------
6 REM              MONEY (CONVERTS CHANGE INTO DOLLARS)
8 REM-------------------------------------------------------------
10 PRINT "TYPE IN THE NO. OF NICKELS, DIMES, AND QUARTERS YOU HAVE:"
20 INPUT N,D,Q
30 PRINT "YOU HAVE";.05*N+.1*D+.25*Q;"DOLLARS."
40 END

RUN
TYPE IN THE NO. OF NICKELS, DIMES, AND QUARTERS YOU HAVE:
? 3,5,4
YOU HAVE 1.65 DOLLARS.
Ok
```

Note that we must type in three numbers separated by commas to match line 20.

The computer stores the first number in N, the second number in D, and the third number in Q.

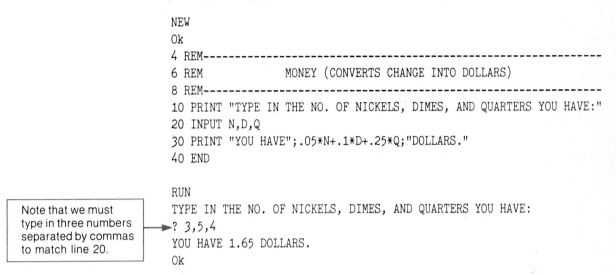

In statement 30, the computer calculates the dollars you have and then prints the result on the terminal.

```
.05*3 = .15
.10*5 = .50
.25*4 = 1.00
        1.65   OUTPUT
```

```
RUN
TYPE IN THE NO. OF NICKELS, DIMES, AND QUARTERS YOU HAVE:
? 3
?Redo from start
? 3,5,4
YOU HAVE 1.65 DOLLARS.
Ok
```

If you forget to type in all the numbers the program asked for, this BASIC prints? Redo from start.

LAB EXERCISE 2.9   File Name: MONEY

Run the preceding program with different values for N, D, and Q.

LAB EXERCISE 2.10   **File Name SUMPROD** _____

Write and run a program that will find both the sum and the product of four numbers. Use two statements like the following:

```
15 PRINT "TYPE 4 NUMBERS SEPARATED BY COMMAS"
20 INPUT W,X,Y,Z
```

to get the numbers from the user.

Special Information about Large Numbers

Look at the following program and run.

```
NEW
Ok


4 REM------------------
6 REM      SCINOT+
8 REM------------------
10 PRINT 30*40*100*1000
20 END

RUN
 1.2E+08
Ok
```

What does 1.2E+08 mean? It is computer *scientific notation* for 120,000,000 (that's one hundred twenty million). Scientific notation is a shorthand for very large (or very small) numbers. Let's see how it works. First recall that

$$10^2 = 10 \times 10 = 100, \quad 10^3 = 10 \times 10 \times 10 = 1000, \quad \text{and so on.}$$

This means that

$$1.2 \times 10^2 = 120, \quad 1.2 \times 10^3 = 1200, \quad \text{and so on.}$$

We can thus see that multiplying 1.2×10^3 is the same as moving the decimal point three places to the right:

$$1.2 \times 10^3 = 1200.$$

In the same way, $1.2 \times 10^8 = 120000000$. Now you can probably see how scientific notation works:

$$1.2E+08 \quad \text{means} \quad 1.20000 \times 10^8, \quad \text{which means} \quad 120000000.$$

In other words, since a computer can't print 10^8 on a terminal, it uses E+08 to mean $\times 10^8$.

The number 8 is called an *exponent,* and E+08 means "times 10 with the exponent positive 8." (The largest possible exponent on most systems is +38.)

▶ *Rule:* E+10 means "move the decimal point 10 places to the *right*."

Special Information about Small Numbers

Now consider the following program* and run.

```
NEW
Ok

4 REM----------------------
6 REM        SCINOT-
8 REM----------------------
10 PRINT ((1/1000)/12)/5280
20 END

RUN
 1.57828E-08
Ok
```

You can perhaps guess what 1.57828E−08 means. It means

1.57828×10^{-8},   which means   .0000000157828.

In case you haven't used negative exponents before, here's how they work:

$$10^{-1} = \frac{1}{10} = .1, \quad 10^{-2} = \frac{1}{10 \times 10} = .01, \quad 10^{-3} = \frac{1}{10 \times 10 \times 10} = .001, \text{ and so on.}$$

This means that

$1.5 \times 10^{-1} = .15, \quad 1.5 \times 10^{-2} = .015, \quad 1.5 \times 10^{-3} = .0015, \quad$ and so on.

We can thus see that multiplying 1.5×10^{-3} is the same as moving the decimal three places to the left:

$1.5 \times 10^{-3} = .0015$

In our program, 1.57828E−08 means 1.57828×10^{-8}, which means

.0000000157828.

► *Rule:* E−10 means "move the decimal point 10 places to the *left.*"

EXERCISES

Find the missing numbers.

2.10 (a) 5.00000E+06 = ___5000000___   (b) 8,000,000 = ___?___

2.11 (a) 8.23000E+08 = ___?___   (b) 27,000,000 = 2.70000E+___?___

2.12 (a) 1.23000E+11 = ___?___   (b) 2,234,000 = 2.23400E+___?___

*This program finds out how wide a one-thousandth-of-an-inch hair is, figured in parts of a mile.

2.13 (a) 1.50000E−07 = $\underline{.00000015}$ (b) .000000732 = 7.32000E−$\underline{\quad ? \quad}$

2.14 (a) 3.75000E−06 = $\underline{\quad ? \quad}$ (b) .0000006 = $\underline{\quad ? \quad}$

2.15 (a) 9.82000E−16 = $\underline{\quad ? \quad}$ (b) .00000000000015 = $\underline{\quad ? \quad}$

2.16 (a) 2.00000E+09 = $\underline{\quad ? \quad}$ (b) 2.00000E−09 = $\underline{\quad ? \quad}$

2.17 (a) 6.30000E+08 = $\underline{\quad ? \quad}$ (b) 6.30000E−08 = $\underline{\quad ? \quad}$

2.18 (a) 3.14159E+11 = $\underline{\quad ? \quad}$ (b) 3.14159E−11 = $\underline{\quad ? \quad}$

2.19 (a) $\underline{\quad ? \quad}$ = 7000000000 (b) $\underline{\quad ? \quad}$ = 0.000000007

2.20 (a) $\underline{\quad ? \quad}$ = 328100000000 (b) $\underline{\quad ? \quad}$ = 0.0000003281

2.21 (a) $\underline{\quad ? \quad}$ = 1000000000 (b) $\underline{\quad ? \quad}$ = 0.00000001

LAB EXERCISE 2.11 **File Name: SLEEP2**

Write and run a program that prints the number of hours, minutes, and seconds that a person has slept. Then see whether you can use your program to answer the following questions: How old does a person have to be in order to have slept a million seconds? a billion seconds?

Review of Section 2.4

- The statement

  ```
  20 INPUT X
  ```

  causes the computer to stop, print a ?, and wait for you to type in a decimal number. Then when you press the RETURN key, the computer continues the program, with the number you typed now stored in the location X.

- The statements

  ```
  15 PRINT "WHAT IS X";
  20 INPUT X
  ```

  cause the computer to print WHAT IS X? and wait for you to type in a number.

- The statement

  ```
  25 INPUT W,X,Y,Z
  ```

  causes the computer to stop, print a question mark, and wait for you to type in four numbers, separated by commas. It puts the first number you type in W, the second in X, the third in Y, and the fourth in Z. If you *don't* type four numbers, it will remind you with a double question mark or some other message (for example, REDO FROM START).

- Very large and very small numbers are printed with scientific notation.

  ▶ *Examples:* 1.34567E+08   means   134567000
  1.34567E−08   means   .00000001324567

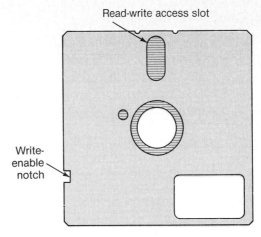

FIGURE 2.1 A microcomputer diskette. The diskette is actually a round piece of magnetically coated plastic that revolves inside the protective jacket shown here. Data is
read (or written) on the diskette through the read-write access slot. If the write-enable
notch is covered with opaque tape, then write operations are prevented.

2.5 Storing Programs on Disk or Tape

IBM

Radio Shack

APPLE

If your computer is equipped to use either hard or floppy disks (also called
diskettes), you'll be able to save the programs you've written as *disk* files. When
you do this, you'll be using something called DOS, which means *disk operating
system*. On Radio Shack computers it's called TRSDOS, on the IBM it's PC-
DOS or MS-DOS, and on the Apple it's called DOS 3.3 or PRODOS.

There are four main uses of DOS that a BASIC programmer should know
about: (1) how to load the BASIC interpreter from disk, (2) how to save and/or
load BASIC program files from disk, (3) how to save and/or retrieve data files
from disk, and (4) how to use DOS commands to manage disk files. We'll examine each of these in turn.

Loading the BASIC Interpreter

This varies with machines, but it's easy to do. Usually you put the diskette
containing DOS in the first drive (called A on the IBM, #0 on the TRS-80, #1 on
the Apple), close the drive door, and turn the power on. After you answer some
questions (or simply press ⟨enter⟩ a few times), the DOS prompt symbol will appear. You then respond by typing BASIC, BASICA, or some such similar command. (On the Apple you may have to type FP, which means "floating point"
BASIC.)

Saving and Loading BASIC Programs

After BASIC is loaded into memory, you can type in a new program, or load an
old one. For example, on the IBM or TRS-80, you load an old program by typing

```
LOAD "ARRDEM2"
```

On the Apple, you don't use the quotation marks. In all cases, the BASIC program that you originally saved with the *file name* ARRDEM2 is brought from the
disk into memory.

Rules for Choosing File Names

When one is using Microsoft BASIC on the IBM or TRS-80 computers, or when one is using the CP/M, MS-DOS, or PC-DOS operating systems, file names can have primary names with up to eight characters, followed by an optional period and a three-character secondary name. The characters allowed are capital letters, numbers, and the following punctuation marks:

```
$ & # @ ! % ' ( ) - \ _
```

Here are some examples of correct and incorrect file names.

Correct	Wrong
PROG7BAS	PROGRAM78
PROGRAM7	BAD:NM
7PROG-XX.OLD	HOLD.FORT

On the Apple, when using DOS 3.3, file names may include spaces and be 1 to 30 characters in length, but the name *must* start with a letter. The only character that may *not* be used is the comma.

Correct	Wrong
DEMO PROG5	5DEMO PROG
NAME PROGRAM	EXTRATERRESTRIAL MODULATOR PROGRAM
FILE#7	FILE,7

To double-check the contents of the program loaded from disk into memory, type LIST ⟨enter⟩. To list it on the printer, type LLIST ⟨enter⟩. If you can't remember which file names are on disk, type FILES ⟨enter⟩ (or possibly CATALOG or DIR).

To enter a new program, type NEW ⟨enter⟩, and then type in the program, line by line. On some machines you can save time here by having BASIC automatically supply the line numbers. You do this with the command AUTO ⟨enter⟩. *Important:* Be sure to turn off the AUTO mode before trying to make corrections, or doing a RUN or LIST. You leave the AUTO mode by typing ⟨ctrl⟩ ⟨break⟩ or ⟨ctrl⟩ ⟨C⟩.

To save either a new program or a modified old program, type

```
SAVE "DEMO5"
```

On the Apple, omit the quotation marks. Here DEMO5 is a name that you invent, using the rules given above. *Caution:* If there is already a file with that name, it will be overwritten by the new version.

Saving and/or Retrieving Data Files

We are going to discuss this subject at some length in Chapters 11 and 12. Until then, just bear in mind the fact that, in addition to BASIC program files, data files may also be saved on disk for later retrieval by a program.

Using DOS Commands to Manage Disk Files

The way you give DOS commands varies considerably from computer to computer. Here's how IBM PC DOS works (it's similar to MS-DOS as used on the Tandy 2000). When you see the A⟩ prompt symbols, you are "talking" to DOS. This prompt appears when you first start up the system. When you type A⟩ BASICA, you leave DOS, and you're then "talking" to BASIC. You can go back to DOS by typing

```
SYSTEM
```

You'll then see the A⟩ prompt again.

Two of the commands you can give DOS are

```
A>DIR    and    A>DIR/W
```

Both commands show you a directory of file names on the disk in drive A (on the Apple, you'd type CATALOG). The form DIR/W gives a "wide" directory, with five file names per line. The result is similar to giving the command FILES while you are in BASIC. To see the file names on the diskette in drive B, you type

```
A>DIR B:    or    A>DIR/W B:
```

You can change the name of a file—say DEMO5.BAS to DEMO6.BAS—with the command

```
A>RENAME DEMO5.BAS DEMO6.BAS
```

You can erase a file by typing

```
A>ERASE JUNK.BAS
```

Similar commands are available in Microsoft BASIC as follows:

```
NAME "DEMO5.BAS" AS "DEMO6.BAS"
KILL "JUNK.BAS"
```

Another useful DOS command is COPY. You can use it to create extra copies of a file. For example, to copy GOLD.BAS from the A drive to the B drive, use

```
COPY GOLD.BAS B:
```

To make an extra copy of GOLD.BAS on A, use

```
COPY GOLD.BAS    XTRAGOLD.BAS
```

There are many other commands available in DOS. Remember, the preceding explanations are for the IBM PC or for computers using MS-DOS, such as the Tandy 2000. For other computers, consult your DOS reference manual.

Saving and Loading Programs on Cassette Tape

Cassette-tape storage systems are less sophisticated than disk systems, but they are considerably less expensive. Here's the general procedure for saving a file you name "2" on tape on a TRS-80.

1. Make sure the program you want saved is in memory by typing LIST.
2. Position the tape cassette to a free space. If the recorder has a counter, make note of its reading.
3. Type CSAVE "2"; *do not type* ⟨enter⟩.
4. Start the tape recorder *recording*. Type ⟨enter⟩.
5. When the computer prints OK, stop the tape recorder.
6. Write the file name and date on the cassette label, along with the reading of the tape counter.

Loading Files from Cassette Tape

1. Turn on the recorder, insert the cassette, and rewind it. Reset the counter to zero. Then use Fast Forward to position the tape a little before the starting counter value for the file "2".
2. Type CLOAD "2", *and type* ⟨enter⟩.
3. Press the Play button on the recorder.
4. When the computer prints OK, stop the recorder.
5. Type LIST to check that you have loaded the program correctly.

If the loading process doesn't work properly, try again with a different play-back volume setting.

2.6   Summary of Chapter 2

■ BASIC key words are combined with line numbers and other components to make BASIC statements (instructions).

■ BASIC commands direct the computer to do something immediately. They need not be part of a statement.

■ RUN is a command that means "execute (carry out) all the BASIC statements currently stored in memory."

■ A BASIC statement consists, in general, of the following components.

⟨line number⟩ ⟨key word⟩ ⟨other components (optional)⟩

Example: 10 PRINT 2 + 2;"IS THE ANSWER."

■ REM (or ´ on some computers) is a key word meaning "ignore the rest of this BASIC statement." It allows labels, comments, blank lines, and so on, to be inserted in a program to help the human reader understand the program.

■ The key word END means "this is the end of the program." It causes the BASIC interpreter to stop execution.

■ Line numbers indicate the order in which statements are to be carried out (unless instructed otherwise). They start at 0 or 1 and go to some specified maximum number, depending on the version of BASIC: 1 to 65000 is typical.

■ PRINT statements have the following form:

⟨ln⟩ PRINT ⟨first item (optional)⟩⟨punctuation⟩⟨second item (optional)⟩...and so on. Examples:

```
10 PRINT "JULY 1985"
15 PRINT
20 PRINT "HERE ARE THE RESULTS"
25 PRINT "--------------------"
30 PRINT 2+2, 10763*313, 1/3,2^16
40 PRINT "NET VALUE=";(4.98+6.75)*.85
```

PRINT statements can calculate an arithmetic expression and print the result. Strings of characters enclosed between quotation marks (") are printed "as is." PRINT statements with no items result in a blank line being displayed (just a carriage return and a line feed).

■ The arithmetic operators in BASIC for addition, subtraction, multiplication, division, and exponentiation are: +, −, *, /, and ^ (or ** on some computers).

■ Calculations are performed according to an agreed-upon order of precedence always applied from left to right: exponentiation first; then any multiplication and division; finally addition and subtraction. Parentheses direct the computer to "do this first" and substitute the results in the expression.

■ Punctuation in PRINT statements may be required if there is more than one item to be printed. Commas spread results out; semicolons keep them close together. Exact spacing depends on the version of BASIC you are using. When no punctuation or just a space is used between items, this generally means the same as a semicolon. Examples, with output:

```
10 PRINT 2,3,4
 2            3            4
10 PRINT 2;3;4
 2 3 4
```

■ Using a comma or semicolon at the end of a PRINT statement means "print whatever is printed next by the program on the same line." That is, the usual carriage return and line feed at the end of a PRINT statement are suppressed.

■ LIST ⟨n-m⟩ directs the computer to display the BASIC program currently in memory from line n to m.

■ NEW commands the computer to erase the program currently in memory (and so be ready for a new program).

■ The LET statement assigns a value to a location in the computer's memory and gives it a label called a variable name. This statement has the form:

```
<ln> LET (optional) <variable name>=<expression>
```

```
10 LET A=10
15 B=7
30 LET D2=A+2*(B-7)/A
```

■ Strings of characters can also be stored in memory using variable names that end with $ (see Chapter 6 for further detail).

```
230 LET S$="SONG"
```

■ Rules for making up names of variables differ from one version of BASIC to another. All BASIC versions accept single letters or a letter and a number. Most also accept two letters. Some accept longer names. Examples:

```
A, X
A1, X0, P9
AB, PS, SQ
SUM1, SUM2, TEMP, XAXIS, YAXIS
```

In those versions of BASIC that allow long variable names, be careful to avoid using reserved words (key words, commands, or function names) as variable names, or in some cases, as part of a variable name.

■ The INPUT statement takes values from the keyboard and assigns them to locations in memory. When INPUT is executed, the computer prints a question mark and waits for the user to type in a value and press ⟨enter⟩.

```
<ln> INPUT <list of variable names>
10 INPUT A
20 INPUT B1,B2,N$
```

■ It's usually a good idea to accompany the INPUT statement with a PRINT statement that explains exactly what values the program expects.

```
100 PRINT "TYPE LENGTH, WIDTH, AND HEIGHT IN FEET (EX. 10,20,8)"
110 INPUT L,W,H
```

■ Scientific notation allows the computer to display very large and very small numbers using a limited number of columns (so they fit more neatly on the screen or paper).

1.2E + 08	is equivalent to	120000000
1.57828E-08	is equivalent to	.0000000157828

■ LLIST is a command similar to LIST, which directs the listing to a printer.

■ To get a printed listing on Apple computers, you use a command that switches all output from the display screen to the printer: PR#1 (assuming the printer interface board is plugged into slot 1). PR#0 switches all output back to the screen.

■ Computers that use floppy disks as a mass storage medium usually have a disk operating system (DOS), a special program that takes care of file storage tasks. On some computers, you must use the DOS to load the BASIC interpreter into memory before beginning to work.

■ FILES is a command that means "display the filenames of all files stored on disk." On the Apple, use CATALOG.

■ The SAVE ⟨filename⟩ command stores the BASIC program currently in memory on disk.

■ The LOAD ⟨filename⟩ command reads a copy of a BASIC program on disk into memory.

2.7 Problems and Programming Projects

1. Simulate running the following program by showing the output that is produced.

   ```
   10 A=10
   20 B=25
   30 A1=A+B
   40 PRINT A;" + ";B;
   50 PRINT"IS EQUAL TO ";A1
   ```

2. Simulate running the following program by showing the output produced.

   ```
   100 X=5: Y=7: Z=X*Y
   110 PRINT X;" MULTIPLIED BY ";Y;
   120 PRINT"IS ";Z
   ```

3. Make changes in the following programs so that they run correctly.

   a)
   ```
   10 PRINT GOOD MORNING
   20 ONE DOG YEAR=7 HUMAN YEARS
   30 PRINT "HOW OLD IS YOUR DOG?"
   40 INPUT
   50 D=7
   60 PRINT "YOUR DOG IS ";D:" HUMAN YEARS OLD"
   ```

   b)
   ```
   100 INPUT X
   110 PRINT"HOW MUCH MONEY DO YOU HAVE"?
   120 PRINT I NEED TO BORROW HALF
   130 Y=X DIVIDED BY Y
   140 PRINT "WILL YOU LEND ME ";Y;" DOLLARS."
   ```

4. Write a program that will add five numbers supplied by the user. Display the total and the average of the numbers.

5. Write a program that calculates the sum and product of five numbers supplied by the user. Print the sum, the product, the ratio of product to sum, and the ratio of sum to product.

6. Write a program that will:
   a) Print a greeting message.
   b) Ask the user for two numbers.
   c) Calculate the product of the numbers.
   d) Ask the user for his/her estimate of the product.
   e) Calculate the difference between (c) and (d).
   f) Tell the user how close his/her estimate was.

7. Write a program that asks the user for the times at bat and the number of hits for three players named ACE, SLUGGER, and ROOKIE. The program should then print the batting average for each player.

8. Write a program that asks the user for the price and the number of tablets supplied per bottle of four brands of vitamin C. The program should then print the price per tablet for each brand.

9. Write a program that calculates and prints the monthly payment for a four-year loan on a car. The car costs $8000. The total interest is calculated as 10% of the original cost for each year of the loan. (This is the add-on method discussed in Chapter 11.) The monthly payment is (cost of car + total interest cost)/48.

10. Modify your program from Problem 9 to allow the user to specify the length of the loan, the cost of the car, and the interest rate.

11. (Sneak Preview of String Variables) All the variables we've used so far correspond to locations in memory where numbers are stored (X, SUM, A3, and so on). BASIC also allows you to store sequences of characters like "STAR DATE 4732" or "SWEET SUE" in memory. These sequences are called *strings*. A BASIC program refers to strings by using variable names which end in a $ sign (X$, SUM$, A3$, and so on). For a preview of how strings can be used—enter, run, and experiment with the following program.

```
10 REM ************************************************
20 REM *     STRNGVAR  (DEMONSTRATES STRING VARIABLES)     *
30 REM ************************************************
40 LET G$="AH YES ... "
50 PRINT "HELLO.  WHAT IS YOUR NAME";
60 INPUT N$
70 PRINT G$;"GOOD MORNING ";N$
80 PRINT "WHAT IS YOUR LUCKY NUMBER TODAY";
90 INPUT LN
100 PRINT G$;"WELL ";N$;", MINE IS HALF THAT (";LN/2;")."

RUN
HELLO.  WHAT IS YOUR NAME? CINDY
AH YES ... GOOD MORNING CINDY
WHAT IS YOUR LUCKY NUMBER TODAY? 45
AH YES ... WELL CINDY, MINE IS HALF THAT ( 22.5 ).
Ok
```

## CHAPTER THREE

Control Structures in BASIC

NEW TOPICS INTRODUCED IN CHAPTER 3

- ■ *Control structures*
- ■ *Looping*
- ■ *Flow charts*
- ■ *STOP*
- ■ *WHILE and WEND*

- ■ *GOTO*
- ■ *IF ... THEN*
- ■ *Program styling*
- ■ *FOR ... NEXT ... STEP*
- ■ *Structured D charts*

3.1   What Is a Control Structure?

The dictionary defines the word *structure* to mean "a complex entity with parts that are organized in some methodical way." In computer programming, the word "structure" is used with a similar meaning, but it's applied in three different ways.

First, computer programs themselves can be viewed as structures, and the process of putting them together according to a well-organized plan is called structured programming. We'll have a lot to say about this subject, particularly in Part II of the book, where we'll note that it's also a good idea to decompose large programs into sub-structures called *program modules.*

Second, the data (numbers and characters) used by programs can be organized in special ways, giving rise to the term *data structures*. Chapter 4 says more about data structures, and explains how to use one- and two-dimensional array structures. Arrays are also used extensively in the programs of Part II. Chapter 10 introduces an advanced data structure called the linked list.

The third use you'll see of the word structure is in the term *control-structure* statement. This is a programming statement that can change the normal flow of control in a program. In other words, it's a statement that can cause a program to abandon the usual rule that "statements are to be executed in the order given by their line numbers."

This chapter is about control-structure statements. The three we'll examine in the first part of the chapter are the GOTO statement, the IF ...THEN statement, and the FOR ... NEXT statement. Let's start with GOTO.

3.2 The GOTO Statement

This is literally a statement that allows you to tell the computer where it can go (at least as far as order of execution goes).

Let's illustrate its use in our second TV-rating program (RAT2 in Section 2.4). We'll put in a statement (line 120) that tells the computer to GO (back) TO line 10 and run the program all over again.

```
4 REM-------------------------------------------------------
6 REM          GOTO (ADDS A 'GOTO' STATEMENT TO RAT2)
8 REM-------------------------------------------------------
10 PRINT "TYPE IN THE TIME SLOT NUMBER:"
20 INPUT N
30 PRINT "INPUT THE TOTAL NUMBER OF VIEWERS:"
40 INPUT A
50 PRINT "TYPE IN THE NUMBER OF ABS VIEWERS:"
60 INPUT B
70 LET C=(B/A)*100
80 PRINT "TIME SLOT NO.","TOTAL VIEWERS-VIEWERS OF ABS";
90 PRINT "-% WATCHING ABS"
100 PRINT N,A,B,C;"%"
110 PRINT
120 GOTO 10
130 END
```

Here's the GOTO statement. You may type either 120 GO TO 10 or 120 GOTO 10

Recall that this makes the computer print an empty line and makes the output look nicer.

Now we don't have to continually type RUN. *But* the computer will go eternally back to line 10, through line 120, back to line 10, and so on. This program puts the computer into an "infinite loop." This means that the computer will try to go through a program (or a part of it) forever unless it is stopped. Infinite loops are not usually a good idea, and we'll see how to avoid them in Section 3.3. But let's examine a little further the consequences of using GOTO to create such loops.

APPLE

Radio Shack

IBM

The first thing we realize is that, before running any program that contains an infinite loop, we should know how to stop the "running" (execution) of the program. Ask someone how to stop it, or read your computer manual, but make sure you know. On many systems (including the Apple), you press ⟨ctrl⟩ ⟨C⟩, which means "hold down the CONTROL key and then press C." On other systems (such as the TRS-80), you use the BREAK key. On the IBM PC, you use ⟨ctrl⟩ ⟨break⟩.

Here's what a run of the preceding program would look like.

```
RUN
TYPE IN THE TIME SLOT NUMBER:
? 2
INPUT THE TOTAL NUMBER OF VIEWERS:
? 36530
TYPE IN THE NUMBER OF ABS VIEWERS:
? 9604
TIME SLOT NO. TOTAL VIEWERS-VIEWERS OF ABS-% WATCHING ABS
 2            36530         9604          26.2907 %
```

```
TYPE IN THE TIME SLOT NUMBER:
? 3
INPUT THE TOTAL NUMBER OF VIEWERS:
? 47867
TYPE IN THE NUMBER OF ABS VIEWERS:
? 16390
TIME SLOT NO. TOTAL VIEWERS-VIEWERS OF ABS-% WATCHING ABS
   3            47867          16390         34.2407 %

TYPE IN THE TIME SLOT NUMBER:
? 4
INPUT THE TOTAL NUMBER OF VIEWERS:
? ^C
Break in 40
Ok
```

See what the GOTO statement did? The computer went back to line 10 and started the program over again.

Either ⟨ctrl⟩⟨C⟩ or ⟨ctrl⟩⟨break⟩ or ⟨break⟩ was pressed here. The notations ⟨ctrl⟩⟨C⟩, ^C, and Control-C all mean the same thing.

Flow Charts

Flow charting is a method of visually showing in what order the computer will run a program. It uses symbols such as

and lines with arrows to create a "map" of what the computer will do. Figure 3.1 is a flow chart of the preceding program.

You can see from Figure 3.1 that the computer will never reach the END statement in this particular program, since the line above it represents the GOTO statement.

Flow charting is especially helpful in planning very complicated programs, since a flow chart makes it easier to follow the logic or sequence of the program. We'll say more about this subject later in this chapter and in Chapter 7.

EXERCISES Simulate computer runs of the next two programs.

3.1 Show the output of INFINITE after five loops, if you input 1 for A.

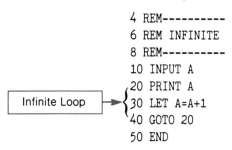

```
4 REM----------
6 REM INFINITE
8 REM----------
10 INPUT A
20 PRINT A
30 LET A=A+1
40 GOTO 20
50 END
```

Infinite Loop

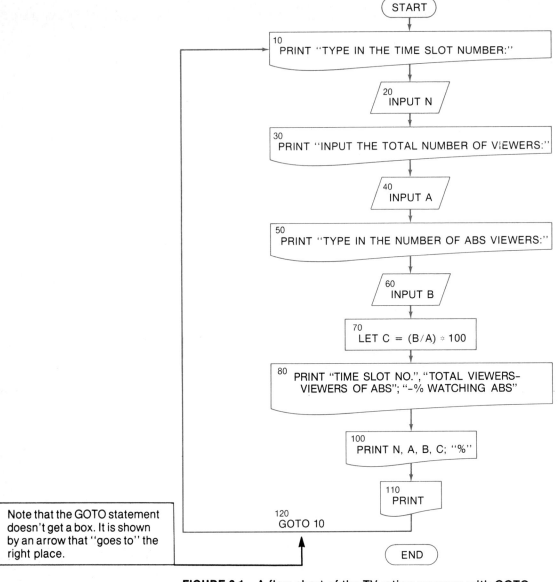

Note that the GOTO statement doesn't get a box. It is shown by an arrow that "goes to" the right place.

FIGURE 3.1 A flow chart of the TV-rating program with GOTO

3.2 Use 1, 2, and 10 for R.

```
4 REM----------------------------------------
6 REM    CIRCLE (FINDS AREA OF A CIRCLE)
8 REM----------------------------------------
10 PRINT "PROGRAM TO FIND AREA OF A CIRCLE"
20 PRINT "TYPE IN THE RADIUS"
30 INPUT R
40 LET A=3.14159*R*R
50 PRINT "AREA =";A
60 GOTO 20
70 END
```

3.3 What is wrong with each of the following "statements"?

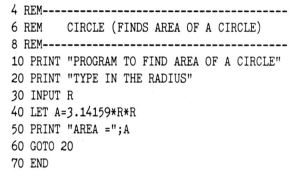

```
10 INPUT 4          40 LET C=B+A,        70 INPUT F AND G
20 LET B=3A         50 INPUT, D,E,       80 LET H="F+G"
30 INPUT C+A        60 PRINT "D/E=;D/E   90 PRINT "H";=H
```

LAB EXERCISE 3.1   File Name: RAT3

There is still one more thing we can do with our television program: Shorten it! One way to do this is to input several numbers in one step, as we did in Section 2.4. So here's our final version.

```
4 REM------------------------------------------------------
6 REM      RAT3 (INCLUDES PRINT, INPUT, LET AND GOTO)
8 REM------------------------------------------------------
10 PRINT "TYPE, IN THIS ORDER:"
20 PRINT "TIME SLOT NO., TOTAL VIEWERS, VIEWERS OF ABS"
30 INPUT N,A,B
40 LET C=(B/A)*100
50 PRINT "TIME SLOT NO.","TOTAL VIEWERS-VIEWERS OF ABS";
60 PRINT "-% WATCHING ABS"
70 PRINT N,A,B,C;"%"
80 PRINT
90 GOTO 20
100 END
```

We are transferring to line 20, not 10, just to make the output a little shorter.

Run this program, using the information from the program RAT1.

▶ *Special Variation:* Change line 20 by putting a semicolon (;) at the end and see what happens.

LAB EXERCISE 3.2   File Name: WAU

You are a dispatch director for Trans Waukegan Airlines. It's your job to give the pilots all the information they need for their flights. One of the things they have to know is the estimated flight time, that is, how long a given flight is expected to take. The pilots also want an estimate of the amount of fuel that will be needed. You're getting tired of just guessing, so—in a small step for mankind and a giant leap for Waukegan—you decide to use the computer.

Write and run a program using the information given in Table 3.1. Your program should produce output like that shown here. (MPH means miles per hour.)

```
RUN
TYPE IN:
FLIGHT NUMBER:? 128
PLANE SPEED (MPH):? 600
DISTANCE (MILES):? 560
WIND SPEED (MPH):? -40

FLIGHT NUMBER: 128
ESTIMATED FLIGHT TIME: 60 MINUTES
FUEL NEEDED: 9960 POUNDS + RESERVE

TYPE IN:
FLIGHT NUMBER:?
```

−40 means a head wind *hindering* the plane's progress.
40 would mean a tail wind that *helped* the plane's progress.

The speed of the plane with respect to the ground is called the *ground speed.* We are assuming that the wind is either a head wind or a tail wind. If there

(continued)

is a tail wind, the ground speed equals the sum of the plane speed and the wind speed. If there is a head wind, you subtract the wind speed from the plane speed, or you do as the computer does, that is, *add the negative number* that represents the speed of the head wind.

Here are the formulas you'll want to use.

Ground speed in miles per minute = (plane speed + wind speed)/60
Time traveled in minutes = (distance in miles)/(ground speed, miles/min.)

Assume that about 166 pounds of fuel are burned for each minute of flight.

Example: Suppose that

Plane speed = 600 mph

Wind speed = 60 mph (this means a tail wind)

Distance = 330 miles

Then:

Ground speed in miles per minute = (600 + 60)/60 = 660/60 = 11 miles per minute

Time traveled in minutes = 330/11 = 30 minutes

Fuel needed = 166*30 = 4980 pounds of fuel

Estimate the flight time and the fuel needed for each of the flights listed in Table 3.1.

TABLE 3.1   Flight Information for Trans Waukegan Airlines

Flight no.	Plane Speed (mph)	Point of Origin Destination	Distance (miles)	Wind Speed (mph)
126	600	Boston - Pittsburgh	483	−45 (head)
381	600	Washington - Los Angeles	2300	−55 (head)
513	600	Denver - Salt Lake City	371	−25 (head)
125	600	Miami - New York	1092	+38 (tail)
120	600	San Francisco - Chicago	1858	+50 (tail)
630	600	Detroit - Seattle	1938	−60 (head)
819	600	Philadelphia - Washington	123	+30 (tail)

Review of Section 3.2

■ Computers execute statements in the order given by the line numbers of the statements. You can *change* this order by using a GOTO statement. A GOTO statement, as the name implies, forces the computer to go to a specific statement anywhere in a program. For example:

```
300 GOTO 179
```

forces the computer to go from statement 300 to statement 179 and continue execution at that point in the program. We say that the program branches to statement 179.

■ Some of the programming techniques illustrated in this section are the following.

1. It's a good idea to use a PRINT statement to tell the person running the program what the INPUT statement is asking for.

2. Instead of always rerunning a program, we can use a GOTO statement to cycle back to the beginning of the program (or to any other point). An even better technique will be shown later. To stop programs caught in a loop, press ⟨ctrl⟩ ⟨C⟩ or ⟨ctrl⟩ ⟨break⟩.

3. Always label an answer. Don't just say 26.290, for example. Make sure it's clear whether 26.290 is the percentage of viewers watching ABS, the weight of your dog, or whatever else you had in mind.

3.3 Statements Using IF...THEN; STOP

Sue is a computer programmer for the state transportation department. She has just been given an assignment: to computerize the process of automobile driver licensing.

She decides that the first thing the computer should do is to look at the applicant's age and determine what type of license (if any) can possibly be issued. Here is what Sue is thinking:

1. IF the person's age is less than 16, THEN the computer should print:

       "NO LICENSE POSSIBLE -- UNDER AGE"

2. IF the person is 16, THEN the computer should print:

       "JUNIOR OPERATOR'S LICENSE POSSIBLE"

3. IF the person is older than 16, THEN the computer should print:

       "OPERATOR'S LICENSE POSSIBLE"

In reality, Sue has set up three test conditions about the applicant's age that can be stated as the following three assertions:

1. The applicant is *younger than* 16.

2. The applicant *is* 16.

3. The applicant is *older than* 16.

One and only one of these assertions can be true for each applicant. Hence it should be possible to program the computer to find out which fits each applicant. Let's first use English "if" sentences to show the logical thinking needed to decide which assertion holds.

For example, suppose that an applicant is 19 years old.

1. IF the applicant is younger than 16,...
   But the applicant is *not* younger than 16; so assertion 1 is *false,* and we continue.

2. IF the applicant is 16,...
   But the applicant is *not* 16; so assertion 2 is *false,* and we continue.

3. IF the applicant is older than 16,...
   The applicant is 19; so assertion 3 is *true.* We therefore decide that the applicant is eligible for a regular operator's license.

The logic behind this thinking can be summarized in the flow chart of Figure 3.2.

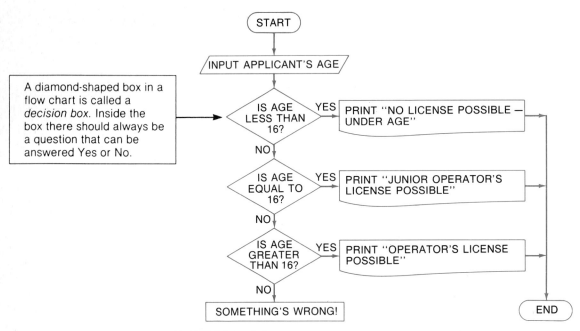

FIGURE 3.2   A flow chart that describes logic in granting drivers' licenses

Another way to describe a decision box is to say that it corresponds to a condition that is either *true* or *false*. Such conditions are described in BASIC by using the symbols <, =, or >, where:

A<16   means that A is less than 16
A=16   means that A is exactly equal to 16
A>16   means that A is greater than 16

Now look again at Figure 3.2. Can you think of an age that would result in the answer No to all three questions in the decision boxes? In other words, can you think of an age that is *not* less than 16, *not* equal to 16, and also *not* greater than 16? Of course not. This tells us that the third decision box is not really needed.

EXERCISE

3.4   Redraw the flow chart in Figure 3.2 so that it uses only two decision boxes.

Before writing her program, Sue decided on one more improvement. Instead of ending the program after checking one applicant, she decided to have the program loop back to the beginning. But to avoid having an infinite loop, she put in a special decision box at the start, which would stop the program any time she typed in 0 (zero). Figure 3.3 shows her new flow chart.

Here's a program based on Sue's flow chart.

```
4 REM---------------------------------------------
6 REM  IFTHEN (BRANCHING WITH SIMPLE IF...THEN)
8 REM---------------------------------------------
10 PRINT "TYPE 0 (ZERO) TO STOP THIS PROGRAM."
20 PRINT
30 PRINT "TYPE IN APPLICANT'S AGE:";
40 INPUT A
```

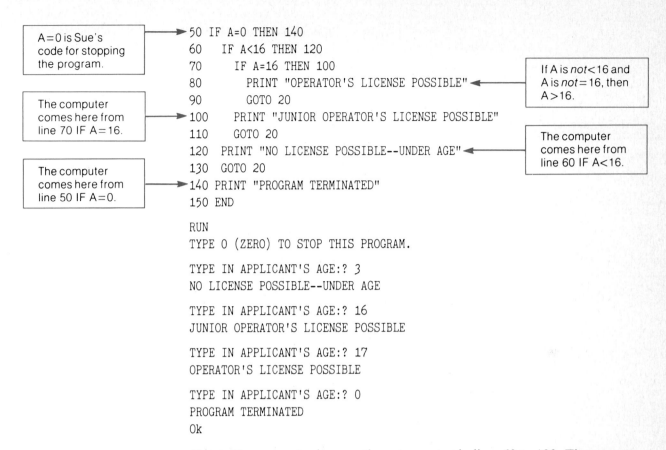

```
50 IF A=0 THEN 140
60    IF A<16 THEN 120
70       IF A=16 THEN 100
80          PRINT "OPERATOR'S LICENSE POSSIBLE"
90          GOTO 20
100      PRINT "JUNIOR OPERATOR'S LICENSE POSSIBLE"
110      GOTO 20
120   PRINT "NO LICENSE POSSIBLE--UNDER AGE"
130   GOTO 20
140 PRINT "PROGRAM TERMINATED"
150 END

RUN
TYPE 0 (ZERO) TO STOP THIS PROGRAM.

TYPE IN APPLICANT'S AGE:? 3
NO LICENSE POSSIBLE--UNDER AGE

TYPE IN APPLICANT'S AGE:? 16
JUNIOR OPERATOR'S LICENSE POSSIBLE

TYPE IN APPLICANT'S AGE:? 17
OPERATOR'S LICENSE POSSIBLE

TYPE IN APPLICANT'S AGE:? 0
PROGRAM TERMINATED
Ok
```

Annotations in figure:

A=0 is Sue's code for stopping the program.

The computer comes here from line 70 IF A=16.

The computer comes here from line 50 IF A=0.

If A is *not* <16 and A is *not* =16, then A>16.

The computer comes here from line 60 IF A<16.

▶ *Note:* The computer ignores the extra spaces in lines 60 to 130. These extra spaces are used to make it easier to see which statements are executed when an IF condition is *not* true. This is one of the techniques used to do what's called styling of the program. Another use of spaces that is recommended for styling purposes is to indent the body of FOR loops, as will be shown in Section 3.4.

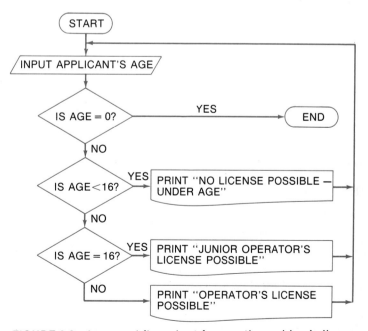

FIGURE 3.3   Improved flow chart for granting a driver's license

Here are examples of three other kinds of conditions that can be used in BASIC:

A> =16   means   A greater than 16 or A equal to 16

A<=16   means   A less than 16 or A equal to 16

A<>16   means   A *not* equal to 16 (on some computers, # can be used
                instead of <>)

The condition A>=18 is true if either A>18 or A=18. Here's an example that shows how you might use such a condition. This example also illustrates the use of the key word STOP. Figure 3.4 shows the flow chart.

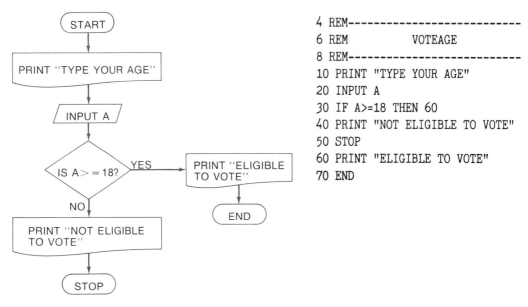

```
4 REM--------------------------
6 REM            VOTEAGE
8 REM--------------------------
10 PRINT "TYPE YOUR AGE"
20 INPUT A
30 IF A>=18 THEN 60
40 PRINT "NOT ELIGIBLE TO VOTE"
50 STOP
60 PRINT "ELIGIBLE TO VOTE"
70 END
```

FIGURE 3.4   Flow chart: Eligible to vote

Using the Key Word STOP

In some versions of BASIC, the last statement in a program *must* be an END statement. To stop execution at any other place, you can use a statement with the key word STOP. However, most recent versions of BASIC allow you to use END anywhere in the program, so you can use either END or STOP to cause execution to stop before the last statement is reached. The main difference is that STOP prints a message telling you the line number where the program stopped. On the other hand, END does something called "closing files," which is useful for the programs that we'll discuss in Chapters 11 and 12.

Making Programs that Use IF . . . THEN Easier to Read

Most versions of BASIC allow you to write IF statements with one or more statements after THEN. This construct helps make the logic of the programs much "cleaner." When several statements follow THEN, they must be separated by a colon (:). (Some versions of BASIC use a backslash (\ ) instead of a colon.) When the IF condition is true, all the statements after THEN are executed. Otherwise, none are executed, and execution continues at the next numbered statement.

The following examples show how to apply this technique to the last two programs. The second example shows how to use the single quote (') as an abbreviation for REM.

```
4 REM-------------------------------------------------
6 REM  IFTHEN2  (BRANCHING WITH EXTENDED IF...THEN)
8 REM-------------------------------------------------
10 PRINT "TYPE 0 (ZERO) TO STOP THIS PROGRAM."
20 PRINT: PRINT "TYPE IN APPLICANT'S AGE:";
30 INPUT A
40 IF A=0 THEN PRINT "PROGRAM TERMINATED": END
50   IF A<16 THEN PRINT"NO LICENSE POSSIBLE--UNDER AGE": GOTO 20
60     IF A=16 THEN PRINT"JUNIOR OPERATOR'S LICENSE POSSIBLE": GOTO 20
70       PRINT "OPERATOR'S LICENSE POSSIBLE": GOTO 20

RUN
TYPE 0 (ZERO) TO STOP THIS PROGRAM.

TYPE IN APPLICANT'S AGE:? 3
NO LICENSE POSSIBLE--UNDER AGE

TYPE IN APPLICANT'S AGE:? 16
JUNIOR OPERATOR'S LICENSE POSSIBLE

TYPE IN APPLICANT'S AGE:? 17
OPERATOR'S LICENSE POSSIBLE

TYPE IN APPLICANT'S AGE:? 0
PROGRAM TERMINATED
Ok


4 '--------------------------
6 '          VOTEAGE2
8 '--------------------------
10 PRINT "TYPE YOUR AGE"
20 INPUT A
30 IF A>=18 THEN PRINT "ELIGIBLE TO VOTE": STOP
40 PRINT "NOT ELIGIBLE TO VOTE"

RUN
TYPE YOUR AGE
? 14
NOT ELIGIBLE TO VOTE
Ok
RUN
TYPE YOUR AGE
? 18
ELIGIBLE TO VOTE
Break in 30
Ok
```

EXERCISES

3.5   Here is part of a program.

```
10 LET B=16
20 LET C=24
30 LET D=48
40 ----------
50 ----------
60 ----------
   ------------
```

Table 3.2 shows ten versions of line 40. In each case, decide whether the condition is true or false, and indicate the next statement to which the program will branch.

TABLE 3.2

Statement 40:	Condition Is:	Branch To:
1. 40 IF D>B THEN 60	TRUE (48>16)	60
2. 40 IF B=D THEN 60	FALSE (16 is not equal to 48)	50
3. 40 IF B/8=D/C THEN 60	TRUE WHY?	?
4. 40 IF B<>D THEN 60	? WHY?	?
5. 40 IF D<=2*C THEN 60	TRUE WHY?	?
6. 40 IF D/B>=D/C THEN 80	? WHY?	?
7. 40 IF 3*D<>2*B THEN 80	? WHY?	?
8. 40 IF B*D<=C*D THEN 80	? WHY?	?
9. 40 IF C + B<40 THEN 80	? WHY?	?
10. 40 IF B*B>=D*D THEN 80	? WHY?	?

3.6   Pretend you are a computer and simulate running the following program. Although it makes an interesting puzzle, this is really an example of how *not* to write programs. The haphazard use of GOTO (or IF...THEN) statements as shown here is bad practice, and it should be avoided in serious programming.

```
4 REM---------------------
6 REM          PUZZLE
8 REM---------------------
10 LET F=10
20 IF 18<2*F THEN 50
30    PRINT "WAS"
40    GOTO 170
50 LET G=20
60 IF G/F<>4/2 THEN 80
70    PRINT "THIS"
80 GOTO 120
90 PRINT "NEVER"
100 PRINT "A"
110 GOTO 70
```

```
120 PRINT "PROGRAM"
130 LET F=F-7
140 IF F/2<=1.5 THEN 20
150 PRINT "EVER"
160 IF F/2>1.5 THEN 80
170 PRINT "RUN"
180 IF G+F<25 THEN 220
190   PRINT "SPOT"
200   PRINT "RUN"
210   LET F=F+1
220 IF G-F<=F+F THEN 190
230 PRINT "CORRECTLY."
240 END
```

LAB EXERCISE 3.3   **File Name: MATHQUIZ**

Here is a program that is short, yet it gives a long addition quiz (20 questions). Draw a flow chart and then run it. (You might also try changing it to a multiplication quiz.)

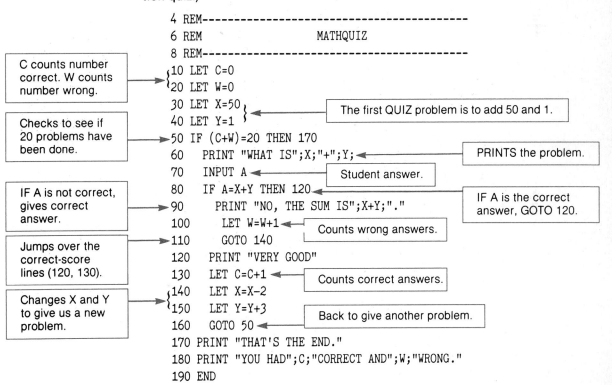

C counts number correct. W counts number wrong.

Checks to see if 20 problems have been done.

IF A is not correct, gives correct answer.

Jumps over the correct-score lines (120, 130).

Changes X and Y to give us a new problem.

```
4 REM------------------------------------------
6 REM                    MATHQUIZ
8 REM------------------------------------------
10 LET C=0
20 LET W=0
30 LET X=50
40 LET Y=1
50 IF (C+W)=20 THEN 170
60   PRINT "WHAT IS";X;"+";Y;
70   INPUT A
80   IF A=X+Y THEN 120
90     PRINT "NO, THE SUM IS";X+Y;"."
100    LET W=W+1
110    GOTO 140
120   PRINT "VERY GOOD"
130   LET C=C+1
140   LET X=X-2
150   LET Y=Y+3
160   GOTO 50
170 PRINT "THAT'S THE END."
180 PRINT "YOU HAD";C;"CORRECT AND";W;"WRONG."
190 END
```

The first QUIZ problem is to add 50 and 1.

PRINTS the problem.

Student answer.

IF A is the correct answer, GOTO 120.

Counts wrong answers.

Counts correct answers.

Back to give another problem.

▶ *Note:* In most versions of BASIC, lines 10 and 20 are unnecessary. Numeric variables automatically have the value 0 to begin with.

LAB EXERCISE 3.4   **File Name: MATHQ2**

Rewrite MATHQUIZ using the form of IF...THEN that allows several statements (instead of a line number) after THEN. For example, you can use

```
80  IF A=X+Y THEN PRINT "VERY GOOD":C=C+1:GOTO 140
```

Looping

Let's discuss another use of the IF...THEN statement. Suppose that we wish to print the squares of all the whole numbers from 1 to 10. (The square of 2 is 2 × 2, or 4.) We could say:

```
10 PRINT 1*1
20 PRINT 2*2
30 PRINT 3*3
     .
     .  }  There would be six additional statements here.
     .
100 PRINT 10*10
110 END
```

But we can write a much *shorter* program that will do the same thing, as shown in Figure 3.5 and the following program.

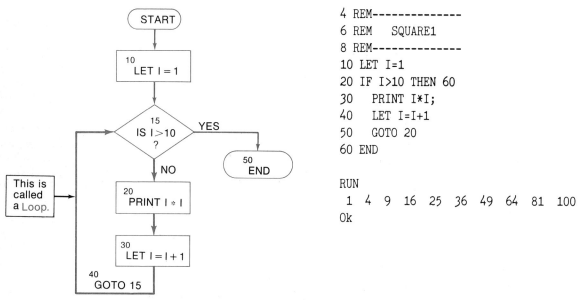

```
4 REM-------------
6 REM    SQUARE1
8 REM-------------
10 LET I=1
20 IF I>10 THEN 60
30    PRINT I*I;
40    LET I=I+1
50    GOTO 20
60 END

RUN
  1  4  9  16  25  36  49  64  81  100
Ok
```

FIGURE 3.5 Flow chart: the squares of whole numbers from 1 to 10, and a corresponding BASIC program. Note that the program would be the same length if we decided to print the squares of the whole numbers from 1 to 100, or any other range.

You can see from the flow chart of Figure 3.5 that the program controls the looping (repetition) of a group of statements. Let's take a closer look at how it works.

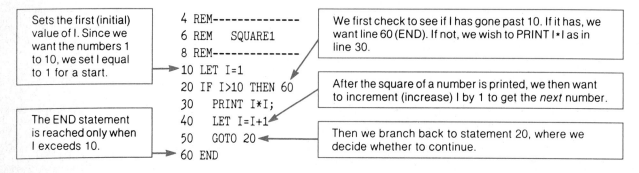

Step 20 uses IF...THEN to *test* whether the program is finished. We put our test right at the start of the program. (It is also possible to put it other places.) Note that IF...THEN provides a neat way of escaping from a loop. In other words, there won't be an infinite loop.

Summary

You can avoid infinite loops in your programs by using IF...THEN statements together with statements that *increment* the loop variable.

It's somewhat analogous to the situation in which a bus driver travels a "loop" around an area of the city, over and over. Each time he passes the starting point, he presses a lever to *increment* his trip counter. He gets out of the loop and heads for the garage when his counter shows 10 trips.

LAB EXERCISE 3.5   File Name: SQUARE20

Change the preceding program to print out the squares of the numbers from 10 to 30.

LAB EXERCISE 3.6   File Name: QUIZ1

Write (off-line) a QUIZ program on any subject (music, history, physics, mathematics, accounting, and so on) that appeals to you. You can use the following program as an example. Your program should be at least as long, and it should keep score. Include enough directions so that anyone can run your program. When you are sure it's ready, try it on-line with a friend.

Sample QUIZ Program   (Sample Run Is Given on Page 72)

```
4 '-----------------------------------------------------------
6 ' QUIZ1  (USES EXTENDED IF...THEN)
8 '-----------------------------------------------------------
10 S=0
20 PRINT "HERE IS A LIST OF SIX NAMES IN MUSIC. YOU WILL BE"
30 PRINT "ASKED FOUR QUESTIONS; ANSWER EACH WITH THE NUMBER"
40 PRINT "CORRESPONDING TO THE CORRECT NAME."
50 PRINT "1. BEATLES         2. ENRICO CARUSO"
60 PRINT "3. BOB DYLAN       4. LUDWIG VAN BEETHOVEN"
70 PRINT "5. JOHANN S. BACH  6. LOUIS ARMSTRONG"
90 PRINT: PRINT "WHO WROTE NINE SYMPHONIES?"
100 INPUT A
110 IF A=4 THEN S=S+1: PRINT"RIGHT!": GOTO 130
120   PRINT "NO, BEETHOVEN (4) IS THE ANSWER."
130 PRINT: PRINT "NAME A FORMER MAJOR 'ROCK' GROUP."
140 INPUT B
150 IF B=1 THEN S=S+1: PRINT"CORRECT!": GOTO 170
160   PRINT "NO, BEATLES (1) IS THE ANSWER."
170 PRINT: PRINT "A FAMOUS ITALIAN OPERA STAR WHO DIED IN 1921 WAS:"
```

(continued)

```
180 INPUT C
190 IF C=2 THEN S=S+1: PRINT"YES!!": GOTO 210
200   PRINT "NO, ENRICO CARUSO (2) IS THE ANSWER."
210 PRINT: PRINT "WHO WAS 'SATCHMO'?"
220 INPUT D
230 IF D=6 THEN S=S+1: PRINT"GREAT!": GOTO 250
240   PRINT "NO, LOUIS ARMSTRONG (6) IS THE ANSWER."
250 PRINT "OK, YOUR SCORE OUT OF A POSSIBLE 4 IS";S;"."
260 IF S=4 THEN PRINT"YOU HAD A PERFECT SCORE.  CONGRATULATIONS!!!": END
270   PRINT "HOPE YOU HAD FUN.  MAYBE NEXT TIME YOU CAN DO BETTER."
```

Here is a sample run of the QUIZ program shown on page 71.

```
HERE IS A LIST OF SIX NAMES IN MUSIC. YOU WILL BE
ASKED FOUR QUESTIONS; ANSWER EACH WITH THE NUMBER
CORRESPONDING TO THE CORRECT NAME.
1. BEATLES         2. ENRICO CARUSO
3. BOB DYLAN       4. LUDWIG VAN BEETHOVEN
5. JOHANN S. BACH  6. LOUIS ARMSTRONG

WHO WROTE NINE SYMPHONIES?
? 1
NO, BEETHOVEN (4) IS THE ANSWER.

NAME A FORMER MAJOR 'ROCK' GROUP.
? 2
NO, BEATLES (1) IS THE ANSWER.

A FAMOUS ITALIAN OPERA STAR WHO DIED IN 1921 WAS:
? 3
NO, ENRICO CARUSO (2) IS THE ANSWER.

WHO WAS 'SATCHMO'?
? 5
NO, LOUIS ARMSTRONG (6) IS THE ANSWER.
OK, YOUR SCORE OUT OF A POSSIBLE 4 IS 0 .
HOPE YOU HAD FUN.  MAYBE NEXT TIME YOU CAN DO BETTER.
Ok
```

Review of Section 3.3

The IF...THEN statement is one of the most important statements in programming. It allows a computer program to "decide" whether the next statement to be executed is the one right below, or the one that the THEN part mentions. Some examples of correct IF...THEN statements are:

```
 23 IF A<4 THEN 200
 97 IF C>=9*A THEN 320
126 IF R=S+T THEN 560
516 IF V<>M+1 THEN 680
```

The parts of the IF...THEN statement (see Figure 3.6) are:

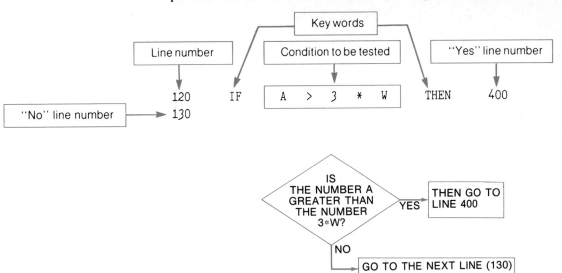

FIGURE 3.6 Flow-chart representation of the above IF ...THEN statement

■ The extended IF...THEN works similarly, but takes the following form:

```
220 IF condition THEN statement1: statement2: statement3: ...
```

If the condition is true, *all* the statements after THEN are executed. If it is false, *none* will be executed. Control then passes to the next numbered statement.

3.4 Statements Using the Key Words FOR and NEXT; STEP

The FOR and NEXT statements were invented to simplify the writing of programs that do the same kind of thing over and over again—in other words, programs that contain loops. This means that FOR and NEXT can help you write short programs that produce lots of output.

The IF...THEN statement can also be used to write programs with loops, but using FOR and NEXT is easier in those cases to which it applies. Let's compare using the two methods to print the squares of the first ten natural numbers.

Looping with IF...THEN

```
4 REM--------------
6 REM    SQUARE1
8 REM--------------
10 LET I=1
20 IF I>10 THEN 60
30    PRINT I*I;
40    LET I=I+1
50    GOTO 20
60 END
```

Looping with FOR and NEXT

```
4 REM--------------
6 REM    SQUARE2
8 REM--------------
10 FOR I=1 TO 10
20    PRINT I*I;
30 NEXT I
40 END
```

These two programs do the same thing:

- They both start I out equal to 1.
- They both PRINT I*I, and then increase I by 1.
- They both continue to print the square of I until I exceeds 10.
- Then they both stop.

When run, both programs produce the same output.

```
RUN
 1  4  9  16  25  36  49  64  81  100
Ok
```

Notice that FOR and NEXT are *both* used in the second program. They are always used as a pair.

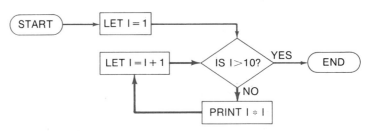

```
10 FOR ...


30 NEXT ...
```

We can see the "loop" in the first program (the one that uses IF...THEN) by drawing a flow chart like that in Figure 3.7. We can also see that when the number I gets larger than 10, the IF statement will throw the computer out of the loop. The heavy lines show where the looping takes place.

FIGURE 3.7   Flow chart, showing use of IF ...THEN to control a loop

This looping idea works the same way in a FOR-NEXT loop, except that the computer automatically does

    the *incrementing step:*   (LET I=I+1)

and

    the *testing step:*   (IS I>10?)

Here's a description of the FOR-NEXT version of the same program.

BASIC	ENGLISH
`4 REM------------`	
`6 REM   SQUARE2`	
`8 REM------------`	
`10 FOR I=1 TO 10`	Let I=1; if I<=10, print I*I,
`20    PRINT I*I`	go back and get the next I(=2); if I<=10, print I*I
`30 NEXT I`	go back and get the next I(=3); if I<=10, print I*I
`40 END`	and so on, until we have printed I*I for I=10.

Are you confused? The above explanation of FOR-NEXT loops is from a computer viewpoint. Let's look at FOR-NEXT loops from a human viewpoint, and also show how looping can apply to whole groups of statements.

Using FOR . . . NEXT to Repeat Blocks of Statements

Let's write a "program" to describe what really happens when a person does something several times. For example, suppose that we want someone to clap hands and sing a little tune five times. A "program" that we might try is the following.

1. FOR each number from 1 to 5, you're going to do something. Let's start with 1.
2. Clap your hands and sing a tune.
3. Go back and get the NEXT number, but stop if it is greater than 5.

Someone following our "program" would do the following.

① Start with 1
Check: Is 1 greater than 5?
No
Clap and sing

② Go on to the NEXT number: 1+1=2
Check: Is 2 greater than 5?
No
Clap and sing

③ NEXT number — LET the number equal 2+1=3
Check: Is 3 greater than 5?
No
Clap and sing

④ NEXT I — LET I=I+1=3+1=4
Check: Is 4 greater than 5?
No
Clap and sing

⑤ NEXT I — LET I=I+1=4+1=5
Check: Is 5 greater than 5?
No
Clap and sing

NEXT I — LET I=I+1=5+1=6
Check: Is 6 greater than 5?
Yes
Stop!

This English "program," simple though it is, gives you some idea of how FOR and NEXT work in BASIC.

Summary

The FOR and NEXT statements are used to count for the computer while it does something over and over.

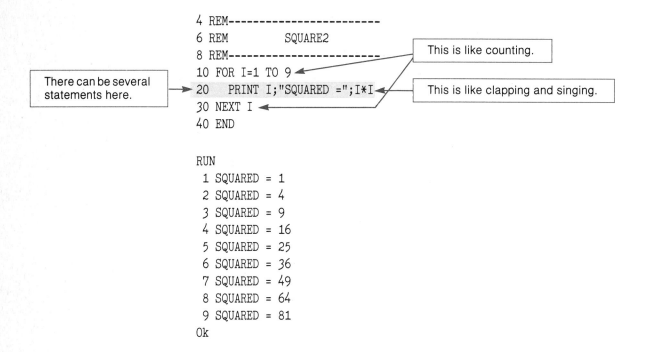

```
4 REM-----------------------
6 REM          SQUARE2
8 REM-----------------------
10 FOR I=1 TO 9
20    PRINT I;"SQUARED =";I*I
30 NEXT I
40 END
```

This is like counting.

This is like clapping and singing.

There can be several statements here.

```
RUN
 1 SQUARED = 1
 2 SQUARED = 4
 3 SQUARED = 9
 4 SQUARED = 16
 5 SQUARED = 25
 6 SQUARED = 36
 7 SQUARED = 49
 8 SQUARED = 64
 9 SQUARED = 81
Ok
```

Here's an example that has four statements *between* the FOR and NEXT statements. These four statements are called the *body* of the loop.

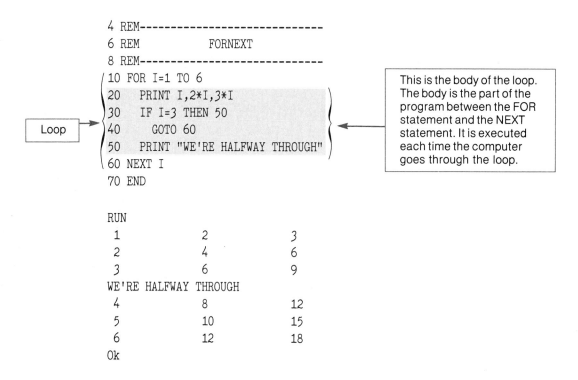

```
4 REM----------------------------
6 REM           FORNEXT
8 REM----------------------------
10 FOR I=1 TO 6
20    PRINT I,2*I,3*I
30    IF I=3 THEN 50
40       GOTO 60
50    PRINT "WE'RE HALFWAY THROUGH"
60 NEXT I
70 END
```

Loop

This is the body of the loop. The body is the part of the program between the FOR statement and the NEXT statement. It is executed each time the computer goes through the loop.

```
RUN
 1            2            3
 2            4            6
 3            6            9
WE'RE HALFWAY THROUGH
 4            8            12
 5            10           15
 6            12           18
Ok
```

Using STEP to Modify FOR . . . NEXT Statements

A FOR statement doesn't have to start with 1. Look at the following.

```
4 REM----------
6 REM FORNEXT1
8 REM----------
10 FOR M=2 TO 5
20   PRINT M
30 NEXT M
40 END

RUN
 2
 3
 4
 5
Ok
10 FOR M=5 TO 6
RUN
 5
 6
Ok
10 FOR M=163 TO 165
RUN
 163
 164
 165
Ok
```

We are changing only line 10. The rest of the program remains the same.

If you were told to count to 10 by 2's, you would say:

2 4 6 8 10

How about counting from 1 to 9 by 2's?

1 3 5 7 9

Or count from 2 to 11 by 4's:

2 6 10

Note that the lower number (1 in "from 1 to 9") is the first value, and the number you are counting by is then *added* to it to get the next number. You then check to see if the new number is greater than the upper limit (9 in "from 1 to 9").

For someone counting from 2 to 11 by 4's (2, 6, 10), the next number would have been 14. But 14 is greater than the upper limit, 11, and so it is *not* included.

We can include a similar idea in the FOR statement by using the additional key word STEP:

```
FOR Z=1 TO 7 STEP 2
```

means counting from 1 to 7 by 2's.

```
4 REM------------------
6 REM     FORNEXT2
8 REM------------------
10 FOR Z=1 TO 7 STEP 2
20   PRINT Z
30 NEXT Z
40 END
```

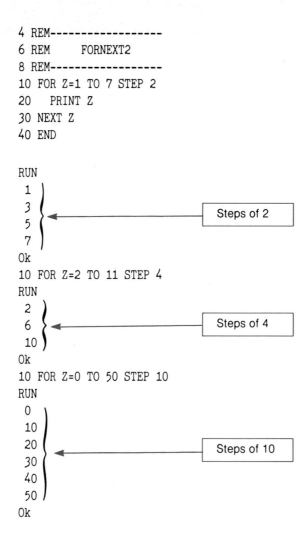

```
RUN
 1
 3
 5
 7
Ok
10 FOR Z=2 TO 11 STEP 4
RUN
 2
 6
 10
Ok
10 FOR Z=0 TO 50 STEP 10
RUN
 0
 10
 20
 30
 40
 50
Ok
```

Steps of 2

Steps of 4

Steps of 10

▶ *Note:* Unless there is a STEP part in the FOR statement, the computer assumes that the values are to be *increased by* 1. 10 FOR I = 1 TO 4 *means the same as* 10 FOR I = 1 TO 4 STEP 1.

Here's an example of "stepping backward."

```
NEW
Ok


4 REM-----------------------------------
6 REM                FORNEXT3
8 REM-----------------------------------
10 FOR Z=10 TO 0 STEP -1
20   PRINT Z
30 NEXT Z
40 PRINT "***********BLAST-OFF***********"
50 END
```

```
RUN
 10
  9
  8
  7
  6
  5
  4
  3
  2
  1
  0
************BLAST-OFF************
Ok
```

Notice that when you are "stepping backward," the larger number in the FOR statement comes first, and the step carries a minus sign:

```
FOR Z=⑩ TO 0 STEP -1
```

On the other hand, when you are "stepping forward," the larger number comes second:

```
FOR I=2 TO ⑪ STEP 3
```

Really, then, we can say that each FOR statement determines an ordered set of values for a particular variable:

```
10 FOR F=1 TO 3
```

determines the set {1,2,3} for the variable F, to be assigned in that order.

```
10 FOR P=2 TO 8 STEP 2
```

determines the set {2,4,6,8} for the variable P, to be assigned in that order.

EXERCISES

3.7   For each FOR statement, write the set of values that will be used.

FOR statement	Variable	Set of values
FOR L=3 TO 9 STEP 3	L	{3,6,9}
FOR G=1 TO 9 STEP 2	G	{1,3,5,7,9}
FOR Y2=3 TO 8 STEP 3	?	?
FOR W=314 TO 817 STEP 200	?	?
FOR B7=3 TO 16 STEP 5	?	?
FOR R=1 TO 6 STEP 6	?	?
FOR M8=3 TO 27 STEP 6	?	?

3.8 Now, given a variable and a set of values, write an appropriate FOR statement.

Variable	Set of values	FOR statement
Q	{1,4,7,10}	FOR Q = 1 TO 10 STEP 3
P	{18,25,32,39,46}	?
K3	{200,201,202,203,204}	?
X	{1,1.1,1.2,1.3,1.4,1.5,1.6,1.7}	?
N4	{10,8,6,4,2}	?
D6	{3,8,13,18,23,28}	?

Look at the following programs and then answer the questions after each.

3.9
```
4 REM-------------------
6 REM       HELLO
8 REM-------------------
10 FOR P=8 TO 30 STEP 6
20   PRINT "HELLO"
30 NEXT P
40 PRINT "GOOD-BYE"
50 END
Ok
```

How many Hello's will be printed? How many Goodbyes will be printed?

3.10
```
4 REM-------------------
6 REM       NUMBERS
8 REM-------------------
10 FOR L=3 TO 19 STEP 4
20   PRINT L-2
30   PRINT L+2
40 NEXT L
50 END
Ok
```

How many numbers will be printed in all? Now print the numbers out.

3.11 Find the two errors in the following "program."

```
10 FOR F=36 TO 34 STEP 2
20 PRINT F
30 NEXT G
40 END
```

Using Variables in FOR-NEXT Statements

Here's a simple program that will print out five rows of ten asterisks each.

```
4 REM-------------------
6 REM       STARROW
8 REM-------------------
10 FOR I=1 TO 5
20   PRINT "**********"
30 NEXT I
40 END
```

```
RUN
*********
*********
*********
*********
*********
Ok
```

That's simple enough. Now let's change the program as follows.

```
9 INPUT R
10 FOR I=1 TO R
```

With this change, we can have different numbers of rows printed out. Watch.

```
RUN
? 3
*********⎫          Since R = 3, line 10 becomes
*********⎬  ⟵ 10 FOR I=1 TO 3
*********⎭          and three rows of asterisks are printed.
Ok
RUN
? 4
*********⎫          Since R = 4, line 10 becomes
*********⎬  ⟵ 10 FOR I=1 TO 4
*********⎪          and four rows of asterisks are printed.
*********⎭
Ok
```

Now that we know that we can put a variable in a FOR statement, let's change the program again.

```
4 REM-----------------------------------------------------------
6 REM                          STARROW2
8 REM-----------------------------------------------------------
10 PRINT "HOW MANY BLOCKS OF ASTERISKS DO YOU WANT";
20 INPUT T
30 FOR H=1 TO T
40    PRINT "HOW MANY ROWS OF ASTERISKS DO YOU WANT IN BLOCK";H;
50    INPUT R
60    FOR I=1 TO R
70       PRINT "*********"
80    NEXT I
90 NEXT H
100 END
Ok
```

The preceding program illustrates nested FOR loops. As the name implies, nested loops are loops nested, or included, within other loops. In the above program, we have the FOR-NEXT loop with H, and within *that* loop, the FOR-NEXT loop with I. The two loops work like this.

(Leaving out
the other steps)

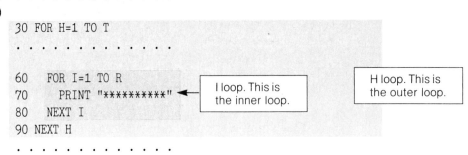

```
. . . . . . . . . . . .

30  FOR H=1 TO T

. . . . . . . . . . . .

60    FOR I=1 TO R
70      PRINT "**********"
80    NEXT I
90  NEXT H

. . . . . . . . . . . .
```

I loop. This is
the inner loop.

H loop. This is
the outer loop.

When the computer reaches the FOR statement in line 30, it sets H = 1 and
then continues, as usual, executing the *body* of that loop. But it just so happens
that the body of the H loop is another FOR-NEXT loop—the I loop. So the computer now must go through the body of the I loop, over and over, until I is greater
than R (the number of rows of asterisks wanted).

When I is greater than R, the computer skips to the line right after the NEXT
I, just as it would in any FOR loop. The line the computer skipped to is the
NEXT H, which returns the computer to line 30 (finally!). Now it sets H = 2 and
repeats the whole process again.

You might compare this with the way an odometer in a car works. The
tenth-mile dial must go through all the ten digits *before* the mile dial moves one
digit.

The best way to understand what a computer does with nested FOR loops is
to run the program and study the output. Here is a sample run.

```
RUN
HOW MANY BLOCKS OF ASTERISKS DO YOU WANT? 3
HOW MANY ROWS OF ASTERISKS DO YOU WANT IN BLOCK 1 ? 4
**********
**********
**********
**********
HOW MANY ROWS OF ASTERISKS DO YOU WANT IN BLOCK 2 ? 2
**********
**********
HOW MANY ROWS OF ASTERISKS DO YOU WANT IN BLOCK 3 ? 6
**********
**********
**********
**********
**********
**********
Ok
```

Do you see that the computer went through the H loop three times? And that
each time the H loop was executed, the I loop was run first four, then two, and finally six times? If you keep in mind that the *body* of the H loop includes the I
loop, this is easier to understand.

EXERCISES   Run each program by hand.

3.12

```
 4 REM----------------------
 6 REM         COMPUTER
 8 REM----------------------
10 PRINT "THIS IS A COMPUTER"
20 FOR K=1 TO 4
30   PRINT "NOTHING CAN GO"
40   FOR J=1 TO 3
50     PRINT "WRONG"
60   NEXT J
70 NEXT K
80 END
```

(Now you'll understand Program 1 in Section 1.10.)

3.13

```
 4 REM------------------
 6 REM      PATTERN
 8 REM------------------
10 FOR W=2 TO 8 STEP 2
20   PRINT "*   *   *"
30   FOR X=18 TO 20
40     PRINT "  *   *"
50   NEXT X
60   PRINT "*   *   *"
70 NEXT W
80 END
```

A Special Trick

You know that using the semicolon (;) at the end of a PRINT statement (so that the computer does not give a new line feed) can create interesting effects. We can use this idea in printing out rows of asterisks.

```
 4 REM-----------
 6 REM   TRICK
 8 REM-----------
10 FOR I=1 TO 5
20   PRINT "*";
30 NEXT I
40 END


RUN
*****
Ok
```

Here the semicolon caused the five asterisks to be printed on the same line.

EXERCISES   Run each program by hand, and show the output.

3.14

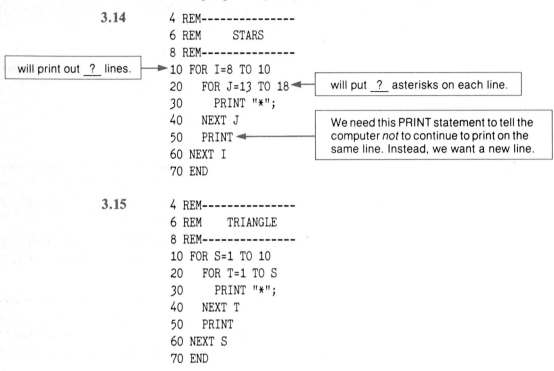

```
4 REM--------------
6 REM     STARS
8 REM--------------
10 FOR I=8 TO 10
20    FOR J=13 TO 18
30      PRINT "*";
40    NEXT J
50    PRINT
60 NEXT I
70 END
```

will print out __?__ lines.

will put __?__ asterisks on each line.

We need this PRINT statement to tell the computer *not* to continue to print on the same line. Instead, we want a new line.

3.15

```
4 REM--------------
6 REM     TRIANGLE
8 REM--------------
10 FOR S=1 TO 10
20    FOR T=1 TO S
30      PRINT "*";
40    NEXT T
50    PRINT
60 NEXT S
70 END
```

LAB EXERCISE 3.7   File Name: STARS

Enter and run the program in Exercise 3.14.

LAB EXERCISE 3.8   File Name: TRIANGLE

Enter and run the program in Exercise 3.15.

LAB EXERCISE 3.9   File Name: BLOCKS

Write and run a program that will print three rectangles, each having four rows of seven asterisks each, using nested loops.

LAB EXERCISE 3.10   File Name: GRADE

Write a program (off-line) that plots a bar graph of the grades on a quiz. After you have perfected your program, try it on-line. The output might look like this, where each unit is represented by ⟨*⟩.

```
RUN
INPUT GRADES. TYPE 101 WHEN FINISHED.
? 85
? 90
? 100
? 95
? 85
? 55
? 100
? 75
? 60
? 75
? 20
? 40
? 65
? 70
? 75
? 101

     GRADES         DISTRIBUTION
     0 TO 20        <*>
    21 TO 40        <*>
    41 TO 60        <*><*>
    61 TO 80        <*><*><*><*><*>
    81 TO 100       <*><*><*><*><*><*>

AVERAGE GRADE WAS 72.6667
Ok
```

If you need some ideas, try running this experimental program.

```
4 REM-----------------------
6 REM          GRADE1
8 REM-----------------------
10 PRINT "INPUT GRADES. ";
20 PRINT " TYPE 101 TO STOP."
30 LET T=0
40 INPUT G
50 IF G>100 THEN 90
60    IF G<70 THEN 40
70    LET T=T+1
80    GOTO 40
90 PRINT "70 TO 100",
100 FOR K=1 TO T
110   PRINT "<*>";
120 NEXT K
130 END
```

A more advanced program that prints a bar graph will be shown in Section 6.4.

LAB EXERCISE 3.11   File Name: BOOSTER _____

Write a program (off-line) to solve the following problem. Then run it on-line.

You are an engineer helping to design a new amusement park ride. The layout looks like Figure 3.8.

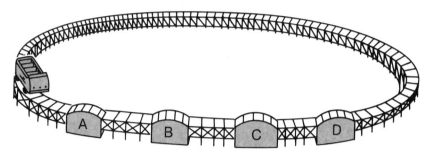

FIGURE 3.8   Booster stations

A given car starts to the left of point A with a certain starting speed. Then it continues along the track, passing booster stations A, B, C, D, then A, B, C, D again, and so on. Every time the car passes station A, B, C, or D, its speed is increased 10% by a gear rotating below the track. If, for instance, the car is traveling at 5 miles per hour coming into station B, when it leaves B, it will be traveling at 5+.1*5=5.5 miles per hour.

The ride is designed so that the car goes around ten times before the power is cut and the car coasts to a halt. The designers are unsure as to the speed at which the car should start. Some say 2 miles per hour, others say 5 miles per hour. They turn to you for advice.

What are you going to do? Probably the best idea would be to make a chart of the various starting speeds of the car, and, for each starting speed, show what the final speed of the car would be. This suggests writing a program to complete Table 3.3.

TABLE 3.3

Starting speed (miles/hour)	Final speed (after 10th trip around)
.5	?
1.0	?
1.5	?
2.0	?
2.5	?
3.0	?
3.5	?
4.0	?
4.5	?
5.0	?
5.5	?
6.0	?

► *Hints:* You will need *nested* FOR *loops*. The *outer* loop will control the increasing starting speed.

```
(FOR S=.5 TO 6 STEP .5)
```

The *inner* loop will calculate the speed after 40 "boosts."

```
(FOR B=1 TO 40)
```

3.5   Other Control Statements; Structured Flow Charts

Many versions of BASIC have additional control statements that extend those we've just discussed. These will be summarized in Chapter 6, but here's a quick preview of one of them. It's called the WHILE statement. The main reason for introducing it here is to compare it with IF...THEN and FOR...NEXT. You'll see that WHILE is just one more way of controlling the same kind of loops we have already discussed.

Here's a comparison of the loop structures we've already seen with WHILE. The programs all do exactly the same thing, namely, print a table of five cubes.

```
10 REM   IFCUBE (TABLE OF CUBES USING AN IF...THEN LOOP)
20 K = 1
30 IF K>5 THEN 70
40    PRINT K;" CUBED = ";K*K*K
50    LET K=K+1
60    GOTO 30
70 PRINT "*** DONE ***"

10 REM   FORCUBE (TABLE OF CUBES USING A FOR...NEXT LOOP)
20 FOR K = 1 TO 5
30    PRINT K;" CUBED = ";K*K*K
40 NEXT K
50 PRINT "*** DONE ***"

10 REM   WHILECUB (TABLE OF CUBES USING A WHILE LOOP)
20 K = 1
30 WHILE K<=5
40    PRINT K;" CUBED = ";K*K*K
50    K=K+1
60 WEND
70 PRINT "*** DONE ***"
```

You'll notice that the WHILE loop is very close to the IF...THEN loop. There are two differences. The first is that the condition tested is K<=5 instead of K>5. These are called complementary conditions, since K<=5 is the same as NOT(K>5).

The second, more subtle difference is that the GOTO is hidden in the WHILE loop (it's also hidden in the FOR...NEXT loop). The loop just keeps repeating between WHILE and WEND ("while end") until the condition K<=5 is no longer true. The reason for inventing control structures that keep GOTO out of the hands of programmers will be discussed in Chapter 7. For now, we'll just note that GOTO should be used carefully; otherwise long programs can easily become tangled masses.

Structured Flow Charts

The flow-chart symbols shown in Section 3.2 date back to the early days of computing. In 1972, two computer scientists named Bruno and Steiglitz wrote an article advocating flow charts based on the use of "higher-level" symbols. In particular, they argued for flow charts that never had to show lines and arrows that corresponded to GOTO branches. They used the name *structured* D *charts* in honor of Edsger Dijkstra, another computer scientist who had written about the confusion that could be caused by an undisciplined use of GOTO statements. Since then, there have been several variations on these charts. They all fall under the heading of *macro flow charts,* that is, flow charts in which the individual boxes are made general enough to suppress confusing detail.

We'll discuss the GOTO problem further in Section 7.1, and macro flow charts in Section 7.2. Suffice it to say for now that GOTO-type branching can't really be eliminated. It can be *controlled* (by the discipline of the programmer), or *hidden* (by the use of constructs like the WHILE statement). The symbols used in the structured D charts (or in macro flow charts) are pictorial ways of implementing hidden GOTO constructs. In general, the goal of such charts is to describe the flow of control in programs as a sequence of actions that start at the top, and go down to the end without any confusing backtracking.

Here are three flow charts (corresponding to the three programs at the beginning of this section) that illustrate this idea. The first one (Figure 3.9) explicitly shows the branching caused by the GOTO and IF ... THEN statements. The other two flow charts (Figures 3.10 and 3.11) show how D charts suppress this detail.

The circle symbol Ⓐ used on the D charts shows the start (top) of a repetitive control structure. The triangle symbol ⚠ indicates the end (bottom) of a repetitive control structure. The letter inside (A in our example) indicates the point to

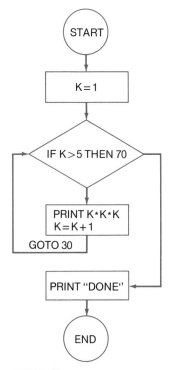

FIGURE 3.9

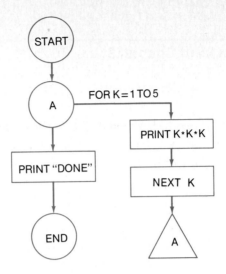

FIGURE 3.10

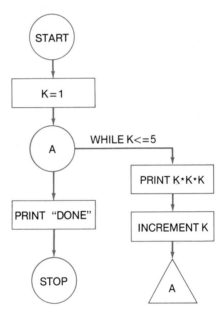

FIGURE 3.11

return to after finishing the repetitive action. Details of *how* the repetition is accomplished are not shown. It's like a boss writing a memo that says "I don't care how you do it, just get me five contracts prepared and don't come back until they're finished."

Should you use D charts? Do professionals use them? Surprisingly, the evidence* is that professional computer scientists tend not to use flow charts. They prefer something called *pseudocode* instead. (Pseudocode will be explained in Section 7.2, and illustrated for a variety of programs in Part II.) However, it's still a good idea to try your hand at flow charts of various kinds, and make up your own mind about how helpful they are.

---

*One of the most highly regarded books on this subject is *A Discipline of Programming* by Edsger Dijkstra. It contains dozens of very elegant programs, but not a single flow chart of any kind.

3.6 Summary of Chapter 3

■ Control-structure statements are those that can change the normal flow of control in a program. They can cause program statements to be executed in an order other than that given by their line numbers.

■ The GOTO statement sends control to the line number indicated. Execution continues from that point in the program.

```
<ln> GOTO <ln>
100 GOTO 10
```

■ Flowcharts show visually the order in which statements are executed. Tasks are described in different-shaped boxes and connected by arrows indicating the flow of control.

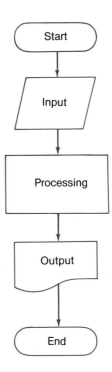

■ More than one BASIC statement may be placed after one line number in most versions of BASIC. Such multiple statements must be separated by a colon (or backslash in some versions of BASIC).

```
10 A=0: B=0: D1=1: D2=1
10 A=0\ B=0\ D1=1\ D2=2
```

■ The conditional statement, using the key words IF...THEN, allows programs to make "decisions" based on whether a condition is true or false. It has two forms:

Form 1: <ln> IF <condition> THEN <ln>

Form 2: <ln> IF <condition> THEN <one or more statements>

```
 20 IF A<4 THEN 200
 90 IF C>9*A THEN PRINT "TOO HIGH" :GOTO 70
120 IF R=S+T THEN PRINT "DONE"
```

If the condition is true, control is passed to the line number indicated (Form 1) or all the statements after THEN are executed (Form 2). If the condition is false, items after THEN are ignored and execution continues at the next numbered statement.

The flowchart symbol for a conditional statement is:

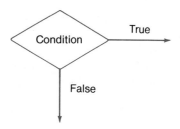

■ Conditional expressions can be formed in BASIC using relational operations =, <>, >, <, >=, <=.

A=16	means	"A equals 16"
A<>16	means	"A is not equal to 16"
A>16	means	"A is greater than 16"
A<16	means	"A is less than 16"
A>=16	means	"A is greater than or equal to 16"
A<=16	means	"A is less than or equal to 16"

■ One can stop execution anywhere in a program with the statement STOP.

```
100 IF X>=X1 THEN PRINT "OK": STOP
```

■ Some versions of BASIC allow a third form of IF...THEN, as follows:

<ln> IF <condition> THEN <clause 1> ELSE <clause 2>

Each clause may be one or more BASIC statements. If the condition is true, clause 1 is executed and clause 2 is ignored. If the condition is false, then clause 2 is executed and clause 1 is ignored. Execution then continues at the next numbered statement. See Chapter 6.

■ An important use of control-structure statements is to cause a block of statements to be repeated a specified number of times. This structure can be visualized as a "finite loop" in the flow of control.

■ To control the number of repetitions in a finite loop, a variable can be initialized outside the loop, and then increased by 1 each time there is a pass through the loop. This is called incrementing (increasing) the loop variable or counter.

■ The key words FOR and NEXT automate finite looping and counting. The general form is as follows.

<ln> FOR <variable name> = <n> TO <m>
<lns> <statements to be repeated>
<ln> NEXT <variable name>

```
10 FOR X=5 TO 10
20  PRINT "SIZE"; X; "SHOES AVAILABLE"
30 NEXT X
```

The variable name in the FOR statement acts as the loop variable or counter; n is its first or initial value; m is the final value wanted. Each time through the loop, the variable is tested to see if it is greater than m, the final value. If the variable is less than or equal to m, the statements between FOR and NEXT are repeated. If it is greater than m, control passes to the statement after the NEXT statement. The block of repeated statements is sometimes called the "body of the loop."

■ The key word STEP can be added to the FOR statement to add a number other than 1 to the loop variable.

```
10 FOR Z=2 TO 100 STEP 2
10 FOR Q=100 TO 1 STEP -10
```

■ The body of a FOR loop can include another FOR loop. This is called a "nested" FOR loop.

```
10 FOR I=1 TO 3
20    FOR J=1 TO I
30       PRINT I,J
40    NEXT J
50 NEXT I
```

■ It is a good idea to indent the body of a FOR loop in order to make the structure of the program clearer to the human reader. In general, whenever control-structure statements are used, indentions should be used to help the reader see where the flow of control is being sent.

■ Flowcharts can be used to show the control logic in a program. Diagrams called macro flowcharts, which depict only the larger ideas and suppress the detail, are also used. Both kinds of charts are useful. Structured D-charts are an example of macro flowcharts.

3.7   Problems and Programming Projects

1. Simulate running the following program segments. For each, show the *output* that is produced.

   (a)
   ```
    50 PRINT"ADDING PRACTICE"
    60 X=5: Y=4
    70 PRINT"WHAT IS ";X;" PLUS ";Y
    80 INPUT Z
    90 IF Z<>(X+Y) THEN 80
   100 PRINT"VERY GOOD."
   ```

   (b)
   ```
   10 X=3: Y=3*X^2: Z=Y+(4+X^2)*3
   20 PRINT X,Y,Z
   ```

2. The following program doesn't work. Rewrite it so that it produces the promised output.

```
10 PRINT"THIS PROGRAM CALCULATES INTEREST EARNED AT 7%"
20 PRINT"ANNUAL INTEREST COMPOUNDED DAILY."
30 INPUT B
40 PRINT"TELL ME HOW MUCH MONEY YOU HAVE"
50 PRINT"HOW MANY DAYS BEFORE YOU NEED IT"
60 INPUT D
70 D=1
80 I=B*7
90 B=B+I
100 D=D+1
110 IF D<B THEN 70
120 PRINT"YOU WILL HAVE ";B;" DOLLARS AFTER ";D;"DAYS."
```

3. Write a program that will calculate the population of an area in the year 2000. Assume that the population of the region was 1,000,000 in 1985 and that is has an annual growth rate as input by the user. Run the program for growth rates of 0.5, 1, 2, and 4%.

4. Write a program that calculates the population of a region at a time to be stipulated by the user. The user will also supply the initial population, starting time, growth rate, and name of the region.

5. Write a program to find the interest on $1000 that is left in a bank for 10 years. The interest rate is 7½ % per year and is added to the balance once each year.

6. Modify the program that you wrote for Problem 5 so that the user can supply the starting balance, the duration, and the interest rate.

7. Write a program to calculate the balance in a savings account on which interest is compounded daily. Have the user supply the initial balance, interest rate, and amount of time that the money is in the bank. The output should be in the form of monthly statements that show the interest credited every 30 days.

8. Write a program to handle a savings account on which interest is compounded daily and calculated day in to day out. Allow deposits and withdrawals. Have the user input the initial balance, interest rate, and the amount and time of deposits and withdrawals. Do not allow the balance to go below zero.

9. Write a program to help a salesperson who has a station at which there are only $5 and $1 bills and also quarters and pennies with which to give change. Have the user supply the cost of a purchase and the amount tendered. Have the program calculate the amount of change to be given, followed by a list of the bills and coins in which the change should be given.

10. Write a program that calculates the least number of bills that can be given in change for a purchase that costs less than $100 and is also an exact number of dollars. A $100 bill is given to pay for the purchase. Have the user supply the purchase price.

11. Write a program that calculates the square root, the square, and the cube of the numbers from 60 to 75. Print the results in a table with the headings and columns of numbers lined up.

12. Write a program that calculates the sales tax, calculated at the local rate for your state (use 6% if your state doesn't have a sales tax), on five items purchased. Have the program ask the user to supply the stock number of the item and the price for each item. Print a table listing the number, price, tax, and total cost for each item. At the bottom of each column, print a total.

► *Note:* If you read ahead to Sections 5.2 and 6.5, you'll find that the above program can be modified to input the *names* instead of stock numbers. Do this if you can.

## CHAPTER FOUR

One- and Two-Dimensional Arrays; Using TAB and PRINT USING

NEW TOPICS INTRODUCED IN CHAPTER 4

- Data structures
- One-dimensional arrays
- DIM
- String variables
- Subscripted variables
- Two-dimensional arrays
- PRINT with TAB
- PRINT USING

4.1 BASIC Data Structures

The dozen key words of BASIC explained in the first three chapters allow one to write an amazingly large variety of programs. In fact, there are very few programming problems that can't be solved with this minimal vocabulary—at least theoretically. But that's like saying that there are very few construction jobs that can't be handled with the dozen or so tools found on a home workbench—at least theoretically. In practice, a modern craftsman can get a lot more done, and with surer results, if he or she has access to a full range of more sophisticated tools: everything from power saws to precision lathes to diamond-tipped drills.

In this and the next chapter we're going to add to the arsenal of tools in your programming tool kit by introducing BASIC statements based on an additional dozen or so key words. We'll also introduce some of the *library functions* available in BASIC, each one of which acts like a special-purpose processing tool.

However, as you may suspect, we would be headed toward some kind of overkill if all we did was pile on the new tools. What good are fancy construction tools without fancy construction materials? To respond to this question, we'll start out in Sections 4.2 and 4.4 by introducing two new and versatile kinds of "material," on which all of our programming tools can be exercised. They are called one- and two-dimensional arrays, respectively, and they are examples of what are in general called data structures.

What is a data structure? It's simply a way of picturing or *organizing* in one's mind the storage scheme used for the numbers and/or characters manipulated by a BASIC program. The only data structure we've used so far is the *simple variable*. This was pictured in Section 2.3 as being something like a mailbox—a location in memory where our program stored one piece of data, either numerical data like −43 or 3.1416, or string (character) data like ''@'' or ''wow!''

The *arrays* introduced in this chapter are ''structures'' that make it easy to store whole collections of data. We can picture a one-dimensional array as a stack of mailboxes, sequentially numbered from top to bottom. To work with the contents of a given box—say the third one down—we can use a notation like BOX(3). A two-dimensional array is like a whole wall full of boxes, numbered according to what *row* and what *column* the box is in. For example, BOX(2,3) refers to the contents of the box in the second row down and the third column over.

```
BOX(1,1)     BOX(1,2)     BOX(1,3)     BOX(1,4)
BOX(2,1)     BOX(2,2)     BOX(2,3)     BOX(2,4)
BOX(3,1)     BOX(3,2)     BOX(3,3)     BOX(3,4)
```

To see why this is an important idea, let's take a look at some specific examples of how arrays are used in BASIC.

4.2 Subscripted Variables; Using DIM

Up to this point we have been getting along pretty well with variable names like X, A, B4, or F8. Some versions of BASIC allow even longer names, like AMT, BIN3, or CHARLIE7. Let's call these *simple variables*. Unfortunately, one soon finds that simple variables aren't flexible enough for more advanced programs. To show why, let's use an example:

Take-a-Chance International Airlines

Suppose that TACI-Air has one flight each day of a 31-day month, and that there are three passenger seats available on each plane (it's a very small airline). We want to run a reservation office where a person can request a seat for any day in the month.

One way to do this is to set up a board as shown in Table 4.1, with A as the name of the variable where we store the number of seats available on March 1, B the seats available on March 2, and so on. When we start, we let A=3, B=3, and so on. If a passenger requests a ticket for March 1, we look at our board, say OK, and sell him the ticket. Then we change the value of A to 2.

TABLE 4.1 Seats Available for Month of March on TACI Airlines

1	2	3	4	5	6	7
A = 3	B = 3	C = 3	D = 3	E = 3	F = 3	G = 3
8	9	10	11	12	13	14
H = 3	I = 3	J = 3	K = 3	L = 3	M = 3	N = 3
15	16	17	18	19	20	21
O = 3	P = 3	Q = 3	R = 3	S = 3	T = 3	U = 3
22	23	24	25	26	27	28
V = 3	W = 3	X = 3	Y = 3	Z = 3	A1 = 3	B1 = 3
29	30	31				
C1 = 3	D1 = 3	E1 = 3				

Let's try automating our system so that a ticket agent can use a terminal to make reservations. A program to do this might start out as follows:

```
10 LET A=3
20 LET B=3
30 LET C=3
40 LET D=3
   ...
```

Hold it! Do you see that we'd need 31 LET statements just to assign the starting values for each day? That's one of the problems with simple variable names. We have the job of not only choosing the names, but also of storing values in the locations they label, one at a time. If we were doing the airline reservations for the whole year, we'd need 365 separate LET statements to assign starting values.

Another trouble with using simple variable names in this example is that they're not very logical. Why should A stand for March 1, or P for March 16? We need a way of naming variables that will get the *computer* to help choose the names, and that will generate names that will fit the application better.

Let's look at the situation more closely. As any calendar shows, a month is a collection of days. March is a collection of 31 days. We refer to a specific day in March by its number, for instance, March 12 or March 27.

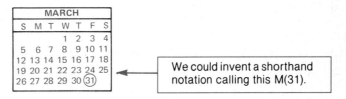

We could invent a shorthand notation calling this M(31).

In a similar way, we can set up a collection of computer variables. This collection is called an array. Arrays also have names: the "M array" or "H array," for example. And (just as with months) we can talk about a specific *member* (also called an *element*) of the array by using an array name followed by a number in parentheses, for example, M(8) or H(12). These symbols are called subscripted variables (the number is the subscript):

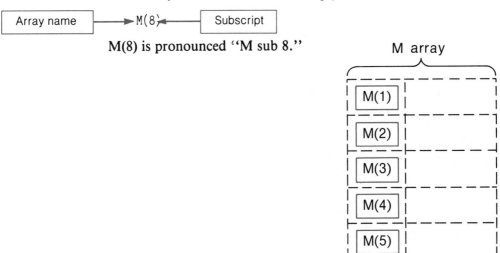

Array name ⟶ M(8) ⟵ Subscript

M(8) is pronounced "M sub 8."

M array

M(1)
M(2)
M(3)
M(4)
M(5)

Note 1: If your version of BASIC allows long variable names, these can also be used for array names. Examples: MONTH(2), MX10(5), SALLY(17).

Note 2: In order to distinguish between an entire array and an element of the array, we will later use the notation M( ) for the entire array, and M(J) for the Jth element of the array.

One of the best things about subscripted variables is that they help the computer keep track of where things are stored. This is because the computer "knows" that M(8) is the 8th member of the array M (just as we know that March 8 is the 8th day of March). Also, just as we know that there are 7 days of March before March 8, the computer "knows" that there are 7 members of the M array before M(8). We'll soon see how useful this is. But first let's note that there is a crucial difference between simple and subscripted variables.

The Difference Between Simple and Subscripted Variables

H8, a simple variable, is *not* the same as H(8), a subscripted variable. The difference is something like that between the name

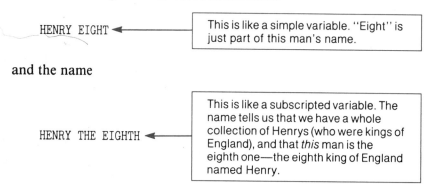

and the name

There is one similarity between simple and subscripted variables: Both store values. That is, M(8) is a label for a memory location that can store a value (for example, 429).

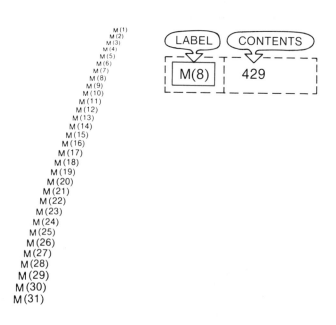

Most computers have enough storage room for arrays with quite a few members. However, it is up to us, in our programs, to indicate how many members of the array we'll need. For instance, in TACI-Air, we'll need 31 variables, one for each day of March. We warn the computer that we'll need 31 subscripted variables by using a *dimension* statement, as follows:

```
10 DIM M(31)
```

This says "Reserve space for 31 variables called M(1), M(2), and so on up to M(31)." [*Note:* Most versions of BASIC also reserve space for one extra variable called M(0), but we won't use it in this example.]

In general, any time you have a subscript larger than 10, you must use a DIMension statement. After warning the computer, you can use the subscripted variables anywhere in the program.

Let's illustrate all of this by writing the complete TACI-Air program. First, let's picture a reservation board that uses subscripted variables:

MARCH

M(1) = 3	M(2) = 3	M(3) = 3	M(4) = 3	M(5) = 3	M(6) = 3	M(7) = 3
M(8) = 3	M(9) = 3	M(10) = 3	M(11) = 3	M(12) = 3	M(13) = 3	M(14) = 3

This says that there are 3 seats available on March 8.

. . . and so on . . . up to M(31) = 3

This time we have stored the *number* of seats for the first day in M(1), for the second day in M(2), . . . , for the sixteenth day in M(16), . . . , and so on. That's logical, isn't it? Here's how we do this in BASIC.

This dimension statement reserves 31 locations in memory.

```
 4 REM------------
 6 REM    DIM
 8 REM------------
10 DIM M(31)
20 FOR D=1 TO 31
30 LET M(D)=3
40 NEXT D
```

The trick is to write
30 LET M(D) = 3
and ask the computer to make D = 1, 2, 3, . . . , 31.

We can now assign our 31 starting values with only four statements!
Here's the complete reservation program.

```
 4 REM----------------------------------------------------
 6 REM             AIRLINE1 (CHECKS SEAT AVAILABILITY)
 8 REM----------------------------------------------------
10 DIM M(31)
20 FOR D=1 TO 31
30    LET M(D)=3
40 NEXT D
50 PRINT
60 PRINT "TYPE THE DAY IN MARCH REQUESTED AND THE NUMBER OF SEATS."
70 INPUT D,N
80 IF M(D)>=N THEN 120
90    PRINT "SORRY, ONLY";M(D);"SEAT(S) AVAILABLE."
100   PRINT " FOR MARCH";D;". MAKE ANOTHER REQUEST."
```

This line checks to see if there are as many seats as you wish on the day you requested. [M(D) is the number of seats left on day D.] If there are, then the ticket agent is authorized to issue a ticket (line 120) and the number of seats is reduced by N (line 130).

(continued)

```
110  GOTO 50
120 PRINT "RESERVATION O.K.--ISSUE";N;"TICKET(S) FOR MARCH";D;"."
130 LET M(D)=M(D)-N
140 PRINT "STILL";M(D);"EMPTY SEAT(S) ON MARCH";D;"."
150 PRINT "NEXT REQUEST PLEASE."
160 GOTO 50
170 END


RUN


TYPE THE DAY IN MARCH REQUESTED AND THE NUMBER OF SEATS.
? 5,2
RESERVATION O.K.--ISSUE 2 TICKET(S) FOR MARCH 5 .
STILL 1 EMPTY SEAT(S) ON MARCH 5 .
NEXT REQUEST PLEASE.


TYPE THE DAY IN MARCH REQUESTED AND THE NUMBER OF SEATS.
? 18,1
RESERVATION O.K.--ISSUE 1 TICKET(S) FOR MARCH 18 .
STILL 2 EMPTY SEAT(S) ON MARCH 18 .
NEXT REQUEST PLEASE.


TYPE THE DAY IN MARCH REQUESTED AND THE NUMBER OF SEATS.
? 5,2
SORRY, ONLY 1 SEAT(S) AVAILABLE.
  FOR MARCH 5 . MAKE ANOTHER REQUEST.


TYPE THE DAY IN MARCH REQUESTED AND THE NUMBER OF SEATS.
? 6,2
RESERVATION O.K.--ISSUE 2 TICKET(S) FOR MARCH 6 .
STILL 1 EMPTY SEAT(S) ON MARCH 6 .
NEXT REQUEST PLEASE.


TYPE THE DAY IN MARCH REQUESTED AND THE NUMBER OF SEATS.
? ^C
Break in 70
Ok
```

We decide to stop the input by pressing CTRL and C together.

Notice that this program does not keep a record of the reservations from one run to the next. A more practical program would use files, as discussed in Chapter 11.

There is another interesting feature of subscripted variables that you should know about: The subscript can be any expression, that is, a combination of variables and numbers joined by the operators $*$, $/$, $+$, $-$, and $\uparrow$.

▶ *Examples:* X(K+1),   X(K-1),   B(2*J+1)

EXERCISES

4.1 In each row, circle the variable name or names that are the same as the underlined name. For example, you would circle G(4*3) and G(2*6) in row 1.

G(12)	G(4*3)	G(14)	G12	G(2*6)		G(12+10)	
M9	M(9)	M(2*4.5)	M	M(4+5)		M9	M(16−7)
P(3)	P(6−3)	P(3)	P3	P(1+2)		P(4−2)	P(27/9)
L(4)	M(4)	L(16/4)	L4	L(1+1+1+1)			L(128/32)
Z(16)	Z(160/10)	Z16	Z	Q(16)		Z(256/16)	

4.2 Simulate running the following program.

```
4 REM--------------------------------
6 REM SUBSCRPT (SUBSCRIPTED VARIABLES)
8 REM--------------------------------
10 DIM Q(24)
20 LET M(1)=2
30 LET M(2)=8
40 LET M(3)=16
50 LET Q(4)=10
60 LET Q(6)=20
70 LET Q(24)=130
80 PRINT M(1)+M(3)
90 PRINT M(1+2)
100 PRINT M(1)+M(2)
110 PRINT Q(4*6)
120 PRINT Q(4)*Q(6)
130 PRINT Q(10+14)
140 PRINT M(28-25)
150 PRINT M(6-4)
160 PRINT Q(24/6)
170 PRINT Q(24)/Q(6)
180 PRINT M(2+1)+M(3-1)+Q(8-4)+Q(3+3)
190 END
```

4.3 Simulate running the following program.

```
4 REM----------------------------------------------
6 REM    SQUARE (CALCULATES SQUARES OF NUMBERS)
8 REM----------------------------------------------
10 REM  PROGRAM TO PRINT SQUARES OF ANY 5 NUMBERS
20 PRINT "TYPE IN 5 NUMBERS, ONE FOR EACH '?':"
30 FOR I=1 TO 5
40   INPUT N(I)
50 NEXT I
60 PRINT "YOUR NUMBERS","SQUARES OF YOUR NUMBERS"
70 FOR K=1 TO 5
80   PRINT N(K),N(K)*N(K)
90 NEXT K
100 END
```

4.4   Simulate running the following program.

```
4 REM-------------------------------------------------------
6 REM FIBNACCI (GENERATES NUMBERS IN FIBONACCI SERIES)
8 REM-------------------------------------------------------
10 REM  PROGRAM TO GENERATE 10 FIBONACCI NUMBERS
20 LET A(1)=1
30 PRINT A(1);
40 LET A(2)=1
50 PRINT A(2);
60 FOR J=3 TO 10
70   LET A(J)=A(J-1)+A(J-2)
80   PRINT A(J);
90 NEXT J
100 END
```

▶ *Note:* Fibonacci was a mathematician born in Pisa, Italy, in 1180. The numbers named after him are still used today in higher mathematics.

LAB EXERCISE 4.1   **File Name: TRACK**

An athlete can run the 100-yard dash in 12 seconds. How fast is he going in miles per hour (mph)?

You can calculate his speed as follows:

100 yards = 300 feet = 300/5280 = .0568 mile
12 seconds = 12/3600 = .00333 hour

So his speed is

D/T = .0568/.00333 = 17.0455 mph

That's a lot of arithmetic, especially if you want to figure out speeds for a list of athletes. Let's use the computer.

Here is a program that prints the speeds for as many runners as you wish, and then gives the average speed.

After studying it and the sample run, see if you can modify the program so that it prints the average of only those athletes you specify. For example, you might want the average of the three highest speeds (that is, athletes 2, 4, and 5). Can you do this by letting the user input the subscripts of the variables he or she wants averaged?

```
4 REM-------------------------------------------------------
6 REM    TRACK1 (CALCULATES ATHLETES' SPEEDS FOR 100 YARDS)
8 REM-------------------------------------------------------
100 DIM T(20)
110 LET S=0
120 PRINT "HOW MANY TRACK 'TIMES' DO YOU WISH TO ENTER (<20)";
130 INPUT N
140 PRINT "AFTER EACH '?' ENTER A TIME (IN SECONDS) FOR THE";
150 PRINT " 100-YARD DASH."
```

```
160 FOR I=1 TO N
170   PRINT "ATHLETE #";I;
180   INPUT T(I)
190   LET S=S+T(I)
200 NEXT I
210 PRINT
220 PRINT "HERE ARE THE TIMES AND SPEEDS:"
230 PRINT "ATHLETE #","TIME (SEC)","SPEED (MILES PER HOUR)"
240 FOR I=1 TO N
250   PRINT I,T(I),(300/5280)/(T(I)/3600)
260 NEXT I
270 PRINT
280 PRINT "AVERAGE TIME WAS";S/N;"SECONDS."
290 PRINT "THE AVERAGE SPEED WAS";(300/5280)/((S/N)/3600);"MPH."
300 END

RUN
HOW MANY TRACK 'TIMES' DO YOU WISH TO ENTER (<20)? 5
AFTER EACH '?' ENTER A TIME (IN SECONDS) FOR THE 100-YARD DASH.
ATHLETE # 1 ? 15.3
ATHLETE # 2 ? 12.0
ATHLETE # 3 ? 14.1
ATHLETE # 4 ? 9.8
ATHLETE # 5 ? 11.3

HERE ARE THE TIMES AND SPEEDS:
ATHLETE #      TIME (SEC)      SPEED (MILES PER HOUR)
1              15.3            13.36898
2              12              17.04545
3              14.1            14.50677
4              9.8             20.87198
5              11.3            18.10137

AVERAGE TIME WAS 12.5 SECONDS.
THE AVERAGE SPEED WAS 16.36364 MPH.
OK
```

> S is used to find the SUM of all the "times." The average time will then be S/N.

(arrow points to line 190)

LAB EXERCISE 4.2 **File Name: AIRLINE1**

Run the TACI-Air reservation program for several customers.

LAB EXERCISE 4.3 **File Name: AIRLINE2**

Add the following statements to your airline program and see what happens when you type 0, 0 as the last input.

```
75 IF D=0 THEN 162
162 PRINT
164 PRINT "SEATS LEFT FOR THE MONTH OF MARCH ARE (DAY,SEATS):"
165 FOR D=1 TO 31
166 PRINT D;M(D);"   ";
168 NEXT D
```

Sneak Preview

LAB EXERCISE 4.4   File Name: BUBBLE1 _____

Here's a good example of the value of subscripts. The following program *sorts* a collection of numbers into ascending (increasing) order. (Chapter 7 will explain the program.) Try running it, and then see if you can write a similar program to put numbers into descending (decreasing) order.

```
4 REM----------------------------------------------------------------
6 REM          BUBBLE1  (SORTS NUMBERS INTO ASCENDING ORDER)
8 REM----------------------------------------------------------------
100 PRINT "PROGRAM TO SORT A LIST OF NUMBERS INTO ASCENDING ORDER"
110 DIM A(100)
120 PRINT "HOW MANY NUMBERS TO BE SORTED (MAX=100)";
130 INPUT N
140 IF N>100 THEN 120
150 PRINT "TYPE IN THE LIST OF NUMBERS ONE AT A TIME:"
160 FOR I=1 TO N
170   INPUT A(I)
180 NEXT I
200 REM=========================================================
210 REM          ROUTINE TO USE BUBBLE SORT ON A()
230 LIMIT=N                       'N ITEMS TO BE SORTED
240 SPOT=0                        'START "DO UNTIL NO SWAPS" LOOP
250   FOR K=1 TO LIMIT-1          'START PASS THROUGH DATA
260     IF A(K+1)>=A(K) THEN 310  'NO SWAP NEEDED
270       TEMP=A(K+1)             'SWAP, STEP 1
280       A(K+1)=A(K)             'SWAP, STEP 2
290       A(K)=TEMP               'SWAP, STEP 3
300       SPOT=K                  'REMEMBER WHERE WE SWAPPED
310   NEXT K                      'CONTINUE PASS THRU DATA
320 IF SPOT=0 THEN 420            'FINISHED'
330   LIMIT=SPOT                  'ELSE CHANGE LIMIT
340   GOTO 240                    'CONTINUE "DO UNTIL" LOOP
400 REM=========================================================
410 REM   ROUTINE TO PRINT N ITEMS, 3 ITEMS/LINE, 13 COLS/ITEM
420 PRINT"*** HERE ARE THE SORTED NUMBERS ***"
430 FOR J=1 TO N
440   T=J-3*INT((J-1)/3)
450   PRINT TAB(13*T-12);A(J);
460   IF T>=3 THEN PRINT
470 NEXT J
490 PRINT
500 PRINT"*** DONE ***"
RUN
PROGRAM TO SORT A LIST OF NUMBERS INTO ASCENDING ORDER
HOW MANY NUMBERS TO BE SORTED (MAX=100)? 5
TYPE IN THE LIST OF NUMBERS ONE AT A TIME:
? 3.25
? 4.68
? 98.32
? .78
? 12.5
```

```
*** HERE ARE THE SORTED NUMBERS ***
 .78          3.25          4.68
 12.5         98.32
*** DONE ***
Ok
```

► *Challenge:* Combine the program BUBBLE1 with the program TRACK1 to put the athletes' records in the order of first place, second place, and so on, and then to give the average time for the first three places.

4.3 Two-Dimensional Arrays

A new mayor of Ashbank has just been elected. One of his main campaign promises was to make Ashbank a safer place to live. His first directive is to the police department: Cut down the number of traffic accidents. So the police commissioner's first move is an order to his computing division: Get statistics on the number of accidents at each intersection.

Figure 4.1 is a map of downtown Ashbank. Let's look at the map, and then help ABC (the Ashbank Bureau of Computing) to analyze the problem.

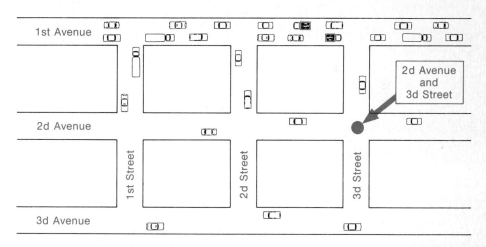

FIGURE 4.1   Downtown Ashbank

First, we'll need an easy way to refer to a particular intersection.

Second, we'll have to be able to associate the number of accidents at a given intersection with the name of that intersection.

We could letter the intersections with simple variables, or we could use subscripted variables. Which shall it be? Well, the downtown area is rapidly expanding, so our method should make it easy to add other intersections in the future. Also, the streets already have numbers. Why not use them?

We could refer to the intersections by first giving the name of the avenue, and then the name of the intersecting street. The intersection marked with a heavy dot in Figure 4.1 is "2d Avenue and 3d Street."

Variables with Double Subscripts

This suggests that it would be nice to have a second type of subscripted variable, one that has *two* subscripts. Here's what these variables look like in BASIC.

$N(2,3)$ = the number of accidents at 2d Avenue and 3d Street

$N(1,2)$ = the number of accidents at 1st Avenue and 2d Street

     and so on

Just like single-subscript variables, double-subscript variables store values. So if, in the past year, 23 accidents have taken place at 2d Avenue and 3d Street, we can say:

```
LET N(2,3)=23
```

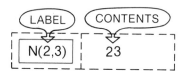

If 21 accidents occurred at 1st Avenue and 2d Street, we can say:

```
LET N(1,2)=21
```

We can think of these storage locations as if they were arranged in a table. The *contents* are the numbers of accidents at each intersection.

Street / Avenue	1st Street	2d Street	3d Street
1st Avenue	46 accidents	21 accidents	72 accidents
2d Avenue	13 accidents	28 accidents	23 accidents
3d Avenue	16 accidents	18 accidents	34 accidents

The usual practice is to enter these numbers into the computer by rows, that is, in the order

```
46, 21, 72, 13, 28, 23, 16, 18, 34
```

The best way to compare the safety of the different intersections is to find each intersection's percentage of the total accidents in Ashbank. If we found, for instance, that 37% of the accidents happen at one intersection and 21% happen at another, then it would be clear that the former intersection for some reason is much more dangerous.

So we write the following program.

```
4 REM-----------------------------------------------------------
6 REM                        ASHBANK
8 REM-----------------------------------------------------------
10 PRINT "TYPE IN THE NUMBER OF ACCIDENTS AT EACH INTERSECTION"
20 PRINT "IN THE ORDER 1ST AVENUE AND 1ST STREET, 1ST AVENUE AND"
30 PRINT "2ND STREET, AND SO ON."
```

```
40 LET T=0
50 FOR A=1 TO 3
60   FOR S=1 TO 3
70     INPUT N(A,S)
80     LET T=T+N(A,S)
90   NEXT S
100 NEXT A
110 PRINT
120 PRINT " AVE   AND  STREET","% OF TOTAL"
130 FOR A=1 TO 3
140   FOR S=1 TO 3
150     PRINT A;"AVE  AND ";S;"ST ",(N(A,S)/T)*100;"%"
160   NEXT S
170 NEXT A
180 PRINT
190 PRINT "1ST AVE'S PERCENTAGE IS";(N(1,1)+N(1,2)+N(1,3))/T*100;"%."
200 PRINT "2ND AVE'S PERCENTAGE IS";(N(2,1)+N(2,2)+N(2,3))/T*100;"%."
210 PRINT "3RD AVE'S PERCENTAGE IS";(N(3,1)+N(3,2)+N(3,3))/T*100;"%."
220 END
```

```
RUN
TYPE IN THE NUMBER OF ACCIDENTS AT EACH INTERSECTION
IN THE ORDER 1ST AVENUE AND 1ST STREET, 1ST AVENUE AND
2ND STREET, AND SO ON.
? 46
? 21
? 72
? 13
? 28
? 23
? 16
? 18
? 34
```

Challenge: Can you add a PRINT statement (similar to line 150) at line 65 to clarify these input requests?

AVE	AND	STREET	% OF TOTAL
1 AVE	AND	1 ST	16.9742 %
1 AVE	AND	2 ST	7.74908 %
1 AVE	AND	3 ST	26.5683 %
2 AVE	AND	1 ST	4.79705 %
2 AVE	AND	2 ST	10.3321 %
2 AVE	AND	3 ST	8.48708 %
3 AVE	AND	1 ST	5.90406 %
3 AVE	AND	2 ST	6.64207 %
3 AVE	AND	3 ST	12.5461 %

```
1ST AVE'S PERCENTAGE IS 51.2915 %.
2ND AVE'S PERCENTAGE IS 23.6162 %.
3RD AVE'S PERCENTAGE IS 25.0923 %.
Ok
```

You can see that 1st Avenue clearly has the most accidents—more than 50% of all the accidents in Ashbank. There should no longer be any doubt that 1st Avenue needs some traffic lights!

The most complex parts of the program are the nested FOR loops in lines 50–100 and 130–170. Let's make a table to see how the nested FOR loops select the various elements of N( ).

```
FOR A=1


                  (A) (S)



    FOR S=1   N(1,1)   1st Ave. and 1st St.
        =2    N(1,2)   1st Ave. and 2d St.
        =3    N(1,3)   1st Ave. and 3d St.


FOR A=2


    FOR S=1   N(2,1)   2d Ave. and 1st St.
        =2    N(2,2)   2d Ave. and 2d St.
        =3    N(2,3)   2d Ave. and 3d St.


FOR A=3


    FOR S=1   N(3,1)   3d Ave. and 1st St.
        =2    N(3,2)   3d Ave. and 2d St.
        =3    N(3,3)   3d Ave. and 3d St.
```

Line 80 finds the total number of accidents in Ashbank.

Line 150 prints the percentage of all accidents happening at each intersection.

And lines 190–210 find the percentages of accidents by *avenues*.

LAB EXERCISE 4.5   File Name: ACCIDENT

Change and run the preceding program for a town that has 16 intersections (4 avenues and 4 streets) with data as follows:

	1st Street	2d Street	3d Street	4th Street
1st Avenue	3 accidents	8 accidents	6 accidents	2 accidents
2d Avenue	2 accidents	14 accidents	11 accidents	9 accidents
3d Avenue	2 accidents	4 accidents	5 accidents	3 accidents
4th Avenue	1 accident	3 accidents	2 accidents	0 accidents

DIMension Statements with Double-Subscript Variables

Just like single-subscript variables, double-subscript variables must have DIMension statements if subscripts greater than 10 are to be used. Suppose, for example, that you wanted to run ACCIDENT for a town with 15 avenues and 20 streets. Then you would need to add the statement:

```
35 DIM N(15,20)
```

► *Warning:* Since this requires 336 memory locations, it might not work on some computers. [The reason that there are 336 locations is that subscripts actually start at 0 (zero), so there are 16 rows and 21 columns.]

► *Suggestion:* Always use a DIM statement with arrays, even when 10 or fewer elements are needed. This makes your programs easier to read and understand.

4.4   Using TAB in PRINT Statements

If you're bored with numbers, PRINT with TAB is the answer. PRINT with TAB allows you to make graphs, to draw designs, to plot curves, and to have fun generally.

Here's how it works: You have to tell the computer two main things:

- What to print
- Where to print it

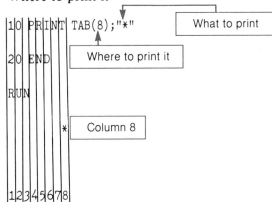

The 8 is the horizontal position (or *column*) on the terminal. Most terminals have 80 columns, numbered from 1 to 80.

Statement 10 tells the computer to go to column 8 and print an asterisk (*) there. The statement

```
10 PRINT TAB(14);"*"; TAB(20);"*"
```

would cause the computer to print two asterisks, one in column 14 and one in column 20. That's the general idea. Now for some specifics.

Rules for Using PRINT TAB

1. You can print anything at the specified position. Nonnumeric characters must be placed within quotation marks; numbers do not need quotation marks.

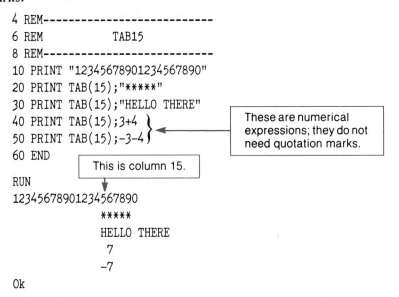

```
4 REM-------------------------
6 REM            TAB15
8 REM-------------------------
10 PRINT "12345678901234567890"
20 PRINT TAB(15);"*****"
30 PRINT TAB(15);"HELLO THERE"
40 PRINT TAB(15);3+4
50 PRINT TAB(15);-3-4
60 END

RUN
12345678901234567890
              *****
              HELLO THERE
              7
              -7

Ok
```

These are numerical expressions; they do not need quotation marks.

This is column 15.

 Notice that (except on the Apple) the computer leaves a space in front of a number for a sign, either positive (+) or negative (−). But it does not *print* a + sign, only a − sign. Therefore the 7 is actually printed in column 16.

2. A variable can be used to tell the computer where to print. For example, if X equals 10,

```
PRINT TAB(X);"*"
```

means the same as:

```
PRINT TAB(10);"*"
```

If M equals 64,

```
PRINT TAB(M);"*"
```

means the same as:

```
PRINT TAB(64);"*"
```

You can also specify several columns in which the computer is to print. (See the next example.)

3. Once TAB has been used to move to a given position, it cannot be used to move backward. Only TABs to further positions along a line are carried out. For instance:

```
4 REM--------------------------------------------------
6 REM                        TAB
8 REM--------------------------------------------------
10 PRINT "12345678901234567890"
20 PRINT TAB(5);"*";TAB(10);"+";TAB(15);"-"
30 END

RUN
12345678901234567890
    *    +    -
Ok
```

To illustrate multiple TABs on a line, let's use an example. One simple design to print is a tree. Here is a listing and a run of a tree program.

```
4 REM--------------------------------------
6 REM                     TREE
8 REM--------------------------------------
10 PRINT TAB(35)"*"
20 FOR I=1 TO 10
30   PRINT TAB(35-I)"*"TAB(35+I)"*"
40 NEXT I
50 PRINT TAB(35-I)"***********************"
60 FOR I=1 TO 3
70   PRINT TAB(33)"+"TAB(37)"+"
80 NEXT I
90 PRINT TAB(33)"+++++"
100 END

RUN
```

This prints the tree trunk. → { lines 60-80 }

This is the base of the tree. → line 50

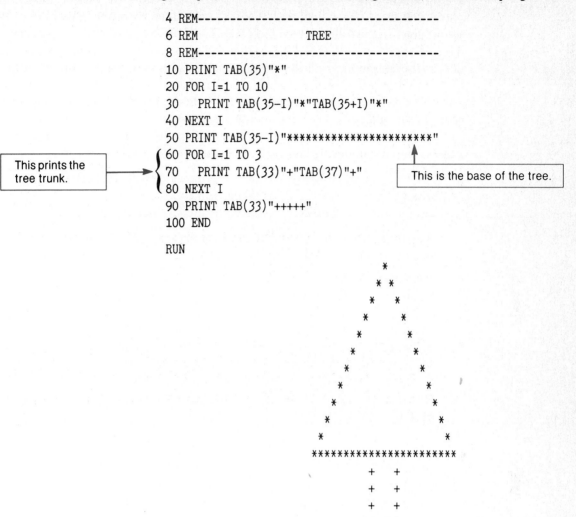

The first FOR loop causes the computer to print 10 pairs of asterisks. The positions of the two asterisks in each row are:

I	TAB(35 − I)	TAB(35 + I)
1	34	36
2	33	37
3	32	38
4	31	39
5	30	40
⋮	⋮	⋮
10	25	45

In line 50, I = 11, so the tree base starts at column 24.

► **Warning:** This program won't work properly on a 40-column display. To fix it, reduce all TAB arguments by about 20 (for example, change 35 to 15, 33 to 13, and 37 to 17).

APPLE

Restrictions on the Use of PRINT TAB

If a statement uses TAB(X) followed by TAB(Y), but Y is *less than* X, most computers will print a new line, with TAB(Y) calculated from the beginning of the second line. In the following example, the TAB(10) in line 40 puts the plus sign in the first line of output. The TAB(5) that follows cannot be executed on the same line, so the computer prints the "*" in the fifth column of the next line of output. However, the minus sign and "40" can be placed on the same line of output, since the numbers used (called *arguments*) with the last two TABs on line 40 are each greater than any TAB arguments previously used on that line.

If the argument of TAB is not an integer, the number is rounded to the nearest whole number. In line 50 of the example,

	PRINT TAB(10.8) is taken to mean	PRINT TAB(11)
whereas	TAB(10.2) is taken to mean	TAB(10)
but	TAB(19.9) is taken to mean	TAB(20)

Also notice that lines 20 and 30 produce the same result, showing that semicolons aren't really needed in PRINT statements between strings and TAB.

```
4 REM---------------------------------------------------
6 REM                           TAB?
8 REM---------------------------------------------------
10 PRINT "123456789012345667890"
20 PRINT TAB(5);"*";TAB(10);"+";TAB(15);"-";TAB(20);"20"
30 PRINT TAB(5)"*"TAB(10)"+"TAB(15)"-"TAB(20)"30"
40 PRINT TAB(10)"+"TAB(5)"*"TAB(15)"-"TAB(20)"40"
50 PRINT TAB(10.8)"?"TAB(10.2)"?"TAB(10)"?"TAB(19.9)"50"
60 END
```

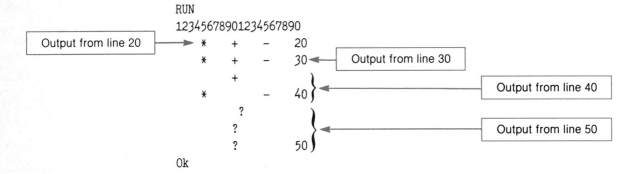

LAB EXERCISE 4.6 **File Name: TREE2**

Modify the program TREE to print a tree that is about twice as tall as the one shown on page 111.

LAB EXERCISE 4.7 **File Name: BRAKE**

Write a program that makes a "graph" of the distance it takes a car to stop if it is going 10, 15, 20, . . . , 80 miles per hour. Use the formula

Distance needed to stop (in car lengths) = .01*S*S

(S = speed in miles per hour). Or, in BASIC,

```
LET D=.01*S*S
```

Here's a sample output.

```
RUN
DISTANCES NEEDED TO STOP A CAR AT VARIOUS SPEEDS

SPEED          DISTANCE (EACH + REPRESENTS ONE CAR LENGTH)
     ++++++++++++++++++++++++++++++++++++++++++++++++++++++++++++++++++++++++
 10 *
 15  *
 20    *
 25     *
 30      *
 35       *
 40        *
 45         *
 50          *
 55           *
 60            *
 65             *
 70              *
 75               *
 80                                                                       *
     ++++++++++++++++++++++++++++++++++++++++++++++++++++++++++++++++++++++++
Ok
```

If you need some help, first try this simple program:

```
10 LET S=40
20 LET D=S*S*.01
30 PRINT S;TAB(D+3);"*"
```

Section 9.4 presents a further discussion of the use of TAB in programs that produce graphical output.

4.5 PRINT USING

Many versions of BASIC have a special form of the PRINT statement that produces "formatted" output. It allows you to specify the format (or arrangement) of items in a line of output, and avoid some of the limitations of the standard spacing for numbers and characters. In particular, you can specify the number of decimal digits to be printed, the position of the decimal, the size of the field, and the position of the digits within that field. You can also specify the size of fields containing alphanumeric (text) information. Here's a simple example that shows how it works.

```
4 REM----------------------------------------
6 REM                 PRUSING
8 REM----------------------------------------
10 REM DEMONSTRATION OF PRINT USING
20 F$=">>> ###.#### =\           \"
30 PRINT USING F$;355/113;"PI APPROXIMATION"
40 PRINT USING F$;1/3;"ONE THIRD DISCOUNT"
50 PRINT USING F$;1000/4;"QUARTERLY AMOUNT"
60 END

RUN
>>>    3.1416 = PI APPROXIMAT
>>>    0.3333 = ONE THIRD DIS
>>> 250.0000 = QUARTERLY AMO
Ok
```

The format for the output of this program is defined in line 20, with the string variable F$. String variables are indicated in BASIC by adding a dollar sign to the variable name. The word string refers to a sequence of characters placed between quotation marks. In this case it consists of some characters we want to *always* show up in the output, such as the three arrowheads >>> and a space, and the = sign, surrounded by spaces. Our string also has two "placeholders" for *variable* information that we want to appear in the output. The first one, ###.####, holds a place for a number that is to be formatted in a field of eight positions: three digits, a decimal point, and four more digits. The second placeholder is written as two backslash symbols with 11 spaces between. This reserves space for text (string) information, allowing a total of 13 characters to appear at this position in the output. You can see how these two placeholders work by studying the run of the program, and comparing lines 30, 40, and 50 with the actual output produced.

Placeholders for PRINT USING

Here's a list of all the special symbols that can be used as placeholders in PRINT USING, followed by another example of PRINT USING.

!	Prints only the first character of a string
\ \	Prints 2 + m characters of a string, where m = the number of spaces between the backslashes (the TRS-80 uses % for \ )
&	A variable-length string field
#	Represents one digit position
.	Represents the decimal point
+	Prints the sign of the number at this position
−	After a numeric field, prints a trailing minus
**	Fills the leading spaces with asterisks
$$	Prints $ to the left of the number in this field
**$	Combines the two previous signs
,	Before the decimal, prints commas every third digit
^^^^	After the digit-position characters, prints in exponential format as E + nn
_	Prints the next character "as is"

```
100 '----------------------------------------------------------------
110 '    PRUSING2   (PRINT USING APPLIED TO CHECKBOOK DATA)
120 '----------------------------------------------------------------
130 ' NOTE: # IS ONE OF THE SPECIAL 'PRINT USING' FORMAT SYMBOLS
140 ' TO ACTUALLY PRINT A # (OR ANY OTHER SPECIAL SYMBOL), USE _#
150 F$="CK_# ###: ##/##/##  \                    \ $$###.##"
160 PRINT">>>  FORMATTED DISPLAY OF CHECKBOOK DATA  <<<"
170 PRINT"-----------------------------------------------"
180 FOR K=1 TO 3
190    READ M,D,Y,D$,A
200    PRINT USING F$;K+100,M,D,Y,D$,A
210 NEXT K
220 DATA 3,20,84,"AJAX COMPUTER SUPPLIES",67.3
230 DATA 5,15,85,"EMBASSY LOUNGE",9
240 DATA 12,20,86,"FRIENDLY FINANCING FIDUCIARY CO.",683.875

RUN
>>>  FORMATTED DISPLAY OF CHECKBOOK DATA  <<<
-----------------------------------------------
CK# 101:  3/20/84  AJAX COMPUTER SUP    $67.30
CK# 102:  5/15/85  EMBASSY LOUNGE        $9.00
CK# 103: 12/20/86  FRIENDLY FINANCIN   $683.88
Ok
```

Simulating PRINT USING

PRINT USING is not available in all versions of BASIC (for example, Applesoft BASIC doesn't have it). You can simulate some of its features by combining the use of the TAB( ) function (Section 4.4) with certain string functions (Section 6.5). An example of this technique is shown in the program RCDSHELL (Section 8.5).

4.6   Summary of Chapter 4

- A data structure is a storage scheme used to organize the data (numbers and/or characters) manipulated by a BASIC program.

- A one-dimensional array is a data structure that consists of a collection of variables, all with the same variable name. The variables are differentiated from one another by a number called a subscript. For example: A(1), A(2), A(3), and so on; YAXIS(1), YAXIS(2), YAXIS(3), and so on. Another name for this data structure is a one-dimensional table. It is analogous to a numbered list of items of data.

- A two-dimensional array is a collection of double-subscripted variables with the same variable name and two subscript numbers. It can be visualized as a table of data items arranged as rows and columns.

- The DIM statement (for "dimension") reserves space in memory for arrays.

```
10 DIM X(50), Y(50), A(50,50)
```

Arrays with subscript numbers less than 10 need not be dimensioned; however, it is a good practice to do so.

- The TAB (⟨n⟩) function allows you to indicate in what column you wish to have the next item printed.

  ```
  100 PRINT TAB(10); I; TAB(15);C
  ```

- The PRINT USING statement allows you to create a format for your line of output. It has the form:

  ⟨ln⟩ PRINT USING ⟨format string⟩; ⟨list of items⟩

  ```
  140 F$=">>> ###.#### = \              \"
  150 PRINT USING F$; X1, "FIRST QUARTER"
  ```

  Special characters within the format string such as #, ., and \ hold open a place for numbers or strings that are to be printed.

- To find the largest (MAX) and smallest (MIN) elements of an array A(), first set MAX and MIN = A(1). Then use a loop to change them to their correct values.

  ```
  10 MAX=A(1): MIN=A(1)
  20 FOR K=2 TO N
  30   IF A(K)>MAX THEN MAX=A(K)
  40   IF A(K)<MIN THEN MIN=A(K)
  50 NEXT K
  ```

4.7   Problems and Programming Projects

1. Write a program that inputs a list of ten numbers and assigns them to a one-dimensional array. Have your program find the smallest and largest numbers in the array and print them. (See Section 6.5 for some ideas on finding smallest and largest values.)

2. Modify your program from Problem 1 so that it moves the smallest value to the beginning of the array and the largest value to the end of the array. Your program should then print out the modified array.

3. Extend your program from Problem 2 so that it successively repeats the process on the unordered central part of the array until all the elements are in order of increasing value (smallest to largest) from the beginning to the end of the array.

4. Write a program that enters the grade information shown below through input statements. Find the average grade for each student, and print the information in a table.

Student #1	26, 38, 32, 27, 36
Student #2	17, 32, 44, 22, 30
Student #3	32, 18, 17, 37, 32
Student #4	28, 26, 27, 27, 26
Student #5	25, 30, 35, 20, 15

   ▶ *Suggestion:* If there are 40 students with five test grades each, define a two-dimensional array with

   ```
   DIM G(40,5)
   ```

   to store the grades. Element G(I,J) should hold the grade for test J, student #I.

5. Extend the program of Problem 4 so that it also prints a table showing the individual grades and average grades as *percentages*. To do this, your program must also input the maximum possible grade for each test. For example, if the maximum grade for test J is 50, and a student receives 35, then the percentage grade for that student on test J is 100*35/50 = 70.

6. Further modify the program of Problem 5 so that it also prints a table of letter grades, where A is 90–100%, B is 80–89%, C is 70–79%, D is 60–69%, and F is 0–59%.

7. Extend the program for Problem 6 so that it also prints the class averages for each test and the class average for the average percentages of students.

8. Simulate running the following program.

```
10 DIM A(5,4) 'HOLDS DATA FOR 5 ATHLETES
20 T$(1)="PLAYER #  ": T$(2)="WINS      ": T$(3)="LOSES     "
30 FOR I=1 TO 5
40   FOR J=1 TO 3: PRINT T$(J);:INPUT A(I,J): NEXT J
50   PRINT: A(I,4)=A(I,2)/(A(I,2)+A(I,3))
60 NEXT I
70 PRINT " TO SORT ON PLAYER #   TYPE 1"
80 PRINT "           ON WINS     TYPE 2"
90 PRINT "           ON PERCENTAGE TYPE 3"
100 INPUT X: IF X=3 THEN LET X=4
110 FOR I=1 TO 4
120   FOR J=1 TO 5-I: IF A(J,X)<=A(J+1,X) THEN 160
130     FOR K=1 TO 4
140       T=A(J,K): A(J,K)=A(J+1,K): A(J+1,K)=T
150     NEXT K
160   NEXT J
170 NEXT I
175 PRINT" PLAYER #"," WINS"," LOSES"," PERCENTAGES"
180 FOR I=1 TO 5
190   FOR J=1 TO 4: PRINT A(I,J),: NEXT J: PRINT
200 NEXT I
210 END
Ok
```

▶ *Note:* Lines 20 and 40 make use of a *string array* called T$(). Each element of the array holds the sequence of characters between quote marks that are assigned in line 20. For further information about string arrays, see Section 6.5.

9. (*Difficult*) Modify the program of Problem 4 so that the table of grades is printed in sorted order, from the highest average to the lowest. (For some help in doing this, read ahead to Section 8.5.)

Professional BASIC

## CHAPTER FIVE

BASIC Tools for Professional Programming; String Variables

NEW TOPICS INTRODUCED IN CHAPTER 5

- *READ ... DATA*
- *String variables*
- *SQR, INT, ABS, RND*
- *DEF FN*
- *GOSUB*

- *RESTORE*
- *Library functions*
- *SIN, COS, TAN, ATAN, LOG, EXP*
- *ON ... GOTO*
- *ON ... GOSUB*

5.1 The Plan for Part II

The four chapters of Part I might be thought of as a get-acquainted course in BASIC. The eight chapters of Part II, on the other hand, are meant to be a guide to building on that acquaintance, with the objective of giving you a professional command of BASIC, and of program design in general. Part II will present three kinds of information.

1. New, extended features of BASIC will be introduced and illustrated. You can think of these extensions as professional tools that make it possible (even easy) for you to handle just about any programming challenge you will meet.

2. A set of principles and techniques for designing large and complicated programs will be explained. These are part of a systematic, one-thing-at-a-time method called structured program design.

3. A variety of professional-level applications written in BASIC will be shown, including sorting and searching, simulations, games, graphics, data encryption, word processing, business calculations, and file-oriented data-processing programs.

In this chapter and in Chapter 6, we'll start on the first part of this plan by introducing several new tools. The first of these is the READ ... DATA facility.

This is a more powerful feature than meets the eye. It not only allows for the convenient storage of data in a program, but it helps the programmer understand (and clearly distinguish) the concept of *program structure* versus that of *data structure*. There will be more on this subject in Section 7.4. For now, let's just concentrate on how to use READ and DATA.

5.2   READ and DATA Statements; RESTORE; String Variables

We've discussed the INPUT statement as one way of getting data values into a program. When you use the INPUT statement, the computer types a ? and then waits for you to type in a value. After you type it in and press RETURN, the computer then stores that number in its memory. But, if you have a lot of data that won't change from run to run, there is a better method for getting information into the computer. This method uses the READ and DATA statements.

Look at the following program.

```
4 REM------------
6 REM      READ
8 REM------------
10 READ A,B,C,D
20 LET X=A*B*C+D
30 PRINT "X =";X
40 DATA 2,3,4,10
50 END

RUN
X = 34
Ok
```

How did that work? The key word READ tells the computer that some variables follow that need to have values assigned. To find their values, the computer searches for a DATA statement in which the values are listed.

So, in our example, at line 10, the computer "sees" the key word READ, and then the A. It searches for a DATA statement, finds it, and then stores the first value in the DATA statement in location A.

```
10 READ A, ...
20
30
40 DATA 2, ...
```

The computer finds values for B and C and D in the same way.

```
10 READ A,B,C,D
20
30
40 DATA 2,3,4,10
```

When finished with line 10, the computer has given A the value 2, B the value 3, C the value 4, and D the value 10. At line 20, using A, B, C, and D, it calculates the value of X (X = 2*3*4 + 10 = 34).

Here's another example that illustrates the same idea.

```
4 REM--------------          F equals 23
6 REM     READ1
8 REM--------------          G equals 32
10 READ F,G,H,M
20 PRINT F+G+H+M             H equals 10
30 DATA 23,32,10,1
40 END                       M equals  1
Ok
                                    66
 66
Ok
```

There are several interesting variations possible with READ ... DATA statements:

1. We can have more than one READ statement for one DATA statement. The various READ statements use the values in the DATA statement one by one. When a value has been used, it cannot be used again (unless you use the word RESTORE, as will be explained shortly). For example:

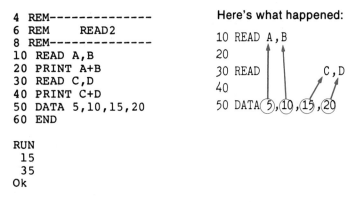

```
4 REM--------------
6 REM     READ2
8 REM--------------
10 READ A,B
20 PRINT A+B
30 READ C,D
40 PRINT C+D
50 DATA 5,10,15,20
60 END

RUN
 15
 35
Ok
```

2. We can also have several DATA statements. It does not matter to the computer where the DATA statements are located in the program, or how many DATA statements are used. The computer combines all the DATA statements into one big list of values, which will be used one by one by the READ statements. So

50 DATA 2,3,4,5   is the same as   50 DATA 2
                                   51 DATA 3,4
                                   52 DATA 5

► *Query:* Is   50 DATA 2
                51 DATA 4,3
                52 DATA 5

the same as the first two examples?

► *Answer:* No, since the numbers are not in the same *order* as in the original DATA list.

Here's another example of several READ and DATA statements in one program:

```
4  REM--------------
6  REM      READ3
8  REM--------------
10 READ A,B
20 PRINT A+B
30 READ C,D,E
40 DATA 5
50 PRINT A+C+E-D
60 DATA 10
70 DATA 15,20
80 DATA 25
90 END

RUN
 15
 25
Ok
```

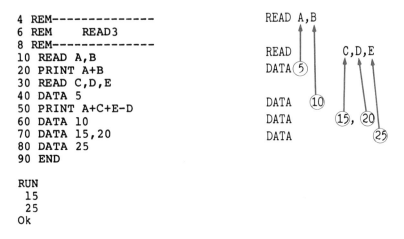

3. Two other situations can arise.
   a) One is that there are fewer variables in the READ statement than values in the DATA statements. In this case, only the values in the DATA statement needed by the READ statements are used.

```
4  REM--------------------
6  REM          READ4
8  REM--------------------
10 READ A,B
20 PRINT B-A
30 READ C,D,E
40 PRINT C*D*E+B-A
50 DATA 1,4,5,20,10,97,33
60 END

RUN
 3
 1003
Ok
```

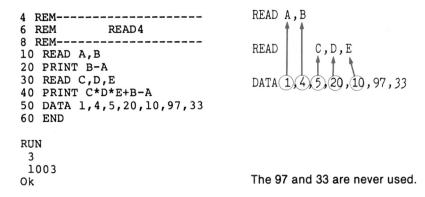

The 97 and 33 are never used.

   b) On the other hand, there may be fewer values in the DATA statements than variables in the READ statements. If the computer finds that it needs more values than are provided, it halts the running of the program, and types a message that says: "OUT OF DATA." For example:

```
4  REM--------------
6  REM      READ5
8  REM--------------
10 READ A,B
20 READ C
30 PRINT A+B+C
40 DATA 5,10
50 END

RUN
Out of DATA in 20
Ok
```

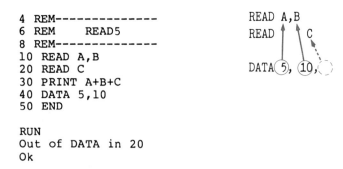

The moral is that the *programmer* must make sure that variables and data match.

4. It is possible to use the same data over and over by using the RESTORE statement. The RESTORE statement is particularly useful when the same data are to be used at several places in the program. Here's an example.

```
4 REM---------------------------
6 REM            RESTORE
8 REM---------------------------
10 READ A,B,C
20 PRINT "TOTAL COST IS";
30 PRINT A+B+C;"."
40 PRINT "SEPARATE COSTS ARE:";
50 RESTORE
60 READ X
70 PRINT X;
80 GOTO 60
90 DATA 5,7,9
100 END

RUN
TOTAL COST IS 21 .
SEPARATE COSTS ARE: 5  7  9
Out of DATA in 60
Ok
```

This uses up all the data.

This restores the data items so that they can be used again.

A Quick Summary of READ ... DATA

- For giving many variables values, READ-DATA statements are usually more efficient than INPUT or LET statements, especially if the program is to be run several times.

- The READ statement names the variables in which the values are to be stored.

- The DATA statement contains the values that will be stored in the variables.

- It's the programmer's responsibility to make sure that the variables in the READ statement match the values in the DATA statement.

EXERCISES Simulate running each of the following programs.

5.1
```
4 REM---------
6 REM  RDEX1
8 REM---------
10 LET A=12
20 PRINT A
30 READ A,B
40 PRINT A*B
50 DATA 8,10
60 END
```

5.2
```
4 REM---------------------------
6 REM            RDEX2
8 REM---------------------------
10 FOR I=1 TO 5
20 READ A,B
30    PRINT I;A;B
40 NEXT I
50 DATA 2,4,4,8,6,12,8,16,10,20
60 END
```

5.3
```
4  REM-------------
6  REM       RDEX3
8  REM-------------
10 READ A,B,C,D
20 PRINT A*B
30 PRINT D/C
40 PRINT B+C
50 DATA 2,24,12,36
60 END
```

5.4
```
4  REM-------------
6  REM       RDEX4
8  REM-------------
10 READ M,T,F,W
20 PRINT M+W
30 PRINT W*M
40 IF T/F>10 THEN 60
50 STOP
60 PRINT M+W
70 DATA 1,15
80 DATA 3,1
90 END
```

5.5
```
4  REM-------------------
6  REM          RDEX5
8  REM-------------------
10 DATA 5,10,15
20 READ R,S
30 PRINT R+S
40 READ T
50 RESTORE
60 READ U,V,W
70 IF T=U THEN 120
80    IF S=V THEN 100
90       GOTO 130
100    PRINT "YOU´RE RIGHT"
110    GOTO 130
120 PRINT "YOU´RE WRONG"
130 END
```

LAB EXERCISE 5.1   File Name: WEATHER1

When the United States Weather Bureau (now the National Weather Service) was established in 1870, records of weather patterns were kept for the first time. Temperature patterns were determined in part by comparing average monthly temperatures from year to year. At the Marquette, Michigan, station, the average monthly temperatures for 1874 and 1875 were as given in the following table.

Average Temperature Readings in Degrees Fahrenheit

Month	JAN	FEB	MAR	APR	MAY	JUNE	JULY	AUG	SEPT	OCT	NOV	DEC
	1	2	3	4	5	6	7	8	9	10	11	12
Year												
1874	19.0	18.9	23.3	29.6	51.3	58.1	65.3	64.4	60.0	45.7	29.9	21.0
1875	5.9	1.3	19.4	33.3	48.5	56.7	63.0	61.5	52.8	39.9	28.5	25.7

Using READ-DATA statements, write a program that finds the difference between temperatures in 1874 and 1875 for each month.

▶ *Hint:* Arrange the DATA statements like this.

```
100 DATA 19.0,18.9,23.3,29.6,51.3,58.1,65.3,64.4,60.0,45.7,29.9,21.0
110 DATA 5.9,1.3,19.4,33.3,48.5,56.7,63.0,61.5,52.8,39.9,28.5,25.7
```

Then read the data for each year [FOR I = 1 TO 12, READ A(I), NEXT I—for the months in 1874; FOR I = 1 TO 12, READ B(I), NEXT I—for the data from 1875]. In a loop, find the difference between each A(I) and B(I) and print it out. A part of a run might look like this.

Month	1874	1875	Difference (Degrees)
1	19.0	5.9	−13.1
2	18.9	1.3	−17.6
3	23.3	19.4	− 3.9
. . .	. . .	. . .	. . .

LAB EXERCISE 5.2   File Name: WEATHER2

Change your program so that if a given month in 1875 is warmer than the same month in 1874, the program prints out:

```
MONTH (number) IS WARMER BY ? DEGREES
```

If it's colder, print out

```
MONTH (number) IS COLDER BY ? DEGREES
```

LAB EXERCISE 5.3   File Name: SURVEY

Write a program that tabulates opinions taken from a questionnaire of the following type (or invent questions of your own choice).

Name: _____ Age: ___ Male ☐ Female ☐

1. The President should be a woman.
   1 = Agree
   2 = Disagree
   3 = No opinion
2. April 15 should be a holiday.
   1 = Agree
   2 = Disagree
   3 = No opinion
3. Schools should remain open all summer.
   1 = Agree
   2 = Disagree
   3 = No opinion

Your program should use a separate DATA statement for each person who fills out a questionnaire. The numbers in each DATA statement should mean the following (use 1 for male, 0 for female):

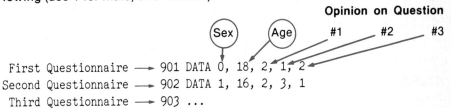

```
First Questionnaire  ⟶  901 DATA 0, 18, 2, 1, 2
Second Questionnaire ⟶  902 DATA 1, 16, 2, 3, 1
Third Questionnaire  ⟶  903 ...
```

(continued)

A run of your program should look like the following.

```
RUN
DATA GATHERED ON QUESTIONNAIRE

                             AGREE     DISAGREED     NO OPINION
 1   FEMALE VOTE:            1         5             4
     MALE VOTE:              5         2             3
     UNDER AGE 16 VOTE:      4         1             1
 2   FEMALE VOTE:            2         6             2
     MALE VOTE:              5         3             2
     UNDER AGE 16 VOTE:      1         4             1
 3   FEMALE VOTE:            5         4             1
     MALE VOTE:              3         6             1
     UNDER AGE 16 VOTE:      1         4             1
Ok
```

Here's *part* of the program that produced this run.

```
. . . . . . . . . . . . . . . . . .
130 READ N
140 FOR I=1 TO 3
150   FOR J=1 TO 3
160     LET X(I,J)=0
170       LET Y(I,J)=0
180       LET Z(I,J)=0
190   NEXT J
200 NEXT I
210 FOR I=1 TO N
220   READ S,A
230   FOR J=1 TO 3
240     READ C
250     IF S=1 THEN 280
260       LET X(J,C)=X(J,C)+1
270       GOTO 290
280     LET Y(J,C)=Y(J,C)+1
290     IF A>=16 THEN 310
300       LET Z(J,C)=Z(J,C)+1
310   NEXT J
320 NEXT I
330 FOR I=1 TO 3
340   PRINT I;TAB(5)"FEMALE VOTE:"TAB(30)X(I,1);
350   PRINT TAB(43)X(I,2)TAB(56)X(I,3)
. . . . . . . . . . . . . . . . . . . . .

700 DATA 20
710 DATA 0,15,1,2,1
720 DATA 0,33,2,3,1
730 DATA 1,21,1,1,2
740 DATA 0,22,2,2,3
750 DATA 1,36,3,1,1
760 DATA 1,14,2,2,2
770 DATA 0,13,3,2,2
780 DATA 0,55,3,3,1
790 DATA 1,49,1,3,2
800 DATA 1,32,3,1,1
810 DATA 0,44,2,2,2
820 DATA 1,56,3,2,2
830 DATA 0,32,2,2,1
. . . . . . . . . . . . . . . . .
```

LAB EXERCISE 5.4   File Name: SURVEY1

Modify your program so that it prints the *percentage* of people who voted in each category.

String Variables in BASIC

In computer work, the word *string* refers to a sequence of characters such as "HI THERE", "GLOB73", or "BIFF!!!#BAM@@!". The characters may be letters, numbers, or punctuation marks. Quotation marks are used to mark the beginning and end of strings, but they are not part of the string itself. Strings can be stored in BASIC by using string variables. These are chosen by the programmer in the same way as numeric variables, except that a $ sign is placed at the end. Here's an example showing how to use string variables in LET, INPUT, and PRINT statements.

```
10 LET A$ = "GOOD MORNING  "
20 PRINT "WHAT'S YOUR NAME";
30 INPUT N$
40 PRINT A$;N$
RUN
WHAT'S YOUR NAME?  HEATHCLIFF
GOOD MORNING HEATHCLIFF
```

Notice that we put a space at the end of the string "GOOD MORNING ". That's because the semicolon in line 40 forces the strings in A$ and N$ to print close together.

Here's an example showing how to use strings in DATA statements, where the string "ZZZ" is used to mark the end of data.

```
10 REM    PARTY   (USES READ ... DATA WITH STRINGS)
20 PRINT "PARTY LIST"
30 PRINT "----------"
40 A$ = "DEAR "
50 B$ = ":  PLEASE COME TO MY PARTY"
60 READ X$
70 IF X$="ZZZ" THEN STOP
80    PRINT A$;X$;B$
90    GOTO 60
100 DATA "JIM", "DEBBIE", "SHERRILYN"
110 DATA "PAUL", "PASCAL", "NICHOLAS", "ZZZ"
RUN
PARTY LIST
----------
DEAR JIM:  PLEASE COME TO MY PARTY
DEAR DEBBIE:  PLEASE COME TO MY PARTY
DEAR SHERRILYN:  PLEASE COME TO MY PARTY
DEAR PAUL:  PLEASE COME TO MY PARTY
DEAR PASCAL:  PLEASE COME TO MY PARTY
DEAR NICHOLAS:  PLEASE COME TO MY PARTY
Break in 70
Ok
```

We'll return to the subject of string variables in Sections 6.5 and 6.6. Chapters 10, 11, and 12 will show several professional applications of strings.

5.3   Some "Library" Functions in BASIC: SQR, INT, ABS, RND; Mathematical Functions

Like most things in computer programming, functions are easier to use than to explain. However, it will help if we take the time to introduce some new terminology—words like *function, argument,* and *value.* This will make it possible to give an accurate description of exactly what happens when you use functions in a program.

Functions are actually small programs stored inside the computer. There are quite a few of these available in BASIC, and the *collection* of functions that you can call on is often called a *library* of functions. In this section, we'll discuss four of the library functions found in every version of BASIC.

Finding Square Roots (SQR)

The function SQR gives you the square root of a number. You supply a number that is called the argument. SQR then returns the *value* of the function—which is the square root of the number. So we have:

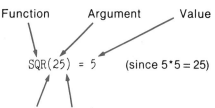

Function   Argument   Value

$$SQR(25) = 5 \qquad (\text{since } 5*5 = 25)$$

The argument is always enclosed in parentheses.

► *Note:* In general, you can use a function at any place in a program in which a variable is used. *Except:* You can never use a function on the *left* side of a LET statement (because a function is not a location in which you can store a value).

Here's an example showing the use of the SQR function.

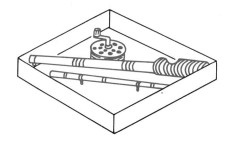

► *Problem:* How long can sections of a fishing rod be if they are to fit into a flat rectangular box?

► *Answer:* From geometry, we know that the "diagonal" of such a box is given by

Diagonal = square root of $(L \times L + W \times W)$

In BASIC, we would say:

```
LET D=SQR(L*L+W*W)
```

Here's a program that uses this formula, with the lengths in inches.

```
4 REM----------------------------------------------------------------
6 REM                                  BOX
8 REM----------------------------------------------------------------
10 PRINT "TYPE THE LENGTH OF BOX, WIDTH OF BOX, AND LENGTH OF SECTION:"
20 INPUT L,W,R
30 LET D=SQR(L*L+W*W)
40 IF D<R THEN 70
50    PRINT "THE FISHING ROD WILL FIT."
60    STOP
70 PRINT "THE FISHING ROD WON´T FIT."
80 PRINT "THE DIAGONAL OF THE BOX IS ONLY";
90 PRINT D;"INCHES."
100 END

RUN
TYPE THE LENGTH OF BOX, WIDTH OF BOX, AND LENGTH OF SECTION:
? 20,15,28
THE FISHING ROD WON´T FIT.
THE DIAGONAL OF THE BOX IS ONLY 25 INCHES.
Ok
```

Notice in statement 30 that the *argument* of the SQR function is allowed to be an expression.

When using functions, you should be aware of the *order* in which the computer does things. Operations within the argument of the function are done first, then the function is evaluated. And finally, all other arithmetic operations in the statement are done in the usual order.

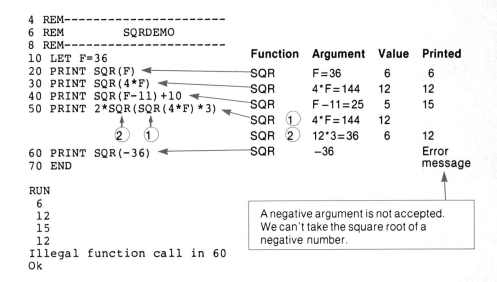

LAB EXERCISE 5.5   **File Name: PIZZA**

Suppose that you are a very neat eater, and take only 1-square-inch bites when consuming a pizza.

Question: How many such bites are in a pizza that is 10 inches in diameter?

Answer: $A = \pi \times R \times R = 78.5397$ square-inch bites, as found in the following program.

(*continued*)

```
4  REM-----------------------------------------------------------------
6  REM                          PIZZA
8  REM-----------------------------------------------------------------
10 INPUT D
20 LET R=D/2
30 LET A=3.14159*R*R
40 PRINT "THERE ARE";A;"SQUARE-INCH BITES IN A(N)";D;"INCH PIZZA."
50 END

RUN
? 10
THERE ARE 78.5398 SQUARE-INCH BITES IN A(N) 10 INCH PIZZA.
Ok
```

Your problem is to improve the given program so that you can also input the price of the pizza. The program should then tell you both the number of square-inch bites and the *cost* per bite. Use your program to find out which is the best buy: an 8-inch pizza @ $1.75, a 10-inch pizza @ $2.00, or a 12-inch pizza @ $3.50.

LAB EXERCISE 5.6   File Name: DIAMETER

Now let's look at the reverse problem: How big a pizza (that is, how large in diameter) do you need to feed a crowd of P people if each person is to get a given number (call it B) of 1-square-inch bites?

Some information you'll need:

The radius of a pizza with A square inches of eating is given by

```
LET R=SQR(A/3.14159)
```

Pizzas are ordered by their diameter D, and D = 2*R.

Write a program that allows you to input the number of people coming to your pizza party, and the number of 1-square-inch bites each person is to get.

The output should be like the following.

```
RUN
HOW MANY PEOPLE AT YOUR PARTY? 10
HOW MANY SQUARE-INCH BITES EACH? 31
IF YOU ORDER 1 PIZZA(S), THE DIAMETER SHOULD BE AT LEAST 19.8672 INCHES.
IF YOU ORDER 2 PIZZA(S), THE DIAMETER SHOULD BE AT LEAST 14.0482 INCHES.
IF YOU ORDER 3 PIZZA(S), THE DIAMETER SHOULD BE AT LEAST 11.4703 INCHES.
  .
  .
  . ◄──────    Output should continue until the diameter goes below 8 inches.
  .
  .
```

Taking the Integer Part of an Expression (INT)

Another function in the BASIC library is one that takes the *integer* part of its argument. INT(N) is defined on most computers as the greatest integer less than or equal to N. If N is not an integer, then INT(N) is the closest integer to the *left* of N, pictured on the usual horizontal number line. If you look at this number line, you'll see that

```
INT(2.3)=2
INT(.8)=0
```

If N is an integer, then INT(N) = N.

► *Question* What does INT(2.3) give you? How about INT(−.5)?

► *Answer*

1. If the argument is positive, then the largest whole number "to the left" can be found by chopping off the decimal part. Therefore INT(2.3) = 2.

2. If the argument is negative, then the largest whole number contained in the argument is still the integer "to the left" of the argument. Therefore INT(−.5) = −1.

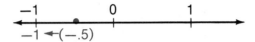

Now let's look at a few uses of the INT function.

To find out whether a whole number is even or odd, we can use the INT function very nicely.

```
4 REM----------------------
6 REM            INT
8 REM----------------------
10 INPUT N
20 IF INT(N/2)=N/2 THEN 50
30    PRINT "ODD"
40    GOTO 10
50 PRINT "EVEN"
60 GOTO 10
70 END

RUN
? 11
ODD
? 56
EVEN
? ^C
```

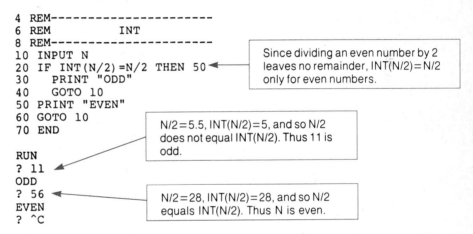

Since dividing an even number by 2 leaves no remainder, INT(N/2)=N/2 only for even numbers.

N/2=5.5, INT(N/2)=5, and so N/2 does not equal INT(N/2). Thus 11 is odd.

N/2=28, INT(N/2)=28, and so N/2 equals INT(N/2). Thus N is even.

The INT function is often used in another way. Let's say we had $10.00 and wanted to divide it equally among three people. How much would each person get? The following program gives the answer.

```
4 REM----------
6 REM    INT1
8 REM----------
10 LET A=10/3
20 PRINT "$";A
30 END

RUN
$ 3.33333
Ok
```

But money is expressed with only two decimal places. We'd like $3.33 instead of $3.33333. How do we chop off the extra 3's?

We want two digits after the decimal point. So we multiply by 100, take the INT part, and then divide by 100.

```
INT(100*3.33333)/100
 =INT(333.333)/100
 =333/100
```

But 333/100 = 3.33, which is what we wanted. (This program doesn't say who gets the extra penny.)

How could we obtain only one decimal place? Simply multiply by 10, take the integer part, and then divide by 10:

```
4 REM----------
6 REM     INT2
8 REM----------
10 LET A=10/3
20 LET A=INT(100*A)/100
30 PRINT "$";A
40 END
```

INT(10*3.33333)/10
=INT(33.3333)/10
=33/10
=3.3

▶ *Note:* In general, if you want a number to have N decimal places (and it has more than N places), use the following:

```
INT((10↑N)×old number)/(10↑N)
```

If you want the value rounded, use

```
INT((10↑N)×old number+.5)/(10↑N)
```

Taking the Absolute Value (ABS)

ABS is a BASIC function that returns the absolute value of a number, that is, the value without regard to sign. The function is written ABS(X).

```
ABS(10)=10
ABS(0)=0
ABS(-10)=10
ABS(-427)=427
```

Notice that ABS(15 – 10) = 5 and ABS(10 – 15) = 5.
Try the following program to see why that's useful.

LAB EXERCISE 5.7   File Name: ELEVATOR _____

Run the following program for various input values.

```
4 REM----------------------------------------------------------------
6 REM                            ELEVATOR
8 REM----------------------------------------------------------------
10 PRINT "THIS PROGRAM ASSUMES A BUILDING WITH 15 FEET BETWEEN FLOORS."
20 PRINT "WHAT FLOOR IS THE ELEVATOR ON";
30 INPUT A
40 PRINT "TO WHICH FLOOR IS IT GOING";
50 INPUT B
60 PRINT "THE NUMBER OF FEET THE ELEVATOR WILL TRAVEL IS";
70 PRINT 15*ABS(A-B);"."
80 END

RUN
THIS PROGRAM ASSUMES A BUILDING WITH 15 FEET BETWEEN FLOORS.
WHAT FLOOR IS THE ELEVATOR ON? 18
TO WHICH FLOOR IS IT GOING? 8
THE NUMBER OF FEET THE ELEVATOR WILL TRAVEL IS 150 .
Ok
```

The Random-Number Function (RND)

One of the most interesting functions in BASIC is the random-number function RND. RND causes the computer to select a "surprise" number between 0 (zero) and 1. In other words, a number like .032145, .285467, or .765321.

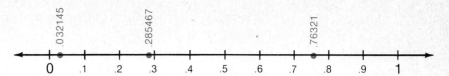

It's as though the computer spun a wheel of chance to get the *value* for the RND function. We're never quite sure what number will be selected.

The precise use of this function varies slightly among computers, and the best way to find out about it is to check your computer manual, ask your instructor, or (best of all) experiment. Here are some suggestions.

The general form of the function is RND(X). On some computers, the value of X is not important. On other computers, it makes a difference. You'll see how this works in a moment. But first you should try an experiment. Run the following program *twice*.

Radio Shack

IBM

► *Note:* If you are using a TRS-80 computer, use RND(0) instead of RND(1) in all the programs in this book. If you are using an IBM PC, you can use RND instead of RND(1).

```
4 REM-------------
6 REM        RND
8 REM-------------
10 FOR K=1 TO 5
20    PRINT RND(1),
30 NEXT K
40 END
```

Here's the result of the preceding experiment on two different computer systems, which we'll call A and B.

Computer A

```
RUN
 .984546      .901591      .727313      6.83401E-03   .96943
Ok
RUN
 .448163      .86774       .0331043     .603678       .7789
Ok
```

Computer B

```
RUN
 .245121      .305003      .311866      .515163       .0583136
Ok
RUN
 .245121      .305003      .311866      .515163       .0583136
Ok
```

Computer A produced a completely *different* set of random numbers on each run. For the applications in this book, this is preferred. If your computer acted like computer A, you're all set!

If your computer acted like computer B, there are three things you can try doing to make it act like computer A, producing a real "surprise" on every run.

1. On some systems, you add a statement containing RND(−1) at the beginning of the program. Run this program twice.

```
4 REM-------------
6 REM        RND1
8 REM-------------
10 LET X=RND(-1)
20 FOR K=1 TO 5
30    PRINT RND(1),
40 NEXT K
50 END
```

2. On other systems, the way to get different random numbers on every run is to add statement 9 as follows:

Radio Shack

    9 RANDOMIZE   (On the TRS-80, use RANDOM)

The rest of the program stays the same.
On the IBM PC, use

IBM

    9 RANDOMIZE TIMER

3. If none of the above works, there is a somewhat clumsy way of making each run be "almost" a surprise. It takes five extra statements, as follows.

```
4  REM-----------------------------------------------------
6  REM                           RND2
8  REM-----------------------------------------------------
10 PRINT "TYPE THE SECOND HAND'S POSITION ON THE WALL CLOCK";
20 INPUT S
30 FOR J=1 TO S
40    LET X=RND(1)
50 NEXT J
60 FOR K=1 TO 5
70    PRINT RND(1),
80 NEXT K
90 END

RUN
TYPE THE SECOND HAND'S POSITION ON THE WALL CLOCK? 26
 .86774        .0331043      .603678       .7789          .286546
Ok
RUN
TYPE THE SECOND HAND'S POSITION ON THE WALL CLOCK? 45
 .22558        .745547       .257104       .930092        .453242
Ok
```

The user typed in 26 after the first run to indicate that the second hand on a clock "happened" to show 26 seconds past the minute. Lines 7, 8, and 9 then forced the computer to run down its list of random numbers to the 26th one before printing anything in line 20. On the second run, since the clock happened to show 45 seconds, a different number in the list was used as the starting point.

One last thing: If your computer acts like A, and you *want* it to act like B, try experiment 1. This technique works in reverse on some computers!

An Application of RND

Now let's look at a program that uses RND. We'll write a computer program that "simulates" the tossing of a coin eight times. We'll assume that the random numbers are evenly distributed between 0 and 1. Since there are two possible results of a coin toss (head or tail), let's decide that if R<= .5, it represents a head, and that if R>.5, it represents a tail (we could just as well reverse this choice).

```
4  REM----------------------------
6  REM              HEADS
8  REM----------------------------
10 RANDOMIZE
20 FOR I=1 TO 8
30    LET R=RND(1)
40    IF R>.5 THEN 70
50    PRINT "  TAILS"
60    GOTO 90
70      LET H=H+1
80      PRINT " HEADS"
90 NEXT I
100 PRINT "NUMBER OF HEADS =";H
110 END
```

To get different tosses on different runs, your computer may require that you omit this step, or instead use
        10 LET X = RND(−1)

```
RUN
Random number seed (-32768-to 32767)? 123
 HEADS
   TAILS
 HEADS
   TAILS
 HEADS
   TAILS
 HEADS
   TAILS
NUMBER OF HEADS = 4
Ok
```

The seed 123 is used by RANDOMIZE in somewhat the same way as the position of the second hand is used in RND2.

Just as if you tossed a real coin, the order of heads and tails is random. If you run the program several times, it is highly probable that the average number of heads will be approximately equal to the average number of tails.

Making RND(1) More Useful

RND(1) generates decimals between 0 and 1. Frequently, though, we prefer integers between two other numbers. For instance, to simulate rolling a die, we might want to generate random integers from 1 to 6 (1, 2, 3, 4, 5, or 6).

What can we do? Well:

RND(1) gives numbers between 0 and 1 (not including 1)
6*RND(1) gives numbers between 0 and 6 (but not including 6)
INT(6*RND(1)) gives integers from 0 to 5
INT(6*RND(1) + 1) gives integers from 1 to 6, which is what we wanted.

In general, INT($(b + 1 - a)$*RND(1)$ + a$) gives the integers from a to b inclusive. In the preceding example, $a = 1$, $b = 6$, and we have:

```
INT((6+1-1)*RND(1)+1)
```

EXERCISES   Write programs that each generate ten random integers of the following kinds.

5.6   Integers from 5 to 20 inclusive   5.9   Integers from 1 to 100 inclusive

5.7   Integers from 9 to 15 inclusive   5.10   Integers from −50 to 50 inclusive

5.8   Integers from 1 to 3 inclusive

LAB EXERCISE 5.8   File Name: COIN

Write a program that simulates tossing a coin 100 times. *Suggestion:* Using HEADS as a guide, put a semicolon at the ends of lines 50 and 80, and add a line that prints the number of tails. Also experiment with changing R>.5 to R>= .5.

LAB EXERCISE 5.9   File Name: RAND

Compare your solution to Exercise 5.6 with the following program by running them both.

```
 4  REM----------------------
 6  REM           RAND
 8  REM----------------------
10  RANDOMIZE
20  FOR I=1 TO 10
30    PRINT INT(16*RND(1)+5);
40  NEXT I
50  END
```

LAB EXERCISE 5.10   File Name: DICE

Write a program that simulates the throwing of two dice. It should produce results similar to the following.

```
RUN
Random number seed (-32768-to 32767)? 246
FIRST DIE       SECOND DIE     TOTAL
     4               2            6
     1               4            5
     6               2            8
     4               5            9
     4               4            8
     1               6            7
     5               3            8
     6               1            7
     4               5            9
     1               2            3
Ok
```

LAB EXERCISE 5.11   File Name: GUESS

Write a program that asks two players to guess which number between 1 and 100 the computer randomly picked. The program should give 10 points to the player who was closest. If the computer's number is picked exactly, 100 points should be given, and the program should stop. A run might look like the following:

```
RUN
Random number seed (-32768-to 32767)? 1234
EACH OF TWO PLAYERS IS TO GUESS A NUMBER FROM 1 TO 99
THE PLAYER WHO IS CLOSEST TO THE COMPUTER'S CHOICE
IS GIVEN 10 POINTS.  O.K.  HERE WE GO!!
PLAYER #1? 47
PLAYER #2? 78
SCORE:  PLAYER #1 10 POINTS; PLAYER #2 0 POINTS.

LET'S TRY AGAIN.
PLAYER #1? 31
PLAYER #2? 9
SCORE:  PLAYER #1 20 POINTS; PLAYER #2 0 POINTS.

LET'S TRY AGAIN.
PLAYER #1? ^C
Break in 60
Ok
```

Mathematical Functions in BASIC

Most versions of BASIC also include a variety of mathematical functions. These include:

LOG(X)	Logarithm of X to the base 10
EXP(X)	The number e raised to the Xth power
SIN(X)	The sine of the angle X
COS(X)	The cosine of the angle X
TAN(X)	The tangent of the angle X
ATN(X)	The angle whose tangent is X

All angles must be expressed in radians. Several examples showing use of the SIN and COS functions to produce interesting graphics will be shown in Chapter 9. A formula for using LOG(X) to calculate logarithms to the base 2 (or any other base) is shown in Section 5.4.

5.4   Defining Your Own Functions with DEF FN

Most versions of BASIC have a facility for defining "homemade" functions, provided that they can be expressed as a single assignment statement. (Multiline functions are also sometimes available, but not in Microsoft BASIC.)

Here's a simple example showing how to define and use a function that returns (gives you) the cube of a number.

> This defines the value to be calculated for any argument A.

> The variable used for the argument on the left must also be used on the right.

> This value of X becomes the argument of FNCUBE in line 10.

```
10 DEF FNCUBE(A) = A*A*A
20 FOR J=1 TO 3
30   PRINT "WHAT IS X";
40   INPUT X
50   PRINT "X CUBED IS"; FNCUBE(X)
60 NEXT J
```

Line 10 is where the function is defined. You must use the key word DEF followed by a function name made up of FN plus a variable name *you* choose. You can then call on this function later in the program by using it as though it were a regular variable.

In general, any expression may be used on the right side of a DEF FN statement. This expression may also use other functions. For example, here's how to define a function that returns a logarithm to the base 2:

```
DEF FNLB2(X) = LOG(X)/LOG(2)
```

Section 8.4 will mention one possible application for this function.

Sneak Preview

You can also use DEF to define functions that use *string variables*. Here's an example showing how to use a function called FNU$ to convert all the lower-case letters in a string to upper-case (capital) letters. This example may not make much sense to you now, since it uses four of the built-in string functions of BASIC (CHR$, ASC, LEN, and MID$) that won't be discussed until Section 6.5. You'll be reminded to take another look at this program in Section 8.3, when we discuss the sorting of strings.

```
10 DEF FNU$(X$)=CHR$(ASC(X$)-32*INT(ASC(X$)/97))
20 PRINT "TYPE ANY STRING, INCLUDING LOWER CASE LETTERS"
30 INPUT X$
40 PRINT "YOUR ORIGINAL STRING WAS"
50 PRINT X$
60 Z$=X$
70 GOSUB 100
80 PRINT "YOUR STRING CONVERTED TO UPPER CASE IS"
90 PRINT U$
99 END
100 '----- SUBROUTINE TO CONVERT TO UC -----
110 U$=""
120 FOR Q=1 TO LEN(Z$)
130   U$=U$+FNU$(MID$(Z$,Q,1))
140 NEXT Q
150 RETURN
```

(continued)

```
RUN
TYPE ANY STRING, INCLUDING LOWER CASE LETTERS
? Puttin´ On the Ritz!!
YOUR ORIGINAL STRING WAS
Puttin´ On the Ritz!!
YOUR STRING CONVERTED TO UPPER CASE IS
PUTTIN´ ON THE RITZ!!
Ok
```

5.5 ON...GOTO...or GOTO...OF...

Imagine that you are writing an American history quiz program. The computer asks multiple-choice questions, you type in the number of your choice, and then the computer tells you not only whether you are right or wrong, but also why.

A sample question is: Who was the first man to walk on the moon?

Suppose that four choices (also called *cases*) are given:

1. Alan Shepard
2. John Glenn
3. Neil Armstrong
4. Buzz Aldrin

Let's call your answer X. You will type either a 1, 2, 3, or 4 for X. We could then say:

```
208 IF X=1 THEN 220
209 IF X=2 THEN 230
210 IF X=3 THEN 240
211 IF X=4 THEN 250
```

> These send the computer to special places in the program that tell you why your specific answer was right or wrong.

But in BASIC, we can condense those four lines into one line:

```
210 ON X GOTO 220, 230, 240, 250
```

When the computer reaches line 210, it should have a value of X (previously input by you) that's 1, 2, 3, or 4.

Line 210 says: If X = 1, the computer will go to the *first* line number, or line 220. If X = 2, the computer will go to the *second* line number, or 230. If X = 3, it will go to the *third,* or 240. If X = 4, it will go to the *fourth,* or 250.

Because the ON...GOTO statement selects one of several possible cases, it is called a *case-structure* statement. (The ON...GOSUB statement explained in Section 5.7 is also a case-structure statement.) Here's a listing that illustrates use of the ON...GOTO statement (see line 260) in our quiz program. Each of the multiple-choice answers corresponds to one case.

> If you type a number whose rounded value is less than 1 or greater than 4, the computer will go to line 270, which reminds you of the rules.

```
4 REM-----------------------------------------------------------
6 REM                              SPACE
8 REM-----------------------------------------------------------
200 PRINT "WHO WAS THE FIRST MAN TO WALK ON THE MOON?"
210 PRINT "1) ALAN SHEPARD"
220 PRINT "2) JOHN GLENN"
230 PRINT "3) NEIL ARMSTRONG"
240 PRINT "4) BUZZ ALDRIN"
250 INPUT X
260 ON X GOTO 290,320,350,380
270 PRINT "PLEASE TYPE IN 1, 2, 3, OR 4."
280 GOTO 250
290 PRINT "NO, SHEPARD WAS THE FIRST AMERICAN TO GO INTO"
300 PRINT "SPACE; ARMSTRONG IS THE ANSWER."
310 GOTO 400
320 PRINT "WRONG; GLENN WAS THE FIRST AMERICAN TO ORBIT THE"
```

```
330 PRINT "EARTH; ARMSTRONG IS THE ANSWER."
340 GOTO 400
350 PRINT "RIGHT!! ON JULY 20, 1969, ARMSTRONG BECAME THE"
360 PRINT "FIRST MAN TO WALK ON THE MOON."
370 GOTO 400
380 PRINT "NO; ALDRIN WAS THE SECOND MAN--ABOUT HALF AN HOUR"
390 PRINT "AFTER ARMSTRONG."
400 END
```
In a longer program, this would be the next question.

```
RUN
WHO WAS THE FIRST MAN TO WALK ON THE MOON?
1) ALAN SHEPARD
2) JOHN GLENN
3) NEIL ARMSTRONG
4) BUZZ ALDRIN
? 3
RIGHT!! ON JULY 20, 1969, ARMSTRONG BECAME THE
FIRST MAN TO WALK ON THE MOON.
Ok
```

The GOTO...OF...Statement

Some computers use the key words

```
GOTO ... OF ...    instead of    ON ... GOTO ...
```

The GOTO...OF...statement looks like this:

```
210 GOTO X OF 220, 230, 240, 250
```

Again, if X is 1, the computer will go to the first line number, or 220; if X is 2, it will go to line 230, and so on.

So the two possible forms are:

```
210 ON X GOTO 220, 230, 240, 250
```

or

```
210 GOTO X OF 220, 230, 240, 250
```

Check—perhaps by trying them on your computer, or by reading your computer manual—which form your computer uses. They do exactly the same thing.

In most versions of BASIC, X may be an arithmetic expression. For example, the following statement is legal:

```
210 ON 2*J+1 GOTO 220, 230, 240, 250
```

In this example, the expression $2*J + 1$ plays the same role as X did in the preceding example.

But what happens if X (or the expression) does not have a value of 1, 2, 3, or 4? The preferred answer is that the programmer shouldn't let this happen. However, if it does, most versions of BASIC use certain "default" rules. In Microsoft BASIC, if the value of X is less than zero or greater than 255, an error message is printed. If X is in the range from 0 to 255, but it's not an integer, the value of X is rounded off. Thus $X = 3.4$ is treated as though it were 3, but $X = 3.5$ is treated as though it were 4. If, after rounding, X is equal to zero, or if X exceeds the number of line numbers in the statement, Microsoft BASIC "falls through" to the next executable statement. In BASIC PLUS, however, this condition is treated as an error.

LAB EXERCISE 5.12   File Name: MELODY _____

Use RND and ON K GOTO to write a program that generates eight bars (measures) of melody as follows: Begin with "DO RE MI," end with "MI RE DO," and generate randomly six bars in between.

```
RUN
DO RE MI
SOL FA MI
SOL FA MI
MI SOL FA
MI SOL FA
RE FA MI
SOL FA MI
MI RE DO
Ok
```

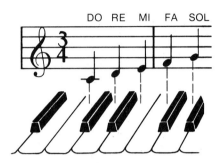

Here's one solution.

```
100 REM--------------------------
110 REM              MELODY
120 REM--------------------------
130 RANDOMIZE
140 PRINT "HERE IS YOUR MELODY!!"
150 PRINT "DO RE MI"
160 FOR I=1 TO 6
170    LET K=INT(3*RND(1)+1)
180    ON K GOTO 190,220,250
190    '
200    PRINT "RE FA MI"
210    GOTO 270
220    '
230    PRINT "MI SOL FA"
240    GOTO 270
250    '
260    PRINT "SOL FA MI"
270 NEXT I
280 PRINT "MI RE DO"
290 END
```

> On TRS-80 computers, use RND(0) here.

After you have run the program, write the melody out in three-quarter time, using regular musical notation, as shown in the diagram.

LAB EXERCISE 5.13   File Name: SONG _____

Write a program that randomly generates four lines of melody, with four bars in each line. Allow all seven notes (DO, RE, MI, FA, SOL, LA, TI) to be used. (*Hint:* Use nested FOR loops as discussed in Section 4.3.)

5.6   GOSUB and RETURN

There are times when the same type of calculation may be needed at various points in a program. Instead of retyping the statements needed for this calculation each time, we can write a subroutine (a part of a major program) that performs the needed calculations. The GOSUB statement is then used to branch to this subroutine from any point in the program. The RETURN statement is used to tell the computer that the subroutine is finished, and the program should now resume execution where it left the *main program*. It works as shown here.

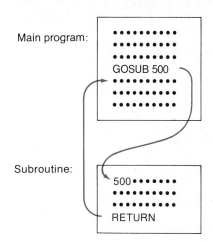

Another use of subroutines is to enable several persons to work on the same large program simultaneously. Each person writes a subroutine to do part of the program. Then a main program links all these subroutines together.

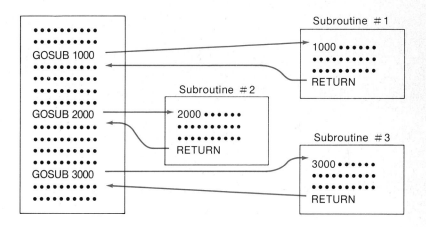

Here is an example of a quiz program that uses GOSUB.

```
4 REM---------------------------------------------------------
6 REM                         GOSUB
8 REM---------------------------------------------------------
100 REM---------------MAIN PROGRAM---------------
110 PRINT "IN THIS PROGRAM YOU WILL BE ASKED FOUR QUESTIONS."
120 PRINT
130 PRINT "AFTER EACH QUESTION, TYPE THE NUMBER OF THE ANSWER"
140 PRINT "YOU BELIEVE TO BE CORRECT."
150 PRINT
160 PRINT "1. ONE OF THE LONGEST CASES OF HICCOUGHING LASTED:"
170 PRINT TAB(10);"1) 3 DAYS";TAB(40);"3) 8 WEEKS"
180 PRINT TAB(10);"2) 2 WEEKS";TAB(40);"4) 8 YEARS"
190 LET A=4
200 GOSUB 9000
210 PRINT "2. THE LARGEST DISH EVER PREPARED WAS:"
220 PRINT TAB(10);"1) FRIED ELEPHANT";TAB(40);"3) BOILED HIPPO"
230 PRINT TAB(10);"2) ROAST CAMEL";TAB(40);"4) BAKED RHINO"
240 LET A=2
250 GOSUB 9000
260 PRINT "3. ROBERTO CLEMENTE LAST PLAYED FOR WHAT TEAM?"
```

Main program

(continued)

```
270 PRINT TAB(10);"1) CHICAGO";TAB(40);"3) ST. LOUIS"
280 PRINT TAB(10);"2) PITTSBURGH";TAB(40);"4) BOSTON"
290 LET A=2
300 GOSUB 9000
310 PRINT "4. ´LOVE´ IS A TERM IN WHAT SPORT?"
320 PRINT TAB(10);"1) GOLF";TAB(40);"3) BILLIARDS"
330 PRINT TAB(10);"2) SOCCER";TAB(40);"4) TENNIS"
340 LET A=4
350 GOSUB 9000
360 PRINT "THAT´S ALL THE QUESTIONS FOR NOW."
370 PRINT "OUT OF FOUR QUESTIONS YOU ANSWERED";C;"CORRECTLY"
380 PRINT "AND";W;"INCORRECTLY."
390 STOP
9000 REM----------------SUBROUTINE---------------
9010 PRINT "TYPE THE NUMBER OF YOUR ANSWER:"
9020 INPUT R
9030 IF A=R THEN 9070
9040    PRINT "NO, THE ANSWER IS NUMBER";A;"."
9050    LET W=W+1
9060    GOTO 9090
9070 PRINT "WOW--THAT´S RIGHT."
9080 LET C=C+1
9090 PRINT
9100 RETURN
9110 END
```

Subprogram

It's important that you have STOP or END before the first subroutine in a program. Otherwise the main program will run into the subroutine incorrectly.

Here's a sketch of how the quiz program works.

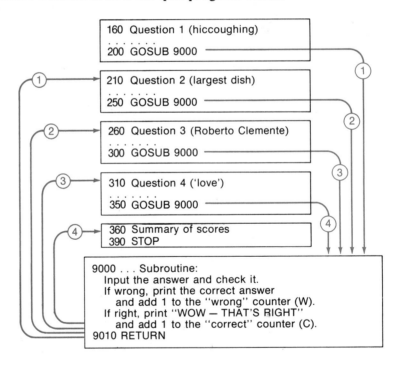

In this program, lines 160 to 350 present four *different* quiz questions. The subroutine always does the same thing: It allows the student to input an answer, it checks the answer, and it keeps score. Notice that the correct answer is always found in the variable A.

Here's a run of the program GOSUB:

```
RUN
IN THIS PROGRAM YOU WILL BE ASKED FOUR QUESTIONS.

AFTER EACH QUESTION, TYPE THE NUMBER OF THE ANSWER
YOU BELIEVE TO BE CORRECT.
```

```
1. ONE OF THE LONGEST CASES OF HICCOUGHING LASTED:
        1) 3 DAYS                  3) 8 WEEKS
        2) 2 WEEKS                 4) 8 YEARS
TYPE THE NUMBER OF YOUR ANSWER:
? 1
NO, THE ANSWER IS NUMBER 4 .

2. THE LARGEST DISH EVER PREPARED WAS:
        1) FRIED ELEPHANT          3) BOILED HIPPO
        2) ROAST CAMEL             4) BAKED RHINO
TYPE THE NUMBER OF YOUR ANSWER:
? 1
NO, THE ANSWER IS NUMBER 2 .

3. ROBERTO CLEMENTE LAST PLAYED FOR WHAT TEAM?
        1) CHICAGO                 3) ST. LOUIS
        2) PITTSBURGH              4) BOSTON
TYPE THE NUMBER OF YOUR ANSWER:
? 2
WOW--THAT´S RIGHT.

4. ´LOVE´ IS A TERM IN WHAT SPORT?
        1) GOLF                    3) BILLIARDS
        2) SOCCER                  4) TENNIS
TYPE THE NUMBER OF YOUR ANSWER:
? 4
WOW--THAT´S RIGHT.

THAT´S ALL THE QUESTIONS FOR NOW.
OUT OF FOUR QUESTIONS YOU ANSWERED 2 CORRECTLY
AND 2 INCORRECTLY.
Break in 390
Ok
```

Summary of the GOSUB and RETURN Statements

At a GOSUB statement, the computer:

- Goes to the subroutine.

- Works through the subroutine until it finds a RETURN statement.

- Then it branches back to the statement *right after* the GOSUB that sent it to the subroutine in the first place.

5.7 ON K GOSUB...

The ON K GOSUB...statement works in a manner similar to ON K GOTO.... The difference is that each line number must correspond to a subroutine. When K = 1, the program branches to the first subroutine. When K = 2, it goes to the second, and so on. In each case, when it encounters the RETURN at the end of the subroutine, the program then automatically goes back to the line right after the ON K GOSUB...statement.

Here's an example showing how ON K GOSUB could be used as part of a card-game program. The suit and number of the card are selected by two random numbers. The ON...GOSUB statement is used to translate the suit numbers into an actual card name. Since five cards are selected, this program could be used to deal hands in a poker simulation.

```
4 REM------------------------
6 REM           CARDS
8 REM------------------------
10 RANDOMIZE
20 FOR I=1 TO 5
30    LET K=INT(4*RND(1)+1)
40    LET L=INT(13*RND(1)+1)
50    ON K GOSUB 100,150,200,250
60    PRINT TAB(20);"THAT IS CARD #";I
70 NEXT I
80 PRINT "THIS IS YOUR HAND!"
90 STOP
100 REM----SUBROUTINE #1----
110 PRINT L;"OF HEARTS. ";
120 RETURN
150 REM----SUBROUTINE #2----
160 PRINT L;"OF CLUBS. ";
170 RETURN
200 REM----SUBROUTINE #3----
210 PRINT L;"OF DIAMONDS. ";
220 RETURN
250 REM----SUBROUTINE #4----
260 PRINT L;"OF SPADES. ";
270 RETURN
280 END

RUN
Random number seed (-32768-to 32767)? 234
 1 OF HEARTS.      THAT IS CARD # 1
 6 OF SPADES.      THAT IS CARD # 2
 1 OF CLUBS.       THAT IS CARD # 3
 7 OF CLUBS.       THAT IS CARD # 4
 10 OF SPADES.     THAT IS CARD # 5
THIS IS YOUR HAND!
Break in 90
Ok
```

LAB EXERCISE 5.14   **File Name: QUIZ2**

Write a quiz program using your own questions (and answers).

LAB EXERCISE 5.15   **File Name: QUIZ3**

Get eight students to work on a longer quiz, with each person contributing three questions. Student #1 should use line numbers in the 1000's, student #2 in the 2000's, and so on.

LAB EXERCISE 5.16   **File Name: CARDS1**

The program CARDS uses the numbers from 1 to 13 to represent all the cards of a given suit. Modify it so that 1 prints as ACE, 11 as JACK, 12 as QUEEN, and 13 as KING.

5.8 Summary of Chapter 5

- The READ statement stores a value in memory as a named variable. It finds the value in a DATA statement. Values in DATA statements are read, one at a time, into variable locations, in the order in which they appear in the DATA statement. These two statements have the general form:

  ⟨ln⟩ READ ⟨list of variable names⟩
  ⟨ln⟩ DATA ⟨list of values⟩

  ```
  150 READ A, A$, B, B$
  600 DATA 2.98, "ORANGES", 1.95, "PEACHES"
  ```

- The RESTORE statement allows the program to reread data that has already been used by a READ.

  ```
  350 RESTORE
  360 READ A, A$, B, B$
  ```

- Functions are small programs that accomplish particular tasks. BASIC includes a collection of useful functions, sometimes called its "library functions." Examples: SQR (⟨n⟩) returns the square root of n. SIN (⟨x⟩) returns the sine of the angle x. You supply the value within parentheses, called the "argument of the function." The value that is returned by the function can be used anywhere in an expression that a variable may be used.

  ```
  10 A=SQR(B)
  100 SX=(SIN(X)+10)/.5
  ```

- The function INT (⟨n⟩) returns the greatest integer less than or equal to n.

  ```
  100 PRINT INT (1.5), INT (-1.5)
   1              -2
  ```

- The function ABS (⟨n⟩) returns the absolute value of n, that is, the number n with a positive sign.

  ```
  100 PRINT ABS(1.5), ABS(-1.5)
   1.5            1.5
  ```

- The function RND or RND (⟨n⟩) returns a random, "surprise" number. Its operation varies among versions of BASIC. It is a good idea to experiment with your version by running the following experimental program several times.

  ```
  10 FOR X=1 TO 5
  20  PRINT RND      (or RND(1), RND(0) RND(-1), RND(6), and so on)
  30 NEXT
  ```

- The key word RANDOMIZE (or RANDOM on some computers) can be used to make the RND function behave differently for each run.

- You may define your own functions in BASIC using the statement:

  ⟨ln⟩ DEF FN⟨function name⟩(⟨argument list⟩) = ⟨expression⟩

  The rules for making up the function name are the same as for a variable name. The defining expression can include other functions.

  ```
  20 DEF FNA(A)=(SIN(A)+30)/.5
  ```

■ The statement ON...GOTO sends control to different parts of a program, depending on the value of an expression. Its form is:

⟨ln⟩ ON ⟨expression⟩ GOTO ⟨list of line numbers⟩

```
150 ON Q GOTO 160, 170, 180, 190, 200
```

In the example shown here, Q = 1 sends control to line 160, Q = 2 to line 170, and so on, up to Q = 5, which sends control to line 200. A value outside this range usually sends control to the next numbered line after the ON...GOTO statement.

■ A subroutine is a section of a larger program than can be called on with the statement GOSUB. Control is sent to the subroutine, which does whatever task it is designed to do. Then control is returned to the statement after the one from which the subroutine was called. The general form of the statements is

⟨ln⟩GOSUB⟨line number XXX⟩

```
        .
        .
        .
```

⟨ln XXX⟩ ⟨first line of the subroutine⟩
⟨lns⟩ ⟨subroutine⟩
⟨ln⟩ RETURN

■ ON...GOSUB works just as ON...GOTO does, except that each line number in the list must indicate a subroutine. Control is returned to the statement following ON...GOSUB.

5.9 Problems and Programming Projects

1. Simulate a run of the following program by showing the output produced.

```
10 '-----------------------------------
20 '      INTDEMO (SHOWS USE OF 'INT')
30 '-----------------------------------
100 PRINT TAB(3);"X";TAB(8);"INT(X)";
110 PRINT TAB(19);"X/3";TAB(27);"INT(";
120 PRINT "100*X/3)"
130 FOR X=-2 TO 2 STEP .5
140    PRINT X;TAB(10);INT(X);TAB(17);
150    PRINT X/3;TAB(30);INT(100*X/3)
160 NEXT X
999 END
```

2. Simulate a run of the following program by showing the output produced.

```
10 '-----------------------------------
20 'BATAVG (USES READ..DATA STATEMENTS)
30 '-----------------------------------
100 PRINT "PLAYER #","AT BAT";"   ";
110 PRINT "HITS";"    ";"BAT.AVG."
120 READ N,B,H
130 PRINT N,B;"      ";H;"     ";H/B
140 GOTO 120
150 DATA 1,50,19
160 DATA 2,43,10
170 DATA 3,51,13
180 DATA 4,49,17
190 END
```

3. Simulate a run of the following program by showing the output produced.

```
10 ´**********************************************************
20 ´*         PERMDEMO (DEMONSTRATES PERMUTATIONS)          *
30 ´**********************************************************
100 FOR I=1 TO 3
110   FOR J=1 TO 3
120     IF (I-J)=0 THEN 170
130       FOR K=1 TO 3
140         IF (I-K)*(J-K)=0 THEN 160
150           PRINT I;J;K
160       NEXT K
170   NEXT J
180 NEXT I
999 END
```

4. Simulate a run of the following program by showing the output produced.

```
10 ´**********************************************************
20 ´*      SIMSTRNG (SIMULATES USE OF STRING VARIABLES)     *
30 ´**********************************************************
100 ´    THIS PROGRAM SHOWS HOW TO PRINT ALL PERMUTATIONS
110 ´    OF 4 STRINGS WITHOUT USING STRING VARIABLES
120 FOR I=1 TO 4
130   FOR J=1 TO 4
140     IF (I-J)=0 THEN 290
150       FOR K=1 TO 4
160         IF (I-K)*(J-K)=0 THEN 280
170           FOR L=1 TO 4
180             IF (I-L)*(J-L)*(K-L)=0 THEN 270
190               ON I GOSUB 510,610,710,810
200               PRINT " & ";
210               ON J GOSUB 510,610,710,810
220               PRINT " & ";
230               ON K GOSUB 510,610,710,810
240               PRINT " & ";
250               ON L GOSUB 510,610,710,810
260               PRINT
270           NEXT L
280       NEXT K
290   NEXT J
300 NEXT I
310 GOTO 999
500 ´
510 PRINT "VANILLA";
520 RETURN
600 ´
610 PRINT "CHOCOLATE";
620 RETURN
700 ´
710 PRINT "WALNUT";
720 RETURN
800 ´
810 PRINT "ORANGE";
820 RETURN
900 ´
999 END
```

5. Write a program that will randomly generate 300 numbers in the range 1 to 99. It should add up the numbers in each of the subranges 1–33, 34–66, and 67–99. It should also count how many of the numbers are in each of the three subdivisions. Report the totals of these calculations and also the sum of all 300 numbers.

6. Modify the program for Problem 5 to generate a stipulated number of random numbers. Have the user specify the range of the numbers, and the subdivisions within this range.

7. Write a program to calculate the population of a lifeform after 25 generations. The lifeform has an initial population of 10 males and 10 females. The females of the species produce offspring on the basis of the male-female balance of their own generation. When the generation contains more females than males, each female produces three offspring. When there are not more females than males, each female produces only one offspring. Offspring have an even chance of being either male or female. The parent generation dies before their offspring produce a new generation.

8. Modify the program for Problem 7 to have the females produce three offspring when there are at least as many females as males, and only one when there are fewer females than males. Test your program for different numbers of offspring under the conditions stated.

9. Modify the program for Problem 8 to have the user stipulate the starting population, the duration of the program, and the rate at which offspring are produced.

10. You have ten $20 bills with which to make four purchases, each of which is less than $50 in value. You can pay for any purchase with any money you have after paying for each of the previous purchases. Write a program that will randomly generate the prices of the four purchases, accept the user's input to pay for the purchases, calculate the change given for each purchase, and list the remaining change in terms of the bills and coins that you have after the shopping trip.

11. Write a program that will calculate the various possible costs of items if it is possible to get one of the following discounts depending on the volume ordered: 5%, 10%, 15%, 17.5%, and 20%, when ordered in quantities of 5 to 9, 10 to19, 20 to 49, 50 to 99, and 100 or more, respectively. Print a table that shows the unit price at each of these different rates for items that have single-item prices ranging from $5 to $60 in steps of $5.

## CHAPTER SIX

Extended BASIC and Its Application

NEW TOPICS INTRODUCED IN CHAPTER 6

- *Advanced data types: DEFINT, DEFSNG, DEFDBL, DEFSTR*
- *Boolean expressions: AND, OR, NOT*
- *More about WHILE and WEND*
- *String arrays*
- *Concatenation of strings*
- *IF . . . THEN . . . ELSE statements*
- *String variables; LINE INPUT*
- *String functions*

6.1 The Dialects of BASIC; Extended BASIC; BASIC Data Types

As mentioned in Chapter 1, BASIC was originally developed as a simple programming language for beginners. The first version was designed in 1964 by John Kemeny and Thomas Kurtz of Dartmouth College, for use by college students with no previous experience in computer programming. It was based on the syntax of more advanced languages, primarily Algol.

Since then, various improvements and additions have been made, resulting in the establishment, by the American National Standards Institute, of a standard BASIC dialect, usually called the ANSI Standard version.*

However, many versions of BASIC go beyond this standard. The best known of these is Microsoft BASIC, a product of the Microsoft Corporation. Microsoft BASIC includes the standard vocabulary and syntax as a subset, while adding numerous extra features. In the chapters ahead, we'll be exploring these extra features, showing how they make it possible to apply what was once a beginner's language to just about any programming task you can imagine.

---

*The document ANSI X3.60, "American National Standard for Minimal BASIC" (1978), defines "core" BASIC, while the document ANSI X3J2/82-17 defines the 1982 extension of the core. In June of 1984 this was updated to ANSI X3J2/84-26. For further information, write to ANSI, 311 First Street, N.W., Suite 500, Washington, DC 20001. In 1984, Kemeny and Kurtz announced their own extended version, called TRUE BASIC.

Computers That Use Extended BASIC

Heathkit

Microsoft has adapted its version of BASIC to most of the low-cost microcomputers. Radio Shack, Apple, IBM, Commodore, Tandy, Zenith, Heathkit, Kaypro, AT&T, and many other computers use a Microsoft BASIC. In addition, Microsoft sells BASIC directly to computer owners. The most powerful Microsoft products are the disk versions of BASIC that are compatible with the popular operating systems CP/M and MS-DOS.

The Microsoft implementation of BASIC goes under several names, including MS-BASIC, Level II BASIC, GW-BASIC, BASIC-80, and MBASIC. The MS-BASIC interpreter comes in several sizes. One of the largest is called BASICA or ZBASIC (for IBM Advanced BASIC or Zenith BASIC).

There is also an extended BASIC available from Digital Equipment Corporation, called BASIC PLUS. It is very similar to Microsoft BASIC. The main differences are in the statements used to handle random-access files (see Appendix C).

The main additions found in extended versions of BASIC fall into five categories.

1. Extended data types (discussed in Section 6.2)
2. Extended control structures (discussed in Sections 6.3 and 6.4)
3. Extended string features (discussed in Sections 6.5 and 6.6)
4. Extended graphics features (discussed in Chapter 9)
5. Extended data-file capabilities (discussed in Chapters 11 and 12)

6.2 Extended Data Types

There are actually four different kinds of data that can be used in extended BASIC.

1. Single-precision real numbers like 314.159 or 3.14159E2
2. Double-precision real numbers like 3141.592653589794 or 3.1415926589793D3, where D3 means *10^3
3. Integers like 26, −483, 0, 32767, −32768
4. Strings like "Smith, John", "BANG!!!", "345LUPGZIG"

From the point of view of the computer, the main difference between these different data types is the amount of storage space they take in memory. The fundamental storage unit in any computer is the bit (which means binary digit). It can store only one of two values, usually written as 0 and 1. A much more practical unit of storage is the byte, which consists of eight bits. It can be used to represent 256 different kinds of information, since there are 256 different ways you can write a pattern of 0's and 1's. For example, the letter A is usually represented as the byte 01000001. When strings are stored in memory, one byte is used for each character. For example, the string ENTERPRISE-X.3 takes 14 bytes of memory. (Behind the scenes, BASIC also allocates three additional bytes for each string: two for its address and one for its length).

How about integers? They take two bytes each, which allows the storage of 65,536 different integers (why?), ranging from −32,768 to 32,767. For reasons we won't go into here, single-precision "real" numbers (also called *floating-point numbers*) use four bytes each, while double-precision real numbers take eight bytes each.

"Good grief!" you cry. "Whatever happened to the good old simple BASIC I've been using all this time?"

Fear not. You don't actually have to know all these details. They can be handled by BASIC itself, as follows.

If you use a variable name ending with no special symbol [like SUM, ARRAY(9), X3], BASIC will automatically use the single-precision data type (which is what you want most of the time anyway). You can also *insist* on single precision, by using the ! symbol at the end of a variable name—like ANS!, SCORE!(I), M5!.

If you put the % symbol at the end of a variable name [for example, COUNT%, TALLY%(K), X3%], then BASIC will set up just enough space to store an integer under each such name.

If you use the # symbol at the end of a variable name [for example, PI#, AMT#(J), Y9#], then BASIC will set up enough space to store a double-precision number under each such name.

If you use the $ symbol at the end of a variable name [for example, NAME$, BUT$(N), Z8$], then BASIC will allow you to store strings using these names.

Here's an example to illustrate the use of the !, %, #, and $ suffixes.

```
10 '-------------------------------------
11 '    DTDEMO1   (DEMO 1 OF DATA TYPES)
12 '-------------------------------------
20 A=1+1/3
30 B!=1+1/3
40 F%=1+1/3
50 K#=1+1#/3#
60 Q$="1+1/3"
70 Z$=" IS THE TEST FORMULA"
80 PRINT A, B!
85 PRINT F%, K#
90 PRINT Q$; Z$

RUN
 1.333333       1.333333
 1              1.333333333333333
1+1/3 IS THE TEST FORMULA
Ok
```

In a long program, typing lots of #, %, and $ signs can be a bother. In such cases, you can use the DEFINT, DEFSNG, DEFDBL, and DEFSTR statements to define the data types of a whole range of variables. For example, the statement DEFINT X,Y defines any variable whose name starts with X or Y to be of type integer. You can also define a whole range of variables, as in DEFINT M-Q, which means "define all variables with names starting with any of the letters M, N, O, P, Q to be of type integer." The other data types can be defined in a similar way, using DEFSNG, DEFDBL, and DEFSTR. Here's an example showing such definitions. Notice that double-precision *constants* (like 1# and 3# in line 50) must still use the # prefix.

```
10 '-------------------------------------
11 '    DTDEMO2  (DEMO 2 OF DATA TYPES)
12 '-------------------------------------
15 DEFSNG A,B
16 DEFINT F
17 DEFDBL K
18 DEFSTR L-Z
20 A=1+1/3
30 B=1+1/3
40 F=1+1/3
50 K=1+1#/3#
60 Q="1+1/3"
70 Z=" IS THE TEST FORMULA"
80 PRINT A, B
85 PRINT F, K
90 PRINT Q; Z

RUN
 1.333333      1.333333
 1             1.333333333333333
1+1/3 IS THE TEST FORMULA
Ok
```

LAB EXERCISE 6.1   File Name: DEMO1

Run the program DTDEMO1 both with and without the symbols !, %, and #. What difference(s) does this make?

LAB EXERCISE 6.2   File Name: DEMO2

Run the program DTDEMO2 both with and without lines 15, 16, 17, and 18. What difference(s) does this make?

6.3 Extended Control Structures; Boolean Expressions

A *control statement* is one that can alter the sequence of statements executed in a program, depending on the value of a *conditional* expression. The two most common control statements in BASIC are IF statements and FOR statements. These can both be extended by the use of other key words, and by use of *multiple statements*.

Putting Multiple Statements on One Line

You can put several statements on one line of extended BASIC, using the colon to separate statements. You can also omit the key word LET any time you wish. For example, instead of

```
10 LET A=49
20 LET B=68
30 LET C=-12
```

you can write

```
10 A=49: B=68: C=-12
```

A good way to read the colon here is as the words "and also." So this statement says "Let A = 49 and also let B = 68 and also let C = −12."

Here's a one-line FOR loop that uses the colon. It stores the numbers from 1 to 10 in the locations A(1), A(2), A(3), and so on up to A(10):

```
95 FOR K=1 TO 10: A(K)=K: NEXT K
```

The use of the colon should not be overdone. Put on the same line only those statements that are related to the same task. Otherwise your program will become difficult to read.

The Extended IF Statement

The IF statement can be extended in three ways. The first is to allow one or more statements after the word THEN, instead of a line number. Here are two examples.

```
15 IF X>10 THEN Y=5*10
25 IF M=0 THEN PRINT "OUT OF MONEY": M=100
99 ' NEXT STATEMENT
```

In the second example, the colons are used to link together two different statements that are to be executed when the condition M = 0 is true. When the condition is false, *none* of these statements are executed; the program goes on to the next numbered statement.

The second extension of IF...THEN uses the word ELSE to show what should be done when a condition is false. Again, colons can be used to group several statements together.

```
350 IF X>9 THEN PRINT "NO": X=X-1 ELSE PRINT "YES": S=S+X
```

When X>9 is true, both the PRINT "NO" and X = X − 1 statements are executed. When X>9 is false (X< = 9), both the PRINT "YES" and S = S + X statements are executed.

The third extension is to allow several conditions to be used in the conditional part of the IF statement, provided they are joined by the "logical" connectives AND, OR, or NOT. For example,

```
550 IF X=9 AND Y=9 THEN 2000
```

This means that if both conditions are true, then branch to line 2000.

```
660 IF E<20 OR T>99 THEN 3000
```

This means that if either condition is true, then branch to line 3000.

```
770 IF NOT (X=9 AND Y=9) THEN 4000
```

This means that if it's not true that both X = 9 and Y = 9, then branch to line 4000.

A combination of symbols like

```
NOT (X=9 AND Y=9)
```

is called a logical, or Boolean expression (named after the logician George Boole). Such expressions can have one of two values, called TRUE and FALSE. Internally, most versions of BASIC use 0 (zero) to represent FALSE and −1 to represent TRUE.

What to Do If You Don't Have Extended BASIC

Each of the extended statements we've shown so far can be rewritten in minimal BASIC by using several simpler statements. Here are some examples showing how the extended statements just shown can be translated back to minimal BASIC.

Undoing multiple statements per line is easy *except* for IF statements. Just write a new line for each colon (:). For example, the FOR loop we showed as line 95 becomes:

```
95 FOR K=1 TO 10
96   A(K)=K
97 NEXT K
```

The IF...THEN followed by multiple statements is a little trickier to translate. For example, line 25 on page 155 becomes

```
25 IF M=0 THEN 50
30 REM ------- STATEMENTS FOR M NOT=0 GO HERE -------
35 GOTO 99
40 REM -------- STATEMENTS FOR M=0 GO HERE ----------
50 PRINT "OUT OF MONEY"
55 M=100
99 REM -----------CONTINUE PROGRAM HERE------------
```

The IF...THEN...ELSE statement (line 350 on page 155) gets translated in a similar manner.

```
350 IF X>9 THEN 380
355 ------------ ELSE BLOCK -----
360 PRINT "YES"
365 LET X=S+X
370 GOTO 400
375 '
380 REM ------------ THEN BLOCK -----
385 PRINT "NO"
390 LET X=X-1
400 REM ----------- CONTINUE PROGRAM ------
```

The apostrophe used in 375, ', is a shorthand for REM that is allowed in some BASICs. We used it just to space things out for readability.

Here's how the AND connective (line 550) is translated:

```
550 IF X=9 THEN 570
560 GOTO 580
570 IF Y=9 THEN 2000
580 REM---AT LEAST ONE CONDITION NOT TRUE IF AT THIS LINE---(and so on)
2000 REM---BOTH CONDITIONS TRUE IF AT THIS LINE---(and so on)
```

The OR condition (line 660) is translated as follows:

```
660 IF E<20 THEN 3000
665 IF T>99 THEN 3000
```

The logical NOT can be eliminated by using the complementary condition:

```
NOT X=9   becomes   X<>9
NOT X<9   becomes   X>=9
NOT X>9   becomes   X<=9
```

and so on. When NOT modifies a group of conditions (as in line 770), then certain laws of logic (*De Morgan's laws*) tell us that we must use the complementary conditions and also interchange AND with OR, and vice versa. So

```
770 IF NOT (X=9 AND Y=9) THEN 4000
```

should be rewritten as

```
770 IF X<>9 OR Y<>9 THEN 4000
```

This can then be written in minimal BASIC as

```
770 IF X<>9 THEN 4000
775 IF Y<>9 THEN 4000
```

The WHILE and WEND Statements

As mentioned in Chapter 3, some versions of BASIC permit the use of a pair of control statements called WHILE and WEND. These allow you to write loops without using GOTO statements (and without some of the confusion these can cause). For example, to print all the factorials less than 900, you would do the following:

```
10 N=0
20 F=1
30 WHILE F<900
50   PRINT N,F
60   N=N+1
70   F=F*N
80 WEND
90 REM-----BEGIN NEXT PART OF PROGRAM-----
```

This says "repeatedly do everything from line 50 to the WEND ("while end") at line 80 WHILE (as long as) F is less than 900."

This program can be translated into minimal BASIC as follows.

```
10 LET N=0
20 LET F=1
30 REM-----BEGIN SIMULATED WHILE LOOP-----
40  IF F>900 THEN 90
50    PRINT N,F
60    N=N+1
70    F=F*N
80  GOTO 40
90 REM------BEGIN NEXT PART OF PROGRAM-----
```

LAB EXERCISE 6.3   **File Name: CONTROL**

> Enter and run both of the previous programs to see if they produce the same results.

▶ *Note:* The quantity N factorial (written in math books as N!) is N*(N − 1)*(N − 2)*...*2*1. If 0! is defined to be 1, then for N = 1,2,3,..., it's true that

$$N! = N*(N-1)!$$

Thus

$$0! = 1$$
$$1! = 1*0! = 1$$
$$2! = 2*1! = 2$$
$$3! = 3*2! = 6$$
$$4! = 4*3! = 24$$
$$5! = 5*4! = 120 \quad \text{and so on}$$

6.4 Applying the Extended Features of BASIC

The extended features of BASIC discussed in Section 6.3 are valuable aids in reducing the size of programs, while simultaneously increasing their readability. The next listing shows a program that would be much more complicated if it had to be written without the extended IF statement and other similar enhancements to BASIC.

The purpose of the program (called GDSTAT2) is to gather data about the grades on a test, and then to print some statistics about the distribution of grades.

To design a program of this size, it's *not* a good idea to start out by writing BASIC code, even when all the extended features are available. In Chapter 7 we'll be more specific about the techniques that can be used to do the preliminary design work that makes writing the final program much easier. As a preview, we'll illustrate two of these techniques in conjunction with the writing of GDSTAT2.

The first technique is to sketch the appearance of both the input and output you expect *before* writing any BASIC statements. Let's face it: You can no more write a program to "do X" without knowing what X is than you can drive a car to Y without knowing where Y is. It's impossible to write a program until you are clear about what it is supposed to do.

Here's what we want the output of GDSTAT2 to look like.

```
RUN
***  GRADE STATISTICS PROGRAM  ***
WHAT IS THE HIGHEST POSSIBLE GRADE? 50
TYPE LAST NAME, GRADE AFTER EACH ´?´ (0,0 = DONE)
? SMITH,44
? BAKER,49
? JONES,38
? ZILCH,33
```

```
? ADAMS,34
? OSTROSKI,40
? ABEL,34
? CHAN,39
? DAVIDSON,42
? FOX,38
? GEORGE,43
? HELLMAN,36
? KING,32
? LEWIS,26
? REITER,49
? OSWALD,17
? MURPHY,35
? 0,0
*** DONE ***

ECHO CHECK OF NAMES AND GRADES
SMITH          44          FOX          38
BAKER          49          GEORGE       43
JONES          38          HELLMAN      36
ZILCH          33          KING         32
ADAMS          34          LEWIS        26
OSTROSKI       40          REITER       49
ABEL           34          OSWALD       17
CHAN           39          MURPHY       35
DAVIDSON       42
-------------------------------------------------------
PRESS <ENTER> TO SEE STATISTICS
    NUMBER OF GRADES:  17
       MAXIMUM GRADE:  49
       MINIMUM GRADE:  17
       AVERAGE GRADE:  37
        MEDIAN GRADE:  33
STANDARD DEVIATION:   7.661972
-------------------------------------------------------
   BAR GRAPH OF PERCENTILE DISTRIBUTION
-------------------------------------------------------
>=90%  <*><*>
>=80%  <*><*><*><*>
>=70%  <*><*><*><*><*>
>=60%  <*><*><*><*>
<=59%  <*><*>
(GRADES FROM 0 TO 59% ARE INCLUDED IN THE LAST PERCENTILE)
Ok
```

Given this picture of what we want a run of the program to look like, the next step is to see if we can organize the program in terms of several smaller parts—to *modularize* it. The output we've sketched suggests writing GDSTAT2 as a sequence of five modules, as follows.

100 Explain the program; initialize variables

200 Write a loop that gathers input data and stores them in memory. Where possible, do some calculations on the data within the loop.

300 Print back (echo) the data.

400 Calculate and print the desired statistics.

500 Display a bar graph of the distribution of grades.

We've labeled these modules with the numbers 100, 200, 300, 400, and 500 to correlate the modular design with ranges of line numbers in the final BASIC program. Here's a listing of a program based on this design.

```
100 ' -------------------------------------------------------
105 '      GDSTAT2    (GRADE STATISTICS REPORT GENERATOR)
110 ' -------------------------------------------------------
115 DIM NAM$(100), GRADE(100)
125 SUM = 0: SQUARES = 0: NUM=0
130 P(1)=0: P(2)=0: P(3)=0: P(4)=0: P(5)=0
135 PRINT "***  GRADE STATISTICS PROGRAM  ***
140 PRINT "WHAT IS THE HIGHEST POSSIBLE GRADE";
145 INPUT HIGH
147 MAX=0: MIN=HIGH
150 PRINT "TYPE LAST NAME, GRADE AFTER EACH '?' (0,0 = DONE)"
200 '
205 '========== MAIN LOOP TO INPUT & PROCESS DATA ==========
210 INPUT N$,G: IF G>HIGH THEN PRINT"ILLEGAL GRADE":GOTO 210
215 IF N$="0" OR G=0 THEN PRINT"*** DONE ***":GOTO 285
220    NUM = NUM+1 : PCT = G/HIGH
225    GRADE(NUM)=G: NAM$(NUM)=N$
230    IF G>MAX THEN MAX=G
235    IF G<MIN THEN MIN=G
240    SUM=SUM+G
245    SQUARES=SQUARES+G*G
250    IF PCT>=.9 THEN P(1)=P(1)+1
255    IF PCT>=.8 AND PCT<.9 THEN P(2)=P(2)+1
260    IF PCT>=.7 AND PCT<.8 THEN P(3)=P(3)+1
265    IF PCT>=.6 AND PCT<.7 THEN P(4)=P(4)+1
270    IF PCT<.6 THEN P(5)=P(5)+1
275    GOTO 210
280 ================= END OF MAIN LOOP ====================
285 AV=SUM/NUM : SQAV=SQUARES/NUM
300 '
310 PRINT:PRINT"ECHO CHECK OF NAMES AND GRADES"
315 MDL = INT(NUM/2+.6)
320 FOR K=1 TO MDL
325    PRINT NAM$(K), GRADE(K),
330    IF K+MDL > NUM THEN PRINT: GOTO 340
335       PRINT NAM$(K+MDL), GRADE(K+MDL)
340 NEXT K
350 PRINT STRING$(48,"-")
360 INPUT"PRESS <ENTER> TO SEE STATISTICS",DU$
400 '
410 PRINT"   NUMBER OF GRADES: ";NUM
415 PRINT"      MAXIMUM GRADE: ";MAX
420 PRINT"      MINIMUM GRADE: ";MIN
425 PRINT"      AVERAGE GRADE: ";AV
430 PRINT"       MEDIAN GRADE: ";(MAX+MIN)/2
435 PRINT "STANDARD DEVIATION: ";SQR(SQAV-AV*AV)
500 '
510 PRINT STRING$(48, "-")
515 PRINT " BAR GRAPH OF PERCENTILE DISTRIBUTION"
520 PRINT STRING$(48, "-")
525 FOR J=1 TO 5
530    IF J=5 THEN F$="<=##% ":FF=59 ELSE F$=">=##% ":FF=100-10*J
535    PRINT USING F$; FF;
540    FOR K=1 TO P(J):PRINT"<*>";:NEXT K
545    PRINT
550 NEXT J
555 PRINT "(GRADES FROM 0 TO 59% ARE INCLUDED IN THE LAST PERCENTILE)"
```

Using LPRINT

Many versions of BASIC allow the word LPRINT to be used in place of PRINT. The difference is that PRINT sends output to your terminal or video display monitor, while LPRINT sends output to the printer. It's usually a good idea to use PRINT for the interactive part of a program, so that someone sitting at the keyboard can see the results immediately. However, it's better to use LPRINT statements for the report-generating part of the program. The next exercise suggests doing this for GDSTAT2.

EXERCISES

6.1   Modify GDSTAT2 so that the grade statistics are output on a printer. Do this by changing all the PRINT statements after line 300 to LPRINT statements. (Apple users should see page 172.)

6.2   How does GDSTAT2 find the MAX and MIN grades? Suppose you changed line 147 to MAX = −E + 38: MIN = +E + 38. Would you still get the correct MAX and MIN grades in lines 415 and 420?

6.3   Rewrite the BASIC code for module 200 (lines 200–280) without using the extended IF...THEN statement. For example, change

```
230 IF G>MAX THEN MAX=G   to   230 IF G<=MAX THEN 235
250 ... and so on              232     MAX=G
                               235 ... and so on
```

6.4   If your BASIC has the WHILE and WEND statements, rewrite GDSTAT2 to use this control structure to control the main loop.

6.5   More About Strings in BASIC; String Arrays and String Functions

We've previously seen that a string is a sequence of characters like "GOLLY!", "CATCH-22", or "GEPL@#!STOCK". You can store a string with assignment statements, READ and DATA statements, or INPUT statements, as shown in STRDEM1.

```
10 REM  STRDEM1  (STORING STRINGS IN BASIC VARIABLES)
20 LET A$ = ">>> "
30 READ B$, C$
40 PRINT "WHAT IS YOUR NAME";
50 INPUT N$
60 PRINT A$; B$; C$; N$; C$; "...ETC..."
70 END
80 DATA "GOOD MORNING",", "

RUN
WHAT IS YOUR NAME? DAVID
>>> GOOD MORNING, DAVID, ...ETC...
Ok
```

In this example, A$, B$, N$, and C$ are examples of *simple string variables*. In addition, extended BASIC allows the use of whole arrays of string variables.

LAB EXERCISE 6.4   File Name: STRLOOP

Modify STRDEM1 so that it loops back to line 40 until the user types DONE for a name. [*Hint:* You can use strings in IF statements of the form: IF N$ = "DONE" THEN ... and so forth.]

String Arrays

Let's first review the idea of *numerical* arrays. In Section 4.2, the subscripted variables M(1), M(2), ..., M(30) were used to store the number of airline seats available on day 1, day 2, up to day 30. Thus our program used 30 consecutive locations of memory to store these data. We sometimes say that the data in this block are related, or *structured*. All the entries are "seats available," and adjacent memory locations represent adjacent days of the month. This kind of structure goes under several names: *array, linear array, one-dimensional array, vector, one-dimensional table,* or simply *table.*

We've also seen that BASIC allows two-dimensional arrays of numerical data, also called *two-dimensional tables,* or *matrices.* For example, suppose your store sold three flavors of ice cream, and you wanted to keep tabs on the sales of each flavor for the 30 days of the month. Then a natural way to organize or structure these numerical data is to store them in a table with three columns, one for each flavor, and 30 rows, one for each day, using an array of the form S(I,J), where I references a day and J a flavor.

In extended BASIC, you can also store *string* data in arrays, provided the array name ends in a dollar sign ($). Most extended BASICs allow both one-dimensional string arrays, with variable names like N$(K), and two-dimensional string arrays, with variable names like A$(J,I). The idea is that you can store blocks of strings together, where each string can usually be anywhere from 0 to 255 characters long. So N$(1) might contain the three-character string JOE, while N$(2) might contain the 13-character string J.R. SMYTH II (the spaces before and after SMYTH are characters).

▶ *Note:* The notations S(J), S(I,J), A$(K), and A$(I,J) all refer to the elements of arrays. When we wish to talk about the array itself, we'll use the notations S(), S(,), A$(), or A$(,). This latter notation is just a convenient way of referring to an array. It cannot be used in programs.

String Operators and String Functions

Strings can be combined by using the + operator. This is called *concatenation.* If A$ = "ANTI", B$ = "BIOTIC", and C$ = A$ + B$, then PRINT C$ will produce ANTIBIOTIC. To do fancier things with strings, extended BASIC also has a number of string functions. Here are some examples showing how these functions work.

LEFT$(A$,M) gives the leftmost M characters of A$, while RIGHT$(A$,N) gives the rightmost N characters. Try this demonstration program.

```
10 REM  STRDEM2 (USE OF LEFT$, RIGHT$, AND +)
20 A$ = "VARNISH"
30 B$ = "UNABLE"
40 PRINT LEFT$(A$,3) + "I" + RIGHT$(B$,4)

RUN
VARIABLE
Ok
```

MID$(A$,P,N) gives you N characters from the "middle" of A$, starting at position P. So PRINT MID$("PRATFALL",2,3) would give you RAT. Actually P can be any position, including P = 1, so the word middle is a little deceptive. If N is omitted, all the characters of A$ from P to the end are returned.

LEN(B$) gives you the length of B$ (which means the number of characters in B$). LEN("MARY") is 4 and LEN("OSCAR") is 5.

VAL(N$) converts a string made up of decimal digits into a genuine number. This is important when you want to do arithmetic with N$. Here's an example.

```
10 REM   STRDEM3 (USE OF VAL)
20 A$ = "98 CENTS"
30 B$ = LEFT$(A$,2)
40 C = VAL(B$)/100
50 PRINT "TWO TIMES ";A$; " = $"; 2*C

RUN
TWO TIMES 98 CENTS = $ 1.96
Ok
```

ASC(A$) is the ASCII code function. Each character in a string is represented inside the computer as a number called its ASCII code. ASCII means American Standard Code for Information Interchange. To find what this code is and perhaps do something with it, extended BASIC uses the ASC(A$) function. Since only one code can be found at a time, ASC("APPLE") will give you the code for just the first letter, A, which is 65 in decimal notation. So ASC("APPLE"), ASC("ART"), and ASC("A") all return the value 65. To get each of the individual ASCII codes for the characters in a string, you can combine ASC with MID$, as follows.

```
10 REM    STRDEM4 (USE OF ASC)
20 A$ = "APPLE"
30 FOR K = 1 TO LEN(A$)
40 PRINT ASC(MID$(A$,K,1));
50 NEXT K

RUN
 65  80  80  76  69
Ok
```

The function STR$(X) works in a way that is the reverse of VAL, making a string out of X. This is different from STRING$(40," – "), which gives a string of 40 dashes (or any number of any other character).

```
100 ´   STRDEM5  (USE OF STR$ AND STRING$)
110 T$=STRING$(30,"*") : B$=STRING$(30,"=")
120 PRINT"TYPE A 4 DIGIT INTEGER";
130 INPUT N
140 IF N>9999 OR N<1000 THEN PRINT "ILLEGAL INPUT" : GOTO 120
160 N$=MID$(STR$(N),2)
170 PRINT "HERE´S YOUR NUMBER IN VERTICAL FORM"
175 PRINT T$
180 FOR J=1 TO LEN(N$)
190    FOR K=1 TO 30:PRINT MID$(N$,J,1);:NEXT K:PRINT
200 NEXT J
210 PRINT B$

RUN
TYPE A 4 DIGIT INTEGER? 2849
HERE´S YOUR NUMBER IN VERTICAL FORM
******************************
222222222222222222222222222222
888888888888888888888888888888
444444444444444444444444444444
999999999999999999999999999999
==============================
Ok
```

(continued)

```
RUN
TYPE A 4 DIGIT INTEGER? 12345
ILLEGAL INPUT
TYPE A 4 DIGIT INTEGER? 3506
HERE'S YOUR NUMBER IN VERTICAL FORM
******************************
333333333333333333333333333333
555555555555555555555555555555
000000000000000000000000000000
666666666666666666666666666666
==============================
Ok
```

CHR$(X) is a function that gives you the character corresponding to the ASCII code X. Thus PRINT CHR$(65) would print the character A.

▶ *Note:* The ASCII codes from 1 to 32 are used for special control purposes, and usually do not correspond to printable characters.

The printable codes go from 32 to 127. To see what they are, run this program:

```
10 FOR X=32 to 127
20 PRINT X, CHR$(X)
30 NEXT X
```

Appendix A summarizes the ASCII codes.

LAB EXERCISE 6.5   **File Name: VOWELS**

Modify the program STRDEM1 so that it uses LEN and MID$ to determine whether the name entered contains all the vowels. If it does, print the message "Congratulations! You have something in common with Ludwig O'Hare."

6.6   Applications Using Strings and String Arrays

Strings and string arrays play an important role in most of the application programs that are shown in the next six chapters. Some of these are fairly long programs, but that doesn't mean that strings aren't also useful in shorter applications. Here are two examples.

Computer-Generated Names

Have you ever wondered how names are chosen for cereals, detergents, and other consumer products? We'll probably never know, but let's see if a computer program might help.

The next program (SOAP) uses nested FOR loops to generate names beginning with GL and ending with the consonants S, P, T, R, or B. All possible vowels are inserted between GL and the consonant. This gives 25 four-letter words you may never have seen before, but which aren't much worse than those concocted by the advertising agencies on Madison Avenue.

```
4 ´-----------------------------------------------------------------
6 ´                        SOAP
8 ´-----------------------------------------------------------------
100 PRINT: PRINT
110 PRINT "PROGRAM TO GENERATE NAMES BEGINNING WITH ´GL´"
120 FOR I=1 TO 5
130   READ A$(I),B$(I)
140 NEXT I
150 FOR I=1 TO 5
160   FOR J=1 TO 5
170     PRINT "GL";A$(I);B$(J),
180   NEXT J
190   PRINT
200 NEXT I
210 DATA A,S,E,P,I,T,O,R,U,B
220 END
RUN


PROGRAM TO GENERATE NAMES BEGINNING WITH ´GL´
GLAS          GLAP          GLAT          GLAR          GLAB

GLES          GLEP          GLET          GLER          GLEB

GLIS          GLIP          GLIT          GLIR          GLIB

GLOS          GLOP          GLOT          GLOR          GLOB

GLUS          GLUP          GLUT          GLUR          GLUB

Ok
```

The Automated Restaurant

Our second string program shows the elegance of the storage scheme behind string arrays in a rather down-to-earth setting. It uses the computer to translate numerically coded orders at a restaurant (for example, an order for entree #3) into more glowing prose. The trick is to store a phrase like "Veal Cordon Bleu" as the array element ENTREE$(3). From then on, any reference to entree #3 is easily translated into the more elegant phrase stored as the third element of the string array ENTREE$(). Since arrays can also be viewed as tables, such a technique is often called *table lookup*.

Here's a program using table lookup in a restaurant setting, where the gimmick is "a terminal at every table" (no pun intended).

```
4 ´****************************************************************
6 ´          MENU1 (USES STRING ARRAYS FOR AUTOMATIC MENU)
8 ´****************************************************************
10 DIM A$(20),B$(20),A(20)
20 PRINT "+++ THE AUTOMATED RESTAURANT +++"
30 PRINT
40 PRINT "THIS IS ROBOT PIERRE READY TO TAKE YOUR ORDER."
50 PRINT
60 PRINT "TYPE THE NUMBER OF YOUR SELECTION AFTER EACH ´?´."
70 PRINT
100 ´------------INITIALIZE VARIABLES------------
110 D$(1)=">>>>>>": D$(2)="++++": D$(3)="": D$(4)="!!": D$(5)="*"
120 Z$="#=\          \  ($#.##)   "
```

(continued)

```
150 ´------------READ DINNER HEADINGS------------
160 FOR I=1 TO 5
170    READ C$(I)
180 NEXT I
200 ´-----------READ AND PRINT DINNER SELECTIONS---
210 FOR I=0 TO 4
220    FOR J=1 TO 3
230       READ A$(J+3*I),B$(J+3*I),A(J+3*I)
240       PRINT USING Z$;J;B$(J+3*I);A(J+3*I);
250    NEXT J
260    ´-----------GET DINNER SELECTIONS-----
270    INPUT X(I)
280    PRINT
290    ´-----------CALCULATE BILL------------
300    P=P+A(X(I)+3*I)
310 NEXT I
320 PRINT: PRINT
400 ´-----------SEND ORDER TO THE COOK------------
410 PRINT "ORDER TO COOK: ";
420 FOR I=0 TO 4
430    PRINT CHR$(I+65);X(I);"/ ";
440 NEXT I
450 PRINT: PRINT
500 ´-----------PRINT DINNER SELECTIONS------------
510 PRINT "*********  ANNOUNCING  *********"
520 PRINT "  YOUR CUSTOM TAILORED DINNER"
530 PRINT
540 I=0
550    PRINT C$(I+1)
560    PRINT D$(I+1);A$(3*I+X(I));B$(3*I+X(I));
570    IF I=1 THEN PRINT A$(6+X(2));B$(6+X(2));
580    IF I=1 THEN I=I+1
590    PRINT
600    I=I+1
610    PRINT
620 IF I<5 THEN 550
700 PRINT "OH,  YES,  YOUR BILL IS ";USING "$$#.##.";P
710 ´--- CALCULATE TIP AT 15% TO THE NEAREST 10 CENTS ---
720 P1=INT((P*.15+.005)*100)/100
730 P1=INT(P1*10+.9)/10
740 PRINT "YOUR SUGGESTED TIP IS ";USING "$#.##.";P1
750 PRINT
760 PRINT "VERY NICE SERVING YOU.  COME AGAIN."
800 ´-----------DATA------------
810 DATA STARTING WITH, *** FEATURING ***,, AND FOR DESSERT
820 DATA   DOWNED WITH
830 DATA   "CHEF´S SPECIAL ","LIVER PATE",0.50
840 DATA "SWEET PINK-CENTERED ","GRAPEFRUIT",0.60
850 DATA "DELICIOUS ","CONSOMME",0.85
860 DATA "A SIZZLING ","HAMBURGER",1.55
870 DATA "CONTINENTAL ","QUICHE",2.70
880 DATA "A SUCCULENT ","HOT DOG",0.95
890 DATA " DELICATELY SEASONED WITH ","MUSTARD",0
900 DATA " SMOTHERED WITH ","CATSUP",0
910 DATA " SERVED WITH A PIQUANT ","PICKLE",0
920 DATA "MOTHER´S ","APPLE PIE",0.85
930 DATA "CREAMY ","ICE CREAM",0.65
940 DATA "RICH MOIST ","RUM CAKE",0.80
950 DATA "FRESH-BREWED ","COFFEE",0.40
960 DATA "A REFRESHING ","SOFT DRINK",0.50
970 DATA "WHOLESOME VITAMIN-ENRICHED ","MILK",0.45
999 END
```

```
RUN
+++ THE AUTOMATED RESTAURANT +++

THIS IS ROBOT PIERRE READY TO TAKE YOUR ORDER.

TYPE THE NUMBER OF YOUR SELECTION AFTER EACH ´?´.

1=LIVER PATE  ($0.50)   2=GRAPEFRUIT ($0.60)   3=CONSOMME   ($0.85)  ? 1

1=HAMBURGER   ($1.55)   2=QUICHE      ($2.70)   3=HOT DOG    ($0.95)  ? 3

1=MUSTARD     ($0.00)   2=CATSUP      ($0.00)   3=PICKLE     ($0.00)  ? 2

1=APPLE PIE   ($0.85)   2=ICE CREAM  ($0.65)   3=RUM CAKE   ($0.80)  ? 2

1=COFFEE      ($0.40)   2=SOFT DRINK ($0.50)   3=MILK       ($0.45)  ? 1


ORDER TO COOK: A 1 / B 3 / C 2 / D 2 / E 1 /

*********  ANNOUNCING  *********
  YOUR CUSTOM TAILORED DINNER

STARTING WITH
>>>>>>CHEF´S SPECIAL LIVER PATE

*** FEATURING ***
++++A SUCCULENT HOT DOG SMOTHERED WITH CATSUP

AND FOR DESSERT
!!CREAMY ICE CREAM

DOWNED WITH
*FRESH-BREWED COFFEE

OH,  YES,  YOUR BILL IS  $2.50.
YOUR SUGGESTED TIP IS $0.40.

VERY NICE SERVING YOU.  COME AGAIN.
Ok
```

EXERCISES

6.5 Modify SOAP to produce five-letter and/or six-letter words.

6.6 Rewrite MENU1 to store menu items in a two-dimensional array. Columns should correspond to menu categories (for example, appetizer, soup salad, entree, dessert, beverage). Rows should correspond to choices within each category.

LAB EXERCISE 6.6   File Name: SOAP2

Let some friends test-run your modified version of SOAP. On the basis of their reactions, design a program that produces even more interesting output, using combinations of letters you hadn't thought of before.

6.7   The Extended INPUT Statement; Other Extensions; BASICA

The statement LINE INPUT A$ is similar to INPUT A$, except that the user's input may contain commas and leading spaces. Also no "?" prompt is given. Examples of its use are shown in the programs KEYCIPH (Section 10.2) and PLEDGE (Section 12.3).

Both INPUT and LINE INPUT may include prompting messages. For example, INPUT "YOUR NAME"; N$ does the same thing as PRINT "YOUR NAME"; followed by INPUT N$. You can suppress the normal "?" prompt by using a comma instead of a semicolon after the prompt string (for example, INPUT "TYPE YOUR AGE ",A). Finally, if you put a semicolon after INPUT, you suppress the <return> <line feed> usually echoed after the user presses <return>. For a valuable use of this feature, see Section 12.4.

Other Extensions; BASICA

The extended version of BASIC used on the IBM Personal Computer is called BASICA, where the A means advanced. Version 2.0 of BASICA contains more than 150 reserved words (which we earlier called *key words*) for use in commands, statements, and functions. Many of these are for use with special hardware. For example, there are statements that allow you to easily create graphics images in color, statements for creating sound, and statements that allow user input via such devices as joysticks and light pens.

An even larger version of this same advanced BASIC, called GW-BASIC (where GW means "Gee Whiz") is supplied with the TANDY 2000 computer. It seems clear that BASIC is destined to keep on growing. Although it's already one of the most extensive and readily accessible languages in the history of computing, the end of its evolution is still not in sight.

There will be several useful programs in the sections ahead that make use of the extended features of BASIC, including string arrays and string functions. One of the programs in Chapter 10 is entirely about the use of strings in programs that do *word processing*. Another use of string manipulation that is important in modern data processing is in the area of data encryption. Chapter 10 shows how to write a BASIC program that does both *data encryption* and *data decryption*. Chapter 9 will show examples of some of the graphics capabilities of BASICA. Chapters 11 and 12 will illustrate the file features.

EXERCISE

6.7   Modify the program GDSTAT (given in Section 6.4) so that student names are input with LINE INPUT. What advantage does this have over using INPUT? Are there any disadvantages?

6.8   Summary of Chapter 6

■ BASIC uses different storage schemes for different types of data. This is done automatically for the most part, but it is possible for BASIC programs to specify the data type desired. This is done using key words DEFINT, DEFSNG, DEFDBL, and DEFSTR; or one can type definition symbols %, !, #, and $ with variable names.

Data type	Type definition key word	Symbol
Single-precision real number	DEFSNG A	A or A!
Double-precision real number	DEFDBL B	B#
Integer number	DEFINT C	C%
String of characters	DEFSTR D	D$

Type definition statements can be used at the beginning of the program; if they, or the type definition symbols, are used later, they supersede the earlier definition.

⟨ln⟩ DEF⟨type⟩⟨list of initial letters of variable names⟩

```
10 DEFINT A-F, X-Z
```

All variable names beginning with letters in the given range are defined as that type.

■ Multiple statements on one line are allowed in many versions of BASIC. They should be limited to logically related statements.

```
100 FOR I=1 TO 10: READ X(I): NEXT I
```

■ An extended form of IF...THEN is allowed in some versions of BASIC.

⟨ln⟩ IF ⟨condition⟩ THEN ⟨clause 1⟩ ELSE ⟨clause 2⟩

```
35 IF X>Y THEN PRINT "NO": X=X-1 ELSE PRINT "YES": S=S+X
```

Either clause may contain one or more BASIC statements, including other IF statements. If the condition is true, clause 1 is executed and clause 2 is ignored. If the condition is false, clause 2 is executed and clause 1 is ignored.

■ In some versions of BASIC the conditional expression may use Boolean (logical) operators to join two or more relations within a condition.

```
200 IF X=1 AND Y=1 THEN 250
210 IF A<10 OR B>0 THEN PRINT "OK"
220 IF NOT (X>5 OR A<6) THEN 800
```

■ The WHILE statement is available in some versions of BASIC. It has the general form:

⟨ln⟩ WHILE ⟨condition⟩
⟨lns⟩   ⟨statements to be repeated⟩
⟨ln⟩ WEND

The body of the loop is repeated if the condition is true. A statement within the body of the WHILE loop should change the value of a variable in the condition in order that the loop eventually terminate.

■ Strings of characters may be stored as simple variables, arrays, and two-dimensional arrays in much the same way as numeric variables. The type definition character, $, is required unless a type definition statement is used.

```
10 A$="ABCDEFGHIJKLMNOPQRSTUVWXYZ"
20 FOR J=1 TO 6: READ V$(J): NEXT J
30 DATA "A","E","I","O","U","Y"
40 PRINT "NAME, PLEASE"; : INPUT N$
```

String arrays must be dimensioned in the same way as numeric arrays.

■ The string operator, + (called "concatenation"), is used to join strings.

```
10 A$="DE"
20 FOR K=1 TO 3: READ B$(K): NEXT K
30 DATA"LIGHTFUL","LICIOUS","LOVELY"
40 FOR L=1 TO 3
45   C$=A$+B$(L)+"!"
50   PRINT C$
60 NEXT L
```

■ Many string functions are available in BASIC. A brief selection is:

LEN($<b\$>$) returns the length of b$.

VAL($<n\$>$) returns the numeric value of n$ (provided that n$ consists of numeric characters).

LEFT$($<a\$>$,$<m>$) returns *m* characters from a$, starting from the left.

RIGHT$($<a\$>$,$<m>$) returns m characters from a$, starting from the right. (In BASIC PLUS, returns characters from position M to end.)

MID$($<a\$>$,$<p>$,$<m>$) returns m characters from a$, starting from position p.

MID$($<a\$>$,$<p>$) returns all the characters from a$, starting at position p.

CHR$($<n>$) returns the character equivalent of the ASCII code n.

ASC($<a\$>$,) returns the ASCII code for the first character in a$.

■ LINE INPUT $<$string variable$>$ allows one to input a string of characters that includes commas, quotation marks, and leading and embedded spaces. It does not produce a ? prompt.

```
100 LINE INPUT A$
```

6.9   Problems and Programming Projects

1. Find and correct the errors in the following program.

```
5  REM   AGE (TESTS AGE BRACKET)
10 PRINT "AGE = "; INPUT A
20 IF A>=21 OR <=65 THEN 50
30 IF A<21 PRINT "TOO YOUNG": GOTO 20
40 IF A>65 PRINT "TOO OLD": GOTO 20
50 PRINT "ELIGIBLE FOR INSURANCE"
```

2. Show the output of the corrected program AGE for inputs of −5, 0, 5, 20, 21, 22, 64, 65, 66, 999.

3. Consider the following program.

```
5  REM   CHECK (CHECKS RANGE OF INPUT)
10 PRINT "TYPE AN INTEGER FROM 1 TO 10";: INPUT N
20 IF N<>INT(N) THEN PRINT "MESSAGE 0"  : GOTO 10
40 IF N<1 THEN 60 ELSE IF N>10 THEN 70 ELSE GOTO 80
50 PRINT "MESSAGE 1" : PRINT "END" : STOP
60 PRINT "MESSAGE 2" : GOTO 10
70 PRINT "MESSAGE 3" : GOTO 10
80 PRINT "MESSAGE 4"
```

Show the output produced by CHECK for each of five runs, where the input is 0, 11, −1, 10, and 1.5. What words do you suggest for each message?

4. Apply the ideas from the program CHECK to the program AGE so that the program AGE rejects zero or negative input, or input greater than 99. In each case an appropriate message should be printed.

5. Write a program that accepts as input a person's taxable income, and produces as output the tax owed, on the basis of the following IRS tables.

For income over	But not over	Tax =	Of amount over
4,400	6,500	272 + 16%	4,400
6,500	8,500	608 + 17%	6,500
8,500	10,800	948 + 19%	8,500
10,800	12,900	1,583 + 22%	10,800
12,900	15,000	1,847 + 23%	12,900
15,000	18,200	2,330 + 27%	15,000
18,200	23,500	3,194 + 31%	18,200
23,500	28,800	4,837 + 35%	23,500
28,800	34,100	6,693 + 40%	28,800
34,100	41,500	8,812 + 44%	34,100
41,500	------	12,068 + 50%	41,500

6. Using the same table as in Problem 5, write a program that generates a table of taxable income versus tax due for income values of $5000 to $150,000, in steps of $5000. The output should also show the actual percentage of income that the tax represents, as follows.

```
RUN
INCOME        TAX      ACTUAL TAX PERCENT
$  5,000    $   368          7.36%
   10,000       *              *
   15,000       *              *
   20,000       *              *
      *         *              *
      *         *              *
      *         *              *
  150,000    $66,338         44.23%
```

7. (Difficult) Read ahead to the discussion of sorting in Chapters 7 and 8. Then modify GDSTAT2 so that the grade roster is printed in sorted order, first by name, then by grade.

8. Write a program that asks the user for information about what his or her recent activities have been. Store these answers in string variables. The program should then write a series of letters to friends for birthday greetings, mixing a "standard" text with the string variables.

9. Write a program that modifies a children's story to include names of friends, relatives, pets, favorite foods, and toys of a particular child. Such a program would use techniques similar to the letter-writing program. The program could first ask the child for the names of friends, pets, toys, and so forth, and then insert them as variables into a "form story."

10. Write a program that allows the user to play a spelling game like Hangman. For an example of how to do this, see Chapter 4 of the book *A Bit of IBM BASIC* (Addison-Wesley, 1985).

11. Write a program that generates "poems." An example can be found in *BASIC and the Personal Computer* (Addison-Wesley, 1984).

12. Some extended features are not available in Applesoft BASIC. Write a demonstration program that shows how to simulate the effect of the following in Applesoft.

$\boxed{\textbf{APPLE}}$

   a. IF...THEN...ELSE   **b.** LPRINT
   c. LLIST   **d.** PRINT USING
   e. LINE INPUT   **f.** WHILE...WEND

Some suggestions: For **a** use the technique shown on page 156. For **b** and **c**, if you have a printer connected to your Apple as device #1, use the command PR #1 to direct output to the printer; use PR #0 to return output to the video display. Within a program, use the statements

```
          25 PRINT CHR$(4): PR #1
and/or    85 PRINT CHR$(4): PR #0
```

For **d**, study the program RCDSHELL on page 203. For **e**, use the INPUT statement, but instruct the user to enclose all strings in quotes so that a run looks like this:

```
TYPE LAST NAME, FIRST NAME, IN QUOTES? "SMITH, JOE"
```

For **f**, see page 157.

## CHAPTER SEVEN

Secrets of
Professional Programming

NEW TOPICS INTRODUCED IN CHAPTER 7

- *Program design criteria*
- *High-level analysis*
- *Macro flowcharts*
- *Top-down program design*
- *Coding*
- *Bubble Sort*
- *Using MERGE to simulate pipes*

- *Structured program design*
- *Program modularization*
- *Use of pseudocode*
- *Stepwise refinement*
- *Algorithms*
- *Debugging BASIC programs*
- *Scope of variables*

7.1 Criteria for Professional Program Design; the Great GOTO Controversy

The criteria for evaluating the professionalism of computer programs have become more and more demanding over the years. Back in the dark ages of computing—from about 1950 to 1970—any program that actually "ran" was a candidate for being called professional. Today, to be labeled professional, in the full sense of the word, a program must also have several other (and much more demanding) attributes. Let's look at three of these.

1. A program should be *reliable;* that is, it should always produce *correct* results. This is a more difficult requirement than one would suspect. The problem is that modern programs are far more complex than anything envisioned in the early days of computing. As a result, it is entirely possible—in fact (are you ready for this?) entirely *probable*—that a complex program will at some time in its life produce incorrect or unexpected output. The challenge today is to cut that word "probable" down to as small a figure as possible, while facing up to the fact that complexity is growing all the time.

2. A program should be *user-proof;* that is, it should continue to perform intelligently even when supplied with unexpected input. (Whether this "bad" input is entered maliciously or not doesn't matter, although the fact that the term *bulletproof* is often used instead of user-proof will give you some idea of what to expect.)

3. Programs should be *maintainable;* that is, it should be easy to modify or expand them. That's a demanding requirement in itself, but what makes things really tough at this stage is that program maintenance may have to be done by someone other than the original author. Further, when the modifications are finished, both conditions (1) and (2) should still hold.

Enter Structured Programming

Several techniques have been developed over the years for dealing with these problems. You'll see a variety of terms related to these techniques, including Warnier-Orr diagrams, HIPO diagrams, structured D-charts, flowcharts, pseudocode, and structured programming languages (including structured BASIC, structured FORTRAN, and Pascal). In general, the application of these techniques is called *structured programming.*

We'll discuss some of these techniques in the next section, and then illustrate their application in a variety of situations. Although none of these techniques is a cure-all, the results can be very positive when combined with a five-step common-sense procedure we'll call *structured program design.*

To GOTO or Not to GOTO: That May Be the Question

Before getting specific about what the phrase "structured program design" encompasses, let's take a look at one of the things that professional programmers are urged *not* to do. This can be summed up in the dictum "Thou shalt not GOTO." It is felt by some computer scientists that many of the evils of bad programming can be traced to use of the GOTO statement. Some have gone so far as to advocate computer languages in which GOTO is a forbidden word.

On the other hand, Professor Donald Knuth (one of the most brilliant and respected computer scientists of our time) has written several papers showing how valuable an intelligent use of the GOTO statement can be. His point is that GOTO shouldn't be blamed for a program's faults; it's an undisciplined *use* of GOTO that causes the trouble.

To get some feel for what has triggered this controversy, consider the following example.

```
 5 REM GOTO SPAGHETTI
10 PRINT "GOOD MORNING" :N=1:GOTO 40
20 IF N>3 GOTC 100
30 IF A>0 GOTO 10
40 INPUT "TYPE A NUMBER";A
50 IF A<0 GOTO 90
60 IF A>999 GOTO 80
70 PRINT "ONE MORE TIME" : N=N-1 : GOTO 20
80 PRINT "TOO BIG" : GOTO 40
90 PRINT "AH, THAT'S BETTER" : GOTO 70
100 PRINT "**DONE**"
```

Now try to answer the following questions. Can you describe exactly what this program does? Will it ever print "**DONE**"? Can you clarify what it does by drawing a flowchart to describe its logic? Does your flowchart look like a bowl of spaghetti?

You get the idea. This program is bad, not because GOTO is bad, but because GOTO was used without rhyme or reason. Now take a look ahead to the program KEYCIPH in Section 10.2. Although this is an advanced program, and you may not understand it now, the fault is not GOTO. In fact, the use of GOTO in KEYCIPH (see lines 500 and 720) is one of the things in the program you probably *can* understand now. It's used simply and consistently to mean "go back to the main menu." This is an example of a disciplined, and quite valuable, use of GOTO. A reasonable conclusion is that when it comes to GOTO, the proper advice is "Don't knock it, but be even more careful not to abuse it."

EXERCISES

7.1   The program PUZZLE in Section 3.3 was an example of a bad use of GOTO. Can you write a similar program *without* using GOTO at all? The final output results should still be a surprise.

7.2   Can you write a program that has output similar to SPAGHETTI, but that avoids all use of the GOTO statement?

7.2   Techniques for Structured Program Design

The GOTO SPAGHETTI program just shown is confusing for about the same reason that a lecture, an artistic performance, or an engineering project is confusing if it isn't based on a well-structured plan. The plan may not be obvious to observers, but if it isn't there, the overall effect will be one of confusion and aimless wandering. Masterful work is next to impossible without a master plan.

The master plan for a program can be expressed in different formats, using several different structuring techniques. Some of the more popular of these are the following.

1. Detailed flowcharts of the type shown in Sections 3.5 and 3.6. These were very popular in the early days of computing, but their use has decreased since the advent of high-level programming languages.

2. Large-scale or "macro" flowcharts. These concentrate on the major features of the program, leaving the details to either smaller subcharts, or to the BASIC code itself. The macro flowchart given in Section 10.2 for KEYCIPH will illustrate this approach.

3. Program modularization based on a problem-solving technique called stepwise refinement. This is one of the most important and useful of the techniques. The idea is to first decompose a given problem into its major components (the "high-level" analysis). Each of these components may, in turn, be broken into smaller components. When a program is finally written to attack the original problem, it is organized in terms of the same components, with each component expressed as a program module.

    A *module* is nothing more than a small group of BASIC statements that have a clearly defined purpose. It's usually a good idea to give each module a heading that explains what it does. For example, here's a program module to convert ASCII characters to ASCII codes (useful as part of a data-encryption program).

```
999  '============================================================
1000 '
1001 '    SUBROUTINE TO CONVERT CHARS IN TX$ TO ASCII IN TC()
1002 '    ASCII CODES KEPT IN RANGE 32-95 TO AVOID LOWER CASE
1003 '
1010 FOR K=1 TO LEN(TX$)
1020    TC(K)=ASC(MID$(TX$,K,1))
1030    IF TC(K)>95 THEN TC(K)=TC(K)-32
1040 NEXT K
1050 RETURN
2000 '.............................................................
```

This particular module is written as a subroutine, but that's not always necessary. The important thing is to keep the module small enough to focus on one thing, and to be easily understood, modified, or extended.

4. One of the most prevalent techniques used in program design today is the use of pseudocode. Pseudocode is a made-up language that *won't* work on computers because they aren't smart enough to "understand" and translate it (at least at present). There is no standard form for pseudocode. You, the user, can actually "invent" it as you go, provided the result is precise and sensible. Here's an example showing how the first part of a program that allows the user to select from one of three subprograms could be written in pseudocode.

```
INITIALIZE VARIABLES; DIMENSION ARRAYS
PRESENT THE USER WITH A MENU OF 3 CHOICES
GET THE USER'S RESPONSE AND STORE IT IN CHOICE
IF CHOICE=1 THEN DO MODULE 410
    ELSE IF CHOICE=2 THEN DO MODULE 610
        ELSE IF CHOICE=3 THEN DO MODULE 810
            ELSE TELL THE USER THERE ARE ONLY 3 CHOICES AND
            PRESENT THE MENU OPTIONS AGAIN
```

You'll notice that although this pseudocode version is very precise about the process to be performed, it omits a lot of detail. For example, it leaves it up to the programmer to decide what DO means. In BASIC, DO could consist of actual statements, a GOTO statement, a GOSUB statement, or some combination of these. Another example of suppressed detail is seen in the last line, in the phrase PRESENT THE MENU OPTIONS AGAIN. This can be handled in several ways, depending on the programmer's style, the computer language used, and other factors. The important thing is that it be a clear statement of what needs to be done in the final program code.

5. More recently, programmers have relied on use of advanced control structures, such as IF ... THEN [statement1: statement2] ELSE [statement3: statement4]. To see the improvement this can make, take another look at the difference between the programs VOTEAGE and VOTEAGE2 in Section 3.3.

6. Other techniques have been proposed, including IBM's HIPO system and Warnier-Orr diagrams. HIPO is an acronym for Hierarchical Input Processing Output. It's a way of formalizing the idea behind the figure we'll show you in Section 11.2 when we discuss data files. Warnier-Orr diagrams concentrate on symbolizing the data structures (rather than data flow) that describe the problem, and then designing programs around this picture. We won't discuss either of these techniques any further, since they are not particularly appropriate to the applications we'll be covering.

Top-Down and Upside-Down Program Design

The techniques just described are all related to something called top-down program design. It's called this because you start with the big ideas, and then gradually work your way down to the level of greatest detail. It's exactly the same approach that's used by a sculptor who first carves out the big shapes in his work, gradually adding details in a series of successive refinements.

Another technique that has no formal name, but that most professional programmers have discovered on their own, is to think carefully about the *input* and *output* desired before thinking about how to write the program. We like to call this an upside-down technique because beginners often assume that the first thing to do is write the program, and not worry too much about its output until the program is finished. If you invert the process, and spend lots of time first sketching exactly what you want to appear on the output screen (including input prompting messages), you'll be amazed at how much easier it is to write the program that produces this final result.

Here's a summary of a recommended sequence to follow in designing and writing a new program. The set of all five steps given here is a guide to what we have called structured program design, whereas steps 3 and 4 summarize what most books mean by *structured programming*. We'll refer to structured program design often from now on. Whenever you see the colored logo with the word Step—plus a number 1, 2, 3, 4, or 5—you'll know we are referring to *structured program design*.

Step 1 Get a very clear idea of what it is you want to do.

Step 2 Think explicitly about the input and output you want. Exactly what do you want to appear on the screen (or printer)? How does this output relate to the input provided? Make sketches of what you imagine snapshots of output will look like. This step is very similar to what movie makers do when they use a "story board" (a series of artist's sketches) to plan a motion picture film.

Step 3 Write out a master plan for a program that produces the output of step 2, using one or more of the techniques just discussed: flowcharts, macro flowcharts, pseudocode. Here's where you should work in top-down fashion, starting with the biggest ideas of your program and working "downward" to more detail in successive stages.

Step 4 Now translate your master plan into actual BASIC code, one module at a time. Writing a program in BASIC (or any other computer language) is called *coding* because you are really translating human ideas into a limited set of code symbols (like FOR, NEXT, PRINT, and so forth).

Step 5 Run and test the program for a variety of input data. If it doesn't perform as expected, use some of the debugging techniques discussed in the next section, make the fixes they suggest, and try again.

We'll illustrate the use of these five steps in Section 7.4, and in most of the applications in the rest of the book.

EXERCISES

7.3 Apply the five-step process of structured program design to an improved version of the airline-reservation system of Section 4.2.

7.4 Consult a teacher about designing some quiz programs for algebra. [The book *Computer Resource Book—Algebra* (Houghton Mifflin, 1975) has numerous ideas.] Then design such a quiz program, using the five-step process described in this section.

7.5 Repeat the preceding exercise for a subject like history or English literature.

7.3 Debugging BASIC Programs

When something doesn't work—or doesn't work as expected—the program is said to have a *bug*. BASIC is an ideal language for finding bugs, since it allows you to do your detective work interactively, that is, as a continuous cycle of *snoop-deduce-fix-try* operations.

To *snoop,* you use one of two techniques. The first is to plant spies in the guilty program by using PRINT and STOP "trace" statements at judicious points. The second is to use the PRINT statement in direct mode to peek into memory at the end of a bad run. Both of these techniques can be combined with use of the CONT statement to continue execution after a STOP.

The *deducing* part of debugging (like the work of a good detective) is the most difficult. On the basis of the evidence presented by your snooping operations, you must come up with a theory of "whodunit." The culprit may be a flaw in your master plan, or it may be as simple as a typing mistake. Whatever the problem, you've got to identify it before weeding it out.

Once you've made your deductions, *fixing* and *trying* your renovated program is easy—at least in BASIC. You just type in new lines to replace the suspected bad ones, and type RUN.

This process may have to be repeated several times. You'll soon learn to be content with testing one hypothesis about what's wrong at a time. Bugs can sometimes interact and gang up on you, so it's best to pick them off one by one. Here's an example showing how to apply the preceding advice to a program called BUGGY. The program is supposed to take a sentence input by the user and print a list of the words used, with a count of how many letters there are in each word.

```
10 ´    BUGGY (PRINT LENGTH OF WORDS IN A SENTENCE)
11 ´
15 INPUT"WHAT IS YOUR SENTENCE";SN$
20 FOR I=1 TO LEN(SN$)
25    LT$=MID$(SN$,I,1)              ´EXTRACT LETTERS FROM SENTENCE
30    W$(K)=W$(K)+LT$                ´BUILD WORD FROM LETTERS
35    IF LT$=" " THEN K=K+1          ´IF SPACE THEN START NEW WORD
40 NEXT I
45 PRINT"------------------------------"
50 PRINT"WORDS USED         LENGTH OF WORD"
55 PRINT
60 FOR J=1 TO K
65    PRINT W$(J), LEN(W$(J))
70 NEXT J
```

```
RUN
WHAT IS YOUR SENTENCE? HOW NOW BROWN COW
----------------------------------
WORDS USED           LENGTH OF WORD

NOW             4
BROWN           6
COW             3
Ok
```

As you can see from the run of BUGGY, we are getting two kinds of errors. First, the word HOW seems to have been lost. Second, the letter count is wrong for all the words except the last one (COW).

To track down the first bug, we can use some direct-mode statements to see exactly what words were loaded into the array W$(), as follows.

```
PRINT K

3                                            ┌─────────────────────────┐
                                             │ Only 3 words...Hmmm     │
FOR I=1 TO K: PRINT W$(I) : NEXT I           └─────────────────────────┘

NOW                                          ┌─────────────────────────┐
                                             │ What happened to HOW?   │
BROWN                                        └─────────────────────────┘

COW

FOR I=0 TO K: PRINT W$(I): NEXT I

HOW                                          ┌─────────────────────────┐
                                             │ There it is! It's in W$(0)! │
NOW                                          └─────────────────────────┘

BROWN

COW
```

So *that's* what happened. We forgot that BASIC initialized K as zero, so the word HOW was stored in W$(0). To fix this, we can either change line 60 to FOR J = 0 TO K, or add the statement 12 K = 1. Now if we try a run, we'll get the following output.

```
10 ´     BUGGY1 (PRINT LENGTH OF WORDS IN A SENTENCE)
11 ´
12 K=1
15 INPUT"WHAT IS YOUR SENTENCE";SN$
20 FOR I=1 TO LEN(SN$)
25    LT$=MID$(SN$,I,1)            ´EXTRACT LETTERS FROM SENTENCE
30    W$(K)=W$(K)+LT$              ´BUILD WORD FROM LETTERS
35    IF LT$=" " THEN K=K+1        ´IF SPACE THEN START NEW WORD
40 NEXT I
45 PRINT"---------------------------------"
50 PRINT"WORDS USED        LENGTH OF WORD"
55 PRINT
60 FOR J=1 TO K
65    PRINT W$(J), LEN(W$(J))
70 NEXT J

RUN
WHAT IS YOUR SENTENCE? HOW NOW BROWN COW
----------------------------------
WORDS USED           LENGTH OF WORD

HOW             4
NOW             4
BROWN           6
COW             3
Ok
```

That's a little better. But the numbers in the second column are still wrong. To track down the reason for the erroneous lengths of words, let's insert a trace statement.

```
27 PRINT "TRACE OF LT$>>>";LT$;"<<< FOR K = ";K
```

Now let's try a run again.

```
27 PRINT"TRACE OF LT$>>>";LT$;"<<< FOR K =";K
RUN
WHAT IS YOUR SENTENCE? HOW NOW BROWN COW
TRACE OF LT$>>>H<<< FOR K = 1
TRACE OF LT$>>>O<<< FOR K = 1
TRACE OF LT$>>>W<<< FOR K = 1
TRACE OF LT$>>> <<< FOR K = 1
TRACE OF LT$>>>N<<< FOR K = 2
TRACE OF LT$>>>O<<< FOR K = 2
TRACE OF LT$>>>W<<< FOR K = 2
TRACE OF LT$>>> <<< FOR K = 2
TRACE OF LT$>>>B<<< FOR K = 3
TRACE OF LT$>>>R<<< FOR K = 3
TRACE OF LT$>>>O<<< FOR K = 3
TRACE OF LT$>>>W<<< FOR K = 3
TRACE OF LT$>>>N<<< FOR K = 3
TRACE OF LT$>>> <<< FOR K = 3
TRACE OF LT$>>>C<<< FOR K = 4
TRACE OF LT$>>>O<<< FOR K = 4
TRACE OF LT$>>>W<<< FOR K = 4
------------------------------------
WORDS USED        LENGTH OF WORD

HOW            4
NOW            4
BROWN          6
COW            3
Ok
```

Aha! We see that we are including a ⟨space⟩ for K = 1, 2, and 3. Looking at our program shows the reason. Line 35 tests for the ⟨space⟩ *after* it's been added to W$(K) in line 30. The fix is to do this test first—say in line 26—and *skip* line 30 when we find the ⟨space⟩. Here's a list and run of our repaired program, now saved with the file name DEBUGGED.

```
10 ´  DEBUGGED (CORRECTLY GIVES LENGTH OF WORDS IN A SENTENCE)
11 ´
12 K=1
15 INPUT"WHAT IS YOUR SENTENCE";SN$
20 FOR I=1 TO LEN(SN$)
25    LT$=MID$(SN$,I,1)            ´EXTRACT LETTERS FROM SENTENCE
26    IF LT$=" " THEN K=K+1: GOTO 40
30    W$(K)=W$(K)+LT$              ´BUILD WORD FROM LETTERS
40 NEXT I
45 PRINT"-----------------------------------"
50 PRINT"WORDS USED      LENGTH OF WORD"
55 PRINT
60 FOR J=1 TO K
65    PRINT W$(J), LEN(W$(J))
70 NEXT J

RUN
WHAT IS YOUR SENTENCE? HOW NOW BROWN COW
-----------------------------------
WORDS USED      LENGTH OF WORD

HOW            3
NOW            3
BROWN          5
COW            3
Ok
```

The Connection Between Debugging and Structured Programming

One of the major reasons for using the techniques of structured program design is that it's much easier to debug a program that's been carefully planned and written—a program with professional style. Clarity of style makes it easy for a programmer to go back and analyze what's been written, even if the author of the original program hasn't looked at the code for a while. And of course this is of even greater importance when the debugging must be done by someone different from the program author.

It's for this reason that one of the most important techniques to use in program design is *program modularization*. This will be illustrated in several of the programs ahead, particularly those in Chapters 10, 11, and 12. As we mentioned earlier, it basically involves designing programs as collections of smaller, semi-independent units called program modules. If this is done properly, it goes a long way toward isolating your bug-hunting to just one module at a time. In other words, your goal is one of *bug containment*. The analogy to the value of containment in the real extermination business is a good one to keep in mind for your future adventures in program debugging.

LAB EXERCISE 7.1   File Name: BUGAWAY

Find a friend who has a program with a bug in it, and swap it with one of your programs that also has a bug. The idea is that each person should try to debug the other person's program. You'll find this *very* instructive.

7.4 Programs = Algorithms + Data Structures: Bubble Sort Revisited

The "formula" in the heading of this section is adapted from the title of a book by Niklaus Wirth, one of the pioneer advocates (along with E. W. Dijkstra and C. A. R. Hoare) of the discipline called *structured programming*. To illustrate what his formula means, and how the ideas of algorithms and data structures fit in with the five-step process we have called structured program design, we'll take a closer look at the Bubble-Sort program that was introduced informally back in Section 4.2.

An algorithm is something like a recipe. It's a step-by-step procedure that tells you how to produce one or more "output ingredients," starting with zero or more "input ingredients." Each step in the procedure must be unambiguous; that is, it must have only *one* possible interpretation. Further, each step must be do-able on a finite machine in a finite amount of time. The algorithm itself must stop after a finite number of steps.

Computer programs are really special examples of algorithms. For example, the program of Section 4.2 called BUBBLE1 consists of a finite number (about 30) of steps expressed as BASIC statements. It accepts as input anywhere from 0 (zero) to 100 numbers, and then, in a finite amount of time (less than a minute), produces a sorted list of those numbers. Let's analyze the writing of this program in terms of our five-step approach to structured program design.

Step 1

Clarify the idea of what you want to do, and how to go about doing it. The idea here is to sort data, that is, to put data in either numerical or alphabetical order. There are all sorts of schemes (algorithms) for doing this. The one we'll use in this program is often called the bubble-sort algorithm because it causes the smallest (or, if you wish, the largest) piece of data to "bubble" to one end of the list. This is done by successively comparing pairs of data, and swapping them if they're out of order. After the smallest (or largest) piece of data has been moved to one end of the list, the process is repeated by conducting a similar "pass" through the remaining data. Then it's done again on the remaining data, and so on until no more swaps are needed. Here's how the algorithm would work on four numbers. In each pass, we'll swap any pair provided that the second number is less than the first. This will move the largest number to the right ("top") of the list.

	Before	After
Pass 1	[5, 23, −5, 19]	[5, −5, 19, 23]
Pass 2	[5, −5, 19], 23	[−5, 5, 19], 23
Pass 3	[−5, 5], 19, 23	[−5, 5], 19, 23

The square brackets show how each pass can concentrate on fewer and fewer numbers. In pass 1, two swaps were needed (23 with −5, and then 23 with 19). In pass 2, only one swap was needed (5 with −5). On the third pass, no swaps were needed, so the algorithm stopped. The output is the sorted data −5, 5, 19, 23.

Step 2

Sketch the imagined output. We'll assume that the user supplies the input data in response to repeated INPUT requests. (Other versions of the program could read the data from DATA statements, get the data from files, as discussed in Chapters 11 and 12, or even generate the data with RND.) Our imagined run looks like this.

```
RUN
HOW MANY NUMBERS TO BE SORTED?  4
TYPE IN THE NUMBERS, ONE AT A TIME
? 5
? 23
? −5
? 19
*** HERE ARE THE SORTED NUMBERS ***
−5       5       19       23
*** DONE ***
```

Step 3

Write out a master plan for your program. This can be done in successive stages. The first stage shows the plan at the highest level (the "top"), concentrating on the big features of the design. Successive stages then expand on these features, adding detail as we move "down" in the plan.

Figure 7.1 shows stage 1 of the step 3 master plan for our design of Bubble Sort. It indicates both the algorithm and the data structures in one flow diagram. The data-structure usage is shown in square brackets. For more complex programs, it might be worth sketching the data structures in a separate diagram.

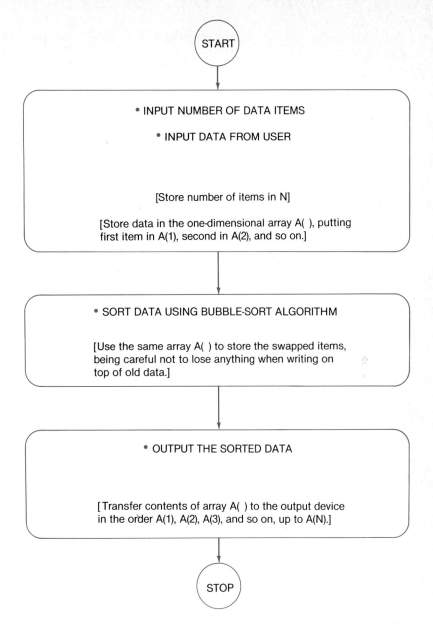

FIGURE 7.1   Stage 1 of the step 3 master plan for design of Bubble Sort

For stage 2 of step 3, we'll refine this diagram by concentrating on one box (module) at a time. The toughest one is the SORT module, so let's attack this. We'll switch techniques here, and show our plan for the SORT module in pseudocode.

SORT Procedure: Using Bubble Algorithm to Sort N Items

1. Set LIMIT = N, where LIMIT means the number of items that have to be compared in each pass.

2. Set SPOT = 0. SPOT will be used in 4.2 below to indicate the spot (value of K) where a swap took place.

3. Do step 4 repeatedly until SPOT remains = 0. Then go to step 5.

4. For K = 1 to LIMIT − 1, do steps 4.1 and 4.2.
   4.1 Compare A(K + 1) with A(K).
   4.2 If they're out of order, swap them and set SPOT = K.

5. Sorting is finished, so go on to the output module.

Line 3 of this pseudocode uses a control structure that is called a DO . . . UNTIL loop in some computer languages. It's not directly available in BASIC, but it can be simulated by using an IF . . . THEN statement at the *bottom* of a loop. This technique will be illustrated in line 320 of the BASIC code of step 4.

Similar stage 2 refinements might be done for the input and output modules of step 3.

For stage 3 of step 3, some of the steps of stage 2 might be refined further. For example, the word "swap" in line 4.2 can be refined into a lower-level procedure, as follows:

SWAP procedure (swaps A with B)

1. Store A in TEMP

2. Store B in A

3. Store TEMP in B

Step 4

Translate step 3 into actual BASIC code. Here's where the skill and art of the programmer come into play. There are usually several "right" ways to do both steps 3 and 4 (just as there are several "right" ways to plan and build a bridge). The code we'll use at this stage is the same as shown earlier in Section 4.2. The particular program lines for the SORT module are as follows, with some comments added. You should compare these with the pseudocode of step 3.

```
200 REM==========================================================
210 REM            ROUTINE TO USE BUBBLE SORT ON A()
230 LIMIT=N                     ´N ITEMS TO BE SORTED
240 SPOT=0                      ´START "DO UNTIL NO SWAPS" LOOP
250    FOR K=1 TO LIMIT-1       ´START PASS THROUGH DATA
260       IF A(K+1)>=A(K)THEN 310 ´NO SWAP NEEDED
270          TEMP=A(K+1)        ´SWAP, STEP 1
280          A(K+1)=A(K)        ´SWAP, STEP 2
290          A(K)=TEMP          ´SWAP, STEP 3
300          SPOT=K             ´REMEMBER WHERE WE SWAPPED
310    NEXT K                   ´CONTINUE PASS THRU DATA
320 IF SPOT=0 THEN 420          ´FINISHED
330    LIMIT=SPOT               ´ELSE CHANGE LIMIT
340    GOTO 240                 ´CONTINUE "DO UNTIL" LOOP
400 REM==========================================================
```

This sorting module can be used as part of any larger program in which N items of data are to be sorted, and the items are stored in the array A(). For example, to test the efficiency of the Bubble Sort algorithm and compare it with other algorithms (which we'll do in Chapter 8), it's convenient to use it as part of a larger program that sorts a large set of random numbers.

Here's a complete listing and run of Bubble Sort that's been modified to sort up to 800 random numbers.

```
4 REM-----------------------------------------------------------------
6 REM       BUBBLE2   (SORTS RANDOM NUMBERS INTO ASCENDING ORDER)
8 REM-----------------------------------------------------------------
100 PRINT "PROGRAM TO SORT A LIST OF NUMBERS INTO ASCENDING ORDER"
110 DIM A(800)
120 PRINT "HOW MANY NUMBERS TO BE SORTED (MAX=800)";
130 INPUT N
140 IF N>800 THEN 120
150 FOR I=1 TO N
160    A(I)=INT(32000-64000!*RND(1))
170 NEXT I
180 PRINT">>> THE UNSORTED NUMBERS ARE:"
190 GOSUB 430
200 REM==========================================================
210 REM            ROUTINE TO USE BUBBLE SORT ON A()
230 LIMIT=N                         'N ITEMS TO BE SORTED
240 SPOT=0                          'START "DO UNTIL NO SWAPS" LOOP
250    FOR K=1 TO LIMIT-1           'START PASS THROUGH DATA
260       IF A(K+1)>=A(K)THEN 310   'NO SWAP NEEDED
270          TEMP=A(K+1)            'SWAP, STEP 1
280          A(K+1)=A(K)            'SWAP, STEP 2
290          A(K)=TEMP              'SWAP, STEP 3
300          SPOT=K                 'REMEMBER WHERE WE SWAPPED
310    NEXT K                       'CONTINUE PASS THRU DATA
320 IF SPOT=0 THEN 350              'FINISHED
330    LIMIT=SPOT                   'ELSE CHANGE LIMIT
340    GOTO 240                     'CONTINUE "DO UNTIL" LOOP
350 PRINT">>> HERE ARE THE SORTED NUMBERS:"
360 GOSUB 430
370 END
400 REM==========================================================
410 REM  SUBROUTINE TO PRINT A(), 3 ITEMS/LINE, 13 COLS/ITEM
430 FOR J=1 TO N
440    T=J-3*INT((J-1)/3)
450    PRINT TAB(13*T-12);A(J);
460    IF T>=3 THEN PRINT
470 NEXT J
490 PRINT
500 RETURN
RUN
PROGRAM TO SORT A LIST OF NUMBERS INTO ASCENDING ORDER
HOW MANY NUMBERS TO BE SORTED (MAX=800)? 17
>>> THE UNSORTED NUMBERS ARE:
-13767        -11720         1142
-31955         -9377        23533
 8369         -5590         23386
-27833         17952        12210
 17095        -25290        -5443
 2441          31764
>>> HERE ARE THE SORTED NUMBERS:
-31955        -27833       -25290
-13767        -11720        -9377
-5590          -5443         1142
 2441           8369        12210
 17095          17952       23386
 23533          31764
Ok
```

Step 5

Run and test the program. This is a good time to go back and run the program BUBBLE1 some more. Can you make it "bomb out," that is, give incorrect results for any special kind of input? Can you modify it to handle string data? How about improving the appearance of the output? Can you write a special version that actually shows all the individual passes being made through the data? Can you combine BUBBLE1 with other programs? This is where you should let your imagination go to work. It's relatively safe to try just about anything, once you have a correct version safely stored away.

LAB EXERCISE 7.2   File Name: BUBBLE5

If you are able to obtain exclusive use of a microcomputer, modify the program BUBBLE2 so that it sorts 5000 random numbers. Since this will take a long time (hours), you should consider letting it run overnight. However, you'll want to keep a record of how long the sort takes, so your best bet is to do this on a computer that has the TIME$ variable (see page 195). Another trick is to add the statement 355 FOR I = 1 TO 500: PRINT CHR$(7): NEXT I at the end of the program. This will act as an alarm to wake you up when it's finished.

7.5   Building Large Programs from Small Ones; Using MERGE

One of the advantages of organizing programs as collections of semi-independent modules is that you can often mix and match the modules. By taking them from several programs, you can create a large variety of new programs.

The basic idea is to arrange the pieces so that the output from one module is "piped" as input to another module. As a matter of fact, some computer operating systems (UNIX and MS-DOS, for example) have a facility for doing such transfers of data between complete programs. The manuals for these systems use the word *pipe* to indicate the connection between the output of one program and the input of another. The arrangement looks like this.

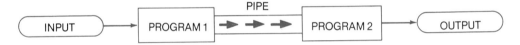

In this section we'll present an example that shows how to simulate this idea by merging two programs together. We'll do this by actually piecing together the programs DEBUGGED and BUBBLE2 (described in the last two sections).

For PROGRAM 1 we'll use DEBUGGED. This takes as its input a sentence typed at the computer keyboard. It breaks the sentence up into words, and produces as its output the individual words of the sentence, stored in the string array W$(). Our combined program then "pipes" the contents of W$() into BUBBLE2, where it is used as input. To make this work, we'll first have to modify BUBBLE2 so that it sorts the elements of a string array rather than a numeric array. This is easy to do. We'll simply replace the numeric array A() with the string array W$(), and TEMP with TEMP$. (Further information about sorting strings can be found in Chapter 8.)

Finally, we'll merge the two programs into a single new program. This can be done in Microsoft BASIC with the command MERGE, provided the second program has been saved as an ASCII file. Also, it is essential that the two programs have nonoverlapping line numbers. Here's the exact procedure to follow.

1. Load DEBUGGED. Modify it as needed, keeping the line numbers less than 100. Then save the modified version with SAVE "DEBUG2".
2. Load and modify BUBBLE2 as needed, keeping the line numbers >= 100. Then save the modified version as an ASCII file with SAVE "BUB2",A.
3. Load the first program back into memory with LOAD "DEBUG2".
4. Merge the two programs in memory with MERGE "BUB2".
5. Save the combination under a new name—say SENTSORT—with SAVE "SENTSORT".

6. Test SENTSORT, making any fixes needed. Here's what your final version might look like.

```
10 ´%%%%%%  SENTSORT (SORTS WORDS IN A SENTENCE)  %%%%%%
11 ´
12 N=1 : DIM W$(100)
15 INPUT"WHAT IS YOUR SENTENCE";SN$
20 FOR I=1 TO LEN(SN$)
25   LT$=MID$(SN$,I,1)              ´EXTRACT LETTERS FROM SENTENCE
26   IF LT$=" " THEN N=N+1: GOTO 40
30   W$(N)=W$(N)+LT$               ´BUILD WORD FROM LETTERS
40 NEXT I
45 PRINT"---------------------------------"
50 PRINT"WORDS USED     LENGTH OF WORD"
55 PRINT
60 FOR J=1 TO N
65   PRINT W$(J), LEN(W$(J))
70 NEXT J
180 PRINT">>> THE UNSORTED WORDS ARE:"
190 GOSUB 430
200 REM=====================================================
210 REM          ROUTINE TO USE BUBBLE SORT ON W$()
230 LIMIT=N                        ´N ITEMS TO BE SORTED
240 SPOT=0                         ´START "DO UNTIL NO SWAPS" LOOP
250   FOR K=1 TO LIMIT-1           ´START PASS THROUGH DATA
260     IF W$(K+1)>=W$(K)THEN 310 ´NO SWAP NEEDED
270       TEMP$=W$(K+1)            ´SWAP, STEP 1
280       W$(K+1)=W$(K)            ´SWAP, STEP 2
290       W$(K)=TEMP$              ´SWAP, STEP 3
300       SPOT=K                   ´REMEMBER WHERE WE SWAPPED
310   NEXT K                       ´CONTINUE PASS THRU DATA
320 IF SPOT=0 THEN 350             ´FINISHED
330   LIMIT=SPOT                   ´ELSE CHANGE LIMIT
340   GOTO 240                     ´CONTINUE "DO UNTIL" LOOP
350 PRINT">>> HERE ARE THE SORTED WORDS:"
360 GOSUB 430
370 END
400 REM=====================================================
410 REM  SUBROUTINE TO PRINT W$(), 3 ITEMS/LINE, 13 COLS/ITEM
430 FOR J=1 TO N
440   T=J-3*INT((J-1)/3)
450   PRINT TAB(13*T-12);W$(J);
460   IF T>=3 THEN PRINT
470 NEXT J
490 PRINT
500 RETURN
RUN
WHAT IS YOUR SENTENCE? TIS A FAR FAR BETTER THING I DO
-----------------------------------
WORDS USED     LENGTH OF WORD

TIS            3
A              1
FAR            3
FAR            3
BETTER         6
THING          5
I              1
DO             2
>>> THE UNSORTED WORDS ARE:
TIS            A              FAR
FAR            BETTER         THING
I              DO
>>> HERE ARE THE SORTED WORDS:
A              BETTER         DO
FAR            FAR            I
THING          TIS
Ok
```

You'll notice that to make this program work, we had to change the variable K used in the original version of DEBUGGED to N. This is because BUBBLE2 expects to find the number of items to be sorted in the variable N, so we had better put that number in N, not K.

This illustrates one of the few defects of BASIC. All the variables have a "global" scope, so the way they are used in one part of a program must be consistent with the way they are used (and what they mean) in all the other parts. To say this another way, most versions of BASIC do not permit use of "local" variables with a private meaning used in only one part of the program. This is because there is no mechanism for automatically passing local values from one place to another. The variables in BASIC are called global because they are all part of one big happy (?) family, and it's up to the programmer to make sure that they always get along with each other.

7.6   Summary of Chapter 7

- A professional program should be reliable, user-proof, and maintainable. This means it should produce correct results, should react intelligently when confronted with unexpected input, and should be easy to modify or expand.

- "Top-down" program design means starting with the big ideas and gradually working down to the level of greatest detail.

- It is important to specify the output desired and the input needed before writing a program.

- Pseudocode is a made-up language that resembles a cross between English and a programming language. Pseudocode does not run on a computer, and has no standard vocabulary. It is a useful tool for top-down program design, and is used by most professional programmers.

- Structured program design involves five steps.
  1. Develop a clear idea of what the program is to do.
  2. Sketch samples of the desired input and output.
  3. Write a master plan for the program, using flowcharts, macro flowcharts, pseudocode, or other techniques, working in a top-down fashion.
  4. Translate the master plan into BASIC code.
  5. Test the program with a variety of data. Find bugs and correct them.

- The debugging process can be described as a "snoop, deduce, fix, and then re-try" cycle that may be repeated many times. Debugging can be aided by use of PRINT trace statements placed at selected points in the program. The PRINT statement can also be used in direct mode after a bad run to inspect the values of variables. If a STOP statement is used after a PRINT trace statement, the command CONT will continue execution.

- Modularization is the design of a program in terms of logically separate parts called modules. If the modules are independent, except for necessary values passed from one module to another, then debugging of incorrect programs is greatly facilitated.

- An algorithm is a step-by-step procedure for producing a specified result from specified inputs (including no inputs). The steps must be unambiguous and finite in number. A computer program is a special case of an algorithm.

- In creating the master plan for a program, you will find it useful to think about both the algorithm and the data structures to be used.

- Programs in BASIC can be loaded together in memory using the commands, LOAD ⟨filename1⟩ and MERGE ⟨filename2⟩.

- In BASIC, variables are global in scope; that is, variables have the same meaning and use throughout a program.

- BUBBLE Sort is an example of an algorithm used to put data in order. It is so named because the algorithm successively causes the largest (or smallest) item of data to move to one end of the list. The Bubble algorithm is not recommended when large quantities of data need to be sorted, since the time it takes can increase as the square of the number of data items.

- To exchange or swap values in two variables, which is done often in sorting programs, do as follows:

```
100 TEMP=A: A=B: B=TEMP
```

TEMP is a temporary resting place for the value in A that is destroyed when the value from B is read into it. The swapping procedure is automated in some versions of BASIC as:

```
⟨1n⟩ SWAP ⟨variable 1⟩, ⟨variable 2⟩
```

7.7 Problems and Programming Projects

1. Write a modified version of BUBBLE2 called BUBBLE3, in which the original data are in an order that is the reverse of what you want the final output to be. This can be thought of as "worst-case" data, since it will make the program do a maximum number of swaps. *Hint:* What does the following loop do?

```
FOR K=1 TO N : A(K)=N-K : NEXT K
```

2. Use BUBBLE2 and BUBBLE3 to compare the time for sorting 800 items of random data with the time for sorting 800 items of data in reverse order.

3. Write a modified version of BUBBLE3 called BUBBLE4, in which the data are already in order. Now compare the time for sorting 800 items that are already ordered with the time for sorting random data, and the time for sorting data in reverse order.

4. Search the computer books and magazines in your library for other sorting algorithms. Write a program based on one of these, and compare its performance with that of BUBBLE2.

5. Add two statistics-gathering statements to BUBBLE2 in the form

```
295 SWP=SWP+1
315 CMP=CMP+1
```

The first statement counts how many swaps are made. The second counts how many comparisons are made. To record these statistics, add statements at the end of the program that print SWP and CMP. Now repeat projects 1, 2, and 3. What can you conclude?

## CHAPTER EIGHT

Professional Searching and Sorting Techniques

NEW TOPICS INTRODUCED IN CHAPTER 8

- *Searching*
- *Shell sort*
- *Swapping*
- *String arrays*
- *Sorting strings*
- *Logarithmic estimate of searching time*
- *Indirect addressing*

- *Sorting business records*
- *Sorting*
- *TIME$*
- *Sequential search*
- *Sorting key*
- *Binary search*
- *Index arrays*
- *Subscripted subscripts*

8.1   Searching and Sorting: What's the Problem?

If a contest were ever held to find the most frequently used algorithms in professional programs, two categories would be right at the top: *searching* and *sorting*. The reason is that business data-processing applications account for a large share of all computer activity, and you can't run a business without using sorted records—lots of them. Even in the years BC (Before Computers), record keeping was at the heart of any business operation. And what did all the clerks in an office do BC? They searched through sorted files for various kinds of records, so that new entries could be made, or old ones changed.

In the years AD (After Digital computers), businesses and government agencies are doing more searching than ever. Also, the number of records being searched has grown astronomically, mostly because of the ease with which data can now be stored in computer-readable form. As a result, there has been great interest in finding faster and more flexible sorting algorithms, along with equally better searching schemes. In this chapter, we'll examine several of these algorithms, and show how to design structured programs on the basis of their use.

8.2   The Shell Sort Algorithm

The Bubble Sort algorithm of Section 7.2 works fine for relatively small amounts of data. However, when you wish to sort several hundred (or even several thousand) items, faster algorithms are available. These have the disadvantage of being more difficult to understand and program, but the results are usually worth the extra trouble.

One sorting algorithm that's highly regarded by professionals, but that is only moderately difficult to program, is called Shell Sort. It's named after its inventor, D. L. Shell, who first described it in an article* dated July 1959. We'll explain and develop it here, using our five-step structured design process.

Step 1

As with Bubble Sort, the idea behind Shell Sort is to swap pairs of data items that are out of order. Unlike Bubble Sort, however, in Shell Sort the items being swapped don't have to be next to each other. When the algorithm begins, a quantity called the GAP is calculated as INT(N/2), where N is the number of items being sorted. For example, if N=8, GAP=4. Items that are GAP units apart are compared, and swapped if out of order. Then GAP is cut in half, and the process is repeated. Here's an example showing the swaps needed for eight data items stored in A(0), A(1), ..., A(7). When finished, the data items are to be in increasing order from A(0) to A(7). (*Note:* We are deliberately using the subscripts from 0 to 7 instead of from 1 to 8 to show that you have this option in BASIC.)

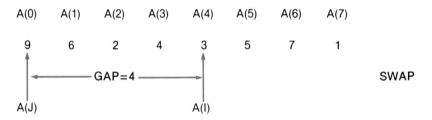

I is a pointer into the "middle" of the data; I is set equal to GAP for a start. J is a pointer to a data item GAP units to the left of I. The algorithm compares A(J) with A(J+GAP), and swaps them if they are out of order. The first time, this gives the following:

```
3      6      2      4      9      5      7      1
```

If there's a swap, the comparison is repeated for J=J−GAP until J "falls off" the left side (which happens right away in our example). We then increase I by 1 (which makes I=5) and repeat the process, as follows.

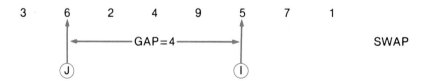

*"A High-Speed Sorting Algorithm," *Communications of the ACM,* July 1959, Vol. 2, pages 30–32.

Repeating two more times (for I=6 and 7), we'll compare 2 with 7 (no swap) and 4 with 1 (swap).

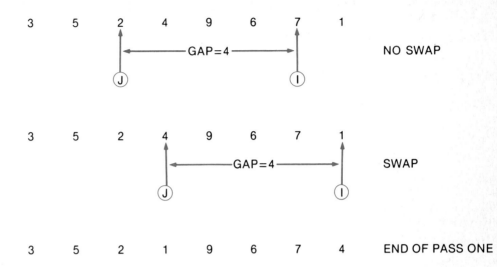

Now we cut the GAP in half, to 2, and start all over. This time I will start at 2, as follows:

Using this reduced gap, we'll go through the data again for I=2, 3, 4, 5, 6, and 7. This time all comparisons will be between data spaced apart by a gap of 2. The following comparisons will be made:

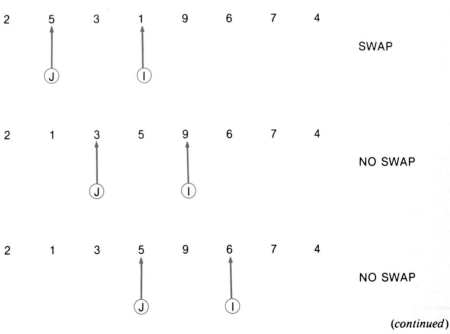

(continued)

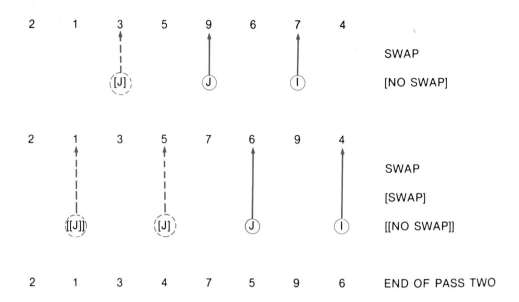

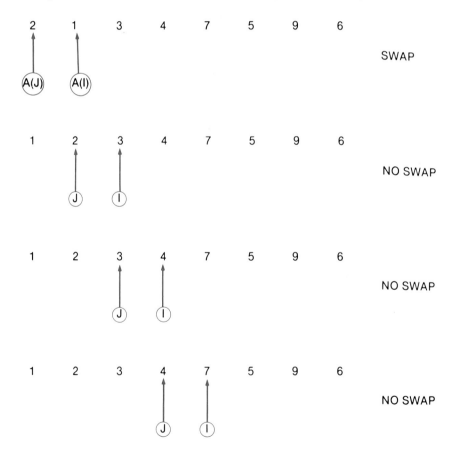

The square brackets show where additional comparisons are made to the left when there's a swap.

Again, the entire process is repeated for GAP=GAP/2. The final pass is made when GAP=1, which means that the comparisons are now made between adjacent items, just as in Bubble Sort. In our example, this happens next, causing the swap of 2 with 1, 5 with 7 and 4, 9 with 6, and 6 with 7, as follows.

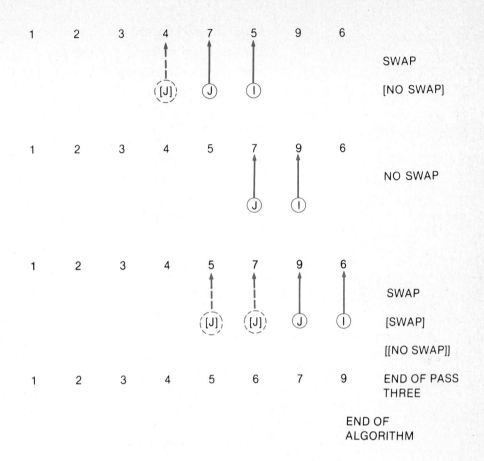

SWAP

[NO SWAP]

NO SWAP

SWAP

[SWAP]

[[NO SWAP]]

END OF PASS THREE

END OF ALGORITHM

<table>
</table>

1	2	3	4	7	5	9	6	SWAP / [NO SWAP]
1	2	3	4	5	7	9	6	NO SWAP
1	2	3	4	5	7	9	6	SWAP / [SWAP] / [[NO SWAP]]
1	2	3	4	5	6	7	9	END OF PASS THREE

Step 2

The output of this program will be the same as that shown for BUBBLE2. That is, we'll show four things:

```
THE UNSORTED DATA
A MESSAGE TO INDICATE THAT THE SORT IS STARTING
A MESSAGE TO INDICATE THAT THE SORT IS FINISHED
THE SORTED DATA
```

The reason for the two messages in the middle is to allow the user to time the sort. On some computers, BASIC has a special variable called TIME$, which shows the current system time. Lines 220 and 360 of the listing in step 4 show how to use this feature. You'll also note that we use RND to generate our unsorted test data.

Step 3

The high-level design of Shell Sort will be given as a series of algorithmic steps A1, A2, and so forth, written in pseudocode. This is a style used by Donald Knuth in his classical books on *The Art of Computer Programming*. We've also used indentions to help show which groups of steps are done "while" a certain condition is true.

A1.   Set GAP=INT(N/2), where N = number of items to be sorted

A2.   While GAP>0, do steps A3 through A10

A3.   Set I=GAP as a pointer into the "middle" of the data

A4.   While I<N, do steps A5 through A9

A5.   Set J=I-GAP as a pointer "gap units" to left of I

A6.   While J>=0, do steps A7 through A8

A7.   If A(J+GAP)>A(J) swap, else goto A9

A8.   Set J=J-GAP to look further left

A9.   Set I=I+1 to move data pointer right

A10.   Set GAP=INT(GAP/2) to cut gap in half

Step 4

Here's the BASIC code that corresponds to step 3, along with a sample run.

```
4 REM-------------------------------------------------------------
6 REM              SHELL2   (SHELL SORT OF RANDOM NUMBERS)
8 REM-------------------------------------------------------------
100 PRINT "PROGRAM TO SORT RANDOM NUMBERS INTO ASCENDING ORDER"
110 DIM A(799)
120 PRINT "HOW MANY NUMBERS TO BE SORTED (MAX=800)";
130 INPUT N
140 IF N>800 THEN 120
150 FOR I=0 TO N-1
160    A(I)=INT(32000-64000!*RND(1))
170 NEXT I
180 PRINT">>> THE UNSORTED NUMBERS ARE:"
190 GOSUB 430
200 REM=========================================================
210 REM              ROUTINE TO USE SHELL SORT ON A()
220 PRINT:PRINT"STARTING TIME OF SORT = ";TIME$
230 GAP=INT(N/2)
240 IF GAP<=0 THEN 360
250    I=GAP                         'INITIALIZE I LOOP
260    IF I>=N THEN 350              'LOOP WHILE I<N
270      J=I-GAP                     'INITIALIZE J LOOP
280      IF J<0 THEN 340             'LOOP WHILE J>=0
290      IF A(J)<=A(J+GAP) THEN 340  'ORDER IS OK, DON'T SWAP
300        TEMP=A(J)                 'SWAP, STEP 1
310        A(J)=A(J+GAP)             'SWAP, STEP 2
320        A(J+GAP)=TEMP             'SWAP, STEP 3
330        J=J-GAP: GOTO 280         'SHIFT J LEFT, CONT. J LOOP
340      I=I+1: GOTO 260             'INCREMENT I, CONT. I LOOP
350    GAP=INT(GAP/2): GOTO 240      'NEW GAP
360 PRINT"  ENDING TIME OF SORT = ";TIME$
370 PRINT: PRINT"SORTED NUMBERS ARE:"
380 GOSUB 430
390 END
400 REM=========================================================
410 REM  SUBROUTINE TO PRINT A(), 3 ITEMS/LINE, 13 COLS/ITEM
430 FOR J=0 TO N-1
440    T=J-3*INT(J/3)
450    PRINT TAB(13*T+1);A(J);
460    IF T>=3 THEN PRINT
470 NEXT J
490 PRINT
500 RETURN
```

```
RUN
PROGRAM TO SORT RANDOM NUMBERS INTO ASCENDING ORDER
HOW MANY NUMBERS TO BE SORTED (MAX=800)? 17
>>> THE UNSORTED NUMBERS ARE:
-13767        -11720         1142
-31955         -9377        23533
  8369         -5590        23386
-27833         17952        12210
 17095        -25290        -5443
  2441         31764

STARTING TIME OF SORT = 16:16:44
  ENDING TIME OF SORT = 16:16:47

SORTED NUMBERS ARE:
-31955        -27833       -25290
-13767        -11720        -9377
 -5590         -5443         1142
  2441          8369        12210
 17095         17952        23386
 23533         31764
```

EXERCISES

8.1 Rewrite the pseudocode steps shown in step 3 of the Shell Sort design, using a decimal notation for step numbers, as illustrated in Bubble Sort (Section 7.4). For example, change A1 and A2 to 1 and 2, change A3 and A4 to 2.1 and 2.2, change A5 and A6 to 2.2.1 and 2.2.2, and so on. Be sure to make the corresponding changes in the "do" and "goto" parts of the pseudocode.

8.2 Rewrite lines 230 to 360 of SHELL2 using WHILE ... WEND control structures in the BASIC code instead of the IF ... THEN structures shown in the listing.

8.3 Sorting Strings

Most business applications involve keeping files of customer accounts, sorted according to some "key" item. This could be an account number, Social Security number, last name, phone number, and so on. Such data items are usually stored as strings, even when they consist mostly of numbers. In other words, we usually save a phone number as P$ = "555-3421," *not* as P = 5553421.

Sorting strings is easy in BASIC. All you have to do is change the numerical array A() to the string array A$(). The following string version of Shell Sort (called STSHELL) illustrates the technique. The data items are input by the user and immediately saved in A$(). When the sorting is finished, the array A$() contains the data in an alphabetized order determined by the order in the ASCII code table of Appendix A.

```
4 REM------------------------------------------------------------
6 REM      STSHELL (SHELL SORT OF STRING DATA IN ARRAY A$())
8 REM------------------------------------------------------------
100 PRINT "PROGRAM TO SORT STRINGS ENTERED BY USER"
110 DIM A$(100)
120 PRINT "HOW MANY STRINGS TO BE SORTED (MAX=100)";
130 INPUT N
```

(continued)

```
140 IF N>100 THEN 120
150 FOR I=0 TO N-1
160    PRINT"STRING #";I;": ";:LINE INPUT A$(I)
170 NEXT I
180 PRINT">>> THE UNSORTED STRINGS ARE:"
190 GOSUB 430
200 REM=========================================================
210 REM          ROUTINE TO USE SHELL SORT ON A$()
220 PRINT:PRINT"STARTING TIME OF SORT = ";TIME$
230 GAP=INT(N/2)
240 IF GAP<=0 THEN 360
250    I=GAP                          'INITIALIZE I LOOP
260    IF I>=N THEN 350               'LOOP WHILE I<N
270      J=I-GAP                       'INITIALIZE J LOOP
280      IF J<0 THEN 340               'LOOP WHILE J>=0
290      IF A$(J)<=A$(J+GAP) THEN 340  'ORDER IS OK, DON'T SWAP
300        TEMP$=A$(J)                      'SWAP, STEP 1
310        A$(J)=A$(J+GAP)                  'SWAP, STEP 2
320        A$(J+GAP)=TEMP$                  'SWAP, STEP 3
330        J=J-GAP: GOTO 280            'SHIFT J LEFT, CONT. J LOOP
340      I=I+1: GOTO 260               'INCREMENT I, CONT. I LOOP
350    GAP=INT(GAP/2): GOTO 240        'NEW GAP
360 PRINT"  ENDING TIME OF SORT = ";TIME$
370 PRINT: PRINT"SORTED STRINGS ARE:"
380 GOSUB 430
390 END
400 REM=========================================================
410 REM  SUBROUTINE TO PRINT A$(), 3 STRINGS/LINE, 26 COLS/ITEM
430 FOR J=0 TO N-1
440    T=J-3*INT(J/3)
450    PRINT TAB(26*T+1);A$(J);
460    IF T>=3 THEN PRINT
470 NEXT J
490 PRINT
500 RETURN
RUN
PROGRAM TO SORT STRINGS ENTERED BY USER
HOW MANY STRINGS TO BE SORTED (MAX=100)? 11
STRING # 0 : SMITH, JOHN
STRING # 1 : MURPHY, PAT
STRING # 2 : JONES, SALLY
STRING # 3 : DELTA, DARLENE
STRING # 4 : CATZ, PASCAL
STRING # 5 : XENIX, KITTY
STRING # 6 : MACGRTUN, A.C.
STRING # 7 : SALAMANDER, JT
STRING # 8 : MONSTYER, NICHOLAS
STRING # 9 : DOYLE, LYNN C.
STRING # 10 : ZILCH, ZZ
>>> THE UNSORTED STRINGS ARE:
SMITH, JOHN             MURPHY, PAT              JONES, SALLY
DELTA, DARLENE          CATZ, PASCAL             XENIX, KITTY
MACGRTUN, A.C.          SALAMANDER, JT           MONSTYER, NICHOLAS
DOYLE, LYNN C.          ZILCH, ZZ

STARTING TIME OF SORT = 15:21:25
  ENDING TIME OF SORT = 15:21:28

SORTED STRINGS ARE:
CATZ, PASCAL            DELTA, DARLENE           DOYLE, LYNN C.
JONES, SALLY            MACGRTUN, A.C.           MONSTYER, NICHOLAS
MURPHY, PAT             SALAMANDER, JT           SMITH, JOHN
XENIX, KITTY            ZILCH, ZZ
Ok
```

EXERCISE

8.3   Will STSHELL work correctly for data that has some strings in upper case and others in lower case? In other words, will "apple" come before "ZENITH"? If not, do you have any ideas about a cure for this problem? [*Hint:* Review Section 5.4.]

LAB EXERCISE 8.1   File Name: STSHELL2

Enter and test STSHELL on your computer. If you do not have the TIME$ feature, omit lines 220 and 360. If you do not have LINE INPUT, see pg. 172.

LAB EXERCISE 8.2   File Name: STSHELL3

Replace lines 220 and 360 of STSHELL with a "beep" feature. On most machines, you can get a beep with FOR K = 1 TO 20: PRINT CHR$(7): NEXT K. Then test the program, using a stopwatch to measure the time between beeps.

8.4   Sequential and Binary Search

Once data items have been stored in a computer's memory—say the names of some popular computer systems stored in a string array A$()—it's easy to search through the data asking the question "Is the string K$ one of the elements of A$()?" K$ is called the *search argument* or *search key*.

The simplest searching technique is one that starts at the beginning of the array and compares K$ to the elements of A$() one by one. This is called sequential search. The program SEQSRCH shows how it works.

```
100 ´-----------------------------------------------------------
110 ´   SEQSRCH   (SEQUENTIAL SEARCH FOR KEY WORD IN STRING ARRAY)
120 ´-----------------------------------------------------------
130 DIM A$(99): N=0
140 READ X$
150 IF X$="$$$" THEN 170
160    N=N+1: A$(N)=X$: GOTO 140
170 PRINT">>> SEQUENTIAL SEARCH IN A$() FOR A GIVEN KEY WORD <<<"
180 INPUT"WHAT IS KEY WORD"; K$: PRINT
190 ´
200 ´---------- SEQUENTIAL SEARCH ROUTINE --------------------
210 M=1
220 IF M>N THEN PRINT "SORRY. "K$" NOT FOUND IN A$()":GOTO 290
230    IF K$=A$(M) THEN HIT=M: GOTO 270
240       M=M+1: GOTO 220
250 ´
260 ´---------- REPORT ON A HIT ------------------------------
270 PRINT">>>>>>>>>       YOU HAVE A HIT      <<<<<<<<<<"
280 PRINT"THE KEY WORD ´";K$;"´ WAS FOUND IN POSITION #";HIT
290 PRINT"************       DONE      *************"
300 ´
310 ´---------- TEST DATA FOR A$() ---------------------------
320 DATA "ABACUS", "BASIC", "CP/M", "EPSON", "GRAPHICS"
330 DATA "IBM", "MICRO", "TANDY", "ZENITH", "$$$"
340 REM   "$$$" IS USED TO SIGNAL END OF DATA
```

(*continued*)

```
RUN
>>> SEQUENTIAL SEARCH IN A$() FOR A GIVEN KEY WORD <<<
WHAT IS KEY WORD? APPLE

SORRY. APPLE NOT FOUND IN A$()
************        DONE        ************
Ok
RUN
>>> SEQUENTIAL SEARCH IN A$() FOR A GIVEN KEY WORD <<<
WHAT IS KEY WORD? ZENITH

>>>>>>>>>        YOU HAVE A HIT        <<<<<<<<<
THE KEY WORD ´ZENITH´ WAS FOUND IN POSITION # 9
************        DONE        ************
Ok
RUN
>>> SEQUENTIAL SEARCH IN A$() FOR A GIVEN KEY WORD <<<
WHAT IS KEY WORD? GRAPHICS

>>>>>>>>>        YOU HAVE A HIT        <<<<<<<<<
THE KEY WORD ´GRAPHICS´ WAS FOUND IN POSITION # 5
************        DONE        ************
Ok
```

Since it does not require that the data be sorted, sequential search is the best approach for many applications. However, it can be very slow when there are several hundred (or thousand) data items. On average, the program has to make N/2 comparisons in a list of N items. For N=100, that's only 50 comparisons, but for N=1000, you can expect 500 comparisons in an average search. And 1000 comparisons would be needed in the worst case (key at the end of the list).

There are several search algorithms that are considerably faster than sequential search. Two of the most widely used are called binary search and tree search. We'll discuss only binary search here.

For N items, binary search requires *at most* $INT(\log_2 N)+1$ comparisons. The quantity $\log_2 N$ means "the power of 2 needed to equal N." For N=1000, $\log_2 N=9.96578$. Thus the *maximum* number of comparisons needed for a binary search of 1000 items is 9+1=10, whereas the maximum number for sequential search is 1000.

The catch to binary search is that the data items must first be sorted. The reason can be seen in Step 1.3 of the following structured design of a program called BINSRCH.

Step 1

The idea behind binary search is similar to that used in finding a name in a phone book. There are four essential stages:

A. Open the "book" to its middle.
B. If the name you want is there, you're finished.
C. If the names you find in the middle are *greater* than the one you want, redefine "book" as the first half; if not redefine "book" as the second half.
D. Go back to stage A.

Each time you go back to stage A, it's as though you started all over with a new phone book that's only half as thick as the previous one. The name "binary" is used to indicate this continual splitting in two. As you can see from stage C, the only way you can be sure that the name you're seeking is in the reduced book is to insist that the names be listed in alphabetical order.

Step 2

The output for this program should first show the key item being sought. If it's found, the output should then show the *position* of the key in the list so that future references to this key can be made directly. (This is like noting that the phone number of someone important is on page 423, seven lines down.) If the key item is not found, the message "NOT FOUND IN LIST" should be printed.

Step 3

A high-level design of our program in pseudocode is as follows.

1.1 Store N items of sorted data in an array A$()

1.2 Get the key item K$ from the user

1.3 Conduct a binary search of A$()

1.4 Print results

A refinement of step 1.3 that shows the binary search is as follows.

1.3.1 Start with LEFT=1 and RIGHT=N

1.3.2 While LEFT<=RIGHT, do steps 1.3.3 through 1.3.5

1.3.3   Calculate MIDDLE=INT((LEFT+RIGHT)/2)

1.3.4   IF K$=A$(MIDDLE), note that we are finished and go to 1.4

1.3.5   IF K$<A$(MIDDLE), reset RIGHT=MIDDLE−1
              else reset LEFT=MIDDLE+1

1.3.6 Print message that K$ was not in the list

Step 4

A coding and sample testing of BINSRCH is shown in the next listing and set of runs.

```
100 '----------------------------------------------------------------
110 '    BINSRCH   (BINARY SEARCH FOR KEY WORD IN STRING ARRAY)
120 '----------------------------------------------------------------
130 DIM A$(99): N=0
140 READ X$
150 IF X$="$$$" THEN 170
160    N=N+1: A$(N)=X$: GOTO 140
170 PRINT">>> BINARY SEARCH IN A$() FOR A GIVEN KEY WORD <<<"
180 INPUT"WHAT IS KEY WORD"; K$: PRINT
190 '
200 '---------- BINARY SEARCH ROUTINE ------------------------
210 L=1: R=N
220 M=INT((L+R)/2)      'MIDDLE OF LIST
230 IF K$=A$(M) THEN HIT=M: GOTO 290
240    IF L=R THEN PRINT "SORRY. "K$" NOT FOUND IN A$()":GOTO 310
250       IF K$<A$(M) THEN R=M-1: GOTO 220
260          L=M+1: GOTO 220
270 '
280 '---------- REPORT ON A HIT ----------------------------
290 PRINT">>>>>>>>>>      YOU HAVE A HIT      <<<<<<<<<<"
300 PRINT"THE KEY WORD '";K$;"' WAS FOUND IN POSITION #";HIT
310 PRINT"************      DONE      ************"
320 '
330 '---------- TEST DATA FOR A$() ------------------------
340 DATA "ABACUS", "BASIC", "CP/M", "EPSON", "GRAPHICS"
350 DATA "IBM", "MICRO", "TANDY", "ZENITH", "$$$"
360 REM  "$$$" IS USED TO SIGNAL END OF DATA
RUN
>>> BINARY SEARCH IN A$() FOR A GIVEN KEY WORD <<<
WHAT IS KEY WORD? APPLE

SORRY. APPLE NOT FOUND IN A$()
************      DONE      ************
Ok
```

(continued)

```
RUN
>>> BINARY SEARCH IN A$() FOR A GIVEN KEY WORD <<<
WHAT IS KEY WORD? ZENITH

>>>>>>>>>        YOU HAVE A HIT       <<<<<<<<<<
THE KEY WORD ´ZENITH´ WAS FOUND IN POSITION # 9
************        DONE        *************
Ok
RUN
>>> BINARY SEARCH IN A$() FOR A GIVEN KEY WORD <<<
WHAT IS KEY WORD? GRAPHICS

>>>>>>>>>        YOU HAVE A HIT       <<<<<<<<<<
THE KEY WORD ´GRAPHICS´ WAS FOUND IN POSITION # 5
************        DONE        *************
Ok
```

EXERCISE

8.4   What is the maximum number of comparisons needed when using binary search on 10,000 items? 100,000 items? Can BASIC be used to find the logarithm of a number to the base 2? [*Hint:* Review Section 5.4.]

LAB EXERCISE 8.3   File Name: BINSRCH2

Enter BINSRCH into your computer, extending the data base it can search by adding new DATA statements. Then test your program with various runs to see if there are any cases in which it fails. (This is step 5 of the structured program design.)

8.5   Sorting Records; Pointers and Indirect Addressing

Consider the following problem. You have accumulated data about the books in your library, and have put together a list of your holdings, as follows.

Author	Title	Cost
1. ZILCH	THE LAST WORD ON COMPUTING	19.95
2. BAKER	COOKING FOR EVERYONE	14.95
3. MELMAN	ENCYCLOPEDIA OF ANTIQUE CARS	45.00
4. DELPHI	PREDICTING THE FUTURE	4.95

Each line in this list is called a data *record*. Each item in a record is called a *field* of the record. Thus our example has four records, with three fields per record.

(The numbers 1, 2, 3, and 4 on the left are not considered part of the record. However, they serve as convenient *pointers* to the records.)

Now suppose you'd like to sort these records. Before you can do this, you must first decide which field should be used to determine the ordering in the sort. Suppose, for example, you decide to sort the records by AUTHOR. This makes AUTHOR the sorting key. You can then apply one of our previous programs—say STSHELL—to the AUTHOR field. However, the *swap* part of the program will have to be extended to swap *all three fields* for pairs of records that are out of order.

The easiest way to make this idea work is to store the data in a two-dimensional array. The rows of the array will correspond to records, while the columns will correspond to the fields of each record. Thus, for 100 records with three fields each, our data structure would be declared as

```
110 DIM A$(100,3)
```

With this definition, the STSHELL swapping routine between rows J and J + GAP is the following.

```
FOR COL=1 TO 3
   TEMP$=A$(J, COL)
   A$(J,COL)=A$(J+GAP, COL)
   A$(J+GAP, COL)=TEMP$
NEXT COL
```

Similar modifications will have to be made in the INPUT and OUTPUT routines. Here's a listing and run to show how the pieces all go together in a program called RCDSHELL (Shell Sort of records).

```
4   REM-------------------------------------------------------------
6   REM        RCDSHELL (SHELL SORT OF STRING RECORDS BY KEY FIELD)
8   REM-------------------------------------------------------------
100 PRINT "PROGRAM TO SORT A 2-D ARRAY OF STRING RECORDS.":PRINT
130 INPUT "HOW MANY RECORDS DO YOU HAVE";N
140 PRINT "EACH RECORD NEEDS AN AUTHORS NAME, BOOK TITLE, AND COST"
150 DIM A$(N,3)
160 PRINT: PRINT
170 B$="                        "
180 FOR I=0 TO N-1
190    PRINT"RECORD #";I+1;": ENTER NAME, TITLE, COST SEPARATED BY COMMAS"
200    INPUT A$(I,1),A$(I,2),A$(I,3)
210    A$(I,1)=LEFT$(A$(I,1)+B$,10)        'THESE LINES SHOW HOW TO
220    A$(I,2)=LEFT$(A$(I,2)+B$,20)        'CONTROL THE SIZE OF STRINGS
230    A$(I,3)=RIGHT$("000"+A$(I,3),5)     'IF YOU DON'T HAVE PRINT USING
240 NEXT I
250 PRINT: PRINT
260 PRINT "WHICH ELEMENT SHOULD BE USED AS THE KEY FOR SORTING?"
270 PRINT "TYPE 1 FOR AUTHOR, TYPE 2 FOR TITLE, TYPE 3 FOR COST"
280 INPUT K
290 PRINT: PRINT
300 PRINT "THE UNSORTED RECORDS ARE:"
310 GOSUB 1000
320 PRINT: PRINT
400 REM========================================================
410 REM         ROUTINE TO USE SHELL SORT ON ARRAY A$(N,E)
420 GAP=INT(N/2)
```

(continued)

```
430  IF GAP<=0 THEN 570
440    I=GAP
450    IF I>=N THEN 560
460      J=I-GAP
470      IF J<0 THEN 550
480        IF A$(J,K)<=A$(J+GAP,K) THEN 550
490          FOR L=1 TO 3
500            TEMP$=A$(J,L)
510            A$(J,L)=A$(J+GAP,L)
520            A$(J+GAP,L)=TEMP$
530          NEXT L
540          J=J-GAP: GOTO 470
550      I=I+1: GOTO 450
560    GAP=INT(GAP/2): GOTO 430
570  REM                 END OF SORTING ROUTINE
600  REM=======================================================
610  PRINT "THE SORTED RECORDS ARE:"
620  GOSUB 1000
630  END
1000 REM-------------------------------------------------------
1010 REM               ROUTINE TO PRINT THE ARRAY
1020 FOR I=0 TO N-1
1030   FOR J=1 TO 3
1040     PRINT A$(I,J);"   ";
1050   NEXT J
1060   PRINT
1070 NEXT I
1080 RETURN
RUN
PROGRAM TO SORT A 2-D ARRAY OF STRING RECORDS.

HOW MANY RECORDS DO YOU HAVE? 4
EACH RECORD NEEDS AN AUTHORS NAME, BOOK TITLE, AND COST


RECORD # 1 : ENTER NAME, TITLE, COST SEPARATED BY COMMAS
? ZILCH,THE LAST WORD ON COMPUTING,19.95
RECORD # 2 : ENTER NAME, TITLE, COST SEPARATED BY COMMAS
? BAKER,COOKING FOR EVERYONE,14.95
RECORD # 3 : ENTER NAME, TITLE, COST SEPARATED BY COMMAS
? MELMAN,ENCYCLOPEDIA OF OLD CARS,45.00
RECORD # 4 : ENTER NAME, TITLE, COST SEPARATED BY COMMAS
? DELPHI,PREDICTING THE FUTURE,4.95


WHICH ELEMENT SHOULD BE USED AS THE KEY FOR SORTING?
TYPE 1 FOR AUTHOR, TYPE 2 FOR TITLE, TYPE 3 FOR COST
? 2


THE UNSORTED RECORDS ARE:
ZILCH       THE LAST WORD ON COM   19.95
BAKER       COOKING FOR EVERYONE   14.95
MELMAN      ENCYCLOPEDIA OF OLD    45.00
DELPHI      PREDICTING THE FUTUR   04.95


THE SORTED RECORDS ARE:
BAKER       COOKING FOR EVERYONE   14.95
MELMAN      ENCYCLOPEDIA OF OLD    45.00
DELPHI      PREDICTING THE FUTUR   04.95
ZILCH       THE LAST WORD ON COM   19.95
Ok
```

EXERCISE

8.5 If your BASIC has PRINT USING, modify RCDSHELL to use this feature in the output subroutine.

LAB EXERCISE 8.4 **File Name: RCDBUB** _____

Design, write, and test a program called RCDBUB. It should be similar to RCDSHELL, except that the bubble-sorting algorithm should be used. Compare the sorting times of RCDBUB and RCDSHELL for 5 records, then for 50 records. What can you conclude?

Index Arrays

The program RCDSHELL suffers from the need to do multiple swapping in order to keep the fields of each record together. An alternative approach is to use a separate *index* array INX(), which holds only the record numbers.

INX() is initialized to hold the numbers 1, 2, 3,..., N. To sort the records, you still do the comparisons using the key field of each record. However, you actually swap the elements of INX(). Then, when it comes time to print the sorted list, you use subscripted subscripts, as follows.

```
FOR ROW=1 TO N
  FOR COL=1 TO 3
     PRINT A$(INX(ROW), COL),
  NEXT COL
  PRINT
NEXT ROW
```

We'll leave the task of finishing this program to you (see Project 7 in Section 8.6). It's suggested that you combine the idea of indexed sorting with the Shell Sort algorithm. An appropriate name for your program might be INXSHELL.

8.6 Summary of Chapter 8

■ Two categories of algorithms frequently used in professional programming are (1) algorithms to sort data and (2) algorithms to search through data for specified items.

■ You can compare searching algorithms by timing them or by calculating the maximum number of comparisons required to find an item.

■ For large quantities of data, the Shell Sort algorithm is faster than Bubble Sort, but it is more complex to program. The items to be compared (and perhaps swapped) are a specified distance apart. This distance, called the gap, is gradually reduced as successive passes through the data are made.

■ Some versions of BASIC have a function that returns the current system time. This can be used to provide timing data when comparing algorithms.

■ In BASIC, sorting and searching string data is no more difficult than sorting and searching numeric data. String arrays are used, and the relations $>$, $<$, and $=$ are used to find the alphanumeric relation between the strings in the array.

■ In business applications, data is usually organized in terms of records. Each record consists of a set of related parts called fields. For example, one business record might contain the fields name, sex, age, address, zip code, and amount paid. To sort records, one makes comparisons on a specified key field.

■ An index array has as its contents pointers (numbers) that reference the records of a file. Since records can be stored as rows of a two-dimensional array, with each field stored in a different column, the following technique could be used to print out a set of records in the order given by an index array, NDX().

```
100 FOR COL=1 TO N
110   FOR ROW=1 TO M
120     PRINT RECORD$(NDX(ROW),COL)
130   NEXT ROW
140 NEXT COL
```

■ A sequential search looks for a given search argument (key item) by using the algorithm "start at the beginning of the list, compare each item in turn with the search argument, continue until you find a match or reach the end of the data." Sequential search does not require that the data be in order, but it can take a long time.

■ Binary search is faster than sequential search, but requires that the data be sorted first. The maximum number of comparisons for a sequential search of 1000 items is 1000. The maximum for a binary search of 1000 (sorted) items is 10.

8.7   Problems and Programming Projects

1. Write a modified version of SHELL2 called SHELL3, in which the original data items are in an order that is the reverse of what you want the final output to be. This can be thought of as worst-case data, since it will make the program do a maximum number of swaps. *Hint:* What does the following loop do?

```
FOR K=1 TO N : A(K)=N-K : NEXT K
```

2. Use SHELL2 and SHELL3 to compare the time for sorting 800 items of random data with the time for sorting 800 items of data in reverse order.

3. Write a modified version of SHELL3 called SHELL4, in which the data items are already in order. Now compare the time for sorting 800 items that are already ordered with the times for sorting random data and reverse-order data.

4. Repeat all the previous experiments for a sorting algorithm (called SORTX) different from Bubble Sort or Shell Sort. This can be your own sort, or one found in another book.

5. Summarize the results of all these experiments, along with the similar experiments in Section 7.7. Summarize the times for the various sorts in a table, as follows.

	Ordered data	Random data	Reverse-order data
Bubble Sort			
Shell Sort			
SORTX			

6. Rewrite SHELL so that the array elements start at A(1) instead of A(0). Then rewrite BUBBLE so that the array elements start at A(0) instead of A(1). *Note:* In most versions of BASIC, the statement

```
DIM A(800)
```

sets aside 801 locations called A(0), A(1), A(2), and so forth, up to A(800). Thus, if you start at A(0), and want only 800 locations, DIM A(799) works just fine. On the other hand, if you insist that there be no element A(0), you can use the statement OPTION BASE 1 in Microsoft BASIC to mean "start at A(1)." In this case, the number of elements available is the same as the number dimensioned.

7. Design, write, and test the program INXSHELL, using the ideas given in Section 8.5. [If you need some help, see the program INSERT2 in *A Bit of Basic* (Dwyer and Critchfield, Addison-Wesley, 1980).]

## CHAPTER NINE

BASIC Simulations, Games, and Graphics

NEW TOPICS INTRODUCED IN CHAPTER 9

- Games
- Electronic spreadsheets
- Graphics in business computing
- Screen coordinates
- Graphics in color
- Transformations: scaling, translation, reflection

- Pixel graphics
- Simulations
- Computer graphics
- World coordinates
- Plotting mathematical curves
- Character graphics

9.1 Simulations versus Games; Electronic Spreadsheets

Simulations, games, and graphics make a natural trio in the study of computer programming. Some of the most interesting and widespread graphics features of computers have been inspired by the needs of simulations and games, while the existence of graphical output has, in turn, inspired new uses for computers.

The main problem programmers face is that the graphics capabilities of computer hardware vary greatly. Interestingly, some of the best graphics features are found on low-cost personal computers, while terminals connected to larger time-sharing systems usually have limited graphics capabilities.

You can, it is true, do some graphing on the screen or paper of terminals using symbols like "*" (asterisk), or even by using whole words to make patterns. However, you are usually limited to 80 or 40 columns and 24 or fewer lines. Real graphics begins when the computer system provides you with a grid of much smaller programmable points (called pixels for "picture elements"). For example, on the IBM Personal Computer, there are 200 rows down the screen, with 320 pixels across each row, while the Tandy 2000 has 400 rows of 640 pixels each. The more pixels there are, the better the resolution (detail) of the graphics. Also, on many machines, color can be specified for each pixel.

IBM

TANDY

Another difficulty programmers face is that the graphics statements available in computer languages are not very powerful. Fortunately, there are extended versions of BASIC that include good graphics features. However, the graphics statements of BASIC are not standardized. For example, to plot a point on a computer's screen, the key words for Radio Shack, Apple, and IBM machines are SET, PLOT, and PSET, respectively. Further, the parameters (coordinates) used with these key words are all expressed differently.

Radio Shack

APPLE

IBM

To illustrate the differences, we will later show comparative examples of graphics on these three microcomputers (the TRS-80, Apple, and IBM). However, we'll also demonstrate a variety of games, simulations, and graphics programs that work on just about any system, since they use the key word PRINT to produce the standard alphanumeric symbols available on all computer output devices.

Games and Simulations

Let's start by clarifying the meanings of "game" and "simulation." The burgeoning computer-game industry has made everyone aware of some of the possibilities in designing computer games. The programs known as simulations are less familiar, although they have been used by professionals for a long time. A computer simulation is a program that *imitates* some process. Usually this is a process that is too complex, expensive, or dangerous to try in its real-world form.

How do games and simulations differ? A game is a process that may or may not relate to real life, but that culminates with a player's winning or losing (and perhaps an opponent's losing or winning correspondingly). There is a goal in the form of points, money, position, and so forth, and there may be a time limit. The scoring system can be based on skill or luck, or on some combination of these factors.

By contrast, a simulation need not have any such goal. It simply imitates some other process, usually by selecting important features of it, and then expressing these in terms of a mathematical model. This model is, in turn, expressed as a computer program. If the original process had a gamelike quality, fine; then the simulation can also be thought of as a game. For example, a simulation program that imitates the behavior of a space vehicle may include landing back on Earth. This can be used to give the simulation a gamelike quality, by assigning various numbers of points for smooth, rough, or disastrous landings.

Electronic Spreadsheets

A common form of simulation used today is a cost projection based on something called the electronic spreadsheet. This is a program that displays a large table of numbers and formulas that depend on each other. By changing one value, and immediately seeing the changes produced in all the others, a user can experiment with different possibilities, asking the question, "What if . . . ?" For instance, the economics of financing a college education on the basis of various assumptions about inflation could be simulated in this way. Questions could be asked about "What if tuition and living expenses increase?" "What if I have to travel greater distances?" And so on. Other factors that could be examined are the cost of loans, the possibility of scholarships, and the possibility of part-time work. The model could be further refined by adding formulas that reflect that as the student grows older, part-time work may be better paid, but, as class work becomes more demanding, the hours of part-time work will have to be cut back. All this can be tried out in many combinations, experimenting with various starting values, rates of change, and other assumptions.

Another example of use of a spreadsheet model would be the simulation of the running of a microcomputer center in a school. Figure 9.1 shows such a simulation expressed in the form of a spreadsheet.

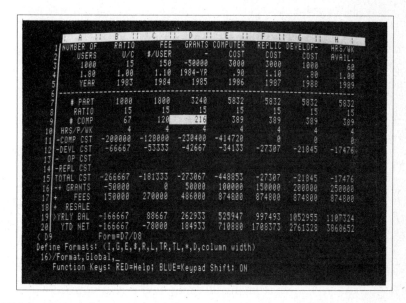

FIGURE 9.1   Output from a spreadsheet program used to model the economics of a microcomputer center. The output is shown as a grid of numbers, but there are also formulas behind most of these numbers. For example, each "cell" in the row showing the cost of computers is backed up by a formula that multiplies the cost per computer by the increment in users per year, and by the computer/user ratio assumed for that year. Changing any one of these quantities causes an immediate change in the entire row. This in turn causes an immediate change in all the bottom-line calculations based on that row.

9.2   A Slot-Machine Simulation

Step 1

The next program emphasizes a feature common to many simulations and games: the use of the random-number generator to simulate probabilistic events. The "step 1" idea behind the program is to simulate (act like) a slot machine with three windows.

A picture of an orange, a lemon, or a cherry appears in each window each time you put in 50 cents and pull the imaginary handle. If all three pictures are the same, you win $3.00. If not, you lose your 50 cents.

One way of figuring your odds for winning is to draw a diagram like that shown in Figure 9.2. The winning combinations are marked with the symbol *. You can see that although there are 27 possible combinations, only three of these are winners.

Here are all the 27 possible paths; the winning combinations are ringed.

(CCC)	CCL	CCO
CLC	CLL	CLO
COC	COL	COO
LCC	LCL	LCO
LLC	(LLL)	LLO
LOC	LOL	LOO
OCC	OCL	OCO
OLC	OLL	OLO
OOC	OOL	(OOO)

A mathematician would say that your probability of winning on this machine is:

$$P = \frac{\text{No. of winning combinations}}{\text{No. of possible combinations}} = \frac{3}{27} = \frac{1}{9}$$

In other words, if you played 90 times, you would win about one-ninth of the time, or 10 times.

Playing 90 times would cost you $45.

Winning 10 times would give you $30.

So you can see that on the average the owner of the machine would make $15 on every 90 plays. In other words, in the long run, on this machine you lose, the owner wins.

Step 2

A good way to plan a simulation program is to write a short scenario, showing what the computer will print as output, and what the user will type as input. Here's an example of such a scenario. (You'll notice that it corresponds to step 2 of the structured program design process explained in Section 7.2.)

1. Announce the purpose and rules of the program.
2. Let the user input how much money he or she will play with.
3. Tell the user *exactly* what keys to press to play the slot machine; or tell the user how to quit, and then wait for a key press.
4. Show the result of the key press, using "pictures" made up of strings of symbols, letters, and spaces. Add sound effects if possible [on most terminals you can use PRINT CHR$(7) to produce a "beep"].
5. Tell the user how much money is left, and allow another play if there's enough money.
6. Display messages for winning, losing, and quitting, as appropriate.

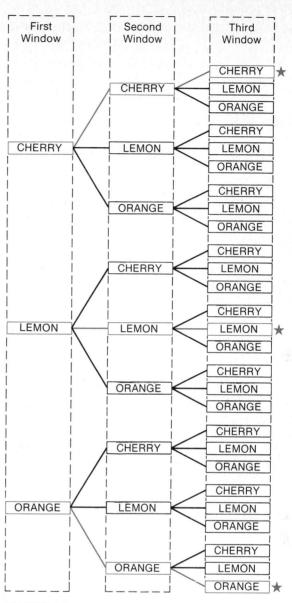

FIGURE 9.2

Step
3

Based on this desired input/output scheme, here's a step 3 high-level design expressed in pseudocode.

A1. Initialize variables: three "picture" strings, an amount of money, a counter for each picture.

A2. Give the user some instructions.

A3. Create a WHILE loop that does A4 as long as:

    a. the user doesn't type ⟨Q⟩ ⟨enter⟩ for quit,

    b. the user has at least .50 left.

A4. For each play:

    a. Subtract .50 from the user's money.

    b. Reset the counters to 0.

c. For I = 1 to 3, do the following: Generate a random integer = 1, 2, or 3. Print a "picture" and produce some sound effects based on that number. Add 1 to a counter for whichever picture string is chosen. Check to see whether the user won (got three of the same) or lost; if the user won, set a flag WF = 1.

d. Tell the user whether he or she won or lost, and produce appropriate sounds.

e. If the user won, add 3 to the money available.

f. In any case, tell the user how much money is left.

A5. After the user quits or runs out of money, display one message for a winner, another for a partial loser, and another for someone who has lost everything.

Step 4

The step 4 BASIC code corresponding to this pseudocode is shown in the next listing, followed by some comments on the code.

```
100 '*******************************************************
110 '            SLOT   (SLOT MACHINE SIMULATION)
120 '*******************************************************
130 RANDOMIZE
140 A$(1)="%% CHERRY %%   "
150 A$(2)="oo LEMON oo   "
160 A$(3)="** ORANGE **   "
170 PRINT "THIS IS A $0.50 SLOT MACHINE."
190 PRINT "PAYOFF IS $3 FOR 3 CHERRIES, 3 LEMONS, 3 ORANGES."
200 PRINT "ALL OTHER COMBINATIONS LOSE."
210 PRINT
220 '------------ ESTABLISH LINE OF CREDIT ----------------
230 INPUT "HOW MANY 50-CENT PIECES DO YOU WANT"; M1: M=M1*.5
240 IF M1<1 THEN PRINT"YOU NEED AT LEAST $0.50 TO PLAY":GOTO 230
260 PRINT "O.K. YOU START WITH ";USING "$$##.##";M
270 PRINT
280 '============ START MAIN LOOP =========================
290 INPUT "TO PLAY PRESS <ENTER>, <Q><ENTER> TO QUIT --";P$
300    IF LEFT$(P$,1)="Q" THEN 540
310    M=M-.5: PRINT                          'SUBTRACT .50
320    FOR I=1 TO 3: C(I)=0: NEXT I           'RESET COUNTERS
330 '------------ GENERATE AND PRINT STRINGS --------------
335    WF=0
340    FOR I=1 TO 3
350       D1=100: L=4: GOSUB 700        'SOUND EFFECTS
360       N=INT(3*RND)+1                'CHOOSE WHICH STRING
370       PRINT A$(N);
380       C(N)=C(N)+1                   'COUNT EACH STRING
385       IF C(N)=3 THEN WF=1           '3 OF SAME WINS
390    NEXT I
400    PRINT: PRINT
450    IF WF=0 THEN PRINT "TOO BAD -- YOU LOST.": GOTO 490
460    D1=0: L=10: GOSUB 700           'SOUND EFFECTS
470    PRINT "GREAT -- YOU WON.": M=M+3
480 '------------ PRINT CURRENT BALANCE -------------------
490    IF M<.5 THEN 640
500       PRINT "YOU NOW HAVE ";USING "$$#.##";M;
510    PRINT
520    GOTO 290
530 '=========== END MAIN LOOP ========================
540 IF M<M1/2 THEN 600
550 '------------ COMMENT FOR WINNER ----------------------
560 PRINT "WELL I GUESS IT IS A GOOD IDEA TO QUIT"
570 PRINT "WHILE YOU ARE AHEAD."
```

```
580 GOTO 660
590 '----------- COMMENT FOR PARTIAL LOSER ---------------
600 PRINT "BEST TO LEAVE BEFORE YOU HAVE LOST EVERYTHING"
610 PRINT "THESE MACHINES JUST KEEP TAKING."
620 GOTO 660
630 '----------- COMMENT FOR THOSE LOSING ALL ------------
640 PRINT "YOU NOW HAVE LESS THAN $0.50 SO YOU HAVE TO QUIT"
650 PRINT "SORRY ABOUT THAT. BETTER LUCK NEXT TIME."
660 PRINT "BYE FOR NOW."
670 END
680 '----------- SOUND EFFECTS SUBROUTINE ---------------
690 'D1 VARIES THE TIMING OF DINGS, L CONTROLS HOW MANY
700 FOR J=1 TO L
710    FOR K=1 TO 170+D1*RND:NEXT K
720    PRINT CHR$(7);
730 NEXT J
740 RETURN
```

Comments on SLOT

The array A$() holds the three picture strings, and N is a random integer from 1 to 3, so A$(N) is a randomly chosen string, and C(N) is a corresponding counter, where C(N) holds the count for appearances of A$(N). When any one of these counters reaches 3, a "winning flag" WF is set to 1. Lines 260 and 500 use PRINT USING with a regular string as well as a print-image string to show the current balance, with a dollar sign next to the amount.

Lines 350 and 460 both call the sound-effects subroutine. In each case, values are put in D1 and L, variables that will be used by the subroutine. This is the usual method of "passing parameters"—that is, setting up values—for a subroutine in BASIC. Remember, the variables used within subroutines in BASIC are not treated separately (technically speaking, they are "global," not "local," variables). So it's up to the programmer to choose names that do not conflict with those in the calling program.

This particular subroutine rings the bell or beeper using the standard ASCII code 7 (⟨ctrl⟩⟨G⟩), printing it (sending it to the terminal) with the CHR$ function. The loop within the loop is a time filler. It executes 170 times, plus a random amount times D1. 170 was the approximate minimum time needed between beeps on our machine before they blended into one long bee-eep! This number should be determined by experiment on your machine.

Notice that this program does not tolerate inputting a lower-case "q" instead of "Q" for "quit," nor does it check for noninteger requests for credit (say 20.5 half dollars, or $10.25, as a starting amount). However, it does "kick the user out" when the money variable goes below .5 in value. Some suggestions on adding better input checking are given later.

The slot-machine program uses no special graphics and will work on either a video display or a hard-copy terminal (although you might use up a lot of paper trying to beat the odds). A suggested area of improvement is to adapt SLOT to a video-graphics screen display, using some of the ideas from the next section. Here's a run of the above hard-copy version.

```
RUN
Random number seed (-32768 to 32767)? 234
THIS IS A $0.50 SLOT MACHINE.
PAYOFF IS $3 FOR 3 CHERRIES, 3 LEMONS, 3 ORANGES.
ALL OTHER COMBINATIONS LOSE.

HOW MANY 50-CENT PIECES DO YOU WANT? 5
O.K. YOU START WITH   $2.50
```

(continued)

```
                    TO PLAY PRESS <ENTER>, <Q><ENTER> TO QUIT --?

                    ** ORANGE **   oo LEMON oo   ** ORANGE **

                    TOO BAD -- YOU LOST.
                    YOU NOW HAVE  $2.00
                    TO PLAY PRESS <ENTER>, <Q><ENTER> TO QUIT --?

                    oo LEMON oo   oo LEMON oo   oo LEMON oo

                    GREAT -- YOU WON.
                    YOU NOW HAVE  $4.50
                    TO PLAY PRESS <ENTER>, <Q><ENTER> TO QUIT --? Q
                    WELL I GUESS IT IS A GOOD IDEA TO QUIT
                    WHILE YOU ARE AHEAD.
                    BYE FOR NOW.
                    Ok
                    RUN
                    Random number seed (-32768 to 32767)? 345
                    THIS IS A $0.50 SLOT MACHINE.
                    PAYOFF IS $3 FOR 3 CHERRIES, 3 LEMONS, 3 ORANGES.
                    ALL OTHER COMBINATIONS LOSE.

                    HOW MANY 50-CENT PIECES DO YOU WANT? 1
                    O.K. YOU START WITH   $0.50

                    TO PLAY PRESS <ENTER>, <Q><ENTER> TO QUIT --?

                    %% CHERRY %%   %% CHERRY %%   ** ORANGE **

                    TOO BAD -- YOU LOST.
                    YOU NOW HAVE LESS THAN $0.50 SO YOU HAVE TO QUIT
                    SORRY ABOUT THAT. BETTER LUCK NEXT TIME.
                    BYE FOR NOW.
                    Ok
                    RUN
                    Random number seed (-32768 to 32767)? 345
                    THIS IS A $0.50 SLOT MACHINE.
                    PAYOFF IS $3 FOR 3 CHERRIES, 3 LEMONS, 3 ORANGES.
                    ALL OTHER COMBINATIONS LOSE.

                    HOW MANY 50-CENT PIECES DO YOU WANT? 5
                    O.K. YOU START WITH   $2.50

                    TO PLAY PRESS <ENTER>, <Q><ENTER> TO QUIT --?

                    %% CHERRY %%   %% CHERRY %%   ** ORANGE **

                    TOO BAD -- YOU LOST.
                    YOU NOW HAVE  $2.00
                    TO PLAY PRESS <ENTER>, <Q><ENTER> TO QUIT --? Q
                    BEST TO LEAVE BEFORE YOU HAVE LOST EVERYTHING
                    THESE MACHINES JUST KEEP TAKING.
                    BYE FOR NOW.
```

LAB EXERCISE 9.1   **File Name: SLOT2**

Enter and run SLOT enough times to enable you to see how much you lose or win over a long period. Then modify the program so that both the player and the house can use other rules. For example, try a version in which both the payoff and the amount lost are multiples of the original amount bet.

9.3 Three Treasure-Hunt Games

It's a natural part of programming to want to create new versions of an already viable program—to keep on adding one more feature. Computer hobbyists have been known to spend years refining one program. Professional programmers don't have the luxury of unlimited time, but they too generally go through many versions of a program before releasing it to the public. This process is greatly aided if the original version of the program was well planned and coded in a clean and tidy manner—another argument for structured program design.

This section presents three versions of essentially the same program. Each version adds new features, but this is easy to do, since the original structure stays constant. The three versions are all based on the idea of finding a hidden "treasure," four squares long and one square wide, on a 10-by-10-square grid, with a limited number of "test holes" allowed. (It's not as easy as you may think. Before tackling the program, see if you can figure out what pattern of test holes will ensure that the area covered contains no buried treasure.)

Treasure Hunt, Version 1

Let's start out with a run of the first program (called TREAS1). It will give you a good idea of the decisions that were made about the interaction of the player with this game.

```
RUN
Random number seed (-32768 to 32767)? 24
THE COMPUTER HAS BURIED A ´TREASURE´ SOMEWHERE
IN A 10 BY 10 GRID.  IT FILLS 4 CONNECTED
SQUARES ACROSS OR DOWN WITHIN THE GRID.
YOU CAN DIG 20 TEST HOLES.  TYPE THE LOCATION OF
THE HOLE AS AN X COORDINATE, A COMMA, AND A Y COORD.
DO YOU WISH TO SEE THE GRID (Y/N)? Y
      Y
      ^
      9  |—— —— —— —— —— —— —— —— —— ——|
      8  |—— —— —— —— —— —— —— —— —— ——|
      7  |—— —— —— —— —— —— —— —— —— ——|
      6  |—— —— —— —— —— —— —— —— —— ——|
      5  |—— —— —— —— —— —— —— —— —— ——|
      4  |—— —— —— —— —— —— —— —— —— ——|
      3  |—— —— —— —— —— —— —— —— —— ——|
      2  |—— —— —— —— —— —— —— —— —— ——|
      1  |—— —— —— —— —— —— —— —— —— ——|
      0   —— —— —— —— —— —— —— —— —— ——
   >X     0  1  2  3  4  5  6  7  8  9

WHERE DO YOU WANT THE FIRST HOLE? 0,0
NOTHING THERE --
NUMBER OF TRIES LEFT: 19
NEXT HOLE? 0,4
NOTHING THERE --
NUMBER OF TRIES LEFT: 18
NEXT HOLE? 4,0
NOTHING THERE --
NUMBER OF TRIES LEFT: 17
NEXT HOLE? 1,3
YOU FOUND IT!
THE TREASURE WAS LOCATED AT ( 1 , 0), ( 1 , 1), ( 1 , 2), ( 1 , 3).
Ok
```

Step 3

You'll notice that to win this first version, all you need is one hit. Here's a design outline for this version.

1. Get a random number seed. Initialize the variable for the number of test holes allowed. Define all variables except strings as integers.

2. Present instructions. Tell the player how to type the input.

3. (Optional) Show the 10-by-10 grid. Number the squares as in algebra: 0 to 9, with 0,0 at the lower left.

4. "Bury the treasure" randomly in four squares across or down.

5. Create a loop that continues as long as (WHILE):
   a. The player has not found the treasure.
   b. The player has test holes left up to the limit set previously.

6. Within the loop:
   a. Ask for player's input.
   b. Check to see whether it matches one of the treasure squares. If it does, end the game. Tell where the rest of the treasure was buried.

Step 4

   c. If it does not, tell the player it doesn't. Also tell the player how many test holes are left.

Here's a BASIC program that follows this outline.

```
100 '------------------------------------------------------------
110 '  TREAS1  (1 HIT WINS)
120 '------------------------------------------------------------
130 DEFINT A-Z: RANDOMIZE: TRY=20
140 PRINT "THE COMPUTER HAS BURIED A 'TREASURE' SOMEWHERE"
150 PRINT "IN A 10 BY 10 GRID.  IT FILLS 4 CONNECTED"
160 PRINT "SQUARES ACROSS OR DOWN WITHIN THE GRID."
170 PRINT "YOU CAN DIG"TRY"TEST HOLES.  TYPE THE LOCATION OF"
180 PRINT "THE HOLE AS AN X COORDINATE, A COMMA, AND A Y COORD."
190 '----------- DISPLAY THE GRID --------------------------
195 INPUT "DO YOU WISH TO SEE THE GRID (Y/N)";A$
196 IF LEFT$(A$,1)="N" THEN 270
200 G1$="|___|___|___|___|___|___|___|___|___|___|"
210 PRINT "      Y"
220 PRINT "      ^         _____"
230 FOR I=9 TO 0 STEP -1: PRINT " "I" "G1$: NEXT I
240 PRINT ">X        0   1   2   3   4   5   6   7   8   9"
250 PRINT
260 '----------- BURY THE TREASURE --------------------------
270 AC=INT(2*RND)                       'DECIDE ACROSS OR UPWARD
280 IF AC=1 THEN UP=0 ELSE UP=1
290 X(1)=INT((7+3*UP)*RND)              'X(1)=0...6 OR  =0...9
300 Y(1)=INT((7+3*AC)*RND)              'Y(1)=0...6 OR  =0...9
310 FOR I=2 TO 4
320    X(I)=X(I-1)+AC                   'INCREASE X VAL. IF AC=1
330    Y(I)=Y(I-1)+UP                   'INCREASE Y VAL. IF UP=1
340 NEXT I
360 PRINT "WHERE DO YOU WANT THE FIRST HOLE";
370 '=========== START DIGGING LOOP ===========================
380 INPUT XDIG,YDIG
390    IF XDIG<0 OR XDIG>9 OR YDIG<0 OR YDIG>9 THEN PRINT"???": GOTO 380
430    GOSUB 650                        'CHECK FOR HIT
440    IF HFLAG=1 THEN PRINT"YOU FOUND IT!":PRINT CHR$(7);:GOTO 580
490    PRINT "NOTHING THERE -- "
```

```
510    TRY=TRY-1: IF TRY=0 THEN 580
520    PRINT "NUMBER OF TRIES LEFT:";TRY
530    PRINT "NEXT HOLE";
540    GOTO 380
550  '============ END DIGGING LOOP ==============================
580  Z$(1)=",": Z$(2)=",": Z$(3)=",": Z$(4)="."
590  PRINT "THE TREASURE WAS LOCATED AT ";
600  FOR I=1 TO 4
610    PRINT USING "(## , ##)\\";X(I);Y(I);Z$(I);
620  NEXT I
630  END
640  '------------ SUBROUTINE TO FIND A HIT ----------------------
650  HFLAG=0
660  FOR I=1 TO 4
670    IF XDIG=X(I) AND YDIG=Y(I) THEN HFLAG=1
680  NEXT I
690  RETURN
```

Some Notes on the Coding of TREAS1

It turns out that "burying" the treasure—that is, selecting four sets of X and Y coordinates within the grid—is an interesting programming problem in itself. To see why, look at the grid.

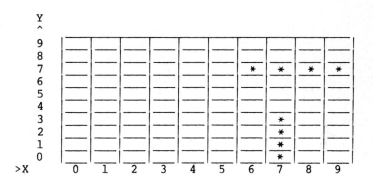

Two examples of possible treasures are shown, one arranged horizontally, the other vertically.

Example 1 (across)   (6,7), (7,7); (8,7), and (9,7)

Example 2 (upward) (7,0), (7,1), (7,2), and (7,3)

Let's assume that the bottom-most, or leftmost, set of coordinates is chosen first, and the rest are added in sequence. In the case of orienting the treasure across, the X values increase by 1, while the Y values stay the same. In the case of an upward orientation, the X values stay the same and the Y values increase. The only hazard is that an X value greater than 6 to start with will put part of an "across" (horizontal) treasure off the grid (starting at 7,7 and ending at 7,10, for instance). The same is true for the Y value of an upward treasure: Starting with Y = 7, 8, or 9 will spill the treasure off the top of the grid.

One solution is to have two separate sections of code for setting "across" (horizontal) and upward (vertical) treasures.

```
270 AC=INT(2*RND)
271 ON AC+1 GOTO 272, 279          'CHOOSE HORIZONTAL OR VERTICAL
272   X(1)=INT(7*RND)              'HORIZONTAL TREASURE
273   Y(1)=INT(10*RND)
274   FOR I=2 TO 4
275       X(I)=X(I-1)+1
276       Y(I)=Y(1)
277   NEXT I
278   GOTO 360
279 X(1)=INT(10*RND)               'VERTICAL TREASURE
280 Y(1)=INT(7*RND)
281 FOR I=2 TO 4
282   X(I)=X(1)
283   Y(I)=Y(I-1)+1
284 NEXT I
360 HIT=0 : PRINT "WHERE DO YOU WANT THE FIRST HOLE";
```

The preceding program will work well, but it contains some inefficiencies. However, it does serve as a good starting point. We notice, for example, that AC is either 0 or 1. If AC = 0,

```
ON AC+1 GOTO 272, 279
```

sends control to a section of code at 272 which buries the treasure *across* the grid. If AC = 1, control is sent to the section at 279, which buries the treasure *upward* on the grid. The actual program listing shown earlier condenses these two sections into one by making use of the special properties of 0 and 1. (Recall that $1*N = N$, $1 + N = N + 1$, $0*N = 0$, $0 + N = N$.) Instead of just using AC to send control to one or the other section of the program, the program uses AC and UP in the calculations for X(1) and Y(1) to make the range 0–6 or 0–9 (depending on whether a horizontal or vertical treasure is planned). In the loop that chooses X(2), X(3), X(4), and Y(2), Y(3), Y(4), AC and UP are used again to automatically determine whether X(I) or Y(I) is incremented.

The subroutine at line 650 checks to see whether the player's input coordinates match one of the treasure coordinates. It is called only once each turn, but this makes the main "digging" loop much more readable. The subroutine sets the value of a "hit flag," HFLAG, to 1 if it finds a match, using the statement

```
IF XDIG=X(I) AND YDIG=Y(I) THEN HFLAG=1
```

EXERCISE

9.1   Can the statement

```
IF XDIG=X(I) THEN IF YDIG=Y(I) THEN HFLAG=1
```

be used to make exactly the same test? Do you prefer one statement to the other? Why?

Treasure Hunt, Version 2

This program (TREAS2) is similar to version 1, except that to win you must now find all four positions of buried treasure. Success is measured by the variable HIT, which must reach 4. The logic of the test for finding a hit is reversed (line 440). This is done simply to make it more convenient to add the new feature: When you hit one square with a treasure buried in it, you do *not* immediately win the game, but continue until you dig up the other three squares. Until you have dug up all four, the program goes on counting hits when you get them, and decrementing the number of tries left.

```
100 '--------------------------------------------------------------
110 '   TREAS2  (4 HITS WIN)
120 '--------------------------------------------------------------
130 DEFINT A-Z: RANDOMIZE: TRY=25
140 PRINT "THE COMPUTER HAS BURIED A 'TREASURE' SOMEWHERE"
150 PRINT "IN A 10 BY 10 GRID.  IT FILLS 4 CONNECTED"
160 PRINT "SQUARES ACROSS OR DOWN WITHIN THE GRID."
170 PRINT "YOU CAN DIG"TRY"TEST HOLES.  TYPE THE LOCATION OF"
180 PRINT "THE HOLE AS AN X COORDINATE, A COMMA, AND A Y COORD."
190 '------------ DISPLAY THE GRID ----------------------------
195 INPUT "DO YOU WISH TO SEE THE GRID (Y/N)";A$
196 IF LEFT$(A$,1)="N" THEN 270
200 G1$="|___|___|___|___|___|___|___|___|___|___|"
210 PRINT "      Y"
220 PRINT "      ^     _____         "
230 FOR I=9 TO 0 STEP -1: PRINT "  "I" "G1$: NEXT I
240 PRINT ">X        0   1   2   3   4   5   6   7   8   9"
250 PRINT
260 '------------ BURY THE TREASURE ---------------------------
270 AC=INT(2*RND)                          'DECIDE ACROSS OR UPWARD
280 IF AC=1 THEN UP=0 ELSE UP=1
290 X(1)=INT((7+3*UP)*RND)                 'X(1)=0...6 OR  =0...9
300 Y(1)=INT((7+3*AC)*RND)                 'Y(1)=0...6 OR  =0...9
310 FOR I=2 TO 4
320   X(I)=X(I-1)+AC                       'INCREASE X VAL. IF AC=1
330   Y(I)=Y(I-1)+UP                       'INCREASE Y VAL. IF UP=1
340 NEXT I
360 HIT=0: PRINT "WHERE DO YOU WANT THE FIRST HOLE";
370 '=========== START DIGGING LOOP ===========================
380 INPUT XDIG,YDIG
390   IF XDIG<0 OR XDIG>9 OR YDIG<0 OR YDIG>9 THEN PRINT"???": GOTO 380
430   GOSUB 650                            'CHECK FOR HIT
440   IF HFLAG=0 THEN 490                  'NO HIT
460     PRINT "YOU FOUND IT!": PRINT CHR$(7);
470     HIT=HIT+1
480     IF HIT<4 THEN 510 ELSE 560
490   PRINT "NOTHING THERE -- "
500 '
510   TRY=TRY-1: IF TRY=0 THEN 580
520   PRINT "NUMBER OF TRIES LEFT:";TRY
530   PRINT "NEXT HOLE";
540   GOTO 380
550 '=========== END DIGGING LOOP =============================
560 PRINT "CONGRATULATIONS, YOU DUG IT ALL UP."
570 '
580 Z$(1)=",": Z$(2)=",": Z$(3)=",": Z$(4)="."
590 PRINT "THE TREASURE WAS LOCATED AT ";
600 FOR I=1 TO 4
610   PRINT USING "(## , ##)\\";X(I);Y(I);Z$(I);
620 NEXT I
630 END
640 '------------ SUBROUTINE TO FIND A HIT --------------------
650 HFLAG=0
660 FOR I=1 TO 4
670   IF XDIG=X(I) AND YDIG=Y(I) THEN HFLAG=1
680 NEXT I
690 RETURN
RUN
Random number seed (-32768 to 32767)? 24
THE COMPUTER HAS BURIED A 'TREASURE' SOMEWHERE
IN A 10 BY 10 GRID.  IT FILLS 4 CONNECTED
SQUARES ACROSS OR DOWN WITHIN THE GRID.
YOU CAN DIG 25 TEST HOLES.  TYPE THE LOCATION OF
THE HOLE AS AN X COORDINATE, A COMMA, AND A Y COORD.
DO YOU WISH TO SEE THE GRID (Y/N)? Y
```

(continued)

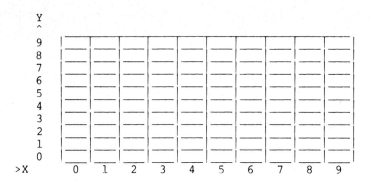

```
WHERE DO YOU WANT THE FIRST HOLE? 0,0
NOTHING THERE --
NUMBER OF TRIES LEFT: 24
NEXT HOLE? 4,0
NOTHING THERE --
NUMBER OF TRIES LEFT: 23
NEXT HOLE? 1,3
YOU FOUND IT!
NUMBER OF TRIES LEFT: 22
NEXT HOLE? 0,3
NOTHING THERE --
NUMBER OF TRIES LEFT: 21
NEXT HOLE? 1,2
YOU FOUND IT!
NUMBER OF TRIES LEFT: 20
NEXT HOLE? 1,1
YOU FOUND IT!
NUMBER OF TRIES LEFT: 19
NEXT HOLE? 1,0
YOU FOUND IT!
CONGRATULATIONS, YOU DUG IT ALL UP.
THE TREASURE WAS LOCATED AT ( 1 ,  0), ( 1 ,  1), ( 1 ,  2), ( 1 ,  3).
Ok
```

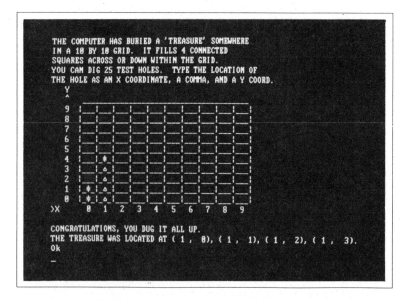

FIGURE 9.3   A run of TREAS3. Finding buried treasure on the 10-by-10 grid is greatly aided if one is able to see the grid. The graphics characters marking the holes and treasure are part of the IBM PC character set.

Treasure Hunt, Version 3

This version (called TREAS3) follows the same game rules as version 2, but it uses the video display (in this case the IBM PC monochrome display) to show the progress of your digging. This makes the game a lot easier to play; see Figure 9.3. Here's a listing of this video-display-adapted version. The techniques shown here can be adapted to other alphanumeric video terminals; see the following pages.

```
100 ´-------------------------------------------------------------
110 ´   TREAS3   (4 HITS WIN, FOR IBM MONOCHROME VIDEO DISPLAY)
120 ´-------------------------------------------------------------
130 DEFINT A-Z: CLS: KEY OFF: RANDOMIZE TIMER: TRY=25
140 PRINT "THE COMPUTER HAS BURIED A ´TREASURE´ SOMEWHERE"
150 PRINT "IN A 10 BY 10 GRID.  IT FILLS 4 CONNECTED"
160 PRINT "SQUARES ACROSS OR DOWN WITHIN THE GRID."
170 PRINT "YOU CAN DIG"TRY"TEST HOLES.  TYPE THE LOCATION OF"
180 PRINT "THE HOLE AS AN X COORDINATE, A COMMA, AND A Y COORD."
190 ´----------- DISPLAY THE GRID ------------------------
200 G1$="|___|___|___|___|___|___|___|___|___|___|"
210 PRINT "    Y"
220 PRINT "    ^          _____"
230 FOR I=9 TO 0 STEP -1: PRINT " "I" "G1$: NEXT I
240 PRINT ">X       0   1   2   3   4   5   6   7   8   9"
250 PRINT
260 ´----------- BURY THE TREASURE ----------------------------
270 AC=INT(2*RND)                       ´DECIDE ACROSS OR UPWARD
280 IF AC=1 THEN UP=0 ELSE UP=1
290 X(1)=INT((7+3*UP)*RND)              ´X(1)=0...6 OR  =0...9
300 Y(1)=INT((7+3*AC)*RND)              ´Y(1)=0...6 OR  =0...9
310 FOR I=2 TO 4
320    X(I)=X(I-1)+AC                   ´INCREASE X VAL. IF AC=1
330    Y(I)=Y(I-1)+UP                   ´INCREASE Y VAL. IF UP=1
340 NEXT I
360 HIT=0: PRINT "WHERE DO YOU WANT THE FIRST HOLE";
370 ´============ START DIGGING LOOP ============================
380 INPUT XDIG,YDIG
390   IF XDIG<0 OR XDIG>9 OR YDIG<0 OR YDIG>9 THEN PRINT"???": GOTO 380
400   COL=XDIG*4+9: ROW=17-YDIG         ´CALC. LOC. ON SCREEN
410   LOCATE ROW,COL: PRINT CHR$(15);   ´DISPLAY HOLE
420   GOSUB 710                         ´ERASE MSG./REPOS.CRSR
430   GOSUB 650                         ´CHECK FOR HIT
440   IF HFLAG=0 THEN 490               ´NO HIT
450     LOCATE ROW,COL: PRINT CHR$(127) ´DISPLAY TREASURE
460     GOSUB 710: PRINT "YOU FOUND IT!": PRINT CHR$(7);
470     HIT=HIT+1
480     IF HIT<4 THEN 510 ELSE 560
490   PRINT "NOTHING THERE -- "
500 ´
510   TRY=TRY-1: IF TRY=0 THEN 580
520   PRINT "NUMBER OF TRIES LEFT:";TRY
530   PRINT "NEXT HOLE";
540   GOTO 380
550 ´=========== END DIGGING LOOP ============================
560 GOSUB 710: PRINT "CONGRATULATIONS, YOU DUG IT ALL UP."
570 ´
580 Z$(1)=",": Z$(2)=",": Z$(3)=",": Z$(4)="."
590 PRINT "THE TREASURE WAS LOCATED AT ";
600 FOR I=1 TO 4
610    PRINT USING "(## , ##)\\";X(I);Y(I);Z$(I);
620 NEXT I
630 END
640 ´----------- SUBROUTINE TO FIND A HIT -------------------
650 HFLAG=0
660 FOR I=1 TO 4
670    IF XDIG=X(I) AND YDIG=Y(I) THEN HFLAG=1
680 NEXT I
```

(continued)

```
690 RETURN
700 '------------ SUBR. TO ERASE MSG. & REPOSITION CURSOR ------
710 LOCATE 20,1
720 FOR J=1 TO 4: PRINT STRING$(50," "): NEXT J
730 LOCATE 20,1: RETURN
```

Comments on the BASIC Code for TREAS3

The first task in any screen-oriented program is to clear the screen and "home" the cursor, that is, send it to the upper left-hand corner. The BASIC command for this on the IBM and TRS-80 computers is CLS. On the Apple, it's HOME. Other systems (or terminals) require two-code sequences. For example, the Zenith Z19 terminal and also Heath computers use the two codes ⟨escape⟩ and ⟨E⟩. Thus in BASIC you can clear the Z19 screen with

```
10 CL$=CHR$(27)+"E"
15 PRINT CL$
```

After clearing the screen, TREAS3 always displays the grid (it does not give the user a choice). In line 400 it calculates a row and column position to be used by a LOCATE statement in line 410 to display the "hole" dug by the player. LOCATE positions the cursor on the screen at a given row and column, where columns are numbered 1 to 80 across, and rows are numbered 1 to 25 downward. (1,1 is at the upper left.) PRINT CHR$(15) displays a special IBM character at that position. For other machines, use PRINT "0". This action is repeated with a different special character if a treasure square is hit (line 450).

The only other difference between TREAS3 and TREAS2 is the subroutine at line 710. It uses LOCATE to position the cursor in row 20 and erase lines 20–24 on the screen by printing strings of 50 spaces. This allows printed messages to be displayed and redisplayed at the same position on the screen. There are two reasons for doing this: (1) It prevents the grid display from disappearing by being scrolled off the top of the screen when lines are printed at the bottom, and (2) it prevents the grid from being overtyped after holes or treasures have been placed there.

How to Calculate Row and Column from X and Y

X, the traditional measure of the "across" (left to right) dimension in graphs, corresponds to *columns* in alphanumeric printing schemes, while Y corresponds to *rows*. However, both X and Y have to be transformed (modified) to obtain the correct column and row numbers.

In TREAS3, X is transformed into a column number in two steps. First we must add 9 to each X value, since all the positions on the grid start nine columns over. You can see this by counting the number of columns from the first column to where the grid begins. Second, since grid values are displayed four columns apart, all X values must be multiplied by 4.

For Y, we have a different problem. The Y values are displayed on adjacent rows, so there's no need to multiply them by anything. However, the grid is displaced downward from the top of the screen, with line 0 of the grid appearing at row 17 of the screen. Thus it would appear that 17 should be added to all Y values.

But wait—our grid Y values increase as you go upward, while the row values on the screen increase as you go downward. The solution to this dilemma is to calculate the row number as 17 − Y. Thus for Y = 0, ROW = 17; for Y = 1, ROW = 16; for Y = 2, ROW = 15; and so on, up to Y = 9, for which ROW = 8.

Notes on Adapting TREAS3 to Other Systems

Note to TRS-80 Users

In the case of the TRS-80, the statement PRINT @ N accomplishes much the same task as LOCATE. The value of N can be calculated from row and column. On the TRS-80 models I and III, columns are numbered 0 to 63, while rows run from 0 to 15, with the 0 in the upper left corner in both cases. PRINT @ requires a number N between 0 and 1023, where N corresponds to a consecutive numbering of character positions. Once you've figured out what row and column you want, the formula ROW*64 + COL can be used to calculate N. For TREAS3, the correct PRINT @ statement would be:

```
PRINT @ (ROW*64+COL);"*";
```

The number 64 should be changed to 80 if you're using an 80-column display (for example, with Model 4 disk BASIC).

TRS-80 users should also remember to use RND(0) instead of RND.

Note to Apple Users

When one is using Applesoft BASIC, placement of the cursor is accomplished with the horizontal and vertical tab functions. Taken together, these operate like a LOCATE statement on the IBM PC, with the difference that they refer to a screen with character positions 1 to 40 left to right and positions 1 to 24 top to bottom. The form of the statement would be:

```
HTAB ROW: VTAB COL: PRINT "*"
```

The size of the grid would have to be reduced slightly to take into consideration the smaller width (for example, by changing 4*XDIG to 3*XDIG). Apple users should remember to use RND(1) instead of RND.

Using Special Characters for Graphics Output

Some computers and terminals have special "graphics characters" to supplement their normal character set. To see if you have any such characters (and what they are), run the following program.

```
100 PRINT "PRESS <ENTER> TO SEE EACH NEW CHARACTER"
110 FOR I=0 TO 255
120    PRINT I;
130    INPUT" -- ";D$
140    PRINT CHR$(I)
150 NEXT I
```

More About Transformations

The process of making the values produced by a program display in proper relation to each other on the video screen (or paper) involves calculations called transformations. These depend on the values you start with (called *world coordinates*) and the values you want to end with (*screen coordinates*). The choice of screen coordinates depends on how the programmer wants the display to appear, and what values the particular computer system will tolerate (that is, how many horizontal and vertical locations you have to work with). Adding or subtracting values shifts the display locations left–right or up–down. This is called *translating* the range of values. Multiplying or dividing to enlarge or contract the display is known as *scaling* the range of values. By subtracting screen coordinates from a fixed value (as we did in TREAS3 for Y), you can flip over the upward orientation of world coordinates to match the downward orientation of screen coordinates. This is called *reflection*. Some further examples of the use of transformations in graphing will be shown in the next section.

LAB EXERCISE 9.2   File Name: TREAS4

Modify TREAS3 for your computer system. Then enter and test it, making any changes (and/or improvements) that are dictated by the system you use, or that are suggested by your instructor.

9.4   Graphics in Business Computing; Scaling Data

Keeping track of trends in such down-to-earth facts as sales or profits can be made a lot easier by turning raw figures into graphs. As a result, many off-the-shelf graphing programs are now available. These produce line graphs, bar graphs, and pie charts, usually in color. The user needs only provide the raw data.

In this section we will show an example of a program that changes raw data into graphical form. It can also show differently scaled ranges on request. Only alphanumeric graphics will be utilized, but the same principles apply to pixel graphics. Only the transformation equations (and the detail of the results) would change.

Rudi's Root-Beer-Barrel Franchise

Suppose you've just bought the franchise for homebrew root-beer barrels for a tristate area. You are also the only salesperson, so a problem that concerns you is the number of *sales* you make versus the number of sales *calls,* that is, actual visits. You have a questionnaire to screen potential customers who inquire by telephone. This helps you decide whether to make the visit. Ideally every visit could result in a sale—but how close to the ideal are you? And are things getting better, or worse, or neither? Here is a run of a program that displays this information in graphical form.

```
RUN
                -- GRAPH OF SALES AND CALLS, 1ST & 2ND QUARTERS --

SALES = $  CALLS = #

        50    60    70    80    90   100   110   120   130   140   150
WEEK    +     +     +     +     +     +     +     +     +     +     +
  1     |  $                                                        #      | R=0.34
  2     |     $                                                    #       | R=0.37
  3     |           $                                            #         | R=0.46
  4     |            $                                         #           | R=0.48
  5     |             $                                     #              | R=0.51
  6     |              $                              #                    | R=0.56
  7     |               $                          #                      | R=0.62
  8     |               $                         #                       | R=0.64
  9     |               $                         #                       | R=0.65
 10     |               $                         #                       | R=0.66
 11     |               $                        #                        | R=0.70
 12     |              $                        #                         | R=0.74
 13     |              $                       #                          | R=0.74
 14     |             $                       #                           | R=0.76
 15     |            $                       #                            | R=0.78
 16     |            $                       #                            | R=0.76
 17     |            $                      #                             | R=0.79
 18     |            $                     #                              | R=0.80
 19     |           $                    #                               | R=0.83
 20     |           $                    #                               | R=0.82
 21     |          $                    #                                | R=0.85
 22     |          $                    #                                | R=0.85
 23     |         $                    #                                 | R=0.86
 24     |        $                    #                                  | R=0.89
 25     |        $                    #                                  | R=0.91
 26     |         $  #                                                   | R=0.94

AVG. SALES =   88.54    AVG. CALLS = 127.92   AVG. SALES/CALLS = 0.71
Ok
```

Barrel Sales, Version 1

The program to produce this output is straightforward in its design. It prints a graph of values read from DATA statements. These are pairs of numbers representing the sales and calls for each of 26 weeks. The program plots them on successive lines by using the TAB function to position the cursor (or print head).

```
100 '**********************************************************
110 '*  BARREL1 (PLOTS GRAPH OF SALES & CALLS VERSUS WEEKS)   *
120 '**********************************************************
130 PRINT TAB(10);" -- GRAPH OF SALES AND CALLS, 1ST & 2ND QUARTERS --"
140 PRINT: PRINT "SALES = $  CALLS = #": PRINT
150 '----- HEADING, 1ST LINE --------------------------------
160 X=0
170 FOR I=50 TO 150 STEP 10
180    PRINT TAB(X*10*.5+6);I;: X=X+1
190 NEXT I
200 PRINT
210 '----- HEADING, 2ND LINE --------------------------------
220 PRINT"WEEK    ";:FOR K=0 TO 10:PRINT"+    ";: NEXT K: PRINT
230 '----- GRAPH DATA ---------------------------------------
240 SUM=0: CSUM=0: RSUM=0
250 FOR X=1 TO 26
260    READ SALES,CALLS
280      R=SALES/CALLS: RSUM=RSUM+R
290      SUM=SUM+SALES: CSUM=CSUM+CALLS
300      PRINT X;TAB(6);"|";
310      PRINT TAB((SALES-50)*.5+8);"$";
320      PRINT TAB((CALLS-50)*.5+8);"#";
330      PRINT TAB(60);"| R="USING"#.##";R
```

(continued)

```
340 NEXT X
350 PRINT: PRINT"AVG. SALES = "USING"###.##";SUM/26;
360 PRINT"   AVG. CALLS = "USING"###.##";CSUM/26;
370 PRINT"   AVG. SALES/CALLS = ";USING"#.##";RSUM/26
380 ´
390 DATA 51,150,55,148,67,145,69,143,71,139,75,134,84,135
400 DATA 85,133,86,132,87,131,90,129,94,127,93,125,96,126
410 DATA 97,125,96,126,97,123,98,122,99,119,97,118,99,116
420 DATA 100,118,101,117,103,116,105,115,107,114
```

The important lines in BARREL1 are lines 170–190, which print the heading numbers, line 220, which prints the cross marks (plus signs), and lines 310 and 320, which plot the sales and calls. The arguments of the TAB function in these two lines determine in which columns the symbols "$" and "#" will be displayed.

We have made a simplifying assumption in planning the BARREL1 program: The number of calls is always greater than the number of sales. This allows us to use two successive tabs within our graphing area, with the confidence that the second will not be less than the first. We also assume in this version of the program that all the values will be within the range displayed. (See BARREL2 and the Project section for ideas on removing these restrictions.)

The numerical assumption used in graphing these data items is that the range of values displayed is 50 to 150; that is, 100 values are possible. The actual number of screen columns to be used is 50. So we must "squeeze" 100 possible values into 50 columns, which means that two values will share one column (or that each value will get half a column). Thus each value must be multiplied by a scaling factor of one-half, that is, by .5. But first we must subtract 50 from each value, since column 1 in our graphing area corresponds to a value of 50. Also our graphing area itself is shifted over to the right eight columns to make room for the week number and a vertical line. These three considerations are combined in the TAB function to create a value that will display a "$" or "#" in the right place in our graph. For example, to plot a symbol corresponding to a value of 51, we use

```
TAB((51-50)*.5+8)=TAB(8.5)
```

TAB() rounds the 8.5 to 9, so the first "$" lands in column 9.

Line 220 places the " + " marker in the eighth column, and in every fifth column after that. This works because we already know that we want eleven crossmarks dividing the 50-column area into 10 intervals. The numbers 50 through 150 could have been distributed across the page in the same way. Instead, however, a formula was used in TAB, as follows (see lines 170 - 190):

```
160 X=0
170 FOR I=50 TO 150 STEP 10
180   PRINT TAB(X*10*.5+6);I; : X=X+1
190 NEXT I
```

This calculates numbers starting at 50, increases them by 10 each time, and places them every fifth column. Using a formula like this is a good idea if we expect to graph to other ranges (as will be seen in the next, more general program).

EXERCISE

9.2   Rewrite line 180 above so that the argument of TAB uses I instead of X.

Barrel Sales, Version 2

This version (BARREL2) is more flexible, since it takes less for granted about the numbers to be plotted. It still uses 50 columns, but the range can be whatever the user types in, from a lower limit A to an upper limit B. So, instead of 50/100, we use 50/B-A for the scaling factor. Heading line 1 and heading line 2 are both calculated using this variable scaling factor, so that the proper scales are shown for both the "standard" run and "customized" runs requested by the user. The graphs themselves also use the quantity 50/(B-A) in positioning the plotting symbols.

```
100 '*****************************************************
110 '*   BARREL2 (PLOTS CUSTOMIZED GRAPH OF SALES & CALLS)    *
120 '*****************************************************
130 PRINT TAB(10);" -- GRAPH OF SALES AND CALLS, 1ST & 2ND QUARTERS --"
140 PRINT: PRINT "SALES = $   CALLS = #": PRINT
150 A=50: B=150: W1=1: W2=26        'COLUMNS USED = 50
160 PRINT"THE RANGE CURRENTLY DISPLAYED IS"A"TO"B
170 INPUT"DO YOU WISH TO SEE A CUSTOMIZED GRAPH (Y/N)";A$
180 IF LEFT$(A$,1)="N" THEN 280
190   INPUT"STARTING WITH WHAT WEEK (1-25)";W1
200     IF W1<1 OR W1>25 THEN PRINT"???";: GOTO 190
210   INPUT"ENDING WITH WHAT WEEK (2-26)";W2
220     IF W2<2 OR W2>26 THEN PRINT"???";: GOTO 210
230   PRINT"WHAT IS THE SMALLEST NUMBER THAT YOU WANT"
240   PRINT"(INSTEAD OF"A;: INPUT") --";A
250   PRINT"WHAT IS THE LARGEST NUMBER THAT YOU WANT"
260   PRINT"(INSTEAD OF"B;: INPUT") --";B
270 '----- HEADING, 1ST LINE ---------------------------------
280 X=0: PRINT
290 FOR I=A TO B STEP 10
300   PRINT TAB(X*10*(50/(B-A))+6);I;: X=X+1
310 NEXT I
320 PRINT
330 '----- HEADING, 2ND LINE ---------------------------------
340 PRINT"WEEK    ";
350 FOR I=0 TO (X-1)
360   PRINT TAB(I*10*(50/(B-A))+8);"+";
370 NEXT I
380 PRINT
390 '----- MOVE DATA POINTER TO STARTING WEEK ----------------
400 FOR I=1 TO W1-1: READ D1,D2: NEXT I
410 '----- GRAPH DATA ----------------------------------------
420 SUM=0: CSUM=0: RSUM=0
430 FOR X=W1 TO W2
440   READ SALES,CALLS
460     R=SALES/CALLS: RSUM=RSUM+R
470     SUM=SUM+SALES: CSUM=CSUM+CALLS
480     PRINT X;TAB(6);"|";
490     IF SALES<A THEN PRINT TAB(7);"<";: GOTO 510
500       PRINT TAB((SALES-A)*(50/(B-A))+8);"$";
510     IF CALLS>B THEN PRINT TAB(59);">";: GOTO 530
520       PRINT TAB((CALLS-A)*(50/(B-A))+8);"#";
530     PRINT TAB(60);"|  R="USING"#.##";R
540 NEXT X
550 PRINT: PRINT"AVG. SALES = "USING"###.##";SUM/26;
560 PRINT"   AVG. CALLS = "USING"###.##";CSUM/26;
570 PRINT"   AVG. SALES/CALLS = ";USING"#.##";RSUM/26
580 '
590 DATA 51,150,55,148,67,145,69,143,71,139,75,134,84,135
600 DATA 85,133,86,132,87,131,90,129,94,127,93,125,96,126
610 DATA 97,125,96,126,97,123,98,122,99,119,97,118,99,116
620 DATA 100,118,101,117,103,116,105,115,107,114
```

(continued)

```
RUN
            -- GRAPH OF SALES AND CALLS, 1ST & 2ND QUARTERS --

SALES = $   CALLS = #

THE RANGE CURRENTLY DISPLAYED IS 50 TO 150
DO YOU WISH TO SEE A CUSTOMIZED GRAPH (Y/N)? Y
STARTING WITH WHAT WEEK (1-25)? 13
ENDING WITH WHAT WEEK (2-26)? 26
WHAT IS THE SMALLEST NUMBER THAT YOU WANT
(INSTEAD OF 50 ) --? 90
WHAT IS THE LARGEST NUMBER THAT YOU WANT
(INSTEAD OF 150 ) --? 120

           90            100           110           120
WEEK       +             +             +             +
  13  |        $                                     >|   R=0.74
  14  |           $                                  >|   R=0.76
  15  |             $                                >|   R=0.78
  16  |           $                                  >|   R=0.76
  17  |            $                                 >|   R=0.79
  18  |             $                                >|   R=0.80
  19  |               $                           #  |   R=0.83
  20  |            $                              #  |   R=0.82
  21  |              $                         #     |   R=0.85
  22  |               $                          #   |   R=0.85
  23  |                $                       #     |   R=0.86
  24  |                   $                   #      |   R=0.89
  25  |                     $                #       |   R=0.91
  26  |                      $            #          |   R=0.94

AVG. SALES =  53.38   AVG. CALLS =  64.62   AVG. SALES/CALLS = 0.45
Ok
```

EXERCISE

9.3   Does the code for BARREL2 contain any inefficiencies? That is, are there any changes one could make to speed up the execution of the program, and/or reduce the amount of BASIC code?

LAB EXERCISE 9.3   **File Name: BARREL3**

Enter and test your own version of BARREL2, making any changes that are needed to exploit the features of your particular computer system.

9.5   Higher-Resolution Graphics

APPLE

Radio Shack

IBM

A good way to show off the advantage of high-resolution (finely detailed) pixel graphics is to plot a mathematical curve. The math functions available in BASIC make this easy to do, particularly if you use the SIN and COS trigonometric functions to display periodic curves. The following three programs (one for the Apple, one for the TRS-80, and one for the IBM PC) all do the same thing, within the resolution limits of each machine: plot a sine wave, along with two reference lines, and give a printed message. In each case, a FOR loop is used to plot a point in every possible pixel column of the display. A scale factor XS is used inside this loop to convert X to a value based on a total screen width equivalent to 4*pi radians, where pi has the value 3.14159. Thus each graph shows two full cycles of the sine function.

Program for the Apple

```
10 REM -------------------------------------------------
20 REM          ASINE (SINE WAVE ON APPLE)
30 REM-------------------------------------------------
35 HOME:VTAB21:PRINT "TO END PROGRAM, PRESS <CTRL><C>"
40 HGR:HCOLOR=2
50 HPLOT 0,0 TO 0,159
60 HPLOT 0,79 TO 279,79
70 HCOLOR=1
80 XS=12.5664/280
90 FOR C=0 TO 279
100    X=C*XS
110    Y=79-79S*SIN(X)+.5
120    HPLOT C,Y
130 NEXT C
140 GOTO 140
```

Program for the TRS-80

```
100 ' -----------------------------------------------
110 '          TSINE (SINE WAVE ON TRS-80)
120 ' -----------------------------------------------
130 CLS
140 FOR V=0 TO 47:SET(0,V):NEXT V
150 FOR H=0 TO 127:(SET (H,23):NEXT H
160 XS=12.5664/128
170 FOR C=0 TO 127
180   X=C*XS
190   Y=23-23*SIN(X)+.5
200   SET(C,Y)
210 NEXT C
220 PRINT @ 862, "PRESS BREAK TO EXIT";
230 GOTO 230
```

Program for the IBM PC

```
100 ' -----------------------------------------------
110 '   ISINE (SINE FUNCTION ON IBM PC)
120 ' -----------------------------------------------
130 CLS: KEY OFF
140 SCREEN 2
150 LINE (0,0) - (0,199)
160 LINE (0,99) - (639,99)
170 '
180 XSCALE=12.5664/640
190 FOR C=0 TO 639
200    X=C*XSCALE
210    Y=99-99*SIN(X)
220    PSET(C,Y)
230 NEXT C
240 '
250 LOCATE 25,36: PRINT "TO END PROGRAM, <CTRL><BREAK>";
260 GOTO 260
```

Here are photos of the output produced by these three programs.

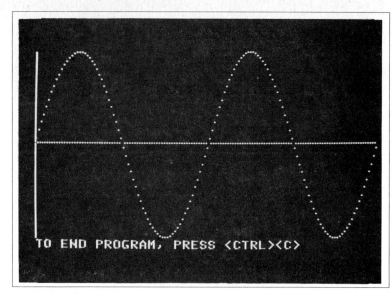

FIGURE 9.4 Output of ASINE produced on an Apple II

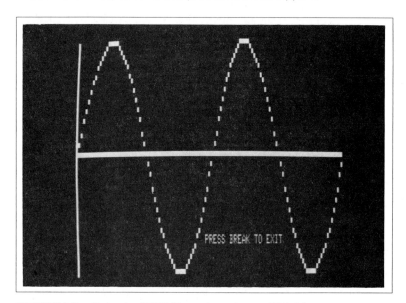

FIGURE 9.5 Output of TSINE produced on a TRS-80

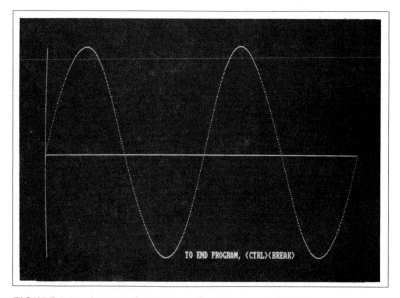

FIGURE 9.6 Output of ISINE produced on an IBM PC

The differing output results of these similar programs can be explained by looking at the different resolutions possible on the screens of the three computers.

The screen of the Apple II, when used with the high-resolution graphics command, can display $280 \times 192 = 53,760$ pixels. Pixels are plotted with HPLOT X,Y.

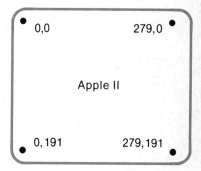

The screen of the TRS-80 has $128 \times 48 = 6144$ pixels. Pixels are plotted with SET (X,Y).

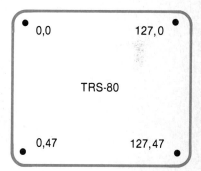

The screen of the IBM PC can display either $320 \times 200 = 64,000$ or $620 \times 200 = 128,000$ pixels. Pixels are plotted with PSET(X,Y). Three colors can be used in the first mode, one in the second.

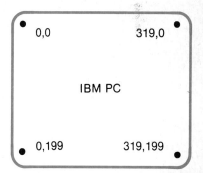

Two computers with even higher-resolution displays are the Zenith Z100 and the Tandy 2000 (both have up to $640 \times 400 = 256,000$ pixels). This resolution is obtained on the Tandy 2000 by using what they call "mode 3." Each pixel in this mode can have one of eight colors.

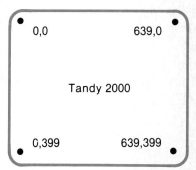

9.6 Graphs in Color that Use Mathematical Functions for Both X and Y

The medium resolution of the IBM PC in its Mode 1 graphics allows the use of several colors. The next two programs (DHARM1 and DHARM2) use Mode 1 on the PC to plot curves of changing color, where both X and Y are determined by the sine function. The results are similar to the patterns often seen on the oscilloscopes that were mandatory props in all the old mad-scientist films. However, DHARM2 goes beyond what's possible on an oscilloscope by plotting short line segments instead of points. The result is an interesting 3-D "ribbon" effect. Incidentally, the technical name for the processes involved here is *double* (or *orthogonal) harmonic motion*. The resulting graphs are also called *Lissajous figures*.

```
100 '------------------------------------------------
110 ' DHARM1  (PLOTS DOUBLE HARMONIC MOTION)
120 '------------------------------------------------
130 CLS: PRINT"TO END PROGRAM, PRESS <CTRL><BREAK>"
140 INPUT"PRESS <ENTER> TO START -- READY";D$
150 SCREEN 1: KEY OFF: COLOR 0,1: CLS
160 LINE (0,99)-(318,99),1        'X AXIS
170 LINE (159,0)-(159,198),1      'Y AXIS
180 DA=.0125                 'ANGLE INCREMENT IN RADIANS
190 '
200 FOR R=0 TO 6.3 STEP DA
210    X=159*SIN(4*R)+159
220    Y=99*SIN(3*R)+99
230    PSET(X,Y),(R MOD 3)+1
240 NEXT R
250 '
260 GOTO 260                 'FREEZE DISPLAY
```

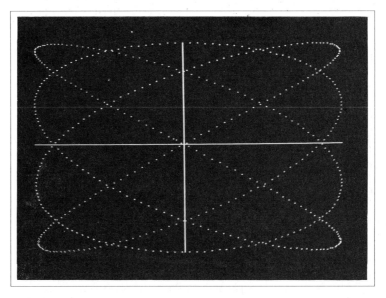

FIGURE 9.7   Photograph of run of DHARM1

```
100 '-------------------------------------------------------------
110 ' DHARM2 (PLOTS 3-D ILLUSION BASED ON DOUBLE HARMONIC MOTION)
120 '-------------------------------------------------------------
130 CLS: PRINT"TO END THE PROGRAM, PRESS <CTRL><BREAK>"
140 INPUT"PRESS <ENTER> TO START";D$
150 SCREEN 1: KEY OFF: COLOR 0,1: CLS
160 LINE (0,99)-(318,99),1      'X AXIS
170 LINE (159,0)-(159,198),1    'Y AXIS
180 DA=.0125     'ANGLE INCREMENT IN RADIANS
190 '
200 FOR R=0 TO 6.3 STEP DA
210    X=159*SIN(4*R)+159
220    Y=90*SIN(3*R)+99
230    LINE(X,Y+9)-(X,Y-9),(R*3.82 MOD 3)+1
240 NEXT R
250 '
260 GOTO 260
```

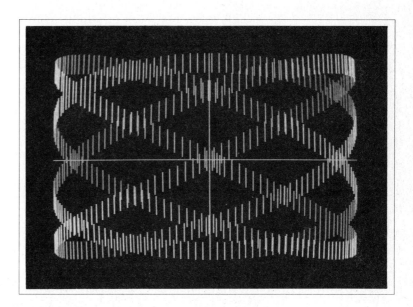

FIGURE 9.8   Photograph of run of DHARM2

EXERCISES

9.4   If you are using a TRS-80, modify DHARM1 to run on it.

9.5   If you are using an Apple II, modify both DHARM1 and DHARM2 to run on it.

LAB EXERCISE 9.4   **File Name: DHARM3**

Run the version of DHARM1 you have modified for your computer to make sure it works reasonably well. Then modify it to produce curves with ratios other than 4 by 3. Do this by changing the numbers 4 and 3 in lines 210 and 220. Also experiment with changing the SIN function to COS.

9.7   Summary of Chapter 9

■ Although some graphics is possible using a standard alphanumeric display, real graphics begins when the programmer can work with a grid of small programmable points called pixels (picture elements). The more pixels there are, the greater the detail (resolution) possible.

■ A simulation is a process that imitates some other process that is too complex, expensive, or dangerous to try in its real-world form. Simulations can frequently be expressed as computer programs that are based on mathematical models of the simulated process.

■ A game is a process that culminates with a player's winning or losing. There is a goal and there may be a time limit. Scoring may be based on skill, luck, or both. A game may or may not imitate a real-life process.

■ A common form of simulation is the cost projection, which is done today using electronic spreadsheet programs. Cost projections ask "What if..." questions regarding income, outgo, rates of change, and so on. When any one value is changed, spreadsheet programs automatically recalculate all the variables in the model being used. The results are then rapidly displayed on the output screen.

■ The RND function is useful when you are writing simulations that depend on a probabilistic model.

■ CLS is a key word that is used in some versions of BASIC to clear the screen and position the cursor at the upper left corner, or "home" position. On the Apple II, the key word HOME is used instead. On other computers, special control sequences such as ⟨esc⟩⟨E⟩ are used.

■ On the IBM, LOCATE ⟨row⟩,⟨col⟩ repositions the cursor. The possible cursor positions are 1 to 80 across by 1 to 25 downward, with the 1,1 position at the upper left.

■ In programming, a flag is a variable whose value changes (usually from 0 to 1) when some event occurs in a program. Later parts of the program may then test this flag to recall what happened earlier.

■ On the TRS-80, PRINT @ ⟨n⟩, ⟨variable name⟩ creates roughly the same effect as LOCATE does on the IBM. Since screen positions on the TRS-80 are numbered 0 to 63 (or 0 to 79) across and 0 to 15 (or 0 to 23) downward, n must be a value 0 to 1023 (or 0 to 1999). On some models the following syntax is also allowed:

    ⟨1n⟩ PRINT @ (⟨row⟩, ⟨col⟩), ⟨variable⟩

■ On the Apple, HTAB ⟨row⟩: VTAB⟨col⟩ is used in much the same way as LOCATE is used on the IBM.

■ Transformations are mathematical operations used to change the position, size, and orientation of graphical images from their representation in "world coordinates" to a representation in "screen coordinates." Changes in position are called translation, changes in size are called scaling, and changes in orientation are called rotation and reflection.

9.8 Problems and Programming Projects

1. Create and test a version of SLOT that uses all the features of a video display. Clear the screen, and prevent scrolling by using cursor-positioning key words or special codes to display output. You must find these in the manual for the computer or terminal you have available, although the ideas shown in TREAS3 will help.

2. Refine SLOT by adding tests (IF statements) that disallow noninteger inputs for money and allow "q" as well as "Q" for quit (see Section 5.4). Adapt the sound-effects subroutine for your local bell or beeper. Find out by experiment how to avoid the blending of beeps into one long bee-eep. If you have a SOUND command, produce melodic signals instead of simple beeps.

3. Extend and generalize SLOT by first asking the user how many pictures (say from 3 to 9) are wanted. Also ask the user to type in what words or symbols are to be shown.

4. Adapt TREAS3 to the video display you have available, using alphanumeric characters and cursor positioning. If you have high-resolution graphics available, use this feature to produce even more interesting pictorial output.

5. Explore the graphics characters you have available, using the program in Section 9.3. Do any of them make the terminal act strangely? Do any of them disable the terminal, forcing you to restart the session? Add IF statements to the program to avoid the offending characters.

6. Extend TREAS3 to make it a two-player game, with players taking turns. Keep records of hits for each player. Also consider whether the number of "test holes" should increase, decrease, or stay the same.

7. In the Barrel Sales Graph, Version 2, the scaling factor is calculated many times. Improve the program by calculating it *outside* the loop once, and then using the variable that holds this value inside the loop.

8. Generalize the Barrel Sales Program so that it's possible for sales to exceed calls on a given line. [*Hint:* Before plotting a line, go to a subroutine that determines whether the number of sales is greater than the number of calls. If it is, TAB to and print the symbol for calls *before* TABing to and printing the symbol for sales.]

## CHAPTER TEN

Writing Large BASIC Programs

NEW TOPICS INTRODUCED IN CHAPTER 10

- *Program modularization*
- *Menu-driven programs*
- *Codes and ciphers*
- *Word processing*
- *Parallel arrays*
- *Module independence*
- *Data encryption*
- *Macro flowcharts*
- *Linked lists*
- *Text editing*

10.1   Modular Program Design; Menu-driven Programs

In Section 10.2 we're going to write a program that enables the user to generate encrypted versions of a text, using an improvement of a classical method called the *Caesar cipher*.

As we'll see, the program involves some fairly unusual ideas, so beginners might consider it difficult to write. What's worse, assuming that it does finally get written, others who look at the program might find it even more difficult to *read*.

And therein lies a lesson: The real test of professional programming is to write programs that not only work correctly and reliably, but that are easy—in fact, a pleasure—to read.

In addition to the pleasure well-written programs can give to reader and writer alike, there's a very practical reason for developing programs that have what one might call *professional style*. The reason is that the terms "professional style" and "clarity of structure" are practically synonymous. So in advocating good style, one is really advocating crystal-clear program structure.

One of the best techniques for achieving such clarity is the concept of program modularization introduced back in Section 7.3. Taken literally, program modularization means splitting a large program into smaller pieces.

However, there's more to the idea than that. In particular, it's important that the modules be as self-contained as possible, and that they do not jump (GOTO) in and out of each other. To say this another way: Although it's important to avoid spaghetti code inside a module, it's even more important to avoid a spaghetti-like interconnection of the modules themselves.

Arranging that modules be self-contained, and that they interact as little as possible, is called achieving *module independence*. In the program applications of this and later chapters, we'll show how to use the idea behind what are called menu-driven programs as a simple but powerful approach to achieving module independence.

10.2   An Example Based on Data Encryption

Let's make these ideas concrete by applying them to a preliminary version of a data-encryption program based on a modular menu-driven structure. As just mentioned, program modularization is a methodical way of breaking the program into clearly defined chunks called program modules. A menu-driven program is one that uses a master menu module to perform a multi-way branch to other program modules, each one of which manages a specific function in the program. Here's what a menu structure might look like for our data-encryption program.

Module 1   Defines the data structures to be used and gives initial values to the data.

Module 2   (The MENU module) Announces the options available to the user of the program. Allows the user to choose the one desired, and then branches to the corresponding module.

Modules 3.1, 3.2, 3.3, 3.4,..., and so forth   Program modules (chunks) that correspond to options 1, 2, 3, 4, and so forth, of the menu.

Modules 4.1, 4.2, 4.3, 4.4,..., and so forth   Common subroutines that some of the above modules can use.

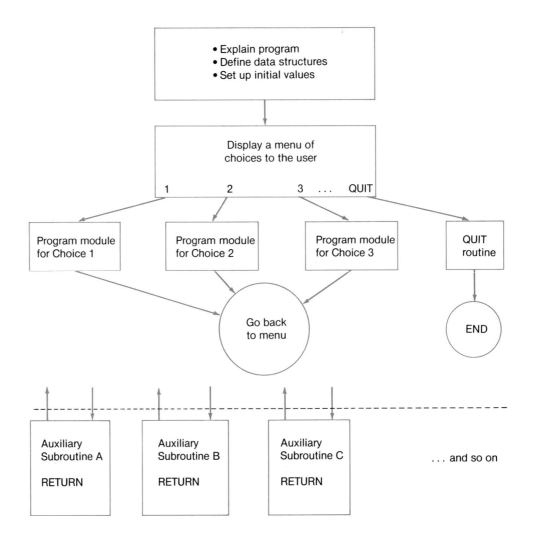

The diagram at the bottom of page 240 is a macro flowchart that shows the relation between these modules. The second module presents the menu of choices. The program flow then consists of a multi-way branch to the corresponding modules.

Before this modularization scheme can be expanded on, you must of course know something about the topic involved—in this case data encryption. So the first step in designing the program is to bone up on the subject addressed by the program. Here the subject is data encryption, which also goes under the names *data encoding* and *data enciphering.*

Step 1

The idea behind this program is to devise a scheme for disguising information. One scheme (which we won't use) is based on the use of *code* words or phrases to transmit arbitrarily defined meanings. When a politician says "We must work vigorously to decrease the deficit," it could be a code that means "Expect higher taxes next year." The file names of programs in this book are a kind of code. You might guess what KEYCIPH is, but to be sure you have to look it up.

Another scheme uses what's called a **cipher.** This is a mathematical transformation that methodically changes the parts of a message. Two types of transformation used are *transposition* and *substitution.* A transposition scheme is one that changes the position of the symbols in a message, turning a word like AGENT into, say, NEGAT.

The second and more useful transformation is substitution. This involves replacing each symbol in the message with another symbol taken from the same set of symbols. The most famous substitution scheme is the Caesar cipher (reportedly used by Julius Caesar), in which each letter of the alphabet is replaced by a letter a fixed distance, R, away. The distance from A to B is 1, A to C is 2, A to D is 3, and so on. The distance going backward in the alphabet is taken as a negative number. So for $R = -1$, IBM becomes HAL. To decipher, you use $R = +1$, changing HAL back to IBM.

Even if you don't know the value of R, the Caesar cipher is easy to crack (decipher), since all the letters have the same R added to them. This means that letters that appear frequently in English, such as E, also appear frequently in the cipher text, and it's easy to guess what they are. A better scheme is one that uses a sequence of values of R (say 7, 3, 5) for successive letters, repeating this *key* pattern as often as needed. But unless the pattern is very long, experts can also crack this kind of cipher. The only theoretically uncrackable cipher is one in which the key is as long as the message, and in which the key is never used more than once. This scheme gives rise to the one-time-pad cipher, in which a fresh, and very long, key is printed on each page of a small book (the pad). Both sender and receiver, who have duplicate copies, use a page once and then destroy it. Such pads, printed on very thin paper with very tiny numbers, have reportedly been rolled up to look like cigarettes. For further information on this subject, the book *The Code Breakers,* by David Kahn [Macmillan, 1973] is recommended.

The program we'll show will be based on use of a key pattern of values for R. For example, if the key pattern is 1, 5, 4, 2, then the message "AGENT g43" will be enciphered in three stages. First we'll change each character in the message to a decimal number corresponding to its ASCII code (see Appendix A for these numbers). This can be done in BASIC with the ASC function. We'll even change the spaces between words to numbers (the ASCII code for "space" is 32). Here's what the first stage does.

Stage 1:	A	G	E	N	T	sp	g	4	3
	↓	↓	↓	↓	↓	↓	↓	↓	↓
	65	71	69	78	84	32	103	52	51

Since some computers use the restricted ASCII range 32 to 95, we'll modify numbers greater than 95 by subtracting 32. In our example, we'll subtract 32 from the 103. If you check Appendix A, you'll see that this changes lower-case g (103) to capital G (71).

Next we'll add the numbers of the key pattern to these ASCII codes in succession, repeating the key as often as necessary. We'll limit the numbers in the key pattern to the 64 integers 0 to 63. If adding any of these key numbers to an ASCII code produces a sum greater than 95 (for example, 95 + 63 = 158), then we'll use the old "secret decoder ring" trick of recycling the sums back into the restricted ASCII range of 32 to 95, as follows.

Original SUM	32 33 34 ... 94 95 96 97 ... 157 158
Recycled SUM	32 33 34 ... 94 95 32 33 ... 93 94

Finally, we'll use the CHR$ function to change from numbers to regular symbols. Here's the result of doing all this to our example, showing that "AGENT g43" becomes "BLIPU%K64".

Stage 2	ASC	65	71	69	78	84	32	71	52	51
	Key	1	5	4	2	1	5	4	2	1
	SUM	66	76	73	80	85	37	75	54	52
		↓	↓	↓	↓	↓	↓	↓	↓	↓
Stage 3	CHR$(SUM)	B	L	I	P	U	%	K	6	4

Step 2

The desired output is as shown in the run of step 4 on pages 245 and 246.

Step 3

These ideas can now be used to create a high-level design in the form of a macro flowchart. Each module in the flowchart (shown on page 243) has been given a range of line numbers that correspond to the BASIC code that will be used in step 4. This makes it a lot easier to both write and read the final program.

Step 4

The following listing and run show the code and output of a BASIC program based on the macro flowchart of step 3. The distinct "chunks" of code in the program correspond to distinct boxes in the flowchart, making it easy to study one section at a time. Most of the code corresponds to the ideas used in the example shown in step 1 for enciphering "AGENT g43". However, there are two additional tricks being used that you should know about.

1. Lines 412–420 and 620–640: Instead of asking the user for a sequence of key numbers, we ask for a key string (for example, BASIC DOG). Subroutine 5010 then changes this into a sequence of LK numbers (LK = 9 for BASIC DOG) in the range 0–63. [*Note:* By modifying subroutine 5010 to calculate a

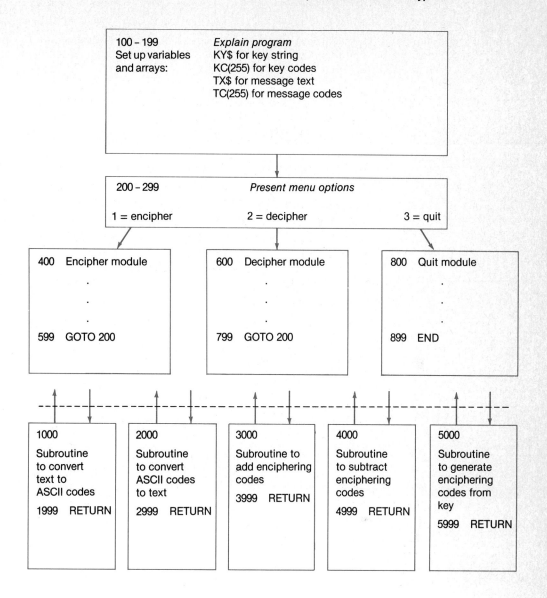

```
100 - 199        Explain program
Set up variables KY$ for key string
and arrays:      KC(255) for key codes
                 TX$ for message text
                 TC(255) for message codes


200 - 299                      Present menu options

1 = encipher          2 = decipher          3 = quit


400   Encipher module     600  Decipher module     800   Quit module
      .                         .                         .
      .                         .                         .
      .                         .                         .
599   GOTO 200            799  GOTO 200           899   END


1000            2000            3000            4000            5000
Subroutine      Subroutine      Subroutine to   Subroutine      Subroutine
to convert      to convert      add enciphering to subtract     to generate
text to         ASCII codes     codes           enciphering     enciphering
ASCII codes     to text                         codes           codes from
                                3999   RETURN                    key
1999   RETURN   2999   RETURN                   4999   RETURN
                                                                5999   RETURN
```

random-number generator *seed* value based on this key string, and then generating LT random numbers based on this seed (LT means length of the text), one could easily implement the one-time-pad scheme. In this case, the GOSUB 5010 should be moved to line 445 (or 665). Why?]

2. Lines 3030 and 4030: These lines use a "modular arithmetic" formula to make the sequence of key numbers stored in KC(N) repeat over and over. For example, suppose that the text has LT = 13 numbers stored in TC(), but the key pattern has only LK = 5 code numbers stored in KC(). Then, as the loop variable M goes through the values 1, 2, 3, 4, 5, 6, 7, 8, 9, 10, 11, 12, 13, the formula

$$N=M-(INT((M-1)/LK))*LK \quad \text{will make} \quad N=1,2,3,4,5,1,2,3,4,5,1,2,3$$

Incidentally, you wouldn't need this formula if you changed subroutine 5010 to generate a one-time pad in KC(), since you would then have LT values in both TC() and KC().

```
100 ´***********************************************************
110 ´*    KEYCIPH    (SIMPLIFIED DATA ENCRYPTION PROGRAM)    *
120 ´***********************************************************
130 KY$="": TX$=""          ´STRING VARIABLES TO HOLD KEY & TEXT
140 DIM KC(255), TC(255) ´ARRAYS FOR ASCII CODES, KEY & TEXT
201 ´------------------------------------------------------------
202 ´                  MENU SELECTION MODULE
203 ´------------------------------------------------------------
210 PRINT: PRINT"*****   MAIN MENU   *****": PRINT
220 PRINT" 1 = ENCIPHER TEXT"
230 PRINT" 2 = DECIPHER TEXT"
240 PRINT" 3 = QUIT PROGRAM"
250 PRINT: PRINT"YOUR CHOICE";: INPUT C
260 ON C GOTO 410, 610, 810
270 PRINT"PLEASE TYPE 1,2,OR 3": GOTO 250
400 ´------------------------------------------------------------
401 ´                  TEXT ENCIPHERING MODULE
402 ´------------------------------------------------------------
410 PRINT: PRINT"ENCIPHER MODE"
412 PRINT">>> ENTER KEY STRING (UP TO 255 CHARACTERS):"
414 LINE INPUT KY$: LK=LEN(KY$)
420 GOSUB 5010          ´GENERATE KEY CODES, STORE IN KC()
430 PRINT">>> ENTER PLAIN TEXT (UP TO 255 CHARACTERS):"
440 LINE INPUT TX$ :  LT=LEN(TX$)
450 GOSUB 1010          ´CHANGE TEXT TO ASCII, PUT IN TC()
460 GOSUB 3010          ´ADD KEY CODES TO TEXT CODES
470 GOSUB 2010          ´CONVERT ASCII TO TEXT, PUT IN TX$
480 PRINT: PRINT">>> ENCIPHERED TEXT IS:"
490 PRINT TX$: PRINT
500 GOTO 210
600 ´------------------------------------------------------------
601 ´                  TEXT DECIPHERING MODULE
602 ´------------------------------------------------------------
610 PRINT: PRINT"DECIPHER MODE"
620 PRINT">>> ENTER KEY STRING (UP TO 255 CHARACTERS):"
630 LINE INPUT KY$: LK=LEN(KY$)
640 GOSUB 5010          ´GENERATE KEY CODES, STORE IN KC()
650 PRINT">>> ENTER ENCIPHERED TEXT (UP TO 255 CHARACTERS):"
660 LINE INPUT TX$: LT=LEN(TX$)
670 GOSUB 1010          ´CHANGE TEXT TO ASCII, PUT IN TC()
680 GOSUB 4010          ´SUBTRACT KEY CODES FROM TEXT CODES
690 GOSUB 2010          ´CONVERT ASCII TO TEXT, PUT IN TX$
700 PRINT: PRINT">>> DECIPHERED TEXT IS:"
710 PRINT TX$: PRINT
720 GOTO 210
800 ´------------------------------------------------------------
801 ´                     QUIT MODULE
802 ´------------------------------------------------------------
810 PRINT"PROGRAM IS TERMINATING WITHOUT SAVING ANY DATA"
820 PRINT"TO USE AGAIN, TYPE ´RUN´"
830 END
997 ´============================================================
998 ´                SUBROUTINES FOR KEYCIPH
999 ´============================================================
1000 ´
1001 ´    SUBROUTINE TO CONVERT CHARS IN TX$ TO ASCII IN TC()
1002 ´    ASCII CODES KEPT IN RANGE 32-95 TO AVOID LOWER CASE
1003 ´
1010 FOR K=1 TO LEN(TX$)
1020   TC(K)=ASC(MID$(TX$,K,1))
1030   IF TC(K)>95 THEN TC(K)=TC(K)-32
1040 NEXT K
1050 RETURN
2000 ´...........................................................
2001 ´    SUBROUTINE TO CONVERT ASCII IN TC() TO CHARS IN TX$
2002 ´
2010 TX$=""
2020 FOR K=1 TO LT
2030   TX$=TX$+CHR$(TC(K))
```

```
2040 NEXT K
2050 RETURN
3000 ´.........................................................
3001 ´    SUBROUTINE TO ADD ENCIPHERING CODES TO TC()
3002 ´    RECALL THAT LT IS LENGTH OF TX$, LK LENGTH OF KY$
3003 ´
3010 FOR M=1 TO LT
3030   N=M-(INT((M-1)/LK))*LK   ´N IS CONGRUENT M MOD LK
3040   TC(M)=TC(M)+KC(N)          ´SO N REPEATS IN STEP WITH M
3050   IF TC(M)>95 THEN TC(M)=TC(M)-64
3060 NEXT M
3070 RETURN
4000 ´.........................................................
4001 ´    SUBROUTINE TO SUBTRACT ENCIPHERING CODES FROM TC()
4002 ´    RECALL THAT LT IS LENGTH OF TX$, LK LENGTH OF KY$
4003 ´
4010 FOR M=1 TO LT
4030   N=M-(INT((M-1)/LK))*LK   ´HERE´S THE MOD ARITH TRICK
4040   TC(M)=TC(M)-KC(N)          ´AGAIN TO RECYCLE KC()
4050   IF TC(M)<32 THEN TC(M)=TC(M)+64
4060 NEXT M
4070 RETURN
5000 ´.........................................................
5001 ´    SUBROUTINE TO GENERATE KEY CODES DERIVED FROM KY$
5002 ´    CODES ARE KEPT IN RANGE 32-95, SHIFTED LEFT TO 0-63
5003 ´
5010 FOR K=1 TO LK
5020   A=ASC(MID$(KY$,K,1))-32  ´SHIFT CODES TO RANGE 0-95
5030   IF A>63 THEN A=A-32      ´TRUNCATE RANGE TO 0-63
5040   KC(K)=A                  ´STORE CODES IN KC()
5050 NEXT K
5060 RETURN
RUN

*****   MAIN MENU    *****

 1 = ENCIPHER TEXT
 2 = DECIPHER TEXT
 3 = QUIT PROGRAM

YOUR CHOICE? 1

ENCIPHER MODE
>>> ENTER KEY STRING (UP TO 255 CHARACTERS):
BASIC DOG
>>> ENTER PLAIN TEXT (UP TO 255 CHARACTERS):
WHEN THE MOON IS RED, THE GEESE FLY HIGH

>>> ENCIPHERED TEXT IS:
9)87CT,4G/0B7CI7O9´%_I7H)O.´&F.CF0HG**:1


*****   MAIN MENU    *****

 1 = ENCIPHER TEXT
 2 = DECIPHER TEXT
 3 = QUIT PROGRAM

YOUR CHOICE? 2

DECIPHER MODE
>>> ENTER KEY STRING (UP TO 255 CHARACTERS):
BASIC DOG
>>> ENTER ENCIPHERED TEXT (UP TO 255 CHARACTERS):
9)87CT,4G/0B/CI7O9´%_I/H)O.´&F.CF0HG**:1

>>> DECIPHERED TEXT IS:
WHEN THE MOON IS RED, THE GEESE FLY HIGH
```

(continued)

```
*****   MAIN MENU    *****

1 = ENCIPHER TEXT
2 = DECIPHER TEXT
3 = QUIT PROGRAM

YOUR CHOICE? 3
PROGRAM IS TERMINATING WITHOUT SAVING ANY DATA
TO USE AGAIN, TYPE 'RUN'
Ok
```

LAB EXERCISE 10.1   File Name: KEYCIPH2

Enter KEYCIPH and test it for a number of different key strings and texts. What happens when a text has more than 255 characters? Do you have any ideas on how to handle this situation? [*Hint:* Consider changing TX$ to a string array.]

10.3 Word Processing

The phrase *word processing* refers to the application of computers to creating and modifying text documents of all kinds.

In order to use a computer system for word processing, you usually need four components:

1. A video terminal (screen and keyboard) for entering and modifying text
2. A letter-quality printer for producing the final output
3. A disk system for storing documents in the form of data files
4. The computer itself, including sufficient memory and the interface circuits needed to connect the terminal, printer, and disk drives

In addition to this hardware, there must also be two kinds of word-processing software.

1. A *text-editing* program (usually just called an editor), that allows you to enter text, change it, delete it, move it around, save it, and/or retrieve it.
2. A *text-formatting* program that takes the text produced by the editor and rearranges margin settings, spacing between lines, paragraph indentions, right justifications, page numbering, and so on, in accordance with your instructions.

The more important of these two programs is the text editor, since you can always format the text to some extent by the way you type it into the editor.

To give you some idea of how the software for word processors functions, the next two sections will show how to write a small text editor in BASIC. Section 10.4 first explains a special data structure (the linked list) that is at the heart of most word-processor text editors. Then Section 10.5 shows how to use this data structure in a BASIC text-editing program called LEDIT1.

These two topics are usually reserved for intermediate or advanced books on programming, so you may wish to postpone study of Sections 10.4 and 10.5 until a later time. However, it is important to note that the *use* of commercial word-processor programs (written by professionals and sold as separate software packages) does not require programming skills at all. In fact, many such software products provide on-line assistance in the form of various "help menus" that appear on the screen as they are needed. Figure 10.1 shows an example of such a menu, along with some text that is being edited with a commercial word-processing program called WordStar.

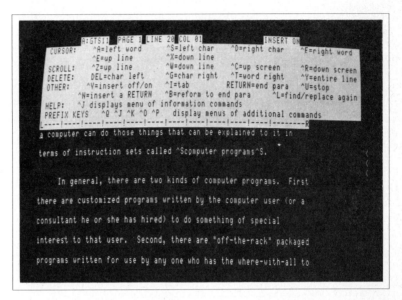

FIGURE 10.1   The screen of a video terminal while the WordStar program is being used. The black-on-white section at the top contains a summary of the commands available for the particular level of editing being done at the point shown. The white-on-black section in the lower part of the screen contains the text being entered and/or edited by the user.

LAB EXERCISE 10.2   File Name: WORDPROC

If you have access to a professional word-processing system, spend some time using it, under the guidance of an experienced user. This will be a valuable experience, and will give you some appreciation of the power of professional software.

10.4   Advanced Data Structures; Linked Lists

The most useful data structure for program applications of all sorts is undoubtedly the *array*. It is especially valuable in BASIC, since both one- and two-dimensional arrays can be used to store strings as well as numbers.

There are, as you may suspect, applications in which more advanced data structures are useful. The names of some of these structures are *circular queues, LIFO stacks, FIFO queues,* and *linked lists*. (LIFO means Last-in-First-Out, while FIFO means First-in-First-Out. Stacks and queues are areas of memory that function like data "holding areas.")

All these data structures can be simulated in BASIC by using arrays. To illustrate how this works, we'll examine the *linked-list* structure. This structure will turn out to be of particular value in writing the text-editing program of Section 10.5.

A *link* is a number that connects one "chunk" of data with another. If you imagine the pages of a magazine to be the chunks of data, then the number in the phrase "Continued on page xx" is a link. Let's pursue this magazine analogy further to explain what links have to do with text editing.

Assume that you are the magazine's editor, and that you can both *write* and *read* data on the pages of the magazine. We'll also assume that you insist that *every* page have a link at the bottom, and that there be a special cover page (page 1) that tells the editor where to find the first page that contains actual text. Finally we'll assume that there's always a special NOTE TO THE EDITOR that indicates the first page available for *writing* new text. We'll call this page AV, and start out with AV = 2. Here's a picture of what your magazine looks like on the first day, when it starts out as a bunch of blank pages. The number 0 is used as a special link to mean "no more text."

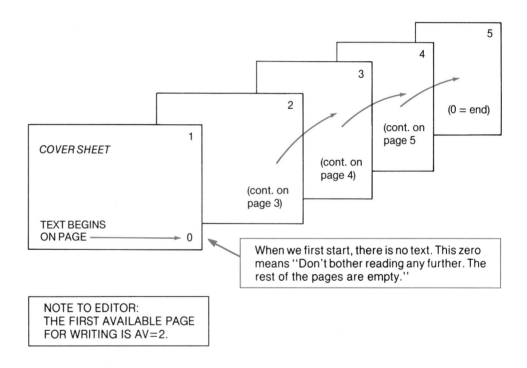

For our text-editor program, it will be better if we use the word *line* instead of page, since a line is a more realistic chunk of text to deal with. Each line will correspond to an entry in a string array T$(). The line number will correspond to the index I. It will be handy to call T$(I) "the Ith slot in the T$() array." The links are stored in a separate "forward-pointer" array FP(). This can be pictured as sitting right next to T$(). For this reason, T$() and FP() are sometimes called *parallel arrays*.

Here's what these arrays look like initially in a program that dimensions them for an editor that can handle up to 100 lines of text.

I	T$()	FP(I)
1		0
2		3
3		4
. . .		. . .
98		99
99		100
100		0

AV = 2

Although this structure is made up of two parallel arrays, it can also be viewed as a linked list. This is because it defines a list of strings in T$() that are linked together by the numbers in FP(). The two most important operations in using a linked list with an editor are *appending* (or adding) lines of text and *deleting* lines of text. For example, here's what the arrays will look like after you initially append four lines of text.

I	T$(I)	FP(I)
1	(not used)	2
2	To succeed, (1) Be honest	3
3	(2) Be thrifty	4
4	(3) Be industrious	5
5	(4) Eat creamed spinach.	0
6		7
7		8
. . .		. . .
100		0

AV = 6

To help illustrate a tricky point, we used a text that had numbers in it corresponding to the order in which the text was initially entered. For example, the text ''(4) Eat creamed spinach.'' was the fourth line initially entered. Note that the numbers in the text are not the same as the slot numbers given by I. Also note that after we added our four lines of text, the zero link shifted from slot 1 to slot 5.

Now let's see what happens when the editor decides to squeeze in a new line right after the current second line. For example, suppose you want to make "because it saves money" the new third line of text. One way to handle this request would be to move the last two lines down, in order to open up a space. A much easier (and, as we'll see, more powerful) approach is to put the new text in the first available space, which is at present $AV = 6$, and then change the links in such a way that the order in which lines of text are to be read can be obtained from the links. Here's what we'll have.

I	T$(I)	FP(I)
1	(not used)	2
2	To succeed, (1) Be honest	3
3	(2) Be thrifty	6
4	(3) Be industrious	5
5	(4) Eat creamed spinach.	0
6	because it saves money	4
7		8
.		.
.		.
.		.
100		0

$AV = 7$

To read the text now, look at the number in FP(1) to find out where the text starts, and then follow the links. Doing this will give you slots 2, 3, 6, 4, 5. If you want to know the implicit line numbers—that is, numbers that say in what order the text will eventually be printed—you'll have to count as you go down the list "1, 2, 3, 4, 5." Notice that the text "(3) Be industrious" is now the *fourth* line in this counting sequence.

To delete a line, all you do is readjust the links to point around the deleted line, and then put the slot number of the deleted line at the top of the list of available space (in AV). You don't have to erase the contents of the deleted line, since that will happen automatically the next time a new line is appended at AV. (When something is stored in computer memory, the old contents are always erased.)

EXERCISES

10.1 Reproduce the last diagram on a piece of paper. Then do a hand simulation (that is, write in the results by hand) of further changes in the linked list that correspond to adding two more sentences to the original sentence.

10.2 Continue Exercise 10.1, this time showing what the linked list looks like after the second of your three sentences is deleted.

10.5   Writing a Line-Editor Program in BASIC

Here's a program that uses the data structure just discussed in a line-editor program. As you can see, the program uses a menu-driven modular design. The selections available from the menu are all one-letter commands related to text editing.

The program is called a *line* editor because the menu commands specifically allow you to enter, delete, or change one line at a time. A better approach would be to write what's called a *screen-oriented* editor program. This allows you to move a pointer called the cursor around the screen, editing any part of a line you wish. We won't show such a program because (1) it would have to be written in terms of the characteristics of one specific computer screen, and (2) it wouldn't work on the printer-type terminals still found on some time-sharing systems.

```
10 '**********************************************************
20 '*                LEDIT1 (LINE EDITOR PROGRAM)           *
30 '**********************************************************
100 ' SOME SYSTEMS WILL NEED TO CLEAR SPACE FOR STRING VARIABLES
110 ' IF YOU NEED IT REPLACE THESE LINES WITH: 100 CLEAR 5000
120 DEFINT A-Z                        'ALL VARIABLES ARE INTEGERS
130 CL=0: HL=0
140 DIM FP(100)                       'LINKED LIST
150 DIM T$(100)                       'TEXT BUFFER
200 '-------------------------------------------------------
210 '            GIVE DIRECTIONS TO THE USER
220 '-------------------------------------------------------
230 GOSUB 820: PRINT "CURRENT LINE NUMBER NOW = 0.  TO APPEND TEXT"
240 PRINT "AT LINE # 1 RESPOND   CMD? A   AFTER? 0"
250 PRINT ".............................."
300 '-------------------------------------------------------
310 '         INITIALIZE POINTERS FOR THE LINKED LIST
320 '-------------------------------------------------------
330 AV=2: FP(1)=0
340 FOR I=2 TO 99
350    FP(I)=I+1
360 NEXT I
370 FP(100)=0
400 '-------------------------------------------------------
410 '              GET A COMMAND FROM THE USER
420 '-------------------------------------------------------
430 PRINT "CMD?";: LINE INPUT;L$
440 L1=CL: L2=CL
500 '-------------------------------------------------------
510 '              INTERPRET THE USER'S COMMAND
520 '-------------------------------------------------------
530 IF L$="E" THEN END
540 IF L$="H" THEN PRINT: GOSUB 830: GOTO 430
550 IF L$="V" THEN 930
560 IF L$="I" THEN 1030
570 IF L$="A" THEN V$="AFTER" ELSE IF L$="G" THEN V$="WHERE" ELSE V$="FROM"
580 PRINT TAB(10); V$;: INPUT; L1: L2=L1
590 IF L$="A" THEN 600 ELSE 610
600 PRINT: GOTO 1210
610 IF L$="G" THEN 2430
620 PRINT TAB(20); "TO";: INPUT L2
630 IF L$="C" THEN 1630
640 IF L$="D" THEN 2030
650 IF L$="L" THEN 2430
660 IF L$="P" THEN 2830
670 IF L$="R" THEN 3230
680 IF L$="T" THEN 3830
690 IF L$="S" THEN 4830
```

(continued)

```
710 PRINT "NO SUCH COMMAND": GOTO 430 ´GET NEXT COMMAND
800 ´-----------------------------------------------------------
810 ´                  H COMMAND (HELP SUBROUTINE)
820 ´-----------------------------------------------------------
830 PRINT "AFTER ´CMD?´ TYPE A(PPEND), C(HANGE), D(ELETE), E(ND)"
840 PRINT "G(OTO), H(ELP), I(NFORMATION), L(IST), P(RINT)"
850 PRINT "R(ESTRUCTURE), S(PACE), T(AB), OR V(ERIFY)."
860 PRINT "RESPOND TO OTHER ? PROMPTS WITH A LINE #. RESPONDING"
870 PRINT "WITH ´ENTER´ GIVES CURRENT LINE #. USE ´I´ CMD TO"
880 PRINT "FIND THE CURRENT LINE #.  TYPE PERIOD (.) TO EXIT A(PPEND)"
890 RETURN                              ´CONTIUE WITH PROGRAM
900 ´-----------------------------------------------------------
910 ´             V COMMAND (VERIFY CURRENT LINE #)
920 ´-----------------------------------------------------------
930 PRINT USING"##:";CL;
940 PRINT T$(CP)
950 PRINT: GOTO 430                      ´GET NEXT COMMAND
1000 ´-----------------------------------------------------------
1010 ´        I COMMAND (GIVES INFORMATION ABOUT LINE #S)
1020 ´-----------------------------------------------------------
1030 PRINT TAB(5)
1040 PRINT "CURRENT LINE IS #";CL;"   HIGHEST LINE IS #"; HL
1050 PRINT: GOTO 430                     ´GET NEXT COMMAND
1200 ´-----------------------------------------------------------
1210 ´              A COMMAND (APPEND AFTER LINE L1)
1220 ´-----------------------------------------------------------
1230 PRINT USING "##>"; L1+1;: LINE INPUT B$
1240 IF LEN(B$)=0 THEN B$=" "
1250 IF B$="." THEN 1390
1260 IF AV=0 THEN PRINT "BUFFER FULL": GOTO 1390
1270 CL=L1+1
1280 I=1: K=1
1290 IF FP(I)=0 OR K=CL THEN 1320       ´I IS LINE POINTER
1300 I=FP(I): K=K+1: GOTO 1290          ´K IS LINE COUNTER
1310 ´
1320 J=AV: AV=FP(J)                     ´RESET PTR TO AVAILABLE SPACE
1330 FP(J)=FP(I)                        ´CHANGE OLD LINK
1340 FP(I)=J                            ´SET NEW LINK
1350 T$(J)=B$                           ´STORE USER´S TEXT IN TEXT BUFFER
1360 CP=J: HL=HL+1                      ´CP IS PTR TO CURRENT LINE
1370 IF CL=HL THEN HP=CP
1380 L1=CL: GOTO 1230
1390 PRINT: GOTO 430                     ´GET NEXT COMMAND
1600 ´-----------------------------------------------------------
1610 ´              C COMMAND (CHANGE LINES L1 TO L2)
1620 ´-----------------------------------------------------------
1630 CL=L1
1640 IF L2>HL THEN PRINT "2ND LINE TOO HIGH": GOTO 1750
1650 I=1: K=1
1660 IF FP(I)=0 OR K=CL THEN 1690
1670 I=FP(I): K=K+1: GOTO 1660
1680 ´
1690 IF FP(I)=O THEN PRINT "NO SUCH LINE": GOTO 1750
1700 CP=FP(I)
1710 PRINT USING "##:";CL;
1720 PRINT T$(CP)
1730 PRINT USING "##>";CL;: LINE INPUT T$(CP)
1740 IF CL<L2 THEN CL=CL+1: GOTO 1650
1750 PRINT: GOTO 430                     ´GET NEXT COMMAND
2000 ´-----------------------------------------------------------
2010 ´              D COMMAND (DELETE LINES L1 TO L2)
2020 ´-----------------------------------------------------------
2030 CL=L1
2040 IF L2>HL THEN L2=HL
2050 FOR C=0 TO L2-L1
2060 I=1: K=1
2070 IF FP(I)=0 OR K=CL THEN 2100
2080 I=FP(I): K=K+1: GOTO 2070
```

```
2090 ´
2100 IF FP(I)=0 THEN PRINT "NO TEXT TO DELETE": GOTO 2160
2110 J=FP(I): FP(I)=FP(J)
2120 FP(J)=AV: AV=J
2130 HL=HL-1: CP=I
2140 IF HL=CL THEN HP=CP
2150 NEXT C
2160 CL=L1-1: IF CL<0 THEN CL=0
2170 PRINT: GOTO 430                        ´GET NEXT COMMAND
2400 ´------------------------------------------------------------
2410 ´              L COMMAND (LIST LINES L1 TO L2)
2420 ´------------------------------------------------------------
2430 I=FP(1):K=1
2440 IF L2>HL THEN L2=HL
2450 IF I=0 THEN PRINT "BUFFER EMPTY": GOTO 2530
2460 IF K<L1 THEN 2490
2470 PRINT USING "##:";K;
2480 PRINT T$(I)
2490 CP=I: I=FP(I): K=K+1
2500 IF K>L2 THEN 2520
2510 GOTO 2460
2520 CL=K-1
2530 PRINT: GOTO 430                        ´GET NEXT COMMAND
2800 ´------------------------------------------------------------
2810 ´              P COMMAND (PRINT TEXT ON LINE PRINTER)
2820 ´------------------------------------------------------------
2830 I=FP(1): K=1
2840 IF L2>HL THEN L2=HL
2850 IF I=0 THEN PRINT "BUFFER EMPTY": GOTO 2940
2860 PRINT "TURN PRINTER ON --- READY";: INPUT Z$
2870 IF K<L1 THEN 2900
2880 CP=I
2890 LPRINT T$(I)
2900 I=FP(I): K=K+1
2910 IF K>L2 THEN 2930
2920 GOTO 2870
2930 CL=K-1
2940 PRINT: GOTO 430                        ´GET NEXT COMMAND
3200 ´------------------------------------------------------------
3210 ´              R COMMAND (RESTRUCTURE LINES L1 TO L2)
3220 ´------------------------------------------------------------
3230 PRINT "COMMAND NOT AVAILABLE"          ´TO BE ADDED LATER
3240 PRINT: GOTO 430                        ´GET NEXT COMMAND
3800 ´------------------------------------------------------------
3810 ´              T COMMAND (SETS TAB FOR LINES L1 TO L2)
3820 ´------------------------------------------------------------
3830 PRINT "COMMAND NOT AVAILABLE"          ´TO BE ADDED LATER
3840 PRINT: GOTO 430                        ´GET NEXT COMMAND
4400 ´------------------------------------------------------------
4410 ´              ROUTINE TO SIMULATE LINE INPUT
4420 ´------------------------------------------------------------
4430 ´ADD SIMULATION OF LINE INPUT HERE IF NEEDED
4800 ´------------------------------------------------------------
4810 ´  S COMMAND (INSERTS SPACES BETWEEN LINES FROM L1 TO L2)
4820 ´------------------------------------------------------------
4830 PRINT "COMMAND NOT AVAILABLE"          ´TO BE ADDED LATER
4840 PRINT: GOTO 430                        ´GET NEXT COMMAND
9999 END
RUN
AFTER ´CMD?´ TYPE A(PPEND), C(HANGE), D(ELETE), E(ND)
G(OTO), H(ELP), I(NFORMATION), L(IST), P(RINT)
R(ESTRUCTURE), S(PACE), T(AB), OR V(ERIFY).
RESPOND TO OTHER ? PROMPTS WITH A LINE #. RESPONDING
WITH ´ENTER´ GIVES CURRENT LINE #. USE ´I´ CMD TO
FIND THE CURRENT LINE #.  TYPE PERIOD (.) TO EXIT A(PPEND)
CURRENT LINE NUMBER NOW = 0.   TO APPEND TEXT
AT LINE # 1 RESPOND   CMD? A   AFTER? 0
```

(continued)

```
.................................
CMD?A    AFTER? 0
 1>SHOPPING LIST
 2>A. MOM???
 3>B. UNCLE HARRY, CIGARS
 4>C. AUNT MATILDA, SCARF
 5>D. KIDS, COMPUTER
 6>.
```

Important: To leave A(PPEND) mode and give another command, you must type a period (.).

```
CMD?L    FROM? 1    TO? 9
 1:SHOPPING LIST
 2:A. MOM???
 3:B. UNCLE HARRY, CIGARS
 4:C. AUNT MATILDA, SCARF
 5:D. KIDS, COMPUTER

CMD?C    FROM? 1    TO? 2
 1:SHOPPING LIST
 1>CHRISTMAS SHOPPING LIST
 2:A. MOM???
 2>A. MOTHER, BOOKS

CMD?L    FROM? 1    TO? 9
 1:CHRISTMAS SHOPPING LIST
 2:A. MOTHER, BOOKS
 3:B. UNCLE HARRY, CIGARS
 4:C. AUNT MATILDA, SCARF
 5:D. KIDS, COMPUTER


CMD?D    FROM? 4    TO? 4


CMD?L    FROM? 1    TO? 9
 1:CHRISTMAS SHOPPING LIST
 2:A. MOTHER, BOOKS
 3:B. UNCLE HARRY, CIGARS
 4:D. KIDS, COMPUTER


CMD?A    AFTER? 2
 3>    AND ANTIQUE BOOK CASE
 4>.


CMD?H
AFTER ´CMD?´ TYPE A(PPEND), C(HANGE), D(ELETE), E(ND)
G(OTO), H(ELP), I(NFORMATION), L(IST), P(RINT)
R(ESTRUCTURE), S(PACE), T(AB), OR V(ERIFY).
RESPOND TO OTHER ? PROMPTS WITH A LINE #. RESPONDING
WITH ´ENTER´ GIVES CURRENT LINE #. USE ´I´ CMD TO
FIND THE CURRENT LINE #.   TYPE PERIOD (.) TO EXIT A(PPEND)
CMD?I
    CURRENT LINE IS # 3    HIGHEST LINE IS # 5


CMD?P    FROM? 1    TO? 5
TURN PRINTER ON --- READY?
CHRISTMAS SHOPPING LIST
A. MOTHER, BOOKS
    AND ANTIQUE BOOK CASE
B. UNCLE HARRY, CIGARS
D. KIDS, COMPUTER


CMD?E
Ok
```

EXERCISE

10.3   The heart of LEDIT1 is the A(PPEND) module (lines 1230–1390). Using the text from the example of Section 10.4, trace through the operation of this module. Which lines of the code actually change the links? Is it correct to say that the A(PPEND) module can either append or insert new lines of text? Why?

LAB EXERCISE 10.3   File Name: LEDIT2

Enter LEDIT1 into your computer and save it on disk or tape. Then try using it for a variety of small text-processing tasks (for example, writing a note or drafting a lab report). What new features would you like to see added? What changes would you recommend?

10.6 Summary of Chapter 10

■ Programs should be easy to read. Program modules should be as self-contained as possible. The interconnections between modules should avoid spaghetti-like tangles.

■ An important form of modularity is the menu structure. The master menu module branches (sends control) to various submodules as chosen by the user. The menu may also contain instructions and information about the available choices. Submodules usually branch back to the menu module when they finish.

■ Data encryption, the science of transforming information, has applications in everything from politics to computer science. Encryption schemes can be based on the use of codes or ciphers. A code is a system of arbitrarily defined symbols or words and their meanings. A cipher uses a mathematical process to transform a message; it is more suited to computer use.

■ Word-processing software automates two main tasks: text editing and text formatting. The first makes it easy for the user to enter text, make changes, move text, and retrieve text. The second produces printed documents with headings, margins, spacing, indention, page numbering, and so on, as specified by the user.

■ A linked list is a data structure useful for text-editing programs. Like many specialized data structures—circular queues, LIFO (last-in-first-out) stacks, FIFO (first-in-first-out) queues—a linked list is not directly provided in BASIC, but may be simulated with arrays. Links are values that allow the data in arrays to be manipulated in orders other than that specified by the natural ordering of the subscripts.

■ A line editor allows the user to enter, delete, or change one line at a time. A "screen-oriented" editor allows the user to move the cursor freely around in text displayed on the screen, making changes at the cursor's position. Such editors must be written in terms of the characteristics of each specific computer screen.

10.7 Problems and Programming Projects

1. See if you can identify any programs from Part I of this book as candidates for being extended by making them menu-driven. [*Hint*: Extending a quiz to handle several subject areas is one application that lends itself to a menu-type structure.]

2. See if you can combine some of the programs from Part I into a single menu-driven program, where each part of the menu serves to demonstrate a group of related features of BASIC to a new student of programming.

3. Modify the program KEYCIPH so that it uses the "one-time-pad" system described in step 1. Use the RND function to generate as many key numbers as there are characters in the message. Also allow use of the full set of printable characters with codes from 32 to 126. When an enciphered code becomes greater than 126, subtract a suitable number. This gives you a modular arithmetic, which is exactly the same idea as used on the old "secret-decoder" rings.

4. Notice that LEDIT1 has provision for additional commands. Add as many of these as you can, giving them whatever interpretation you wish. [Example: "Restructure" could be interpreted as a command that means "Redistribute the words of one paragraph so that the lines are all approximately equal in length."]

## CHAPTER ELEVEN

Business Applications; Using Sequential Files in BASIC

NEW TOPICS INTRODUCED IN CHAPTER 11

- Data processing
- Amortization tables
- Disk files
- OPEN
- EOF
- INPUT #

- Loan calculations
- The exponentiation operator
- Sequential files
- CLOSE
- PRINT #

11.1 Computers Mean Business: Formulas, Loans, and Mortgages

One of the largest areas of application for computers is business data processing. As the phrase implies, this encompasses applications that use computers to process the huge amounts of data—both numerical and textual—needed to run a business today.

We've already seen one facet of business data processing: word processing. Although this is an area of great interest to individuals who own personal computers, it is also at the heart of correspondence and form-generating activities in the business world.

The numerical side of data processing may also involve word processing, since it is frequently desirable to produce *output* reports that include both text and numbers. These numbers are generated by formulas that are part of the data-*processing* activity. The formulas must, in turn, be supplied with *input* data before they can produce their results. The three key words just mentioned—*input, processing, output*—are, in fact, at the heart of all data processing.

In this section we'll illustrate this idea with a set of three programs that help the user analyze the costs of taking out a loan with *add-on interest,* with interest on a *declining balance,* and with interest calculated using *amortization* formulas. (This last method is important to anyone who is shopping for a mortgage on a house.) These programs can be described in terms of their input, processing, and output, as shown in Table 11.1.

TABLE 11.1 Cost of Taking Out a Loan

	Input	Processing	Output
Loan with add-on interest	Amount borrowed Time period Interest rate	Uses formula for add-on interest	Equalized monthly payments
Loan with interest on declining balance	Amount borrowed Time period Interest rate	Uses formula for declining-balance interest	Chart of declining monthly payments
Loan based on equal amortized payments	Amount borrowed Time period Interest rate	Uses exponential amortization formula	Chart of equal monthly payments, showing portions for interest and equity

Let us now look at three BASIC programs, corresponding to the data-processing flow in each row of this table.

ADDON: Calculates Cost of Add-on Interest

This program can be designed with pseudocode as follows.

1. Get input: principal P, months M, interest rate R.

2. Process data: R = R∗.01, total interest TI = P∗M∗R/12.

3. Print output: M, P, TI/M, (P + TI)/M, TI, P + TI.

4. Ask if person wants to use program again. If Yes, go to 1; otherwise end the program.

Here's a listing based on this design, together with a sample run.

```
200 ´********************************************************
205 ´*                        ADDON                         *
210 ´********************************************************
215 CLS: A$=" "
220 PRINT"* INSTALLMENT PAYMENTS WITH ADD-ON INTEREST *"
225 ´----------GET INPUT------------------------------------
230 PRINT"AMOUNT BORROWED (PRINCIPAL)";: INPUT P
235 PRINT"NUMBER OF MONTHS TO PAY";: INPUT M
240 IF M <= 0 OR INT(M) <> M THEN 235
245 PRINT"INTEREST RATE PER YEAR (6.5% = 6.5)";: INPUT R
250 ´----------CALCULATE------------------------------------
255 R = R * .01
260 TI = P * M * R / 12                 ´TOTAL INTEREST
265 ´----------PRINT REPORT---------------------------------
270 PRINT
275 PRINT"MONTHS", "PRINCIPAL", "INTEREST", "MONTHLY"
280 PRINT"TO PAY",,               "PER MO.", "PAYMENT"
285 FOR K = 1 TO 60: PRINT"-";: NEXT K: PRINT
290 F1$ ="  ##        $###,###.##      $###,###.##         $###,###.##"
295 PRINT USING F1$; M, P, TI/M, (P+TI)/M
300 PRINT
305 PRINT,,"TOTAL","TOTAL AMOUNT"
310 PRINT,,"INTEREST","PAID BACK"
315 FOR K = 1 TO 60: PRINT"-";: NEXT K: PRINT
320 F2$ ="$###,###.##        $###,###.##"
325 PRINT TAB(29);: PRINT USING F2$; TI, P+TI
330 ´----------AGAIN?---------------------------------------
335 PRINT"AGAIN (Y = YES)";: INPUT A$: IF A$ ="Y" THEN 215
```

```
RUN
* INSTALLMENT PAYMENTS WITH ADD-ON INTEREST *
AMOUNT BORROWED (PRINCIPAL)? 50000
NUMBER OF MONTHS TO PAY? 36
INTEREST RATE PER YEAR (6.5% = 6.5)? 12.75
```

MONTHS TO PAY	PRINCIPAL	INTEREST PER MO.	MONTHLY PAYMENT
36	$ 50,000.00	$ 531.25	$ 1,920.14

		TOTAL INTEREST	TOTAL AMOUNT PAID BACK
		$ 19,125.00	$ 69,125.00

```
AGAIN (Y = YES)? N
Ok
```

In line 215, CLS clears the screen of the video display. This command works on the IBM PC and Radio Shack TRS-80 computers. On the Apple, use HOME. On other machines, you may have to omit this command. Making A$ a blank lets you press ENTER to mean No in response to the input statement in line 335. On some systems, if you have previously input a Y into A$, later pressing ENTER or RETURN will not change this.

In line 260, the total interest is calculated. Since the interest rate is given for one year but the period of the loan is in months, not years, the interest rate R is divided by 12. The quantity R/12 is often called the *monthly interest rate*. The remainder of the calculations are pretty straightforward.

DBINT: Calculates Cost of Declining-balance Interest

The add-on interest method of paying for "renting" money is usually not used on large loans. Instead, interest is charged only on the unpaid balance of the principal. So if two lending institutions quote the same interest rate, but one uses the add-on method and the other the declining-balance method, you will pay much less interest if you use the second method.

Here's a list and run of DBINT.

```
400 '*************************************************
405 '*                    DBINT                      *
410 '*************************************************
415 CLS: A$=" "
420 PRINT"* INSTALLMENT PAYMENTS WITH INT. ON UNPAID BAL. *"
425 '----------GET INPUT----------------------------------
430 PRINT"AMOUNT BORROWED (PRINCIPAL)";: INPUT P
435 PRINT"NUMBER OF MONTHS TO PAY";: INPUT M
440 IF M <= 0 OR INT(M) <> M THEN 435
445 PRINT"INTEREST RATE PER YEAR (6.5% = 6.5)";: INPUT R
450 '----------CALCULATE FIXED QUANTITIES----------------
455 R = R * .01
460 P1 = P/M
465 '----------CALCULATE & PRINT TABLE------------------
470 TI = 0: TP = 0: SP = 0
475 PRINT"MONTH    PRINCIPAL    INTEREST  +  PRINCIPAL  =  MONTHLY"
480 PRINT"NUMBER    OWED        PAYMENT      PAYMENT       PAYMENT"
485 FOR K = 1 TO 60: PRINT"-";: NEXT K: PRINT
490 F3$ =" ##    $###,###.##    $#,###.##    $#,###.##    $#,###.##"
```

(continued)

```
495 FOR J = 1 TO M
500    I1 = P * R / 12
505    PRINT USING F3$; J, P, I1, P1, P1+I1
510    TI = TI + I1
515    TP = TP + P1 + I1
520    SP = SP + P1
525    P = P - P1
527    IF J=M THEN 545
530    IF J/12=INT(J/12) THEN PRINT"--CONTINUE (Y/N)";:INPUT D$ ELSE GOTO 540
535        IF D$ = "N" THEN 545
540 NEXT J: J=J-1
545 PRINT"PRESS <RET> TO SEE TOTALS AFTER";J;"MONTHS--READY";:INPUT D$
550 '----------SUMMARY------------------------------------
555 PRINT TAB(21);"TOTAL          TOTAL          TOTAL"
560 PRINT TAB(21);"INTEREST       PRINCIPAL      PAYMENTS"
565 FOR K = 1 TO 60: PRINT"-";: NEXT K: PRINT
570 F4$ ="$##,###.##      $###,###.##      $###,###.##"
575 PRINT TAB(19);:PRINT USING F4$; TI, SP, TP
580 '----------AGAIN?------------------------------------
585 PRINT"AGAIN (Y = YES)";: INPUT A$: IF A$="Y" THEN 415
RUN
* INSTALLMENT PAYMENTS WITH INT. ON UNPAID BAL. *
AMOUNT BORROWED (PRINCIPAL)? 50000
NUMBER OF MONTHS TO PAY? 360
INTEREST RATE PER YEAR (6.5% = 6.5)? 12.75
```

MONTH NUMBER	PRINCIPAL OWED	INTEREST PAYMENT	+	PRINCIPAL PAYMENT	=	MONTHLY PAYMENT
1	$ 50,000.00	$ 531.25		$ 138.89		$ 670.14
2	$ 49,861.11	$ 529.77		$ 138.89		$ 668.66
3	$ 49,722.22	$ 528.30		$ 138.89		$ 667.19
4	$ 49,583.33	$ 526.82		$ 138.89		$ 665.71
5	$ 49,444.44	$ 525.35		$ 138.89		$ 664.24
6	$ 49,305.55	$ 523.87		$ 138.89		$ 662.76
7	$ 49,166.66	$ 522.40		$ 138.89		$ 661.28
8	$ 49,027.77	$ 520.92		$ 138.89		$ 659.81
9	$ 48,888.88	$ 519.44		$ 138.89		$ 658.33
10	$ 48,749.99	$ 517.97		$ 138.89		$ 656.86
11	$ 48,611.10	$ 516.49		$ 138.89		$ 655.38
12	$ 48,472.21	$ 515.02		$ 138.89		$ 653.91

--CONTINUE (Y/N)? Y

13	$ 48,333.32	$ 513.54		$ 138.89		$ 652.43
14	$ 48,194.42	$ 512.07		$ 138.89		$ 650.95
15	$ 48,055.53	$ 510.59		$ 138.89		$ 649.48
16	$ 47,916.64	$ 509.11		$ 138.89		$ 648.00
17	$ 47,777.75	$ 507.64		$ 138.89		$ 646.53
18	$ 47,638.86	$ 506.16		$ 138.89		$ 645.05
19	$ 47,499.97	$ 504.69		$ 138.89		$ 643.58
20	$ 47,361.08	$ 503.21		$ 138.89		$ 642.10
21	$ 47,222.19	$ 501.74		$ 138.89		$ 640.62
22	$ 47,083.30	$ 500.26		$ 138.89		$ 639.15
23	$ 46,944.41	$ 498.78		$ 138.89		$ 637.67
24	$ 46,805.52	$ 497.31		$ 138.89		$ 636.20

--CONTINUE (Y/N)? Y

25	$ 46,666.63	$ 495.83		$ 138.89		$ 634.72
26	$ 46,527.74	$ 494.36		$ 138.89		$ 633.25
27	$ 46,388.85	$ 492.88		$ 138.89		$ 631.77
28	$ 46,249.96	$ 491.41		$ 138.89		$ 630.29
29	$ 46,111.07	$ 489.93		$ 138.89		$ 628.82
30	$ 45,972.17	$ 488.45		$ 138.89		$ 627.34
31	$ 45,833.28	$ 486.98		$ 138.89		$ 625.87
32	$ 45,694.39	$ 485.50		$ 138.89		$ 624.39
33	$ 45,555.50	$ 484.03		$ 138.89		$ 622.92
34	$ 45,416.61	$ 482.55		$ 138.89		$ 621.44
35	$ 45,277.72	$ 481.08		$ 138.89		$ 619.96
36	$ 45,138.83	$ 479.60		$ 138.89		$ 618.49

--CONTINUE (Y/N)? N

```
PRESS <RET> TO SEE TOTALS AFTER 36 MONTHS--READY?
                  TOTAL            TOTAL            TOTAL
                  INTEREST         PRINCIPAL        PAYMENTS
-----------------------------------------------------------
                  $18,195.30    $  5,000.00    $ 23,195.29
AGAIN (Y = YES)? N
Ok
```

EXERCISE

11.1 Check the ads in your local newspaper for merchandise sold on credit (for example, a TV set for "only $49.95 per month"). Can you tell from the ad what your total payment will be? If not, what added information is needed? How can you tell whether add-on interest is being charged?

LAB EXERCISE 11.1 **File Name: INTEREST**

Enter ADDON into your computer, and save it on tape or disk. Then do the same for DBINT (don't forget to first type NEW). Now use these programs to compare the monthly cost of buying an appliance on credit under each system. Make the comparison for 12, 24, 36, 48, and 60 months.

MORTGAGE: Calculates Equal Mortgage Payments

This program prints out information similar to DBINT, but with a new wrinkle added. Sometimes there is an advantage to having all the payments of a loan be equal, even though interest is being paid on the unpaid balance. This is called an *amortized payment schedule* or an *amortization table*.

An exponential formula is used to calculate the equal monthly payments. Interest is then calculated on the unpaid balance each month, and the principal payment is what is left when this interest payment is subtracted from the monthly payment. The equal-payment formula is found in line 660. It uses the mathematical operation of *exponentiation,* that is, raising to a power. The expression $(1 + R)^M$ means "raise $1 + R$ to the Mth power." Why do this? The answer is a bit complicated. For our purposes, it will be simplest to take the word of the mathematicians who tell us it works (it does). Incidentally, some printers don't have the "^" exponentiation symbol, so they use "]" instead.

Here's a listing and run of MORTGAGE.

```
600 '**************************************************
605 '*                    MORTGAGE                    *
610 '**************************************************
615 CLS: A$=" "
620 PRINT"* AMORTIZATION TABLE *"
625 '----------GET INPUT----------------------------
630 PRINT"AMOUNT BORROWED (PRINCIPAL)";: INPUT P
635 PRINT"NUMBER OF MONTHS TO PAY";: INPUT M
640 IF M <= 0 OR INT(M) <> M THEN 635
645 PRINT"INTEREST RATE PER YEAR (6.5% = 6.5)";: INPUT R
650 '----------CALCULATE FIXED QUANTITIES------------
655 R = R * .01 / 12
660 E = (P * R * (1 + R)^M) / ((1 + R)^M-1)
665 '----------CALCULATE & PRINT TABLE--------------
670 TI = 0: TP = 0: SP = 0
675 PRINT"MONTH   PRINCIPAL    INTEREST   +   PRINCIPAL   =   MONTHLY"
680 PRINT"NUMBER  OWED         PAYMENT        PAYMENT         PAYMENT"
685 FOR K = 1 TO 60: PRINT"-";: NEXT K: PRINT
690 F3$=" ##   $###,###.##    $#,###.##      $#,###.##       $#,###.##"
```

(continued)

```
695 FOR J = 1 TO M
700    Il = P * R
705    Pl = E - Il
710    IF J = M THEN Pl = P: Il = E - Pl
715    PRINT USING F3$; J, P, Il, Pl, E
720    TI = TI + Il
725    TP = TP + Pl + Il
730    SP = SP + Pl
735    P = P - Pl
737 IF J=M THEN 755
740    IF J/12=INT(J/12) THEN PRINT"--CONTINUE (Y/N)";:INPUT D$ ELSE GOTO 750
745      IF D$ = "N" THEN 755
750 NEXT J : J=J-1
755 PRINT"PRESS <RET> TO SEE TOTALS FOR";J;"MONTHS--READY";: INPUT D$
760 ´----------SUMMARY-----------------------------------
765 PRINT TAB(21);"TOTAL              TOTAL              TOTAL"
770 PRINT TAB(21);"INTEREST         PRINCIPAL         PAYMENTS"
775 FOR K = 1 TO 60: PRINT"-";: NEXT K: PRINT
780 F4$="$##,###.##      $###,###.##      $###,###.##"
785 PRINT TAB(19);: PRINT USING F4$; TI, SP, TP
790 ´----------AGAIN?---------------------------------
795 PRINT"AGAIN (Y = YES)";: INPUT A$: IF A$="Y" THEN 615
RUN
* AMORTIZATION TABLE *
AMOUNT BORROWED (PRINCIPAL)? 50000
NUMBER OF MONTHS TO PAY? 360
INTEREST RATE PER YEAR (6.5% = 6.5)? 12.75
MONTH    PRINCIPAL      INTEREST   +   PRINCIPAL   =   MONTHLY
NUMBER   OWED           PAYMENT        PAYMENT         PAYMENT
------------------------------------------------------------
   1   $ 50,000.00    $  531.25    $    12.10    $   543.35
   2   $ 49,987.90    $  531.12    $    12.23    $   543.35
   3   $ 49,975.68    $  530.99    $    12.36    $   543.35
   4   $ 49,963.32    $  530.86    $    12.49    $   543.35
   5   $ 49,950.83    $  530.73    $    12.62    $   543.35
   6   $ 49,938.21    $  530.59    $    12.75    $   543.35
   7   $ 49,925.46    $  530.46    $    12.89    $   543.35
   8   $ 49,912.57    $  530.32    $    13.03    $   543.35
   9   $ 49,899.55    $  530.18    $    13.16    $   543.35
  10   $ 49,886.38    $  530.04    $    13.30    $   543.35
  11   $ 49,873.08    $  529.90    $    13.45    $   543.35
  12   $ 49,859.63    $  529.76    $    13.59    $   543.35
--CONTINUE (Y/N)? Y
  13   $ 49,846.04    $  529.61    $    13.73    $   543.35
  14   $ 49,832.31    $  529.47    $    13.88    $   543.35
  15   $ 49,818.43    $  529.32    $    14.03    $   543.35
  16   $ 49,804.40    $  529.17    $    14.17    $   543.35
  17   $ 49,790.23    $  529.02    $    14.33    $   543.35
  18   $ 49,775.90    $  528.87    $    14.48    $   543.35
  19   $ 49,761.42    $  528.72    $    14.63    $   543.35
  20   $ 49,746.79    $  528.56    $    14.79    $   543.35
  21   $ 49,732.00    $  528.40    $    14.94    $   543.35
  22   $ 49,717.06    $  528.24    $    15.10    $   543.35
  23   $ 49,701.96    $  528.08    $    15.26    $   543.35
  24   $ 49,686.69    $  527.92    $    15.43    $   543.35
--CONTINUE (Y/N)? Y
  25   $ 49,671.26    $  527.76    $    15.59    $   543.35
  26   $ 49,655.67    $  527.59    $    15.76    $   543.35
  27   $ 49,639.92    $  527.42    $    15.92    $   543.35
  28   $ 49,623.99    $  527.25    $    16.09    $   543.35
  29   $ 49,607.90    $  527.08    $    16.26    $   543.35
  30   $ 49,591.64    $  526.91    $    16.44    $   543.35
  31   $ 49,575.20    $  526.74    $    16.61    $   543.35
  32   $ 49,558.59    $  526.56    $    16.79    $   543.35
  33   $ 49,541.80    $  526.38    $    16.97    $   543.35
  34   $ 49,524.83    $  526.20    $    17.15    $   543.35
  35   $ 49,507.69    $  526.02    $    17.33    $   543.35
  36   $ 49,490.36    $  525.84    $    17.51    $   543.35
```

```
--CONTINUE (Y/N)? N
PRESS <RET> TO SEE TOTALS FOR 36 MONTHS--READY?
                      TOTAL            TOTAL          TOTAL
                      INTEREST         PRINCIPAL      PAYMENTS
----------------------------------------------------------------
                      $19,033.36    $    527.13    $ 19,560.48
AGAIN (Y = YES)? N
Ok
```

EXERCISE

11.2 Study the output of the run of MORTGAGE just shown. Notice that at the end of three years (36 months), only $527 of the total $19,560 paid has actually been used to pay off the loan. What can you conclude about 30-year (360-month) mortgages?

LAB EXERCISE 11.2 **File Name: MORT2**

Enter and save the program MORTGAGE. Run it completely to see the payments for all 360 months. How long does it take before half the original loan is paid off? Does this "halfway" point change with different principals or different interest rates?

11.2 Computer Data Files

Many professionals like to refer to computers as *data-crunching machines*. The "crunching" is what we earlier called data processing. The three loan programs of Section 11.1 illustrate this idea nicely. You feed them data about loans, and they then crunch it around to give you back data about the payments you owe each month. Even word-processing programs crunch data. For input they take the words (text) you enter, along with the commands you give to delete or change those words. For output they give back data in the form of words, this time all spruced up according to your editing commands.

For most of the programs in this book, data items are input from the keyboard, and output is sent to either a video monitor or a printer. The main exception we've had so far was the case in which the READ and DATA statements were used to input data (as discussed in Chapter 5). However, it's also possible to input/output data from/to magnetic disks or magnetic tapes. When this is done, the collection of data on the disk or tape is called a computer data file. On most computers used today, files are stored on disks, so you'll also see them referred to as disk data files.

If you are able to use magnetic disks on your computer system, you can now picture the data input/output options open to you in writing programs, as shown in Figure 11.1.

In the remaining sections of this chapter, we'll show you how to use the disk-file features of extended BASIC. These allow you to *write* (that is, *output*) data onto disks, or to *read* (that is, *input*) data from disks.

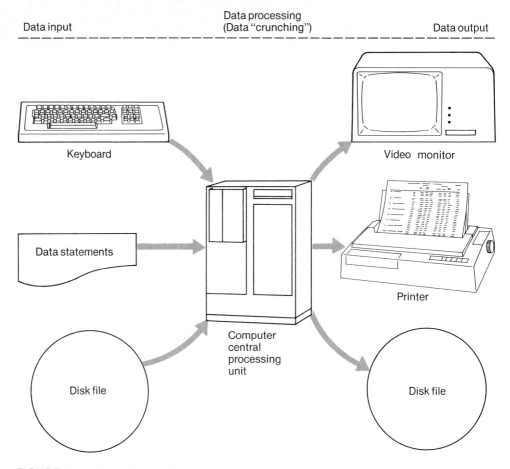

Data input   Data processing   Data output
                    (Data "crunching")

Keyboard

Data statements

Computer
central
processing
unit

Disk file

Video monitor

Printer

Disk file

FIGURE 11.1   Input/output options

Variations in the Disk-File Features of BASIC

TANDY

Radio Shack

IBM

APPLE

DIGITAL

Unfortunately, the disk-file features of BASIC are not standardized. We'll show most of our examples in terms of Microsoft BASIC, which is the same as Level II BASIC and GW-BASIC on Tandy/Radio Shack computers, BASICA on IBM PCs, or MBASIC and GBASIC on CP/M systems such as the Apple II fitted with a CP/M card. For examples of using files on an Apple II using Applesoft BASIC, consult the book *A Bit of Applesoft BASIC,* by M. Critchfield [Addison-Wesley, 1985]. For other machines, you'll have to refer to the instruction manual that accompanies the machine. Appendix C of this book shows file examples written in Applesoft BASIC and BASIC PLUS (Digital Equipment Co.).

Sequential Disk Files: Advantages and Disadvantages

There are two kinds of disk files: sequential files and random-access (also called direct-access) files. We'll start with sequential files because anyone who has used the regular input and print statements of BASIC is already familiar with the ideas behind sequential files.

To begin with, a *file* is a collection of related chunks of information; each chunk is called a record. A familiar example of a file is a collection of addresses kept in a small box on 3x5 file cards. Each card is a *record*. Each record, in turn, is broken into *fields* (Name, Street, City, State, Zip).

If you use a computer for this application, you enter the information into a mailing-list program from the keyboard. To save this information, you can then store it on disk. Later on, you can display it on a video screen or printer as needed. Thus Figure 11.2 shows four forms of exactly the same file idea.

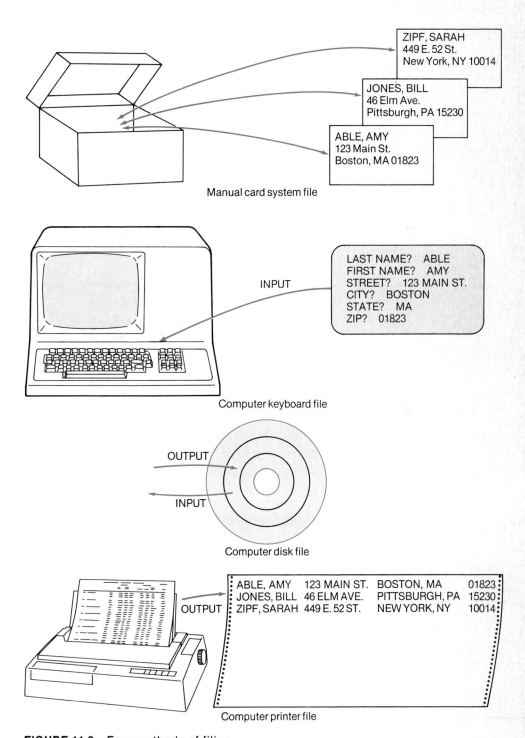

ZIPF, SARAH
449 E. 52 St.
New York, NY 10014

JONES, BILL
46 Elm Ave.
Pittsburgh, PA 15230

ABLE, AMY
123 Main St.
Boston, MA 01823

Manual card system file

INPUT

LAST NAME?   ABLE
FIRST NAME?   AMY
STREET?   123 MAIN ST.
CITY?   BOSTON
STATE?   MA
ZIP?   01823

Computer keyboard file

OUTPUT

INPUT

Computer disk file

OUTPUT

ABLE, AMY   123 MAIN ST.   BOSTON, MA   01823
JONES, BILL   46 ELM AVE.   PITTSBURGH, PA   15230
ZIPF, SARAH   449 E. 52 ST.   NEW YORK, NY   10014

Computer printer file

FIGURE 11.2   Four methods of filing

The reason these can all be called *sequential* files is that the data items go in (or out) in sequence. When you input

123 Main Street

at a keyboard, you first type the 1, then the 2, then the 3, then space, then M, then a, and so on. For output the computer also sends characters to a video display or printer in sequence. Exactly the same idea holds for sequential disk files. These can be used for either input or output (although not at the same time), provided data items go in or out of the files in strict sequence. Further, you must *always* start at the beginning of the file, and work your way forward. This can sometimes be an annoying restriction. It's as though there were a law that said that no matter what name you wanted in a phone book, you *always* had to start looking at the beginning of page 1, moving ahead one name at a time.

This "start at the beginning and go in sequence" restriction will be removed in the next chapter, when we discuss random-access files. However, for many applications, sequential files work just fine, and they have the virtue of simplicity. In fact, you write to (output) or read from (input) sequential files with words like PRINT #1 and INPUT #1 (which are obviously extensions of the familiar words PRINT and INPUT).

11.3   Using Sequential Files in BASIC

The next program (SEQDEMO) shows how to use the sequential-file features of Microsoft BASIC. The program uses INPUT to accept a sequence of product codes, names, and prices from the keyboard, storing the values in the memory variables C$, N$, and P. It then uses PRINT #1 to write each triple (code, name, price) as one record in a sequential file. Next it uses INPUT #1 to read the data from this file back into memory, using PRINT to display each record on the computer's output device.

In addition to INPUT #1 and PRINT#1, you need two more new statements to use sequential files: OPEN and CLOSE. The statement

```
OPEN "O",#1, FL$
```

means open for Output on channel #1 the file having the name FL$. Similarly,

```
OPEN "I",#6, F3$
```

means open for Input on channel #6 the file with the name stored in F3$. Instead of FL$ or F3$, you could use a fixed file name in quotes (like "GROCERY" or "GDATA").

File names are invented by the user, and are limited to eight characters on most systems. However, *inside* the program, files are referred to by an integer channel number (usually from 1 to 15) that the user also chooses. It's something like deciding that instead of always spelling out the full name of a TV station like WOPR-TV, you'll just refer to it by a simple channel number like 1, or 4, or 8.

When you're finished using a file (say the one opened on channel #1), you use the statement

```
CLOSE 1
```

to disconnect the file with the name in FL$ from channel 1, making that number available for other use. Similarly, CLOSE 6 would disconnect the file with the name stored in F3$ from channel 6.

Here's how all these ideas go together in a BASIC program called SEQDEMO.

```
100 ´--------------------------------------------------
101 ´  SEQDEMO (PROGRAM TO CREATE AND ECHO SEQ FILES)
102 ´--------------------------------------------------
110 INPUT "FILE NAME >>>>>>";FL$
120 OPEN "O",1,FL$: NR=1
125 PRINT "ENTER DATA FOR FILE.  TYPE -1 TO QUIT"
130 PRINT "RECORD #";NR;
135   PRINT TAB(12);"PRODUCT CODE >>>";:INPUT C$
137   IF C$="-1" THEN 170
140   PRINT TAB(12);"PRODUCT NAME >>>";:INPUT N$
142   IF N$="-1" THEN 170
145   PRINT TAB(12);"PRICE >>>>>>>>>>";:INPUT P
147   IF P<0 THEN 170
150   PRINT #1, C$;",";N$;",";P
160   NR=NR+1: GOTO 130
170 CLOSE 1: PRINT
175 ´
176 ´-------------------------------------------------
180 PRINT"FILE CHECK: HERE´S DATA ON FILE ";FL$
190 OPEN "I",1,FL$: PRINT: K=0
200 IF EOF(1) THEN 235
210   INPUT #1,M$,Z$,D
220   PRINT USING"\        \ \                \ ##.##";M$,Z$,D
230   K=K+1: GOTO 200
235 PRINT: PRINT "**";K;"RCDS ON FILE **"
240 CLOSE 1: PRINT"** END OF PROGRAM **"
```

```
RUN
FILE NAME >>>>>>? PETSTORE
ENTER DATA FOR FILE.  TYPE -1 TO QUIT
RECORD # 1 PRODUCT CODE >>>? 00024
           PRODUCT NAME >>>? 6´ DOG LEASH
           PRICE >>>>>>>>>>? 12.95
RECORD # 2 PRODUCT CODE >>>? 00078
           PRODUCT NAME >>>? SIZE 16 DOG COLLAR
           PRICE >>>>>>>>>>? 5.95
RECORD # 3 PRODUCT CODE >>>? 00056
           PRODUCT NAME >>>? LARGE RAWHIDE BONE
           PRICE >>>>>>>>>>? 8.95
RECORD # 4 PRODUCT CODE >>>? -1

FILE CHECK: HERE´S DATA ON FILE PETSTORE

00024      6´ DOG LEASH         12.95
00078      SIZE 16 DOG COLLAR    5.95
00056      LARGE RAWHIDE BONE    8.95

** 3 RCDS ON FILE **
** END OF PROGRAM **
Ok
```

EXERCISE

11.3   The program SEQDEMO uses a −1 as a signal that the user is finished entering data. What other special signals might be useful? [*Hint:* Suppose you notice that you have made an error in your input for product code *after* it has been entered. How could you ask for a chance to redo the entire record?]

LAB EXERCISE 11.3   File Name: SEQDEMO2

Enter and save SEQDEMO on your computer system. Try it out for a variety of data. Then see if you can modify the code to allow the "redo" feature suggested in Exercise 11.3.

How SEQDEMO Works

Line 110 gets a file name from the user. Line 120 then opens that file for output on channel #1. (The # sign can be omitted from channel numbers in OPEN and CLOSE statements.) Data items are then gathered from the user in lines 135, 140, and 145, and stored in the variables C$, N$, and P.

Line 150 is where the data items in C$, N$, and P are written sequentially onto the file. Notice that you must also write commas (",") on the file to separate the fields of each record. Line 160 increases the "next record" counter NR, and loops back to line 130 to get data for another record. When the user signals "quit" by typing −1, the file is closed in line 170.

To read the file just created, line 190 opens it for input on channel 1. Line 200 uses the EOF(1) function to see if we're at the *end of file*. If not, line 210 reads the three fields of one record into the variables M$, Z$, and D. The contents of these variables are then printed in line 220. In line 230, the counter K is incremented, and the program loops back to line 200 to see if another record can be read. When the end of file is finally reached, the program goes to line 235, prints the number of records found, and closes the file.

11.4   Adding Data to the End of a Sequential File

As long as a sequential file is open for output, you can continue to write records on it. Each new record is added at the end of the file. However, once you close the file, if you open it again for output, new data items are written at the *beginning* of the file, erasing the old data.

To get around this problem, you can use the following technique.

1. Open the old file (say "OLD") for input.

    ```
    OPEN "I", #1, "OLD"
    ```

2. Open a temporary file "TEMP" for output, using a different channel.

    ```
    OPEN "O", #2, "TEMP"
    ```

3. Read one record from "OLD" (INPUT #1, and so forth).

4. Write it to "TEMP" (PRINT #2, and so forth).

5. Repeat steps 3 and 4 until you reach the end of the file "OLD".

6. Now write the new data to "TEMP". Since you didn't close "TEMP", these data items are added *after* the old data.

7. When finished, close both files:

```
CLOSE 1 : CLOSE 2
```

8. Get rid of OLD with

```
KILL "OLD"
```

9. Change the name of TEMP to OLD:

```
NAME "TEMP" AS "OLD"
```

The file "OLD" now contains both the old and the newly added data.

IBM

► *Note:* The newer versions of Microsoft BASIC (for example, BASICA on the IBM PC) have a special OPEN statement that lets you append data at the end of a sequential file without any of the above machinations. For a file with name FL$ = "OLD", you simply use the statement

```
OPEN "OLD" FOR APPEND AS #1   or   OPEN FL$ FOR APPEND AS #1
```

Then when you use PRINT #1 (or WRITE#1), data items are automatically appended at the end of the file OLD.

APPLE

Applesoft BASIC has a similar facility for appending to the end of files. The code is the following:

```
PRINT CHR$(4); "APPEND OLD"  or  PRINT CHR$(4); "APPEND"; FL$
```

Appendix C gives further information about Applesoft sequential files.

11.5 Summary of Chapter 11

■ Business data processing encompasses such tasks as word processing, cost projection, accounting, record keeping, and calculations needed to carry out specific tasks. This last category includes the calculation of payments on loans at various rates, for various time periods, and under various assumptions about paying off principal.

■ Most data-processing programs are based on the simple structure: (1) get the input, (2) process the data, (3) print the output.

■ Payments on a loan with add-on interest are calculated using the formulas:

Total interest = principal*months*monthly interest rate
Payment = (principal + total interest)/months

■ Payments on a loan with interest on the declining balance are calculated using the formulas:

Interest in any month = remaining principal*monthly interest rate
Payment = interest + principal/months

■ Payments on a loan with amortized payments are calculated using the following formula (where M = number of months and R = monthly rate).

$$\text{Equal monthly payment} = \frac{\text{Principal} * R * (1 + R)^M}{(1 + R)^M - 1}$$

- Business programs commonly use input from and send output to disks or tapes. A collection of data on disk or tape is called a file.

- The information about disk files given in Chapter 11 holds for most micro-computers. Users of Applesoft BASIC or BASIC PLUS should consult Appendix C.

- A file is a collection of related information, each unit of which is called a record. Each record, in turn is broken into fields. In an address file, for example, each address is a record. The fields might be name, street, city and state, and zip code.

- Two kinds of disk file available on computers are sequential files and random- (also called direct-) access files.

- Sequential files are so named because they must be read from (or written to) starting at the beginning and proceeding in sequence. Random-access files allow one to gain access to records by using record number, no matter where a given record is stored in the file.

- The statements required to begin communication with a sequential disk file are:

      <ln> OPEN "O" #<n>, <filename> or
      <ln> OPEN "I" #<n>, <filename>

      ```
      100 OPEN "O", #1, "DATA1"
      100 OPEN "I", #2, FL$
      ```

  These mean "open for output on channel 1, the disk file named DATA1," and "open for input on channel 2, the disk file named FL$." The program then refers to these files by the specified channel numbers.

- The statement: <ln> CLOSE <n> disconnects channel n, and terminates input or output to the file opened on this channel.

- To write to a sequential file, you use the statement:

      <ln> PRINT #<n>, <list of values or variables>

      ```
      150 PRINT #1, C$, ",";N$;",";P
      ```

- To read from a sequential file, you use the statement:

      ⟨ln⟩ INPUT #⟨n⟩, ⟨list of variables⟩

      ```
      210 INPUT #1, M$, Z$, D
      ```

- The function EOF (⟨n⟩) returns a value of True if the end of the file connected to channel n has been reached.

      ```
      200 IF EOF(1) THEN 235
      ```

- To add data to the end of a sequential file that already exists, do the following:

  1. Open the old file for input (to be read from)
  2. Open a new, temporary file and copy the contents of the old file onto the new file
  3. Add the new data to the new, temporary file
  4. Close both files
  5. Get rid of the old file
  6. Change the name of the temporary file to that of the old file

Some versions of BASIC simplify this process by giving the user a new key word APPEND, to be used in the alternative OPEN statement, as follows:

⟨1n⟩ OPEN ⟨filename⟩ FOR APPEND AS #⟨n⟩

```
100 OPEN FL$ FOR APPEND AS #1
```

11.6 Problems and Programming Projects

1. It would be handy to have the three programs ADDON, DBINT, and MORTGAGE as three options within one menu-driven program. Write such a combination program, using subroutines to handle common tasks.

2. Some financial institutions may offer an *adjustable-rate mortgage,* for which the rate of interest can be changed each year. The new rate is determined by some public "index" (for example, 2 percentage points higher than the latest Federal T-bill rate). Modify the program MORTGAGE so that it allows the user to input a new mortgage rate at the end of each 12-month period. Then recalculate the new monthly payment (E), using the remaining months for M and the remaining principal for P. Here's a sample of the kind of output you should get.

```
RUN
* AMORTIZATION TABLE *
AMOUNT BORROWED (PRINCIPAL)? 50000
NUMBER OF MONTHS TO PAY? 360
INTEREST RATE PER YEAR (6.5% = 6.5)? 10.5
```

MONTH NUMBER	PRINCIPAL OWED	INTEREST PAYMENT	+	PRINCIPAL PAYMENT	=	MONTHLY PAYMENT
1	$ 50,000.00	$ 437.50		$ 19.87		$ 457.37
2	$ 49,980.13	$ 437.33		$ 20.04		$ 457.37
3	$ 49,960.09	$ 437.15		$ 20.22		$ 457.37
4	$ 49,939.87	$ 436.97		$ 20.40		$ 457.37
5	$ 49,919.47	$ 436.80		$ 20.57		$ 457.37
6	$ 49,898.90	$ 436.62		$ 20.75		$ 457.37
7	$ 49,878.14	$ 436.43		$ 20.94		$ 457.37
8	$ 49,857.21	$ 436.25		$ 21.12		$ 457.37
9	$ 49,836.08	$ 436.07		$ 21.30		$ 457.37
10	$ 49,814.78	$ 435.88		$ 21.49		$ 457.37
11	$ 49,793.29	$ 435.69		$ 21.68		$ 457.37
12	$ 49,771.61	$ 435.50		$ 21.87		$ 457.37

```
MORE (Y/N)? Y
CURRENT RATE =  10.5
ENTER RATE FOR NEXT YEAR? 12.5
```

13	$ 49,749.74	$ 518.23		$ 14.46		$ 532.69
14	$ 49,735.27	$ 518.08		$ 14.62		$ 532.69
15	$ 49,720.65	$ 517.92		$ 14.77		$ 532.69
16	$ 49,705.89	$ 517.77		$ 14.92		$ 532.69
17	$ 49,690.96	$ 517.61		$ 15.08		$ 532.69
18	$ 49,675.89	$ 517.46		$ 15.23		$ 532.69
19	$ 49,660.65	$ 517.30		$ 15.39		$ 532.69
20	$ 49,645.26	$ 517.14		$ 15.55		$ 532.69
21	$ 49,629.70	$ 516.98		$ 15.72		$ 532.69
22	$ 49,613.99	$ 516.81		$ 15.88		$ 532.69
23	$ 49,598.11	$ 516.65		$ 16.04		$ 532.69
24	$ 49,582.07	$ 516.48		$ 16.21		$ 532.69

```
MORE (Y/N)? Y
```

(continued)

```
CURRENT RATE =  12.5
ENTER RATE FOR NEXT YEAR? 14.5
  25   $ 49,565.85     $   598.92       $   10.78       $   609.70
  26   $ 49,555.08     $   598.79       $   10.91       $   609.70
  27   $ 49,544.17     $   598.66       $   11.04       $   609.70
  28   $ 49,533.13     $   598.53       $   11.17       $   609.70
  29   $ 49,521.96     $   598.39       $   11.31       $   609.70
  30   $ 49,510.65     $   598.25       $   11.44       $   609.70
  31   $ 49,499.21     $   598.12       $   11.58       $   609.70
  32   $ 49,487.63     $   597.98       $   11.72       $   609.70
  33   $ 49,475.90     $   597.83       $   11.86       $   609.70
  34   $ 49,464.04     $   597.69       $   12.01       $   609.70
  35   $ 49,452.03     $   597.55       $   12.15       $   609.70
  36   $ 49,439.88     $   597.40       $   12.30       $   609.70
MORE (Y/N)? N
PRESS <RET> TO SEE TOTALS FOR 36 MONTHS?
                        TOTAL            TOTAL            TOTAL
                        INTEREST         PRINCIPAL        PAYMENTS
-----------------------------------------------------------------
                       $18,624.70     $    572.39      $ 19,197.09
AGAIN (Y = YES)? N
Ok
```

3. Modify the program SEQDEMO so that it uses the techniques shown in Section 11.4 to add new data to the end of a previously created file called ORIG. If there are already data items on ORIG, you must first open a temporary file TEMP for output. Then copy ORIG to TEMP. Next add the new data to the end of TEMP. Finally, close all files, kill the file ORIG, and rename TEMP to ORIG. Extra: How can your program automatically detect whether there really is an old file ORIG to be handled this way? [*Hint:* Study your BASIC manual to see if it has an ON ERROR statement. In this case, does trying to open a nonexistent file for input cause an error? If so, how can this fact be used to branch to a routine that uses TEMP as described above?]

## CHAPTER TWELVE

Random-Access Files

NEW TOPICS INTRODUCED IN CHAPTER 12

- *Random-access files*
- *LSET, RSET, MKS$,*
  CVS, MKI$, CVI
- *Editing data files*

- *OPEN, FIELD, LOF,*
  EOF, GET, PUT, CLOSE
- *Modular design of large file programs*
- *Program stubs*

12.1 Random (Direct) Access Files in BASIC

As was shown in Section 11.2, there are two forms of the OPEN statement used with sequential files. The first opens a sequential file for output, using the form

```
OPEN "O",#1, "TEMP"
```

The second opens a sequential file for input, using the form

```
OPEN "I",#2, "DATA"
```

There is a third form of OPEN that allows use of a much more flexible type of file called the **random-access** or **direct-access file.** When you want random-access files, you use the OPEN statement in the form

```
OPEN "R",1, "MAIL"
```

This opens a file called MAIL for random use on channel 1, and furthermore opens the file for both read and write operations. To see how this works, and why these files are called "random access," you have to understand some of the inner workings of how data transfer takes place when one is using random files.

The main idea behind random-access files is to allow you to move *any* one record from disk to user memory, and vice versa. The record is stored in a portion of memory called a disk I/O buffer. One of these buffers is associated with each channel number. On most systems, a buffer holds 128 bytes (which is the same as 128 characters). The BASIC key words GET and PUT are used to move data from disk to buffer and vice versa, while the key word OPEN is used to say *which* buffer will be used for a given file.

How PUT and GET Work

For example, suppose the file MEMO has six records stored on a disk. You decide to work on some of these records at random, using disk I/O buffer #1. So your program will need the BASIC statement

```
110 OPEN "R",#1, "MEMO"
```

The ''R'' means that this file will be used in random-access mode. You can now ask for any record, and in any order; you don't have to go through the records sequentially.

Figure 12.1 shows what happens when you transfer a record (for example, record 3) from disk and store it in buffer #1, and vice versa.

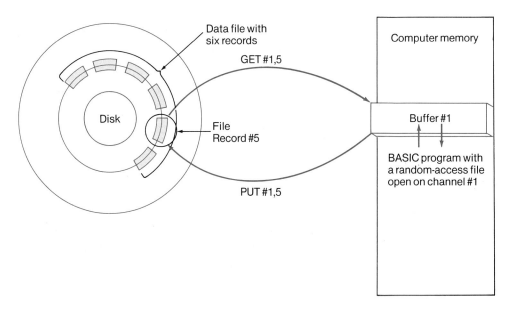

FIGURE 12.1

To make the transfer of record 3 from disk to memory, your program must use a statement like this:

```
310 GET #1,3
```

To reverse the operation, transferring what's in the buffer back to disk (presumably because you've made some changes in the data), your program needs a statement like this:

```
410 PUT #1,3
```

So far, so good. However, once the data items for the desired record have been moved into the buffer, the big question is: How does your program get at them? The answer is that you use the FIELD statement to set up *pointers* to the buffer. These look like names of string variables [such as A$, D$, KE(1)], but they're really just names for different positions in the buffer. For example,

```
210 FIELD 1, 10 AS A$, 30 AS B$, 4 AS C$
```

can be pictured as organizing the buffer as follows:

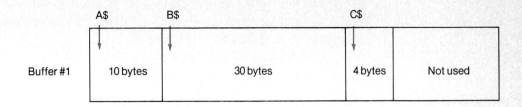

If you next use the statements

```
410 GET #1,3
420 PRINT A$,B$,C$
```

you will then see what's in the third record at the parts of the buffer these names point to, with 10, 30, and 4 bytes printed for A$, B$, AND C$, respectively.

The reverse procedure is a little trickier. For example, suppose you want to store a 10-character word, followed by a 50-character definition, followed by a 2-letter code, putting all three items on record #4 of the file DATA opened for use with buffer #1. To do this, you must first field the buffer, and then load it up with data by using LSET statements, as follows.

```
150 FIELD 1, 10 AS A$, 50 AS B$, 2 AS C$
160 LSET A$="FINIF"
170 LSET B$="SLANG FOR A FIVE-DOLLAR BILL"
180 LSET C$="XX"
190 PUT 1,4
```

LSET is a special *buffer-assignment statement* that must be used when placing data into a buffer. It means "left set," that is, place the leftmost part of the string given in each statement at the position specified by the FIELD statement, using exactly the number of bytes specified. If any bytes are unused, space characters (ASCII 32) are inserted as needed. If there aren't enough bytes fielded in the buffer, the string will be truncated—that is, chopped off—on the right.

Saving and Retrieving Numbers on Random Files

The use of the dollar sign ($) in names of buffer pointers is to remind you that information is usually stored on disk data files as sequences of characters. To store numbers, you must first make them look like a sequence of characters, using the special MKS$() and MKI$() "make into a string" functions. When these strings are later retrieved from disk, they are converted into numbers with the CVS() and CVI() functions. The S in these function names means "single-precision decimal number" (like 3.14159), while the I means "integer number" between −32,768 and 32,767, inclusive. It turns out that single-precision numbers require four bytes when stored as strings, while integer numbers take only two bytes. The next example illustrates the use of MKS$ AND CVS.

12.2   A Simple Example of Random Files

Here's an application that illustrates the use of random-access files in a program called RANDEMO. It allows a user to add new records to a random file, or edit records that already exist. The random-access feature is valuable, since it permits the user to retrieve any record at random, change it if desired, and then write it back on the file. As we'll see in Section 12.4, this makes it easy to *edit* the file, that is, make changes in any of its records.

RANDEMO is based on a simple menu structure, similar to that described in Chapter 10. The user makes choices corresponding to the three options presented in the menu section of the program (lines 350–400). The option chosen then causes the program to branch to the appropriate program module. The choices are to *add* data, *edit* data, or *quit* (end) the program.

The user can return to the menu from either the add module (lines 500–590) or the edit module (lines 600–890) by typing −1 in response to a request for data.

The program starts with a preliminary section (lines 130–240) that requests a file name from the user, opens the file on channel 1, and checks to see whether it is a new or an old file. It can do this because a new file has a length of zero given by the LOF(1) function. [LOF is a BASIC function that returns the length of the file.] If the file is new, the variable RCD is set to 1 (RCD is a variable we have chosen to mean the next available record number), and control then passes to the menu. If the file is an old one, the old data records are read from the file, displayed on the output device, and counted. The end-of-file function EOF(1) is used to test for end of data (line 200), and to cause the program to exit the loop. The highest record with actual data in it will then be RCD-1.

The user is "forced" by the menu to type in A, E, or Q, since line 400 will branch back to the prompt unless one of these commands is given. If Q is typed, the program is stopped in line 390 by the END statement. In most versions of BASIC, END also closes all open files, but it is a good habit to precede END with CLOSE, just in case.

The add module prompts the user for the data to be saved in the next available record (this is record number RCD). Three data items are needed for each record. Each input is tested to see if it is −1, in which case control is sent back to the menu section. Line 575 fills the buffer with the new data, while line 580 writes it to the file opened on channel 1 as record number RCD.

The edit module is a little more complicated. Line 600 anticipates that the user might by mistake try to edit a new (that is, empty) file. If this happens, control is sent back to the menu. If not, the user must type in the record number (R) to be edited. That record is read from the file in line 650, and displayed for the user, who can then decide whether to change it. The user is also allowed to change his or her mind and retype the new data, starting at line 810. When the new data is finally approved by the user, it is moved into the file buffer in line 870, and then written on top of the old record in line 875.

```
100 '-------------------------------------------------------
110 '   RANDEMO (PROGRAM TO CREATE AND EDIT RANDOM FILES)
120 '-------------------------------------------------------
130 INPUT "FILE NAME >>>";FL$
140 OPEN "R",1,FL$
150 FIELD 1, 10 AS B1$, 30 AS B2$, 4 AS B3$
160 IF LOF(1)=0 THEN PRINT"NEW FILE -- ";FL$: RCD=1: GOTO 350
170    PRINT"OLD FILE -- ";FL$
180    RCD=1
190    GET #1,RCD
200       IF EOF(1) THEN 240
210       PRINT "#";RCD;" ";B1$;" ";B2$;" ";CVS(B3$)
220       RCD=RCD+1
230       GOTO 190
240    PRINT"HIGHEST RECORD = ";RCD-1
```

```
340 '--- MAIN MENU ----------------------------------------
350 PRINT
355 PRINT"***  A)DD DATA, E)DIT DATA, OR Q)UIT  **"
360 PRINT"TYPE A, E, OR Q --";
365   A$="": INPUT A$
370   IF A$="A" THEN 500
380   IF A$="E" THEN 600
390   IF A$="Q" THEN CLOSE 1: END
400   GOTO 360
410 '--- ADD MODULE ---------------------------------------
500 PRINT: PRINT "ADD DATA TO FILE."
505 PRINT"TYPE -1 TO RETURN TO MENU."
510 PRINT "RECORD #";RCD;
520   PRINT TAB(12);"PRODUCT CODE >>>";:INPUT C$
530   IF C$="-1" THEN 350
540   PRINT TAB(12);"PRODUCT NAME >>>";:INPUT N$
550   IF N$="-1" THEN 350
560   PRINT TAB(12);"PRICE >>>>>>>>>>";:INPUT P
570   IF P<0 THEN 350
575     LSET B1$=C$: LSET B2$=N$: LSET B3$=MKS$(P)
580     PUT #1,RCD
585     RCD=RCD+1: GOTO 510
590 '--- EDIT MODULE --------------------------------------
600 IF RCD=1 THEN PRINT"NO DATA TO EDIT.": GOTO 500
610 PRINT: PRINT"ENTER RECORD # TO EDIT."
615   PRINT"TYPE -1 TO RETURN TO MENU."
620   INPUT R
630   IF R=>RCD THEN PRINT"TOO HIGH.": GOTO 610
640   IF R<0 THEN 350
650   GET #1, R
680   PRINT"#";R;" ";B1$;" ";B2$;" ";CVS(B3$)
690   PRINT"WANT TO CHANGE (Y/N)";
695   A$="": INPUT A$
700   IF A$="N" THEN 610
705   IF A$="-1" THEN 350
810   INPUT "NEW PRODUCT CODE --";C$
815     IF C$="-1" THEN 350
820     INPUT"NEW PRODUCT NAME --";N$
825     IF N$="-1" THEN 350
830     INPUT"       NEW PRICE --";P
835     IF P<0 THEN 350
836     PRINT"#";R;" ";C$;TAB(13);N$;" ";P
840     PRINT"OK TO SAVE (Y/N)";
850     A$="": INPUT A$
860     IF A$="N" THEN PRINT"ENTER NEW DATA AGAIN":GOTO 810
865     IF A$="-1" THEN 350
870   LSET B1$=C$: LSET B2$=N$: LSET B3$=MKS$(P)
875   PUT #1,R
890   GOTO 610
RUN
FILE NAME >>>? RANDATA
NEW FILE -- RANDATA

***  A)DD DATA, E)DIT DATA, OR Q)UIT  **
TYPE A, E, OR Q --? A

ADD DATA TO FILE.
TYPE -1 TO RETURN TO MENU.
RECORD # 1 PRODUCT CODE >>>? IA45C
           PRODUCT NAME >>>? HAND MOWER
           PRICE >>>>>>>>>>? 49.95
RECORD # 2 PRODUCT CODE >>>? IB79H
           PRODUCT NAME >>>? GLOVES
           PRICE >>>>>>>>>>? 1.49
RECORD # 3 PRODUCT CODE >>>? IC46V
           PRODUCT NAME >>>? THATCHING RAKE
           PRICE >>>>>>>>>>? 12.45
```

(continued)

```
RECORD # 4 PRODUCT CODE >>>? ID55X
           PRODUCT NAME >>>? BUG SPRAY
           PRICE >>>>>>>>>>? 4.95
RECORD # 5 PRODUCT CODE >>>? -1

***  A)DD DATA, E)DIT DATA, OR Q)UIT  **
TYPE A, E, OR Q --? E

ENTER RECORD # TO EDIT.
TYPE -1 TO RETURN TO MENU.
? 3
# 3  IC46V        THATCHING RAKE                    12.45
WANT TO CHANGE (Y/N)? Y
NEW PRODUCT CODE --? IC46V
NEW PRODUCT NAME --? THATCHING RAKE
       NEW PRICE --? 14.95
# 3  IC46V   THATCHING RAKE   14.95
OK TO SAVE (Y/N)? Y

ENTER RECORD # TO EDIT.
TYPE -1 TO RETURN TO MENU.
? -1

***  A)DD DATA, E)DIT DATA, OR Q)UIT  **
TYPE A, E, OR Q --? Q
Ok
RUN
FILE NAME >>>? RANDATA
OLD FILE -- RANDATA
# 1  IA45C        HAND MOWER                        49.95
# 2  IB79H        GLOVES                            1.49
# 3  IC46V        THATCHING RAKE                    14.95
# 4  ID55X        BUG SPRAY                         4.95
HIGHEST RECORD =   4

***  A)DD DATA, E)DIT DATA, OR Q)UIT  **
TYPE A, E, OR Q --? Q
Ok
```

EXERCISE

12.1 Notice in the run of RANDEMO that the user invents the name RANDATA for the data file to be opened and used by this program. Suppose the user had supplied the name RANDEMO instead. Could this lead to disaster? Why? What preventive measure could be taken? [*Hint:* Add a line that reads: 135 IF FL$ = "RANDEMO" THEN ... .]

LAB EXERCISE 12.1   File Name: RANDEMO2

Enter and save RANDEMO. Then try it for a variety of data. Can you use it to create more than one data file? Is this acceptable?

12.3 Applying Random-Access Files to Data Processing; PLEDGE

This section will illustrate the use of random-access files in a menu-driven program called PLEDGE. This is a program that could be used to keep tabs on the pledges made in a fund-raising campaign, whether it be for a public broadcasting station, a church, a college, or a local charity.

The program is menu-driven, which simplifies its writing and later extension. We will illustrate the latter advantage here by deliberately leaving the modules for several of the commands (EDIT, SORT, DELETE, UNDELETE, and ZIP) unwritten. Instead, we'll put in short messages saying that these commands are not implemented yet. This is called writing program *stubs*. It's a simple way of reserving space for adding the new features later on—*after* everything else is working well.

The commands we'll show you how to code are A)DD, E)DIT, P)RINT, and Q)UIT. The ADD command allows you to add new records to a random-access data file. Each record consists of five fields: name, address, Zip code, phone number, and amount pledged. The PRINT command allows you to list all the records on a printer. QUIT lets you leave the program, but only after giving you a chance to save all the data on a disk file. Section 12.4 will discuss the EDIT command.

The principal difference between PLEDGE and the RANDEMO program of Section 12.2 is that the data in PLEDGE will be kept in memory in two arrays called B$(,) and A(). The disk file will not be used until the QUIT command is given, at which time the data will be moved from these arrays to the file.

Conversely, when PLEDGE is first run, any data on the file will be moved from disk into these arrays. From then on, all data processing will be done in terms of the arrays. This has the advantage of simplifying the data-processing parts of the programming (especially for the EDIT and SORT commands), and of making things work more quickly. It has the disadvantage of limiting the size of files to the size of the arrays you dimension. However, with the large amounts of memory being made available at low cost on modern microcomputers, this disadvantage is fast disappearing. (It should also be noted that an advanced technique called file windowing can be used to allow much larger files than the array dimensions would normally permit.)

Here's a list and run of PLEDGE. Study it in conjunction with Section 12.2. When you have a pretty good idea of how it works, move on to Section 12.4, where you'll get further insights into its operation.

```
10  '***********************************************************
15  '*     PLEDGE    (PROGRAM TO COLLECT & SAVE PLEDGE DATA)    *
20  '***********************************************************
25  PRINT "PLEDGE PROGRAM RUNNING ..........."
26  L$=STRING$(63,"*"): DASH$=STRING$(37,"-")
30  DEFINT B-R: DIM B$(100,4), A(100): S=0: N=1
35  INPUT ">>> FILE NAME"; F$: IF LEN(F$)>8 THEN 35
40  OPEN "R",1,F$,80: FF=LOF(1)
45  FIELD 1, 28 AS B1$,28 AS B2$,5 AS B3$,12 AS B4$
46  FIELD 1, 73 AS DUMMY$, 4 AS B5$
50  IF FF=0 THEN PRINT"--- EMPTY FILE ---":GOTO 190
100 '-------------------------------------------------
105 '     ROUTINE TO READ AND DISPLAY THE FILE F$
110 '-------------------------------------------------
115 PRINT "FILE DATA IS BEING LOADED AND ECHOED"
120 PRINT: GET 1,N
125 B$(N,1)=B1$:B$(N,2)=B2$:B$(N,3)=B3$:B$(N,4)=B4$
130 IF LEFT$(B1$,1)="0" THEN 190
135    A(N)=CVS(B5$): S=S+A(N)
140    PRINT ">>> RCD #";N
145    PRINT TAB(9);B1$:PRINT TAB(9);B2$
146    PRINT TAB(9);B3$: PRINT TAB(9);B4$
147    PRINT TAB(9)"PLEDGE = $";A(N)
150    N=N+1: GOTO 120
190 CLOSE 1: PRINT: PRINT"TOTAL PLEDGED = $";S: PRINT
```

(continued)

```
201 '-----------------------------------------------------
202 '                    MAIN MENU
203 '-----------------------------------------------------
210 PRINT L$:PRINT TAB(23);"COMMAND    MENU":PRINT L$:PRINT
215 PRINT"       A = ADD RECORDS        E = EDIT RECORDS"
216 PRINT"       S = SORT PLEDGE LIST   P = PRINT PLEDGE LIST"
217 PRINT"       D = DELETE RECORDS     U = UNDELETE RECORDS"
218 PRINT"       Z = ADD ZIP INFO       Q = QUIT WITH SAVE"
219 PRINT: INPUT"YOUR CHOICE";D$
220 IF D$="A" THEN 315
225 IF D$="P" THEN 415
230 IF D$="Q" THEN 515
235 IF D$="E" THEN 615
240 IF D$="D" THEN 715
245 IF D$="U" THEN 815
250 IF D$="Z" THEN 915
255 IF D$="S" THEN 1015
290 PRINT "TYPE A, E, P, OR Q": GOTO 215
300 '-----------------------------------------------------
305 '      ROUTINE TO ADD RECORDS TO DATA ARRAYS
310 '-----------------------------------------------------
315 PRINT"***** ADDING NEW RECORDS *****"
320 IF N>99 THEN 512
322  PRINT">>> RECORD #";N;" (TYPE 0 TO EXIT)"
325  LINE INPUT "    NAME: ";N$: IF N$="0" THEN 347
330  LINE INPUT " ADDRESS: ";A$: IF A$="0" THEN 347
332  LINE INPUT " ZIPCODE: ";Z$: IF Z$="0" THEN 347
335  LINE INPUT "AC/PHONE: ";P$: IF P$="0" THEN 347
341  INPUT"PLEDGE $ =";A(N): IF A(N)=0 THEN 347
342  B$(N,1)=N$: B$(N,2)=A$: B$(N,3)=Z$: B$(N,4)=P$
345   PRINT: N=N+1: GOTO 320
347 B$(N,1)="0": GOTO 210
400 '-----------------------------------------------------
405 '    ROUTINE TO OUTPUT PLEDGE LIST ON PRINTER
410 '-----------------------------------------------------
415 IF N<=1 THEN PRINT"NO DATA IN MEMORY": GOTO 215
417 INPUT">>> TURN PRINTER ON, THEN PRESS <ENTER>",D:S=0
420 FOR I=1 TO N-1: LPRINT DASH$
430   LPRINT" ";B$(I,1):LPRINT" ";B$(I,2);TAB(33);B$(I,3)
432   LPRINT " ";B$(I,4)
433   LPRINT " >>> PLEDGE = $"A(I):S=S+A(I)
435 NEXT I: LPRINT STRING$(37,"="): LPRINT
440 LPRINT "*** SUM OF PLEDGES = $"S:LPRINT:GOTO 210
500 '-----------------------------------------------------
505 '    ROUTINE TO QUIT AND/OR SAVE DATA
510 '-----------------------------------------------------
512 PRINT "BUFFER SIZE EXCEEDED":B$(N,1)="0"
515 PRINT"QUITTING--DATA WILL BE SAVED ON FILE ";F$
520 INPUT"O.K. TO SAVE (Y/N)";D$:IF D$="N" GOTO 560
525 IF N<=1 THEN PRINT "NO DATA TO SAVE": GOTO 555
530 OPEN "R",1,F$,80
535 FOR K=1 TO N
540   LSET B1$=B$(K,1): LSET B2$=B$(K,2)
542   LSET B3$=B$(K,3): LSET B4$=B$(K,4)
543   LSET B5$=MKS$(A(K))
545   PUT 1,K
550 NEXT K
555 CLOSE:PRINT"**DONE** TO USE AGAIN, TYPE RUN":END
560 INPUT"PROGRAM ENDING WITHOUT SAVE - OK (Y/N)";D$
565 IF D$="Y" THEN GOTO 555 ELSE GOTO 210
600 '======= PROGRAM STUBS FOR FUTURE MODULES   =======
615 PRINT "EDIT NOT AVAILABLE": GOTO 219
715 PRINT "DELETE NOT AVAILABLE": GOTO 219
815 PRINT "UNDELETE NOT AVAILABLE": GOTO 219
915 PRINT "ZIP INFO NOT AVAILABLE": GOTO 219
1015 PRINT"SORT NOT AVAILABLE": GOTO 219
```

```
RUN
PLEDGE PROGRAM RUNNING ............
>>> FILE NAME? TV2
--- EMPTY FILE ---

TOTAL PLEDGED = $ 0

****************************************************************
                        COMMAND   MENU
****************************************************************

        A = ADD RECORDS          E = EDIT RECORDS
        S = SORT PLEDGE LIST      P = PRINT PLEDGE LIST
        D = DELETE RECORDS        U = UNDELETE RECORDS
        Z = ADD ZIP INFO          Q = QUIT WITH SAVE

YOUR CHOICE? A
***** ADDING NEW RECORDS *****
>>> RECORD # 1  (TYPE 0 TO EXIT)
    NAME: SMITH, ALLISON
 ADDRESS: 123 MAIN STREET
 ZIPCODE: 11234
AC/PHONE: 322/555-2341
PLEDGE $ =? 87.50

>>> RECORD # 2  (TYPE 0 TO EXIT)
    NAME: JOHNSON, EDWARD
 ADDRESS: 223 W. 35 STREET
 ZIPCODE: 10022
AC/PHONE: 212/321-5678
PLEDGE $ =? 100.00

>>> RECORD # 3  (TYPE 0 TO EXIT)
    NAME: 0
****************************************************************
                        COMMAND   MENU
****************************************************************

        A = ADD RECORDS          E = EDIT RECORDS
        S = SORT PLEDGE LIST      P = PRINT PLEDGE LIST
        D = DELETE RECORDS        U = UNDELETE RECORDS
        Z = ADD ZIP INFO          Q = QUIT WITH SAVE

YOUR CHOICE? E
EDIT NOT AVAILABLE

YOUR CHOICE? P
>>> TURN PRINTER ON, THEN PRESS <ENTER>
----------------------------------------
 SMITH, ALLISON
 123 MAIN STREET                11234
 322/555-2341
 >>> PLEDGE = $ 87.5
----------------------------------------
 JOHNSON, EDWARD
 223 W. 35 STREET               10022
 212/321-5678
 >>> PLEDGE = $ 100
========================================

*** SUM OF PLEDGES = $ 187.5
****************************************************************
                        COMMAND   MENU
****************************************************************

        A = ADD RECORDS          E = EDIT RECORDS
        S = SORT PLEDGE LIST      P = PRINT PLEDGE LIST
        D = DELETE RECORDS        U = UNDELETE RECORDS
        Z = ADD ZIP INFO          Q = QUIT WITH SAVE
```

(continued)

```
YOUR CHOICE? Q
QUITTING--DATA WILL BE SAVED ON FILE TV2
O.K. TO SAVE (Y/N)? Y
**DONE** TO USE AGAIN, TYPE RUN
Ok
RUN
PLEDGE PROGRAM RUNNING ...........
>>> FILE NAME? TV2
FILE DATA IS BEING LOADED AND ECHOED.

>>> RCD # 1
        SMITH, ALLISON
        123 MAIN STREET
        11234
        322/555-2341
        PLEDGE = $ 87.5

>>> RCD # 2
        JOHNSON, EDWARD
        223 W. 35 STREET
        10022
        212/321-5678
        PLEDGE = $ 100


TOTAL PLEDGED = $ 187.5

****************************************************************
                        COMMAND    MENU
****************************************************************

        A = ADD RECORDS         E = EDIT RECORDS
        S = SORT PLEDGE LIST     P = PRINT PLEDGE LIST
        D = DELETE RECORDS       U = UNDELETE RECORDS
        Z = ADD ZIP INFO         Q = QUIT WITH SAVE

YOUR CHOICE? A
***** ADDING NEW RECORDS *****
>>> RECORD # 3  (TYPE 0 TO EXIT)
    NAME: TALLTREE, MARIA
 ADDRESS: 67 ELM AVENUE
 ZIPCODE: 33021
AC/PHONE: 918/227-9978
PLEDGE $ =? 199.98

>>> RECORD # 4  (TYPE 0 TO EXIT)
    NAME: 0

****************************************************************
                        COMMAND    MENU
****************************************************************

        A = ADD RECORDS         E = EDIT RECORDS
        S = SORT PLEDGE LIST     P = PRINT PLEDGE LIST
        D = DELETE RECORDS       U = UNDELETE RECORDS
        Z = ADD ZIP INFO         Q = QUIT WITH SAVE

YOUR CHOICE? P
>>> TURN PRINTER ON, THEN PRESS <ENTER>
------------------------------------
 SMITH, ALLISON
 123 MAIN STREET                11234
 322/555-2341
 >>> PLEDGE = $ 87.5
------------------------------------
 JOHNSON, EDWARD
 223 W. 35 STREET               10022
 212/321-5678
 >>> PLEDGE = $ 100
------------------------------------
```

```
            TALLTREE, MARIA
            67 ELM AVENUE                 33021
            918/227-9978
            >>> PLEDGE = $ 199.98
            ======================================

            *** SUM OF PLEDGES = $ 387.48


            ************************************************************
                              COMMAND   MENU
            ************************************************************

                    A = ADD RECORDS        E = EDIT RECORDS
                    S = SORT PLEDGE LIST    P = PRINT PLEDGE LIST
                    D = DELETE RECORDS      U = UNDELETE RECORDS
                    Z = ADD ZIP INFO        Q = QUIT WITH SAVE

            YOUR CHOICE? Q
            QUITTING--DATA WILL BE SAVED ON FILE TV2
            O.K. TO SAVE (Y/N)? N
            PROGRAM ENDING WITHOUT SAVE - OK (Y/N)? Y
            **DONE** TO USE AGAIN, TYPE RUN
            Ok
```

LAB EXERCISE 12.2   File Name: PLEDGE1

Enter and save the program PLEDGE. Experiment with using it in conjunction with a real or imagined fund-raising campaign. What additional features are suggested by your experiments?

12.4 Extending PLEDGE to Include an EDIT Function

The listing of PLEDGE shows that we left "stubs" for additional commands called SORT, ZIP, DELETE, UNDELETE, and EDIT. The idea behind ZIP is explained in Programming Project 7 in Section 12.5. The SORT command can be implemented using the techniques explained in Section 8.5. It should produce a sorted index array based on the data in either the B$(,) or A() array, using any field specified by the user as the sorting key. Then when the P command is used, data should be printed in the order last created by SORT. Writing the SORT, DELETE, and UNDELETE modules will be left as "exercises for the reader" (see Problems 5 and 7 of Section 12.6).

The EDIT command can be implemented in a number of ways. We'll illustrate one that is simple and short, but entirely adequate for the purpose. It makes use of the fact that all the data items are in the arrays B$(,) and A(). Thus, if you say you want to edit record 7, the EDIT module will show you what's in *row* 7 of these arrays. It does this one column at a time (note that columns of the arrays correspond to fields in the disk file), asking if any changes are to be made. If you press ⟨ret⟩, no change is made in the array column just displayed. If you type anything else, this overwrites the data in that column of the array. So you're really editing the arrays. But when the QUIT command is given, these edited data items are written back onto the disk file. Hence the disk file itself is effectively edited. Here's the code for the EDIT module.

```
600 '-------------------------------------------------
601 '      ROUTINE TO EDIT RECORDS IN DATA ARRAYS
602 '-------------------------------------------------
615 PRINT"*****  EDITING PLEDGE RECORDS  *****"
616 PRINT"EDIT WHICH RCD # (0 TO EXIT)";:INPUT Q
618 IF Q<=0 THEN 670
620 IF Q>=N THEN PRINT">>> NO DATA PAST RCD #";N-1:GOTO 616
630 PRINT">>> RCD #";Q
631 PRINT TAB(9);"CURRENT DATA";TAB(40);"NEW DATA (<RET> IF OK)"
632 PRINT L$
635 PRINT"   NAME: ";B$(Q,1);TAB(41);"> ";
636 GOSUB 691
637 IF LEN(D$)=0 THEN PRINT B$(Q,1):GOTO 640 ELSE B$(Q,1)=D$:PRINT
640 PRINT"ADDRESS: ";B$(Q,2);TAB(41);"> ";
641 GOSUB 691
642 IF LEN(D$)=0 THEN PRINT B$(Q,2):GOTO 645 ELSE B$(Q,2)=D$:PRINT
645 PRINT"    ZIP: ";B$(Q,3);TAB(41);"> ";
646 GOSUB 691
647 IF LEN(D$)=0 THEN PRINT B$(Q,3):GOTO 650 ELSE B$(Q,3)=D$:PRINT
650 PRINT"AC/PHONE ";B$(Q,4);TAB(41);"> ";
651 GOSUB 691
652 IF LEN(D$)=0 THEN PRINT B$(Q,4):GOTO 655 ELSE B$(Q,4)=D$:PRINT
655 PRINT"PLEDGE = $";A(Q);TAB(41);"> ";
656 INPUT;"",AMT
660 IF AMT=0 THEN PRINT"$";A(Q):PRINT ELSE A(Q)=AMT:PRINT:PRINT
665 GOTO 616
670 GOTO 210
691 LINE INPUT;D$:RETURN
```

LAB EXERCISE 12.3   File Name: PLEDGE2

Add the ROUTINE TO EDIT RECORDS code to PLEDGE. Save the program as PLEDGE2, and then experiment with using it.

12.5   Summary of Chapter 12

▪ To use random-access files, one needs the following statement:

⟨ln⟩ OPEN "R" #⟨n⟩, ⟨filename⟩

```
100 OPEN "R" #1, FL$
```

This opens a random-access file, FL$, for both input (reading) and output (writing) on channel 1. Any record may be accessed by its number and read from or written to.

▪ A buffer area in memory is associated with each random-access channel number. The FIELD statement specifies the pattern for storing values in the buffer:

⟨ln⟩ FIELD ⟨n⟩, ⟨list of pointer variables⟩

```
100 FIELD 1, 10 AS B1$, 30 AS B2$, 4 AS B3$
```

B1$, B2$, and B3$ are used to "point to" positions in the buffer at which data is stored; that is, they allocate space in the buffer.

- A record from a random disk file is brought into the buffer by the following statement.

    ⟨ln⟩ GET #⟨n⟩, ⟨record number⟩

    `410 GET #1, 3`

    Values can then be assigned to variables from the buffer.

    `420 A$=B1$, B$=B2$, C$=CVS(B3$)`

- It is necessary to convert numeric values into strings in order to store them in a random-access file. Integers, single-precision real numbers, and double-precision real numbers take up different amounts of space (numbers of bytes) in the buffer. When assigned to variables for use in the program, such strings must be converted back to numbers. The functions used in this process are as follows.

Variable type	Make into a string	Convert to a number	Bytes taken
Integer	MKI$(⟨n⟩)	CVI(⟨ptr. var.⟩)	2
Single-precision real	MKS$(⟨n⟩)	CVS(⟨ptr. var.⟩)	4
Double-precision real	MKD$(⟨n⟩)	CVD(⟨ptr. var.⟩)	8

- Values are sent to a random disk file by first assigning them to the buffer pointer variables, and then using a PUT statement.

    ⟨ln⟩ LSET ⟨pointer variable⟩=⟨string expression⟩

    `510 LSET B1$=A$: LSET B2$=B$: LSET B3$=MKS$(C)`

    ⟨ln⟩ PUT #⟨n⟩, ⟨record number⟩

    `520 PUT #1, RCD`

- If a newly opened file has a length of 0, that means it has not been used before (has no data in it). This is usually determined by the length-of-file function LOF (⟨n⟩).

    `330 IF LOF(1) THEN 350`

12.6   Problems and Programming Projects

1. Modify the program PLEDGE so that it uses sequential files instead of random-access files. Use the techniques shown in Section 11.4 to add data to an existing file.

2. Using some of the ideas from PLEDGE, write a program that collects and saves data on the parts stored in a warehouse. The program should act as an inventory-control system. There should be a field in each record that holds the number of parts in stock, and another field for cost per part. The menu should have additional commands that allow the user to decrease the number of parts when they are removed from stock, or increase the number when parts are restocked. Add any other features that a warehouse manager might want in order to have accurate information about what parts are on hand, what dollar value they represent, and which items are running low in quantity.

3. Add disk-file S)AVE and L)OAD commands to the editor program LEDIT1 of Chapter 10. You can use the ideas found in PLEDGE to do this using random-access files, or you can adapt the ideas in SEQDEMO if you wish to use sequential files.

4. Add the command Z to the program PLEDGE. This command should allow the user to enter data pairs of the form ZIPCODE, CITY, and STATE. For example, you would enter

```
Zip? 15222
City & State? Pittsburgh, PA
```

These data items should then be saved on a file called ZIPF. When the program runs, it should read this file into an array ZF$(100,2). Then the P command should use this array to print, whenever possible, the city and state for each record.

5. Add the SORT command to PLEDGE, using the approach suggested and illustrated in Section 8.5.

6. Modify the program KEYCIPH (described in Section 10.2) so that it is able to encipher data files. Input to the program should be an ASCII text file. Output should be another ASCII file (the enciphered version). When you have this working, improve it further to use the "one-time-pad" system of data encryption.

7. Add the DELETE and UNDELETE commands to PLEDGE. When the user asks to delete a record, a special character (say X) should be written at the beginning of the record. UNDELETE should remove this character. You'll have to modify the FIELD statement to allow one more byte for the X. The PRINT command should then be modified so that it skips deleted records. Finally, add an option to the QUIT command that allows selected X records to be "purged" during the disk save.

8. Extend PLEDGE so that it also keeps track of the actual amount received on a pledge. It should then be possible to print a list of people who still owe money on their pledge, and the amount due.

9. Add a FIND command to PLEDGE. This should allow the user to specify a name, and receive back a short summary of which records contain that name. To make this work reliably, you'll want to redefine the name field as a last-name field followed by a first-name field. You'll also have to be careful to handle the differences between upper-case (capital) and lower-case letters.

10. Investigate the subject of Data Base Management System (DBMS) software by visiting a computer store and asking if they can demonstrate such a program. For example, one of the more popular DBMS packages is called dBASE II. It can be thought of as a generalization of the program idea behind PLEDGE. It allows you to create files of data based on whatever *record format* you specify. You can then retrieve these data items in various ways, and print reports based on the data. The following listing shows part of the interaction between a user and dBASE II. This is taken from the book *CP/M and the Personal Computer,* by Dwyer and Critchfield [Addison-Wesley, 1983], which contains an extensive treatment of dBASE II and several other professional software packages.

```
. SET PRINT ON
. SET EJECT OFF
. USE LOCKS
. LIST STRUCTURE
STRUCTURE FOR FILE:  A:LOCKS   .DBF
NUMBER OF RECORDS:   00006
DATE OF LAST UPDATE: 07/24/84
PRIMARY USE DATABASE
FLD       NAME      TYPE WIDTH    DEC
001     SERIAL:NUM   C    010
002     ROOMS        C    020
003     HOLDER       C    020
004     DATE         C    008
005     DEPOSIT      N    005      002
006     STATUS       C    003
** TOTAL **               00067
. LIST
00001  X29631    AL110,AL111          BROWN, LORRAINE      9/1/82    0.00 RTN
00002  H45678    AL922,AL923          JOHNSON, MARIE       4/1/79    0.00 RTN
00003  F23456    AL123,AL124          SMITH, ALVA         10/18/83   4.25 ACT
00004  D54473    AL355,AL356          SMITH, GEORGE        9/4/84    5.50 ACT
00005  D58693    AL331,AL332          SMITH, GEORGE        5/9/84    4.50 ACT
00006  E12545    AL255,AL256,AL257    JONES, RALPH         6/18/84   6.50 LST
. DISPLAY FOR HOLDER = ´SMITH´ .AND. DEPOSIT > 5
00004  D54473    AL355,AL356          SMITH, GEORGE        9/4/84    5.50 ACT
. SORT ON DEPOSIT TO TEMP
SORT COMPLETE
. USE TEMP
. LIST
00001  X29631    AL110,AL111          BROWN, LORRAINE      9/1/82    0.00 RTN
00002  H45678    AL922,AL923          JOHNSON, MARIE       4/1/79    0.00 RTN
00003  F23456    AL123,AL124          SMITH, ALVA         10/18/83   4.25 ACT
00004  D58693    AL331,AL332          SMITH, GEORGE        5/9/84    4.50 ACT
00005  D54473    AL355,AL356          SMITH, GEORGE        9/4/84    5.50 ACT
00006  E12545    AL255,AL256,AL257    JONES, RALPH         6/18/84   6.50 LST
. COPY TO LOCKS
00006 RECORDS COPIED
. USE LOCKS
. INDEX ON HOLDER TO LOCKHOLD
00006 RECORDS INDEXED
. USE LOCKS INDEX LOCKHOLD
. LIST
00001  X29631    AL110,AL111          BROWN, LORRAINE      9/1/82    0.00 RTN
00002  H45678    AL922,AL923          JOHNSON, MARIE       4/1/79    0.00 RTN
00006  E12545    AL255,AL256,AL257    JONES, RALPH         6/18/84   6.50 LST
00003  F23456    AL123,AL124          SMITH, ALVA         10/18/83   4.25 ACT
00004  D58693    AL331,AL332          SMITH, GEORGE        5/9/84    4.50 ACT
00005  D54473    AL355,AL356          SMITH, GEORGE        9/4/84    5.50 ACT
. FIND SMITH
. DISPLAY
00003  F23456    AL123,AL124          SMITH, ALVA         10/18/83   4.25 ACT
. DISPLAY
00003  F23456    AL123,AL124          SMITH, ALVA         10/18/83   4.25 ACT
. DELETE RECORD 4
00001 DELETION(S)
. LIST
00001  X29631    AL110,AL111          BROWN, LORRAINE      9/1/82    0.00 RTN
00002  H45678    AL922,AL923          JOHNSON, MARIE       4/1/79    0.00 RTN
00006  E12545    AL255,AL256,AL257    JONES, RALPH         6/18/84   6.50 LST
00003  F23456    AL123,AL124          SMITH, ALVA         10/18/83   4.25 ACT
00004 *D58693    AL331,AL332          SMITH, GEORGE        5/9/84    4.50 ACT
00005  D54473    AL355,AL356          SMITH, GEORGE        9/4/84    5.50 ACT
. RECALL RECORD 4
00001 RECALL(S)
. DELETE RECORD 5
00001 DELETION(S)
. PACK
PACK COMPLETE, 00005 RECORDS COPIED
```

(continued)

```
REINDEXING INDEX FILE - A:LOCKHOLD.NDX
00005 RECORDS INDEXED
. LIST
00001 X29631    AL110,AL111         BROWN, LORRAINE    9/1/82     0.00 RTN
00002 H45678    AL922,AL923         JOHNSON, MARIE     4/1/79     0.00 RTN
00005 E12545    AL255,AL256,AL257   JONES, RALPH       6/18/84    6.50 LST
00003 F23456    AL123,AL124         SMITH, ALVA        10/18/83   4.25 ACT
00004 D58693    AL331,AL332         SMITH, GEORGE      5/9/84     4.50 ACT
. REPORT
ENTER REPORT FORM NAME: LOCKSR1
ENTER OPTIONS, M=LEFT MARGIN, L=LINES/PAGE, W=PAGE WIDTH M=3
PAGE HEADING? (Y/N) Y
ENTER PAGE HEADING: ========== Lock Access List ==========
DOUBLE SPACE REPORT? (Y/N) n
ARE TOTALS REQUIRED? (Y/N) y
SUBTOTALS IN REPORT? (Y/N) n
COL     WIDTH,CONTENTS
001     10,serial:num
ENTER HEADING: Serial #
002     20,rooms
ENTER HEADING: Rooms Accessed
003     20,holder
ENTER HEADING: Name of Holder
004     7,deposit
ENTER HEADING: Deposit
ARE TOTALS REQUIRED? (Y/N) y
005     6,status
ENTER HEADING: Status
006

    PAGE NO. 00001
    07/24/84

                 ========== Lock Access List ==========

    Serial #    Rooms Accessed       Name of Holder   Deposit Status

    X29631      AL110,AL111          BROWN, LORRAINE     0.00 RTN
    H45678      AL922,AL923          JOHNSON, MARIE      0.00 RTN
    E12545      AL255,AL256,AL257    JONES, RALPH        6.50 LST
    F23456      AL123,AL124          SMITH, ALVA         4.25 ACT
    D58693      AL331,AL332          SMITH, GEORGE       4.50 ACT
    ** TOTAL **
                                                        15.25

. quit
*** END RUN    dBASE II    ***
```

The ASCII Codes

Binary Form	Key (and Meaning)	Hexa-decimal Form	Decimal Form	Binary Form	Key (and Meaning)	Hexa-decimal Form	Decimal Form
00000000	^@ (NULL)	0	0	00100000	⟨space⟩	20	32
00000001	^A (SOH)	1	1	00100001	!	21	33
00000010	^B (STX)	2	2	00100010	"	22	34
00000011	^C (ETX)	3	3	00100011	#	23	35
00000100	^D (EOT)	4	4	00100100	$	24	36
00000101	^E (ENQ)	5	5	00100101	%	25	37
00000110	^F (ACK)	6	6	00100110	&	26	38
00000111	^G (BELL)	7	7	00100111	' (quote)	27	39
00001000	^H (BS)	8	8	00101000	(	28	40
00001001	^I (HT)	9	9	00101001	)	29	41
00001010	^J (LF)	A	10	00101010	*	2A	42
00001011	^K (VT)	B	11	00101011	+	2B	43
00001100	^L (FF)	C	12	00101100	, (comma)	2C	44
00001101	^M (CR)	D	13	00101101	- (hyphen)	2D	45
00001110	^N (SO)	E	14	00101110	.	2E	46
00001111	^O (SI)	F	15	00101111	/	2F	47
00010000	^P (DLE)	10	16	00110000	0	30	48
00010001	^Q (DC1)	11	17	00110001	1	31	49
00010010	^R (DC2)	12	18	00110010	2	32	50
00010011	^S (DC3)	13	19	00110011	3	33	51
00010100	^T (DC4)	14	20	00110100	4	34	52
00010101	^U (NAK)	15	21	00110101	5	35	53
00010110	^V (SYN)	16	22	00110110	6	36	54
00010111	^W (ETB)	17	23	00110111	7	37	55
00011000	^X (CAN)	18	24	00111000	8	38	56
00011001	^Y (EM)	19	25	00111001	9	39	57
00011010	^Z (SUB)	1A	26	00111010	:	3A	58
00011011	^[(ESC)	1B	27	00111011	;	3B	59
00011100	^\ (FS)	1C	28	00111100	<	3C	60
00011101	^] (GS)	1D	29	00111101	=	3D	61
00011110	^^ (RS)	1E	30	00111110	>	3E	62
00011111	^_ (US)	1F	31	00111111	?	3F	63

(continued)

Binary Form	Key (and Meaning)	Hexadecimal Form	Decimal Form	Binary Form	Key (and Meaning)	Hexadecimal Form	Decimal Form
01000000	@	40	64	01100000	'	60	96
01000001	A	41	65	01100001	a	61	97
01000010	B	42	66	01100010	b	62	98
01000011	C	43	67	01100011	c	63	99
01000100	D	44	68	01100100	d	64	100
01000101	E	45	69	01100101	e	65	101
01000110	F	46	70	01100110	f	66	102
01000111	G	47	71	01100111	g	67	103
01001000	H	48	72	01101000	h	68	104
01001001	I	49	73	01101001	i	69	105
01001010	J	4A	74	01101010	j	6A	106
01001011	K	4B	75	01101011	k	6B	107
01001100	L	4C	76	01101100	l	6C	108
01001101	M	4D	77	01101101	m	6D	109
01001110	N	4E	78	01101110	n	6E	110
01001111	O	4F	79	01101111	o	6F	111
01010000	P	50	80	01110000	p	70	112
01010001	Q	51	81	01110001	q	71	113
01010010	R	52	82	01110010	r	72	114
01010011	S	53	83	01110011	s	73	115
01010100	T	54	84	01110100	t	74	116
01010101	U	55	85	01110101	u	75	117
01010110	V	56	86	01110110	v	76	118
01010111	W	57	87	01110111	w	77	119
01011000	X	58	88	01111000	x	78	120
01011001	Y	59	89	01111001	y	79	121
01011010	Z	5A	90	01111010	z	7A	122
01011011	[	5B	91	01111011	{	7B	123
01011100	\	5C	92	01111100	|	7C	124
01011101	]	5D	93	01111101	}	7D	125
01011110	^ (up arrow)	5E	94	01111110	~	7E	126
01011111	_ (undrln.)	5F	95	01111111	⟨delete⟩	7F	127

Summary of Extended BASIC

This summary presents BASIC key words, commands, and functions, each followed by a brief explanation, and one or more examples.

Key Words and Commands

The conventions used for key words and commands are as follows:

1. Items in capital letters must be used as shown.

2. Items in lower-case letters enclosed by angle brackets (⟨ ⟩) are supplied by the user.

3. Items enclosed in square brackets ([ ]) are optional.

4. Items followed by ellipses (...) may be repeated any number of times up to the limit of the line length (usually 256 characters).

5. All punctuation must be used as shown (except for ellipses, angle brackets, and square brackets).

In the following, ln = line number, inc = increment, var = variable name, fn = file number, exp = expression, *n*, *m* = numbers. A few key words and commands shown are not available in all versions of BASIC. When a similar function is performed by differing key words, both are included.

- AUTO [⟨ln⟩][,⟨inc⟩]

    Used to generate line numbers after each ⟨enter⟩. Numbering starts with ⟨ln⟩ and increases by ⟨inc⟩. If no values are specified, 10,10 are used. Terminate AUTO by typing ⟨ctrl⟩⟨C⟩, ⟨ctrl⟩⟨break⟩, or ⟨enter⟩⟨enter⟩, depending on your system.

    ```
    AUTO 110,10
    AUTO 1000,5
    ```

■ BLOAD <filename>[,<exp>]

Loads a memory image (binary) file into memory. ⟨exp⟩ is the address in memory where the file is to be loaded. If ⟨exp⟩ is omitted the file is loaded into the location it was saved from. (See BSAVE). Machine language programs are run from within BASIC programs by the CALL statement. For Apple DOS procedures, see Appendix C.

```
190 DEF SEG=&HB800  'IBM SCREEN BUFFER
200 BLOAD "PIX1",0
```

■ BRUN <filename>[,A<address>]

On Apple, loads a binary file into memory starting at ⟨address⟩ and runs it. See Appendix C.

■ BSAVE <filename>,<exp1>,<exp2>

Saves portions of the computer's memory. ⟨exp1⟩ is the address in memory where saving starts. ⟨exp2⟩ is the length, in number of bytes, of the portion to be saved. (See BLOAD.) See Appendix C for Apple DOS procedures.

```
400 DEF SEG=&HB800 'IBM SCREEN BUFFER
410 BSAVE "PIX2",0,&H4000
```

■ CALL <var>[(<var list>)]

Transfers program control to an assembly-language subroutine already located in memory, starting at an address contained in ⟨var⟩. The variables in the list have their values passed to the subroutine.

```
250 SUB1=&HE000
260 CALL SUB1(P,Q,R$,Y+3)
```

■ CATALOG [,S<slot>][,D<drive>]

On the Apple, displays a list of all files on the specified disk drive.

■ CHAIN [MERGE] <filename> [,[<ln exp>][,ALL] [,DELETE <ln-ln>]]

When used without the MERGE option, CHAIN loads a program into memory (erasing the current program) and passes variable values to it from the current program. Execution starts at the specified line number, or else the first line of the program. Only variables previously denoted in a COMMON statement are passed, unless the ALL option is used. DELETE ⟨ln-ln⟩ causes those lines of the new program to be deleted after execution. When CHAIN is used with the MERGE option, the current program is not deleted, but is merged with the new one. See Appendix C for Apple chaining procedures.

```
9999 CHAIN "CHESS12",,ALL
4900 CHAIN MERGE "TAXRPT3",2000,DELETE 2000-3000
```

■ CHDIR <string exp>

On a system with tree-structured directories, allows the user to change the current directory. ⟨string exp⟩ contains special characters and names of subdirectories, depending on the particular tree structures involved. (See your BASIC manual.)

```
CHDIR "TAX1\BUDGET3\ACCT85"
```

■ CLEAR [,<exp1>][<,exp2>]

Sets numeric variables to zero, strings to null, closes all open files. ⟨exp1⟩ sets the highest memory location available to BASIC. ⟨exp2⟩ sets the stack space used by BASIC. (The exact purpose and syntax of this command varies among systems; consult your manual.) *Note:* CLEAR may invalidate a previous DIM statement.

```
10 CLEAR
10 CLEAR, 32768, 3000
10 CLEAR, 32768
10 CLEAR,, 3000
```

■ CLOAD[?] <filename>

Loads a file from cassette tape. CLOAD? verifies a tape by comparing the contents of memory with that of the tape.

```
CLOAD "GRADER1"
CLOAD? "GRADER1"
```

■ CLOAD* <array name>

Loads a numeric array into memory.

```
20 CLOAD* N
```

■ CLS

Clears the screen and sends the cursor to "home" position (upper left corner).

■ COMMON <variable list>

Denotes variables whose values are to be passed to a chained program.

```
100 COMMON P,P$,Q(),Q$()
```

■ CONT

Continues execution after ⟨ctrl⟩⟨C⟩ is typed, STOP or END have been executed, or an error has occurred.

■ CSAVE <string exp>

Saves the program currently in memory on cassette tape, giving it the first character in ⟨string exp⟩ as a name.

```
CSAVE "A"
```

■ CSAVE* <array var>

Saves the values of a numeric array on cassette tape.

```
99 CSAVE* B
```

■ DATA <list of constants>

Contains numeric and string constants to be used by a READ statement.

```
220 FOR I=1 TO 5: READ V$(I),C(I): NEXT I
230 DATA "A",0,"E",0,"I",0,"O",0,"U",0
```

■ DATE$=<string>

See Function DATE$.

■ DEF FN<name> [(<variable list>)]=<function definition>

Defines and names a function written by the user. ⟨name⟩ is any legal variable name. ⟨variable list⟩ are those variables appearing in the definition whose values are passed to the function when it is called. ⟨function definition⟩ is an expression, limited to one line. Variable names appearing in this definition are not global.

```
600 DEF FNX(P,Q)=P^2/Q^3
610 DEF FNEXC$(S$)=S$+"!!!@#!!!"
620 NUM=FNX(A,B)
630 SENT1$=FNEXC$(A$)
```

■ DEFINT <range of letters>
  DEFSNG <range of letters>
  DEFDBL <range of letters>
  DEFSTR <range of letters>

Declares variables beginning with a letter or a range of letters to be of type integer, single precision, double precision, or string, respectively. A later type declaration character (%,!,#,$) takes precedence.

```
100 DEFINT A-Z
100 DEFSTR C
100 DEFDBL D
```

■ DEF USR[<digit>]=<integer exp>

Indicates the starting address of a user-defined machine-language subroutine. ⟨digit⟩ can be 0–9; 0 is assumed if none is given.

```
320 DEF USR=32000
330 DEF USR1=&HF000
```

■ DEF SEG[=<exp>]

Redefines the segment of memory to be used. BLOAD, BSAVE, CALL, PEEK, POKE, and USR statements then refer to addresses given as offsets from the DEF SEG address. ⟨exp⟩ is an address in the range 0–65535. If ⟨exp⟩ is omitted, the current segment is set to BASIC's Data Segment (the user workspace in memory). DEF SEG addresses are commonly given as hexadecimal numbers with a rightmost digit (a zero) deleted, since the segment address is based on a 16-byte boundary. For an example, see BLOAD, BSAVE. On systems in which this feature is not available, CALL, PEEK, POKE, and so forth, specify actual addresses.

■ DELETE <filename>

On Apple, deletes a file from the disk.

■ DELETE <ln>[-][<ln>]

Deletes program lines indicated. Line numbers must exist in the program. The second form (below) deletes all lines up to and including the line indicated. On Apple, use DEL, and a comma instead of dash.

```
DELETE 10
DELETE -50
DELETE 100-200
DELETE 1000-
```

- DEL <ln>[,][<ln>]

   On Apple, deletes program lines.

- DIM <variable list>

   Specifies the maximum values for array variable subscripts. If no DIM statement occurs, the maximum subscript is 10. Subscripts start at 0 unless OPTION BASE 1 is specified. DIM sets all values of the arrays to 0 or null. The maximum number of dimensions and elements varies among systems; typically it is 255 and 32767, respectively. The total number of elements is limited by actual memory.

   ```
   10 DIM A(20), B$(20), C(50,50), D$(50,3)
   ```

- EDIT <ln>

   On some systems, switches to a special editing mode. Consult your manual.

- END

   Terminates program execution, closes all files. END is optional in most versions of BASIC.

- ERASE <array list>

   Eliminates arrays from memory; allows them to be redimensioned.

   ```
   490 ERASE X,Z
   500 DIM X(40), Z(100)
   ```

- ERROR <integer exp>

   Simulates the occurrence of a BASIC error if ⟨integer exp⟩ is the number of an error code already existing (consult your manual). If a nonexistent error number is specified, the user may define the error. ⟨integer exp⟩ must be >0 and <255. (For an example, see ON ERROR GOTO.)

- FILES [<disk:>][<filename>]

   Displays a directory or catalog of files of the named disk. A: is the default disk. All files are displayed if none is specified. If the specified file is not found, a message is printed.

   ```
   FILES "B:*.*"
   FILES "*.BAS"
   FILES "ANIMAL1"
   ```

- FOR <var1>=<exp1> TO <exp2> [STEP<exp3>]

   .
   .
   .

   NEXT [...,<var2>][,var1>]

   The body of statements between FOR and NEXT are executed repeatedly according to the following rules: ⟨var1⟩ is set to ⟨exp1⟩; the statements are executed; ⟨var1⟩ is incremented by ⟨exp3⟩ and its value is checked to see if it's greater than ⟨exp2⟩. If ⟨var1⟩ is not greater, control is passed to the statement after FOR (a repeat); if ⟨var1⟩ is greater, control passes to the statement after NEXT (end of the loop). If ⟨exp1⟩ is initially greater than ⟨exp2⟩ and ⟨exp3⟩ is positive, the body of the statement is skipped. It is also skipped in the reverse case, if ⟨exp3⟩ is negative. If no ⟨exp3⟩ is given, 1 is used. FOR...NEXT loops may be nested, and their NEXT statements may occupy one line.

```
10 P=1 : D=10 : Q=2
20 FOR Y P TO D STEP Q
30  PRINT Y;
40 NEXT Y
50 PRINT:PRINT Y
RUN
1 3 5 7 9
11
Ok

10 FOR T=1 TO 1
20  PRINT T
30 NEXT T
40 PRINT "T=";T
RUN
1
T= 2
Ok

10 FOR T=1 TO 0
20  PRINT T
30 NEXT T
40 PRINT "T=";T
RUN
T= 1
Ok
```

■ GET ⟨string var⟩

On Apple, stores one character input from the keyboard. See function INKEY$.

■ GOSUB ⟨ln⟩
  .
  .
  .
RETURN

Transfers control to a subroutine at ⟨ln⟩. Return statements transfer control back to the statement following the most recent GOSUB. Subroutines may be called from within subroutines. Subroutines must be separated from the main program by END, STOP, or GOTO statements.

```
100 'MAIN PROGRAM
     ...
500 GOSUB 1000
510 PRINT "BACK FROM SUBR. AT 1000"
     ...
990 END
995 'END OF MAIN PROGRAM
1000 '--- SUBROUTINE1 ---
     ...
1090 RETURN
```

■ GOTO ⟨ln⟩

> Transfers control to line ⟨ln⟩.

>> 100 GOTO 300

■ HIMEM: ⟨n⟩

> On Apple, sets the address of the highest memory location available to an Applesoft program.

■ HOME

> On Apple, clears the screen; see CLS.

■ HTAB ⟨n⟩

> On Apple, positions the cursor to the horizontal column specified (1 through 40).

>> 10 HTAB 10: VTAB 20: PRINT "*"

■ IF ⟨exp⟩ THEN ⟨clause1⟩ [ELSE ⟨clause 2⟩]

> Transfers control, based on the value of ⟨exp⟩. ⟨exp⟩ is a logical expression that is either true or false (evaluates to nonzero or zero, respectively). If ⟨exp⟩ is true, ⟨clause1⟩ is executed. If ⟨exp⟩ is false, ⟨clause2⟩ is executed. If ⟨exp⟩ is false and ELSE is not used, execution continues at the next line. ⟨clause1⟩ or ⟨clause2⟩ may consist of: a statement, a compound statement made by joining statements with colon (:), or a line number. **IF statements may be nested in most versions of BASIC (that is, a statement following THEN or ELSE may be an IF statement). If ⟨clause1⟩ consists of a ⟨ln⟩, THEN may be replaced by GOTO.**

>> 100 IF P<=Q THEN 200
>> 100 IF A$="YES" THEN F=1:G=0 ELSE PRINT "WOW!":GOTO 400

■ INPUT[;] [⟨prompt string⟩;] ⟨var1⟩[,⟨var2⟩...]

> Causes the program to print a prompting string (if present), a question mark, and pause. It waits for input from the keyboard, followed by ⟨enter⟩, then assigns values to ⟨var1⟩, ⟨var2⟩, and so forth. Input items should be typed, separated by commas or ⟨enter⟩. ⟨enter⟩, when input alone, causes a 0 or null to be assigned on some systems; on others, it leaves the variable unchanged; on others, execution stops. The optional semicolon suppresses the carriage return/line feed after the user's ⟨enter⟩. Changing the semicolon after the prompting string to a comma suppresses the question mark.

>> 200 INPUT;"ITEM CODE >> ",C$
>> 210 INPUT"   COLOR CODE >> ",C
>> 220 PRINT"THANK YOU."
>> RUN
>> ITEM CODE >> X2365   COLOR CODE >> 44
>> THANK YOU.

■ KILL ⟨filename⟩

> Deletes a file from disk.

>> 10 KILL F1$+".TMP"

■ [LET] <var>=<exp>

Assigns the value of an expression to the variable.

```
A1=14: A2=A1+10: A3=A2*.075: PRINT A1;A2;A3
  14  24  1.8
```

■ LINE INPUT [;][<prompt string>;]<string variable>

Like INPUT, but allows the input of an entire line to a string variable, including commas and spaces (but not trailing spaces). A question mark is not printed unless it is part of the prompting string. The optional semicolon suppresses the carriage return/linefeed sequence after the user's ⟨enter⟩.

```
420 LINE INPUT ">>";A$(J)
```

■ LIST [<ln>][-][<ln>]

Lists at the terminal all or part of the program currently in memory.

```
LIST 10
LIST -200
LIST 200-300
LIST 300-
```

■ LIST [<ln>][,][<ln>]

On Apple, this syntax is also available. Does the same as above.

■ LLIST [<ln>[-[<ln>]]]

Same as LIST, but output is sent to the printer. On Apple, output must be switched to the appropriate slot, using PR# ⟨slot⟩.

```
LLIST 200-300
```

■ LOAD

On Apple cassette systems, used without a filename, loads a file from cassette.

■ LOAD <filename>[,R]

Loads a file from disk into memory, deleting the program currently in memory. Closes all open files and deletes all variables—unless the R option is used. If R is used, the new program will be run after loading, with files kept open and variables preserved.

```
LOAD "QUIZ3"
1000 LOAD "MENU6",R
```

■ LOCATE [<row>][,<col>][,<cursor>][,<start>][,<stop>]

On the IBM PC, positions the cursor to ⟨row⟩ = 1 to 25, ⟨col⟩ = 1 to 40 (or 1 to 80). It also makes the cursor visible (⟨cursor⟩ > = 1) or invisible (⟨cursor⟩ > = 0). ⟨start⟩ and ⟨stop⟩ may be 0 to 13 and indicate the cursor start and stop scan line which changes the size of the cursor.

■ LOCK <filename>
UNLOCK <filename>

On Apple, protects files from deletion or change.

- LOMEM: <n>

    On Apple, sets the lowest address of memory available to a BASIC program.

- LPRINT [<exp1>[,<exp2>...]]
  LPRINT USING <format string>;<exp1>[,<exp2>...]

    Same as PRINT and PRINT USING, except that output is sent to the line printer.

- MERGE<filename>

    Merges the file with a program currently in memory. If no extension is given, .BAS is supplied. The file must have been saved as an ASCII file (see SAVE). Programs are merged line-by-line, with same-numbered lines from the incoming file superseding the ones in memory.

        1000 MERGE "INFO3"

- MID$(<string exp1>,<n>[,<m>])=<string exp2>

    Replaces the characters in <string exp1>, beginning at position <n>, with the characters of <string exp2>. <m> can be used to specify how many characters of <string exp2> to use. The length of <string exp1> is not changed. (See also the function MID$.)

        A$="FREEHOLDER":MID$(A$,5,4)="RUNNING":PRINT A$
        FREERUNNER

- NAME <old filename> AS <new filename>

    Changes the name of a disk file.

        NAME "CHESS1" AS "XCHESS1"

- NEW

    Deletes the program currently in memory and clears all variables.

        NEW

- NULL <n>

    Sets the number of nulls to be sent at the end of each line. Needed on terminals with a slow carriage return.

        NULL 3

- ON ERROR GOTO <ln>

    Turns on error trapping and indicates the line number of an error-handling subroutine. <ln> = 0 turns off error trapping. ON ERROR GOTO 0 occurring within the trapping subroutine causes the standard error message to be printed and causes execution to halt. Errors occurring within the error-handling routine are not trapped.

        60 ON ERROR GOTO 500
        70 IF X$="" THEN ERROR 230
          .
          .
          .
        500 IF ERR=230 THEN PRINT "NULL"
        510 IF ERL=150 THEN RESUME 10

■ ON <exp> GOSUB <ln1>,<ln2> [,<ln3>...]
   ON <exp> GOTO <ln1>,<ln2> [,<ln3>...]

If the rounded value of ⟨exp⟩ is 1, control is transferred to ⟨ln1⟩, if 2, to ⟨ln2⟩, and so forth. For ON...GOSUB, subroutines should be located at ⟨ln1⟩,⟨ln2⟩, and so forth. If the rounded value of ⟨exp⟩ is 0, or greater than the number of line numbers, control passes to the next line. If it is less than 0 or greater than 255, an error results.

```
200 ON X+1 GOSUB 1000, 2000, 3000
```

■ ONERR GOTO <ln>

On Apple, causes a branch to line ⟨ln⟩ if an error is subsequently encountered.

■ OPTION BASE <n>

⟨n⟩ = 0 or 1. Sets the lowest value for array subscripts to 0 or 1 (the default is 0).

```
10 OPTION BASE 1
```

■ OUT <n>,<m>

Sends a byte to a machine output port. Integer expression ⟨n⟩ is the port number; integer expression ⟨m⟩ is the byte to be sent. (See the complementary function INP.)

```
500 OUT 255, $H1A
```

■ POKE <n>,<m>

Writes a byte into a memory location. Integer expression ⟨n⟩ is the address in memory; integer expression ⟨m⟩ is the data to be written. (See the complementary function PEEK.)

```
100 POKE &H5A00, &HFF
200 POKE 16368, X
```

■ PRINT[<exp1>],[<exp2> ...]

Displays data at the terminal. Prints the values of the expression(s), or a blank line if no expressions are present. Punctuation determines the spacing of items. There are differences between versions of BASIC, but in general, a comma causes the next item to be printed in the next print zone (usually 14 columns wide). Repeated commas ''push over'' the item one print zone each. A semicolon causes the next item to be printed immediately after the preceding item. Spaces are usually inserted after numbers, and a space ahead of a number is reserved for the sign. A semicolon at the end of a print statement suppresses the usual line feed/carriage return. In some versions of BASIC, semicolons may be omitted or replaced by a space between items.

```
10 A=3.95: B=.05: C="X2354"
20 PRINT "DISCOUNT PRICE IS  ";A-(A*B);" FOR #";
30 PRINT C$
RUN
DISCOUNT PRICE IS:   3.7525  FOR #X2354
```

■ PRINT USING <format string>; [<exp1>[,<exp2> ...]]

Prints at the terminal the values of the expression(s) using a format specified by special characters in the format string. Characters used may be:

!	Prints only the first character of a string.
\\	Prints 2 + n characters of a string, where n = the number of spaces between backslashes.
&	A variable-length string field.
#	Represents one digit position in the format.
.	Represents the decimal point.
+	Prints the sign of the number at this position.
–	After a numeric field, prints a trailing minus.
**	Fills the leading spaces with asterisks.
$$	Prints $ in front of the number in this numeric field.
**$	Combines the two previous signs.
,	Before the decimal, prints commas every third digit.
^ ^ ^ ^	After the digit-position characters, prints in exponential format as E+nn.
_	Prints next character 'as is'.

```
100 A$="EXPENSES": A1=1234.5: A2=123456!: A3=12.3
110 P$="\                \ ####.## ######, $$##.##"
120 PRINT USING P$; A$,A1,A2,A3
RUN
EXPENSES          1234.50   123,456    $12.30
```

■ RANDOM

On the TRS-80, reseeds the random-number generator.

■ RANDOMIZE [<exp>]

Reseeds the random-number generator. If <exp> is omitted, a message requesting a number is printed. Without RANDOMIZE, the RND function usually generates the same sequence of random numbers each time. (See function RND.)

```
10 RANDOMIZE
10 RANDOMIZE X
```

■ READ <var1>[,<var2>...]

Reads values from data statements and assigns them to variables on a one-to-one basis. Variables may be string or numeric, but DATA values must be in the correct order so that strings are read into string variables, and numbers into numeric.

```
100 READ A, A$, B, C, SALES
```

■ RECALL <array name>

On Apple, retrieves a numeric array stored on cassette tape. See CLOAD*.

■ REM <remark> or ' <remark> or ! <remark>

Allows explanatory remarks to be included with the program listing. REM statements are not executed.

```
10 REM  PROGRAM TO CALCULATE INTEREST
20 '    THE FOLLOWING VARIABLES ARE USED:
500 X=25      'CHANGE THIS VALUE LATER
```

■ RENAME <old filename>,<new filename>[,S<slot>][,D<drive>][,V<val>]

On Apple, renames files. See NAME.

■ RENUM [<ln1>][,ln2][,inc]

Renumbers the program starting with a new ⟨ln1⟩. If ⟨ln2⟩ and ⟨inc⟩ are present, renumbers starting at old ⟨ln2⟩ with increments of ⟨inc⟩. If no values are given, renumbers the entire program starting with 10, with increments of 10. (That is, default is 10,1,10.)

```
RENUM 1000, 500, 5
```

■ RESET

Closes all files and clears the system buffer. May be required when changing diskettes.

■ RESTORE [<ln>]

Allows data to be reread from the beginning of DATA statements. If ⟨ln⟩ is given, allows data to be reread from line ⟨ln⟩.

```
1000 RESTORE 750
```

■ RESUME [<ln>] or [NEXT]

Continues program execution after an error-recovery procedure. RESUME or RESUME 0 continues at the statement that caused the error. RESUME NEXT continues at the statement after that which caused the error. RESUME ⟨ln⟩ continues at ⟨ln⟩. (See ON ERROR GOTO.)

```
RESUME 100
```

■ RETURN

Transfers control to the statement following the most recently executed GOSUB statement. (See GOSUB).

```
1090 RETURN
```

■ RUN [<ln>]
  RUN <filename>[,R]

Executes the program currently in memory. If ⟨ln⟩ is given, starts at ⟨ln⟩. If a filename is given, deletes the file currently in memory, loads the new file from disk, and runs it. Unless option R is used, closes all open files.

```
RUN
100 RUN "PART3",R
```

■ SAVE

On Apple cassette systems, used without a filename, saves a program on cassette.

■ SAVE <filename>[,A or ,P]

> Saves the file in memory on disk. With option A, saves the file in ASCII format; with option P, the file is protected by storing in encoded binary format—it cannot be listed or edited.

```
SAVE "NUTRI1"
SAVE "ANUTRI1",A
SAVE "NUTRISH",P
```

■ STOP

> Terminates program execution.

```
1000 STOP
```

■ STORE <array name>

> On Apple, stores a numeric array on cassette tape. See CSAVE*.

■ SWAP <var1>,<var2>

> Exchanges the value of two variables.

```
A=25: B=3: SWAP A,B: PRINT A;B
3  25
```

■ SYSTEM

> Exits BASIC and returns to the disk operating system.

■ TIME$=<string>

> See function TIME$.

■ TRACE and NOTRACE

> On the Apple, similar to TRON, TROFF.

■ TRON

> Switches on the trace feature.

■ TROFF

> Switches off the trace feature. When the trace debugging aid is on, each line number of the program is printed as it is executed.

■ VERIFY <filename>

> On Apple, checks to see if a file is stored correctly by calculating a new check sum byte and comparing it with the old one.

■ VTAB <ln>

> On Apple, positions the cursor to the vertical line specified (1 through 24).

■ WAIT <port>,<m>[,<n>]

> Suspends execution of a program until ⟨port⟩ develops a certain bit pattern. The pattern is XOR'ed with ⟨m⟩ and AND'ed with ⟨n⟩. If the result is 0 the port is read again. ⟨n⟩ is assumed to be 0 if not present.

```
100 WAIT 250,2 'WAIT UNTIL PORT 250 HAS 00000010
```

■ WHILE <exp>

   .
   .
   .

WEND

Executes the statements below WHILE and above WEND as long as (while) the given expression is true. May be nested to any level.

```
90 WHILE A<B
   ...
   ...
290 WEND
```

■ WIDTH [LPRINT] <integer exp>

Sets the length of the printed line of output. ⟨integer exp⟩ indicates the number of characters. If the LPRINT option is used, line length on the printer is changed; otherwise the terminal line is changed. On some systems "LPT1:" is used instead of LPRINT, and devices other than the terminal and printer may be controlled; see your BASIC manual.

```
10 WD=80: WIDTH WD
20 WIDTH LPRINT 132
```

■ WRITE [<exp1>[,<exp2>...]]

Outputs data to the terminal, separated by commas and with strings enclosed in double quotation marks. Outputs a blank line if no expression is given. A carriage-return line feed is added after the last item.

```
20 WRITE A,B,C$
```

Functions—String and Numeric

Note: x and y represent numeric expressions, i and j represent integer expressions, x$ and y$ represent string expressions, v represents a variable name. Functions shown as part of an assignment statement may be substituted in expressions anywhere the variable type shown could be used. Lower-case letters indicate variable names and arguments supplied by the user; no angle brackets are used.

■ v=ABS(x)

Returns the absolute value of x.

```
A=10: B=25: DIFF=ABS(A-B): PRINT DIFF
   15
```

■ v=ASC(x$)

Returns the ASCII Code (in decimal) of the first character of x$.

```
A$="BEAR": A=ASC(A$): PRINT A$,A
BEAR          66
```

■ v=ATN(x)

Returns the arctangent of x in radians.

```
X=2: Y=ATN(X): PRINT X, Y
 2              1.10715
```

■ v#=CDBL(x)

Converts x to a double-precision number.

```
A=1: B=3: PRINT A/B, CDBL(A)/CDBL(B)
 .333333       .3333333333333333
```

■ v$=CHR$(x)

Returns the character that corresponds to ASCII Code x.

```
110 PRINT CHR$(7)       'RING BELL
120 PRINT CHR$(27)+"E"   'CLEAR SCREEN OF Z19
```

■ v%=CINT(x)

Converts x to an integer; rounds the fraction, if any.

```
NUM=95.67: A%=CINT(NUM): PRINT NUM, A%
 95.67          96
```

■ v=COS(x)

Returns the cosine of x in radians.

```
E=.6: F=2*COS(E): PRINT E, F
 .6              1.65067
```

■ v!=CSNG(x)

Converts x to a single-precision number.

```
TS#=3.141592653589794: PRINT TS#, CSNG(TS#)
 3.141592653589794          3.14159
```

■ v=CSRLIN

Returns the vertical position of the cursor. (See function POS.)

```
100 Y=CSRLIN: X=POS(0)
110 LOCATE 0,0:PRINT"NEW GAME";
120 LOCATE X,Y
```

■ v$=DATE$
DATE$=x$

Returns the date. Contains a 10-character string in the form mm-dd-yyyy. The DATE$ statement sets the date. x$ may be input in the form: mm-dd-yyyy, mm/dd/yyyy, mm-dd-yy, or mm/dd/yy.

```
10 DATE$="6/25/86"
110 TDAT$=DATE$
```

■ ERR

Special variable containing the error code for the last error. (See ERL.)

■ v$=ERR$

On the TRS-80 model IV, returns a system error number and message, or the latest disk-related error, or a null string if there is no error.

■ ERL

Special variable containing number of the line on which the last error occurred. (See ON ERROR GOTO.)

```
20 IF ERR=55 AND ERL=980 THEN RESUME 400
```

■ v=EXP(x)

Returns the value of e raised to the power x (e = 2.71828, the base for the natural logarithms.)

```
X=6: PRINT EXP(1), X, EXP(X)
 2.71828        6              403.429
```

■ v=FIX(x)

Returns the truncated integer part of x.

```
X=-45.93: PRINT X, FIX(X)
-45.93          -45
```

■ v=FRE(x)
  v=FRE(x$)

Returns the number of bytes of memory not being used by BASIC. x and x$ are dummy arguments. FRE with a string forces a house-cleaning of string space, before returning the number of free bytes.

```
PRINT FRE(0)
 31016
10 FRE("")
```

■ v$=HEX$(x)

Returns a string representing the hexadecimal value of x. x is rounded to an integer first.

```
10 J=255: PRINT J, HEX$(J)
RUN
 255            FF
```

■ IN#<slot>

On Apple, switches subsequent input to come from a peripheral connected to ⟨slot⟩. See also Appendix C.

■ v$=INKEY$

Returns the first character typed at the console. Returns a null if no character is pending at the keyboard. The value must be assigned to a string variable before use.

```
100 PRINT"O.K. TO PROCEED (Y/N)?"
110 A$=INKEY$: IF A$="" THEN 110 ELSE PRINT A$
```

■ v=INP(i)

> Returns the byte read from port i. (See also OUT.)
>
> ```
> 100 CHECK=INP(255)
> ```

■ v$=INPUT$(x[,[#]<fn>])

> Returns a string x characters long read from the terminal, or if ⟨fn⟩ is given, from a file. All characters are passed through except ⟨ctrl⟩⟨C⟩, which interrupts the function. No characters are echoed.
>
> ```
> 100 D$=INPUT$(1,#1)
> ```

■ v=INSTR([i,]x$,y$)

> Returns the position at which y$ occurred in x$ (the first occurrence). The search starts at position i (or at 1 if i is not given). If y$ is not found, 0 is returned. 0 is also returned if x$ is null, or i is greater than the length of x$. If y$ is null, i or 1 is returned.
>
> ```
> 10 A$="ARE YOU READY?": B$="YOU"
> 20 PRINT INSTR(A$,B$), INSTR(6,A$,B$)
> RUN
>  5          0
> ```

■ v=INT(x)

> Returns the largest integer less than or equal to x.
>
> ```
> PRINT INT(79.623), INT(-79.623)
>  79          -80
> ```

■ v$=LEFT$(y$,i)

> Returns a substring of y$, i characters long, starting at the left.
>
> ```
> A$="YESSIREE": PRINT LEFT$(A$,1)
> Y
> ```

■ v=LEN(x$)

> Returns the number of characters in x$.
>
> ```
> A$="WITHERSPOON": PRINT LEN(A$)
>  11
> ```

■ v=LOG(x)

> Returns the natural logarithm of x.
>
> ```
> L=45: M=LOG(L): PRINT L,M
>  45          3.80666
> ```

■ v=LPOS(x)

> Returns the position of the line printer head within the line printer buffer. This is not necessarily the physical position of the print head. In some versions of BASIC x is a dummy argument; in other versions, x may indicate which printer is being tested.
>
> ```
> 110 IF LPOS(0)>65 THEN LPRINT CHR$(13)
> ```

■ v=MEM

On the TRS-80, returns the amount of unused memory. Same as FRE(d).

■ v$=MID$(x$,i)
v$=MID$(x$,i,j)

Returns a substring of x$ starting with the ith character and including the rest of the string to the right. If j is specified, returns a substring starting at i, j characters long. (See also the key word MID$.)

```
X$=MID$("FREEHOLDER",5,4): PRINT X$
HOLD
```

■ v$=OCT$(x)

Returns a string representing the octal value of x. x is rounded to an integer first.

```
A=255: PRINT A, OCT$(A)
 255           377
```

■ v=PEEK(i)

Returns the byte read from memory location i. (See also the key word POKE.)

```
100 PRINT PEEK(65535)
```

■ v=POS(x)

Returns the current horizontal cursor position. x is a dummy argument.

```
100 IF POS(0)>80 THEN PRINT CHR$(13)
```

■ PR# <slot>

On Apple, switches subsequent output to go to a peripheral connected to ⟨slot⟩. See also Appendix C.

■ v$=RIGHT$(x$,i)

Returns a substring of x$, i characters long, starting at the right.

```
X$=RIGHT$("BOOKKEEPER",6): PRINT X$
KEEPER
```

▶ *Note:* In BASIC PLUS, RIGHT$ returns all the characters from position i to the end.

■ v=RND
v=RND(x)

Returns a random number between 0 and 1. The same sequence is generated for each run unless RANDOMIZE is used. A value of x > 0 has the same effect as if x were omitted. x = 0 repeats the last number generated, x < 0 restarts the same sequence for any number given. (Check your computer manual for variations of RND on different systems.)

```
10 FOR I=1 TO 5: PRINT RND;: NEXT I
RUN
 .245121  .305003  .311866  .515163  .0583136
RUN
 .245121  .305003  .311866  .515163  .0583136

10 FOR I=1 TO 5: PRINT RND(1);: NEXT I
RUN
 .245121  .305003  .311866  .515163  .0583136
RUN
 .245121  .305003  .311866  .515163  .0583136

10 Z=RND(-3): FOR I=1 TO 5: PRINT RND;: NEXT: PRINT
20 Z=RND(-4): FOR I=1 TO 5: PRINT RND;: NEXT: PRINT
30 Z=RND(-3): FOR I=1 TO 5: PRINT RND;: NEXT: PRINT
RUN
 .709808  .658938  .639327  .0685806  .104624
 .498871  .670127  .98706  .739354  .783018
 .709808  .658938  .639327  .0685806  .104624

10 FOR I=1 TO 5: PRINT RND;: NEXT: PRINT
20 FOR I=1 TO 5: PRINT RND(0);: NEXT: PRINT
30 FOR I=1 TO 5: PRINT RND;: NEXT: PRINT
RUN
 .245121  .305003  .311866  .515163  .0583136
 .0583136  .0583136  .0583136  .0583136  .0583136
 .788891  .497102  .363751  .984546  .901591
```

■ v=ROW(x)

Returns the current vertical cursor position. x is a dummy argument.

■ v=SGN(x)

If x>0, returns 1. If x = 0, returns 0. If x<0, returns −1.

```
100 ON SGN(NUM)+2 GOTO 1000, 2000, 3000
```

■ v=SIN(x)

Returns the sine of x in radians.

```
DSINE=SIN(1): PRINT DSINE
 .841471
```

■ v$=SPACE$(x)

Returns a string of spaces x long.

```
10 FOR S=1 TO 3
20   X$=SPACE$(S): PRINT X$"LINE #"S
30 NEXT S
RUN
 LINE #1
  LINE #2
   LINE #3
```

■ SPC(i)

Prints blanks on the terminal. Used in PRINT statements.

```
10 PRINT SPC(9) "SECTION 3.0" SPC(9) "V 1.5"
```

■ v=SQR(x)

Returns the square root of x.

```
B=25: ROOT=SQR(B): PRINT B, ROOT
 25              5
```

■ v$=STR$(x)

Returns a string representation of the value of x. *Note:* On some systems, STR$(x) includes a leading space for x > = 0, or a leading " −" for x < 0. To eliminate, use MID$(STR$(X),2).

```
NUM=10232: L$=STR$(NUM): PRINT NUM,"!"L$"!"
 10232          ! 10232!
```

■ v$=STRING$(i,j)
  v$=STRING$(i,y$)

Returns a string i long whose characters all have ASCII code j, or which equal the first character of y$.

```
PRINT STRING$(10,65), STRING$(5,"*")
AAAAAAAAAA    *****
```

■ TAB(i)

(Used only in PRINT and LPRINT statements.) Spaces over to position i on the terminal. If i is less than the current position, goes to position i on the next line.

```
100 PRINT TAB(35)"SUMMARY OF STATISTICS"
100 LPRINT TAB(115)"BUDGET REPORT"
```

■ v=TAN(y)

Returns the tangent of y in radians.

```
G=1: S=TAN(G): PRINT S
 1.55741
```

■ v$=TIME
  TIME$=x$

Returns the current time as an 8-character string in the form hh:mm:ss. Hours = 0 to 23, minutes and seconds = 0 to 59. The statement TIME$ sets the time. X$ may be in the form hh, hh:mm, or hh:mm:ss.

■ v=TIMER

Returns a single-precision number representing the number of seconds that have elapsed since midnight or system reset.

```
100 RANDOMIZE TIMER
```

- v=USR(y)
  v=USRn(y)

  Calls the user's assembly language subroutine with the argument y. n = 0 to 9 and corresponds to that given in the DEF USRn statement (if omitted, 0 is assumed).

  ```
  1010 DEF USR5=&HF000
  1020 M=USR5(R/2)
  ```

- v=VAL(x$)

  Returns the numerical value of string x$.

  ```
  S$="   1025.27": PRINT VAL(S$)
   1025.27
  ```

- v1=VARPTR(v2)

  Returns the address of the first byte of data identified with v2.

  ```
  410 A=VARPTR(C)
  1010 A=USR(VARPTR(B))
  ```

- v1=VARPTR(#<fn>)

  Returns the starting address of the disk I/O buffer (or FIELD buffer for random files) assigned to the file opened as ⟨fn⟩.

  ```
  510 B=VARPTR(#1)
  ```

BASIC File-Handling Key Words and Functions

▶ *Note:* Conventions used in these definitions are the same as key words and commands.

- CLOSE [[#]<fn>[,[#]<fn>]...]

  Ends the input-output to a disk file and disconnects the file number from the filename. This frees the numbered buffer associated with the file for input-output purposes. (File number is sometimes called channel number.) Writes the final buffer of output to a sequential file. CLOSE with no argument closes all files. *Note:* In the file-handling statements starting with CLOSE, OPEN, FIELD, PUT, and GET, #fn may be replaced with fn. In all others (PRINT#, INPUT#, PRINT# USING, LINE INPUT#, and WRITE#), the # is mandatory.

  ```
  599 CLOSE 1,2,3
  699 CLOSE #1,#2,#3
  999 CLOSE
  ```

- v#=CVD(<8-byte string>)
  v%=CVI(<2-byte string>)
  v!=CVS(<4-byte string>)

  Converts string values from a random file buffer to double-precision, integer, or single-precision numbers. (See example at FIELD.)

■ v=EOF(<fn>)

End of file. Returns −1 (true) if the end of a sequential file has been reached. (Under CP/M, with random files, if a GET is done *past* the end of file, EOF will return −1.)

```
310 IF EOF(1) THEN 1000
```

■ FIELD [#]<fn>,<n1> AS <var1> [,<n2> as <var2>...]

Allocates space in a random file buffer for use in later GET and PUT statements. ⟨fn⟩ is the number under which the file was opened, ⟨n1⟩ is the number of bytes (characters) allocated for field 1. ⟨var1⟩ is a special string variable that points to the correct place in the buffer. (Do not use buffer variable names in LET or INPUT statements.) Maximum length of the buffer varies, depending on the system, and may be specified in the OPEN statement; usually 128 bytes is the default. *Note:* Field width may also be given as an expression in parentheses.

```
310 OPEN "R",#1,"DATA1",15
320 FIELD #1, 2 AS B1$, 4 AS B2$, 8 AS B3$
340 GET #1
350 A%=CVI(B1$)
360 Z!=CVS(B2$)
370 Q#=CVD(B3$)
390 CLOSE

2040 FIELD #2,(14+2*J) AS D$, 4 AS N$
```

■ GET[#]<fn>[,<record number>]

Reads the specified record from a random disk file into the buffer. ⟨fn⟩ is the number under which the file was opened. If ⟨record number⟩ is omitted, the next record is read.

```
1000 GET #1,29
```

■ INPUT#<fn>,<var1>[,<var2>...]

Reads data items from a sequential disk file, opened for input as ⟨fn⟩, and assigns them to variables. Spaces, carriage returns, and line feeds are treated as delimiters. Strings containing spaces and commas must be surrounded by quotation marks.

```
200 INPUT#2, P$, D$, Q
```

■ LINE INPUT #<fn>,<string var>

Reads an entire record from a sequential disk file to a string variable. ⟨fn⟩ is the number used when the file was opened. All characters up to an ⟨enter⟩ are read into the string variable.

```
300 LINE INPUT#2, B$
```

■ v=LOC(<fn>)

On some systems, this function returns the record number that will be used by the next GET or PUT, if a random file opened to ⟨fn⟩ is referred to. On others, it returns the last record number used. If referring to a sequential file opened to ⟨fn⟩, it returns the number of 128-byte blocks that have been read from or written to since opening. Consult your manual.

```
1000 IF LOC(1)>100 THEN STOP
```

- v=LOF(⟨fn⟩)

    Returns the length of the file opened on channel ⟨fn⟩. On many systems, the length is given as the number of 128-byte records in the file. For further information, see your DOS manual.

```
10 IF LOF(1)>0 THEN PRINT"OLD FILE" ELSE PRINT"NEW FILE"
```

- LSET ⟨string var⟩=⟨string exp⟩

    Moves data from memory to a random file buffer in preparation for a PUT statement. ⟨string var⟩ will have been mentioned in a previous FIELD statement. Left-justifies the string expression in the field. Adds blanks on the right if it is too short; truncates on the right if it's too long. Can also be used to left-justify regular string variables. (See also RSET.)

```
3010 FIELD#1, 2 AS B1$, 4 AS B2$, 9 AS B3$
3020 LSET B1$=MKI(A%)
3030 LSET B2$=MKD(Z!)
3040 LSET B3$=MKD(Q#)
3050 PUT#1
```

- v$=MKD$(⟨x#⟩)
  v$=MKI$(⟨x%⟩)
  v$=MKS$(⟨x!⟩)

    Converts numeric values into strings, in preparation for placing them in a random file buffer. See example at LSET.

- OPEN "O",[#]⟨fn⟩,⟨filename⟩
  OPEN "I",[#]⟨fn⟩,⟨filename⟩
  OPEN "R",[#]⟨fn⟩,⟨filename⟩[,⟨n⟩]
  OPEN "D",[#]⟨fn⟩,⟨filename⟩[,⟨n⟩]

    Allocates a buffer to a disk file to allow for I/O. Specifies a mode: sequential output, O; sequential input, I; or random input/output, R. (On some systems, D is the same as R; D stands for direct input/output.) File number ⟨fn⟩ can be 1 to 15, record length ⟨n⟩ can be set for random files (the default is 128 bytes, which is the maximum allowed). Opening a file for sequential output, O, destroys its current contents.

```
10 OPEN "O",#1,"INFO1"
```

- OPEN ⟨filename⟩ FOR OUTPUT AS [#]⟨fn⟩ [LEN=⟨n⟩]
  OPEN ⟨filename⟩ FOR INPUT AS [#]⟨fn⟩ [LEN=⟨n⟩]
  OPEN ⟨filename⟩ FOR APPEND AS [#]⟨fn⟩ [LEN=⟨n⟩]

    This form of OPEN statement is allowed on some systems, in addition to that above. The first two examples are equivalent to the O and I modes previously shown. The APPEND option allows one to add data to the end of a sequential file.

- OPEN "E",⟨fn⟩,⟨filename⟩

    On the TRS-80, like the APPEND option, allows one to add data to the end of a sequential file ("extending" it).

■ PRINT#<fn>,[USING<format string>;]<exp1>[;<exp2>...]]

Sends data to a sequential file, opened for output as ⟨fn⟩. ⟨format string⟩ consists of special characters as described under PRINT USING. Semicolons, rather than commas, should be placed between expressions; otherwise additional spaces corresponding to the print zones will be written to the disk. Care should be taken so that delimiters are placed, or formatted, between strings sent to the disk. A ",'' or '' '' may be used. If the string data contains commas and spaces, the ASCII code for double quote ('') should be used. (See also WRITE#.)

```
210 PRINT #1, A; A$; ",";B$
510 P$"###.##  \    \  ####.##  \     \"
520 PRINT #1, USING P$;A; A$; B; B$
710 PRINT #1,CHR$(34);A$;CHR$(34);CHR$(34);B$;
        CHR$(34)
```

■ PUT [#]<fn>[,<n>]

Writes record ⟨n⟩ from the buffer to the random file opened as ⟨fn⟩. If ⟨n⟩ is omitted, writes the next available record. See example at LSET.

```
2030 PUT #1,R
```

■ RSET <string var>=<string exp>

Used the same way one uses LSET. Moves data from memory to a random file buffer in preparation for a PUT statement. If string expression is shorter than the string variable, right-justifies it. If string expression is longer, truncates it on the right. (See example at LSET.)

■ WRITE#<fn>,<exp1>[,<exp2>...]

Writes data to a sequential file opened for output as ⟨fn⟩. Expressions must be separated by commas. WRITE sends commas to the disk between items and surrounds strings with quotation marks. A carriage return/linefeed is sent after the last item.

```
500 WRITE#1,A,A$,B,B$
```

Additional BASIC Key Words and Functions on My Computer System

Graphics Key Words and Functions on My System; Escape Sequences

Using Disk Files with Applesoft BASIC and BASIC PLUS

A. Apple Disk-File Key Words and Functions

The information here applies to Applesoft (floating point) BASIC run on a disk system using DOS 3.3. Apple filenames may be up to 30 characters long. The first character must be a letter; the rest may be any typeable character except ^M, comma, or ⟨enter⟩. Control characters are not echoed and may cause problems. For Apple files, the user may specify slot, drive, and volume numbers. Example: MYFILE, S6,D1,V155 refers to the file with the name MYFILE, volume #155, on drive #1 connected to the disk controller in slot #6. Default values for slot and drive are those of the disk and drive you booted the system from, or the last ones set. If volume number is not specified, it is ignored.

When using Disk Operating System commands inside a BASIC program, printing ⟨CTRL⟩⟨D⟩ is a signal that the following characters are to be interpreted as a DOS command, up to the next carriage return. (The ⟨CTRL⟩⟨D⟩ should also have been preceded by a carriage return.) The usual practice is to create a string, D$ = CHR$(4), that is, = ⟨CTRL⟩⟨D⟩. Most Apple DOS commands may be typed by themselves in immediate mode, but must appear in programs in print statements preceded by ⟨CTRL⟩⟨D⟩, as in the following examples.

```
5 D$=CHR$(4)
10  PRINT D$;"CATALOG"
120 PRINT D$;"WRITE MYFILE"
990 PRINT D$;"CLOSE";FL$
```

■ APPEND ⟨filename⟩[,S⟨slot⟩][,D⟨drive⟩][,V⟨vol⟩]

Opens a sequential file, but causes the following WRITE data to be written starting at the end of any existing records.

```
20 PRINT D$;"APPEND";FL$
```

■ BLOAD ⟨filename⟩[,A⟨address⟩][,S⟨slot⟩][,D⟨drive⟩][,V⟨vol⟩]

Loads a binary file into memory at ⟨address⟩ if specified. If not specified, loads it into the address from which it was saved.

```
BLOAD PIX1, A$2000
```

- BRUN <filename>[,A<address>][,S<slot>][,D<drive>][,V<vol>]

  Loads and starts running a binary file at ⟨address⟩. If ⟨address⟩ is not specified, loads it at the address from which it was saved.

- BSAVE <filename>,A<address>,L<n>[,S<slot>][,D<drive>][,V<vol>]

  Stores a segment of memory in a file starting from ⟨address⟩ and ⟨n⟩ bytes long.

  ```
  BSAVE PIX1, A16384,L8192
  BSAVE PIX1, A$4000,L$2000
  ```

- CHAIN

  On the Apple, to run a series of programs without erasing earlier values requires several steps.

  1. BLOAD CHAIN, A12296 loads a program diskette.
  2. BSAVE CHAIN, A12296, L456 saves the CHAIN program onto the diskette holding the programs to be chained.
  3. The first program must then have as its last lines:

  ```
  999 PRINT CHR$(4);"BLOAD CHAIN, A520"
  1000 CALL 520"PART TWO"
  ```

- CLOSE [<filename>]

  Disconnects the buffer and terminates input or output to the file. Used after WRITE, it causes all remaining output characters in the buffer to be sent. Used without a filename, it closes all open files, with the exception of an EXEC file, if any.

  ```
  999 PRINT D$;"CLOSE FILE1"
  ```

- EXEC <filename>[,R<n>][,S<slot>][,D<drive>][,V<vol>]

  Loads and runs a text file made up of PRINT statements containing DOS and BASIC commands, executing the commands as if they were being typed in immediate mode. An EXEC file can run another program and send input to it. If ⟨n⟩ is used, execution will begin at field (program line) ⟨n⟩. Fields are numbered, starting with 0. EXEC does not delete a program currently in memory.

  ```
  EXEC STARTUP2
  ```

- GET <string var>

  Retrieves one character of data from a data file *when used after* OPEN *and* READ.

- IN#<slot>

  Takes all following input from the specified slot. IN#0 switches to input from the keyboard. IN#6 will boot the system if the disk controller is in slot 6.

  ```
  20 PRINT D$;"IN#1"
  ```

- INPUT <var list>

  Retrieves values from a data file *when used after* OPEN *and* READ.

■ MAXFILES <n>

Specifies the number of file buffers that can be active at one time. <n> may be 1 to 16; default at booting is 3. Use MAXFILES before loading a program or at the very beginning of a program, since it erases part of memory. All Apple DOS commands, except IN#, PR# or MAXFILES, require 1 buffer.

```
5 MAXFILES 4
```

■ MON [C][,][I][,][O]
  NOMON [C][,][I][,][O]

Displays subsequent disk activities. Options are C, commands only; I, input only; O, output only. At least one option must be chosen. NOMON turns off MON.

```
10 MON C
900 NOMON
```

■ OPEN <filename>[,S<slot>][,D<drive>][,V<vol>]
  OPEN <filename>,L<n>[,S<slot>][,D<drive>][,V<vol>]

The first form opens a sequential file for input or output, starting at the beginning. The second form opens a random-access file for input and output. In both cases a buffer is set up, and if no file exists by that name, one is created. <n> is the record length, and is required for random files; <n> may be 1 to 32767. See also APPEND.

```
10 PRINT D$;"OPEN FILE1"
```

■ POSITION <filename>[,R<n>]

Moves the pointer in a sequential file to a field <n> fields forward from the current field. (According to the Apple manual, a *field* is a sequence of characters terminated by carriage return; most computer texts call this a *record*. Note the use of R here.) Any following READ or WRITE instructions proceed from that point. Fields are numbered starting with 0.

```
200 PRINT D$;"POSITION";FL$;",R10"
```

■ PR#<slot>

Sends all following output to the specified slot. PR#0 switches output to the screen, PR#1 to a printer—if the printer is connected to slot 1. PR#6 boots the system if the disk controller is in slot 6, as it commonly is.

```
20 PRINT D$;"PR#1"
```

■ PRINT <var list>

Sends values to a data file *when used after* OPEN *and* WRITE.

■ READ <filename>[,B<byte>]
  READ <filename>[,R<records>][,B<byte>]

Causes all subsequent INPUT and GET statements to take information from the specified disk file. If the byte option is used, reading begins at <byte>. If <record> is specified for random files, reading will start at that record. If <byte> is specified for random files, reading will start at that byte in the specified file. READ is terminated by any DOS command or by ⟨CTRL⟩⟨D⟩ alone. A READ command is also terminated by a PRINT.

```
110 D$=CHR$(4):FL$="FILE1"
120 PRINT D$;"OPEN";FL$
130 PRINT D$; "READ";FL$
140 INPUT C$,N$,P
150 PRINT D$;"CLOSE";FL$
```

- WRITE ⟨filename⟩[,B⟨byte⟩]
  WRITE ⟨filename⟩[,R⟨record⟩][,B⟨byte⟩]

Causes all subsequent PRINT statements to send their output to the specified disk file. With the B⟨byte⟩ option, writing begins at ⟨byte⟩. If ⟨record⟩ is specified for random files, writing starts at that record. If ⟨byte⟩ is specified for random files, writing starts at that byte in the specified record. WRITE is terminated by any DOS command or ⟨CTRL⟩⟨D⟩ alone. A WRITE command is also terminated by an INPUT.

```
110 D$=CHR$(4):C$="X49":FL$="FILE1"
115 N$="RAKE":P=6.95
120 PRINT D$;"OPEN";FL$
130 PRINT D$;"WRITE";FL$
140 PRINT C$","N$","P
150 PRINT D$;"CLOSE";FL$
```

Examples of Apple File Handling: A SEQDEMO, A RANDEMO

The program A SEQDEMO illustrates the creation of a sequential file on the Apple. It is virtually the same program as SEQDEMO in Section 11.3. The differences, beyond those dictated by syntax, are as follows. In line 120, the number of records starts at 0. Apple file records are numbered starting with zero. Since we do not access any records by number in this program, it does not matter how we number them, but it's nice to remind oneself of this fact. Lines 180, 182, and 185 add a special record at the end of the file. This is used by the program further on to recognize the end of the file without generating an error (there is no end-of-file function on the Apple). This is done in line 221. K therefore holds the number of records, including this special ending record.

```
100   REM  *** A SEQDEMO ************************
110   INPUT "FILE NAME >>";FL$
115 D$ =  CHR$ (4)
120   PRINT D$;"OPEN";FL$:NR = 0
125   PRINT "ENTER DATA FOR FILE.  TYPE -1 TO QUIT."
130   PRINT "RECORD #";NR;
135   PRINT  TAB( 12);"PRODUCT CODE >>";: INPUT C$
137   IF C$ = "-1" THEN 180
140   PRINT  TAB( 12);"PRODUCT NAME >>";: INPUT N$
142   IF N$ = "-1" THEN 180
145   PRINT  TAB( 12);"PRICE >>>>>>>>>";: INPUT P
147   IF P < 0 THEN 180
155   PRINT D$;"WRITE";FL$
160   PRINT C$","N$","P
165   PRINT D$
```

```
170 NR = NR + 1: GOTO 130
180   PRINT D$;"WRITE";FL$
182   PRINT "$$$""","""$$$""","0
185   PRINT D$;"CLOSE";FL$
187   REM   ------------------------------------
188   PRINT
190   PRINT "FILE CHECK: HERE´S DATA ON FILE ";FL$
195   PRINT D$;"OPEN";FL$
200   PRINT :K = 0
210   PRINT D$;"READ";FL$
220   INPUT M$,Z$,D
221   IF M$ = "$$$" THEN  PRINT D$: GOTO 235
222   PRINT D$
225   PRINT M$; TAB( 7);Z$; TAB( 25);D
230 K = K + 1
232   GOTO 210
235   PRINT : PRINT "** ";K;" RCDS ON FILE **"
240   PRINT D$;"CLOSE";FL$
245   PRINT "** END OF PROGRAM **"
```

A RANDEMO does the same thing as RANDEMO in Section 12.2. The differences are as follows. The first part of the program detects whether the file requested is new or old by using an error routine. (Length-of-file and end-of-file functions are not available on the Apple.) An attempt to read past the end of a file generates an error. Therefore the program always tries to read the file given by the user. When the end of file is reached, this generates an error, and the error routine can tell whether the file is old or new by the value of the record counter RCD. This is not as good a method as using the EOF or LOF functions because *any* error will cause a branch to the error routine. In line 160,⟨CTRL⟩⟨D⟩ is used to terminate reading of data from disk. This is not actually necessary, but it is a good habit to terminate all reads and writes to disk before doing anything else.

```
100   REM  *** A RANDEMO ************************
105   ONERR  GOTO 300
110   INPUT "FILENAME >>";FL$
115 D$ =  CHR$ (4)
120 RCD = 0
130   PRINT D$;"OPEN";FL$;",L35"
140   PRINT D$;"READ";FL$;",R";RCD
150   INPUT C$,N$,P
160   PRINT D$
170   PRINT "#";RCD;" ";C$; TAB( 10);N$;" ";P
180 RCD = RCD + 1
190   GOTO 140
295   REM  --- ERROR ROUTINE --------------------
300   PRINT D$;"CLOSE";FL$: PRINT
320   IF RCD > 0 THEN  PRINT "HIGHEST RECORD = ";RCD - 1: GOTO 350
330   PRINT "NEW FILE -- ";FL$
335   PRINT D$;"OPEN";FL$;",L35"
336   PRINT D$;"WRITE";FL$;",R0"
337   PRINT "FILENAME =";",";FL$;",";"35
338   PRINT D$;"CLOSE";FL$:RCD = 1
340   REM  --- MAIN MENU -------------------------
350   PRINT
355   PRINT "**  A)DD DATA, E)DIT DATA, OR Q)UIT  **"
360   PRINT "TYPE A, E, OR Q --";
365 A$ = "": INPUT A$
370   IF A$ = "A" THEN 500
380   IF A$ = "E" THEN 600
390   IF A$ = "Q" THEN  END
```

(continued)

```
400    GOTO 360
410    REM  --- ADD MODULE -----------------------
500    PRINT : PRINT "ADD DATA TO FILE."
505    PRINT "TYPE -1 TO RETURN TO MENU."
510    PRINT "RECORD #";RCD;
520    PRINT  TAB( 12);"PRODUCT CODE >>";: INPUT C$
530    IF C$ = "-1" THEN 350
540    PRINT  TAB( 12);"PRODUCT NAME >>";: INPUT N$
550    IF N$ = "-1" THEN 350
560    PRINT  TAB( 12);"PRICE >>>>>>>>";: INPUT P
565    IF P < 0 THEN 350
569    PRINT D$;"OPEN";FL$;",L35"
570    PRINT D$;"WRITE";FL$;",R";RCD
575    PRINT C$",",N$",",P
576    PRINT D$;"CLOSE";FL$
577 RCD = RCD + 1: GOTO 510
590    REM  --- EDIT MODULE ----------------------
600    IF RCD = 1 THEN  PRINT "NO DATA TO EDIT.": GOTO 350
610    PRINT : PRINT "ENTER RECORD # TO EDIT."
615    PRINT "TYPE -1 TO RETURN TO MENU."
620    INPUT R
630    IF R = > RCD THEN  PRINT "TOO HIGH.": GOTO 610
640    IF R < 0 THEN 350
649    PRINT D$;"OPEN";FL$;",L35"
650    PRINT D$;"READ";FL$;",R";R
660    INPUT C$,N$,P
670    PRINT D$;"CLOSE";FL$
680    PRINT "#";R;" ";C$; TAB( 12);N$;" ";P
690    PRINT "WANT TO CHANGE (Y/N)";
695 A$ = "": INPUT A$
700    IF A$ = "N" THEN 610
705    IF A$ = "-1" THEN 350
810    INPUT "NEW PRODUCT CODE --";C$
815    IF C$ = "-1" THEN 350
820    INPUT "NEW PRODUCT NAME --";N$
825    IF N$ = "-1" THEN 350
830    INPUT "       NEW PRICE --";P
835    IF P < 0 THEN 350
836    PRINT "#";R;" ";C$; TAB( 13);N$;" ";P
840    PRINT "OK TO SAVE (Y/N)";
850 A$ = "": INPUT A$
860    IF A$ = "N" THEN  PRINT "ENTER NEW DATA AGAIN": GOTO 810
864    IF A$ = "-1" THEN 350
865    PRINT D$;"OPEN";FL$;",L35"
870    PRINT D$;"WRITE";FL$;",R";R
875    PRINT C$",",N$",",P
880    PRINT D$;"CLOSE";FL$
890    GOTO 610
```

The first thing the error routine does is close the file. Then, if the file is new, it is opened again and information is printed on record 0. Then the file is closed again. There are two main reasons for opening and closing files so often in this program. (1) It's good practice not to leave files open too long. A great deal is being done with files behind the scenes and the DOS of some systems can get lost. (2) It's good to keep sections of the program logically independent; therefore the file should be closed before leaving a section. That is why lines 335–338, 569–576, 649–670, and 865–880 open, read or write with the file, and immediately close it. It is usually all right to open and close files before and after a loop, where the loop does nothing but a succession of disk reads or writes.

B. Disk Files in BASIC PLUS

BASIC PLUS supports three kinds of files.

1. **Sequential files** These are quite similar to the sequential files discussed in Chapter 11. You write to or read from them with PRINT #m and INPUT #m statements, where m is a channel number assigned in an OPEN statement of the form

```
OPEN "filename" FOR INPUT AS FILE #m
OPEN "filename" FOR OUTPUT AS FILE #m
```

or simply

```
OPEN "filename" AS FILE #m
```

If the third form is used, BASIC PLUS first tries to open the file for INPUT. If the file does not exist, then it is opened for output instead. To detect the end of file during INPUT, you can either test for special "end" data items you have previously stored on the file, or you can use the ON ERROR GOTO technique illustrated in the APPLE examples given above. The statement for closing a file is CLOSE #m, where m is the channel number.

2. **Virtual array files** These files act like collections of user-accessible arrays. You can access these arrays with regular BASIC statements. For example, you can use INPUT statements to get data from the keyboard and then write it on a file. This is analogous to the way regular INPUT statements are used to get *and* save data in either numeric or string arrays. Conversely, PRINT statements can be used to read data from a file *and* display it on the output device. To use a virtual array file (for example, for use with the two arrays A and W$), you must have an OPEN statement, as shown above, followed by a statement of the form

```
<ln> DIM #<fn>,<variable list>
DIM #1, A(200), W$(100)=64
```

The W$(100) = 64 means that all strings are limited to 64 characters maximum. The allowable lengths are powers of 2 up to 512. The default value is 128. For virtual array files, you use the same OPEN and CLOSE statements as shown in (1) for sequential files. Once a virtual file is open, you write and read to it as though you were working with normal arrays. Example:

```
10 OPEN "TEST" AS FILE#2
20 DIM #2, N(10), CAR$(10)=32
30 FOR I=1 TO 10
40   PRINT "RECORD#";I
50   PRINT "TYPE COST,CAR NAME: "; !PROMPTS USER FOR 2 DATA ITEMS
60   INPUT N(I), CAR$(I)  !GETS DATA FROM KEYBOARD AND THEN WRITES
70 NEXT I                 !IT AS N(I) AND CAR$(I) ON THE FILE "TEST"
80 CLOSE #2
```

Similarly, you could read from this file with a loop that included the statement PRINT N(I), CAR$(I) to *get* data from the file and then display it.

You can also use assignment statements to store/retrieve data on/from virtual array files [for example, N(I) = SUM1 or SUM1 = N(I)]. Other BASIC statements can be used in a similar manner [for example, IF N(I) > 5000 THEN 250].

3. **Record I/O files**   These are quite similar to the Microsoft random-access files discussed in Chapter 12. The statements FIELD, LSET, RSET, PUT, and GET are used as shown in the programs RANDEMO and PLEDGE of Chapter 12. The same OPEN and CLOSE statements shown for sequential files in (1) above are used with record I/O files.

Answers to Selected Exercises

Answers to Selected Exercises (EX), Lab Exercises (LAB), and Problems/ Programming Projects (PPP).

Chapter 2

EX 2.2 **a.** 13   **b.** 13   **c.** 26   **d.** 22   **e.** 66   **f.** 88   **g.** 52

EX 2.4 Program Output:
```
WHAT HAPPENED IN THE YEAR
1776
OR
1945
OR
2001
```

EX 2.6 Values in the chart:
A = 12   B = 8   E1 = 20   E2 = 4   E3 = 96
A = 120   B = 128   W = 248

Program Output:
```
12   8   20   4   96
248
```

EX 2.8
```
10 A=3*4
20 B=10*A
30 PRINT A;B;B/4+6
40 PRINT B+B/4+6
```

EX 2.11 (a) 823,000,000   (b) 2.70000E+07
EX 2.13 (b) 7.32000E−07
EX 2.15 (a) .000000000000000982   (b) 1.50000E−13
EX 2.17 (a) 630,000,000   (b) .000000063

EX 2.19   (a) 7.00000E+09   (b) 7.00000E−09
EX 2.21   (a) 1.00000E+09   (b) 1.00000E−08

LAB 2.2   RUN the program ARITH2. Try some different numbers on the PRINT statements on LINES 110 and 130.

Program Output:

```
HAT SIZES IN DECIMAL FORM
 6.625  6.75  6.875  7  7.125  7.25  7.375
DRILL SIZES
 .03125  .0625  .09375  .125  .15625  .1875
MONEY AFTER DOUBLING $1 FOR 15 DAYS = $ 32768
```

LAB 2.4
```
4 REM--------------------------------------------------------
6 REM         RAT1 (PRODUCES OUPUT FOR TV VIEWER LAB)
8 REM--------------------------------------------------------
10 PRINT "TIME SLOT    TOTAL VIEWERS VIEWERS OF ABS  % WATCHING ABS"
20 LET N=1
30 LET A=31546
40 LET B=8876
45 LET P=B/A*100
50 PRINT N,A,B,P
60 LET N=2
70 LET A=36530!
80 LET B=9604
90 PRINT N,A,B,B/A*100
100 LET N=3
110 LET A=47867!
120 LET B=16390
130 PRINT N,A,B,B/A*100
140 LET N=4
150 LET A=35483!
160 LET B=6379
170 PRINT N,A,B,B/A*100
180 END
```

LAB 2.6   Enter and RUN the program RAT2. Use the DATA from LAB 2.4

LAB 2.8   Enter and RUN the program RETIRE. Try different values for Y. What happens when you enter −1? When you enter 100?

LAB 2.10
```
10 PRINT "THIS PROGRAM WILL ADD AND MULTIPLY NUMBERS."
20 PRINT "TYPE 4 NUMBERS SEPARATED BY COMMAS."
30 INPUT W,X,Y,Z
40 PRINT "THE SUM IS ";W+X+Y+Z
50 PRINT "THE PRODUCT IS ";W*X*Y*Z
60 END
```

PPP 2   Program Output:

```
5  MULTIPLIED BY  7 IS  35
```

PPP 4   A program to add five numbers is shown below.

```
6 REM------------ADDFIVE------------
10 PRINT "PLEASE ENTER FIVE NUMBERS, I WILL ADD THEM."
20 INPUT A,B,C,D,E
30 LET T=A+B+C+D+E
40 LET A1=T/5
50 PRINT "THE SUM OF YOUR NUMBERS IS";T
60 PRINT "THE AVERAGE OF YOUR NUMBERS IS";A1
70 END
```

PPP 6   This program shows a use of the INPUT statement.

```
6 REM------------GUESS------------
10 PRINT "HI THERE! WHAT IS YOUR NAME"
20 INPUT N$
30 PRINT "PLEASE GIVE ME TWO NUMBERS ";N$
40 INPUT A,B
50 LET P=A*B
60 PRINT "WHAT IS THE PRODUCT OF YOUR NUMBERS?"
70 INPUT G
80 LET D=P-G
90 PRINT "I GOT A PRODUCT OF";P;". YOU GOT";G
100 PRINT "THAT IS A DIFFERENCE OF";D
110 PRINT "SEE YOU AROUND, ";N$
120 END
```

PPP 8   This program demonstrates how to use the INPUT and PRINT statements to supply information and display results.

```
6 REM------------VITAMIN------------
10 PRINT "THIS PROGRAM WILL CALCULATE UNIT PRICE OF VITAMIN C"
20 PRINT "FOR EACH BRAND YOU SUPPLY THE COST AND NUMBER OF TABLETS"
30 PRINT "IN EACH BOTTLE."
40 PRINT "FOR BRAND 'W' WHAT IS COST AND THE NUMBER OF TABLETS?"
50 INPUT C1,T1
60 PRINT "NOW THE COST OF BRAND 'X' AND THE NUMBER OF TABLETS?"
70 INPUT C2,T2
80 PRINT "NOW THE COST OF BRAND 'Y' AND THE NUMBER OF TABLETS?"
90 INPUT C3,T3
100 PRINT "AND THE COST OF BRAND 'Z' AND THE NUMBER OF TABLETS?"
110 INPUT C4,T4
120 LET U1=C1/T1
130 LET U2=C2/T2
140 LET U3=C3/T3
150 LET U4=C4/T4
160 PRINT "NOW FOR THE PRICE PER TABLET FOR EACH BRAND!"
170 PRINT
180 PRINT "BRAND","TABLETS","ITEM COST","UNIT COST"
190 PRINT "  -W",T1,C1,U1
200 PRINT "  -X",T2,C2,U2
210 PRINT "  -Y",T3,C3,U3
220 PRINT "  -Z",T4,C4,U4
```

PPP 10 The program written for PPP 9 can be modified as follows.

```
6 REM------------CARLOAN2------------
10 PRINT "THIS PROGRAM CALCULATES PAYMENTS FOR A CAR LOAN."
20 PRINT "WHAT DO YOU WANT THE LENGTH OF THE LOAN TO BE?"
30 INPUT Y
40 PRINT "WHAT IS THE ANNUAL INTEREST RATE? (E.G. FOR 8% TYPE 8)"
50 INPUT I
60 PRINT "WHAT IS THE PRICE OF THE CAR?"
70 INPUT C
80 LET P=C+C*I/100*Y
90 LET M=P/(Y*12)
100 PRINT "THE TOTAL COST OF THE CAR IS $";P
110 PRINT "THE MONTHLY PAYMENTS WILL BE $";M
```

Chapter 3

EX 3.2 Program Output (user input is shown underlined):

```
PROGRAM TO FIND AREA OF A CIRCLE
TYPE IN THE RADIUS
?1
AREA = 3.14159
TYPE IN THE RADIUS
?2
AREA = 12.5664
TYPE IN THE RADIUS
?10
AREA = 314.159
TYPE IN THE RADIUS
?^C
Break in 30
```

EX 3.6 Program Output:

```
THIS PROGRAM WAS RUN CORRECTLY.
```

EX 3.8 FOR statements:

```
FOR P=18 TO 46 STEP 7
FOR K3=200 TO 204
FOR X=1 TO 1.7 STEP 0.1
FOR N4=10 TO 2 STEP -2
FOR D6=3 TO 28 STEP 5
```

EX 3.10 The program will PRINT 10 numbers.

Program Output:

```
1
5
5
9
```

(continued)

```
                        9
                        13
                        13
                        17
                        17
                        21
```

EX 3.12   Program Output:

```
THIS IS A COMPUTER
NOTHING CAN GO
WRONG
WRONG
WRONG
NOTHING CAN GO
WRONG
WRONG
WRONG
NOTHING CAN GO
WRONG
WRONG
WRONG
NOTHING CAN GO
WRONG
WRONG
WRONG
```

EX 3.14   The program will print 3 lines and will put 6 asterisks on each line.

LAB 3.2

```
4 REM--------------------------------------------
6 REM     WAU (GIVES AIRLINER STATISTICS)
8 REM--------------------------------------------
10 PRINT "TYPE IN:"
20 PRINT "FLIGHT NUMBER:";
30 INPUT N
40 PRINT "PLANE SPEED (MPH):";
50 INPUT S
60 PRINT "DISTANCE (MILES):";
70 INPUT D
80 PRINT "WIND SPEED (MPH):";
90 INPUT W
100 PRINT
110 PRINT "FLIGHT NUMBER:";N
120 LET G=(S+W)/60
130 LET T=D/G
140 LET F=166*T
150 PRINT "ESTIMATED FLIGHT TIME:";T;"MINUTES"
160 PRINT "FUEL NEEDED:";F;"POUNDS + RESERVE"
170 PRINT
180 GOTO 10
190 END
```

LAB 3.4
```
4 REM------------------------------------------
6 REM                     MATHQ2
8 REM------------------------------------------
10  C=0: W=0: X=50: Y=1
20 IF (C+W)=20 THEN 80
30    PRINT "WHAT IS";X;"+";Y;
40    INPUT A
50    IF A=X+Y THEN PRINT "VERY GOOD": C=C+1: GOTO 70
60       PRINT "NO, THE SUM IS";X+Y;".": W=W+1
70    X=X-2: Y=Y+3: GOTO 20
80 PRINT "THAT'S THE END."
90 PRINT "YOU HAD";C;"CORRECT AND";W;"WRONG."
100 END
```

LAB 3.8 Program Output:
```
*
**
***
****
*****
******
*******
********
*********
**********
```

LAB 3.10
```
4 REM------------------------------------------
6 REM                  GRADE
8 REM------------------------------------------
10 PRINT "INPUT GRADES. TYPE 101 WHEN FINISHED."
20 INPUT G
30 IF G<21 THEN LET G(1)=G(1)+1
40 IF G>20 AND G<41 THEN LET G(2)=G(2)+1
50 IF G>40 AND G<61 THEN LET G(3)=G(3)+1
60 IF G>60 AND G<81 THEN LET G(4)=G(4)+1
70 IF G>80 AND G<101 THEN LET G(5)=G(5)+1
80 TGRADE=TGRADE+G
90 IF G<>101 THEN 20
100 PRINT
110 PRINT "  GRADES","DISTRIBUTION"
120 PRINT "  0 TO 20",
130 IF G(1)=0 THEN 170
140 FOR I=1 TO G(1)
150    PRINT "<*>";
160 NEXT I
170 PRINT
180 FOR I=1 TO 4
190    PRINT I*20+1;"TO";I*20+20,
200    IF G(I+1)=0 THEN 240
210      FOR J=1 TO G(I+1)
220        PRINT "<*>";
230      NEXT J
240    PRINT
```

(*continued*)

```
250 NEXT I
260 PRINT
270 LET TS=G(1)+G(2)+G(3)+G(4)+G(5)
280 PRINT "AVERAGE GRADE WAS";(TGRADE-101)/TS
290 END
```

PPP 2   The program given in PPP 2 when rewritten will be:

```
6 REM ------------INTEREST3.2------------
10 PRINT "THIS PROGRAM CALCULATES INTEREST EARNED AT 7%"
20 PRINT "ANNUAL INTEREST COMPOUNDED DAILY."
30 PRINT "TELL ME HOW MUCH MONEY YOU HAVE."
40 INPUT B
50 PRINT "HOW MANY DAYS BEFORE YOU NEED IT?"
60 INPUT D
70 X=1
80 I=B*.07/365
90 B=B+I
100 X=X+1
110 IF X<D THEN 80
120 PRINT "YOU WILL HAVE ";B;" DOLLARS AFTER ";X;" DAYS."
130 END
```

PPP 4   A program to calculate population, with the user supplying the information is shown below.

```
6 REM------------POPULATION3.4------------
10 REM THIS PROGRAM CALCULATES POPULATION
20 INPUT "WHAT IS THE NAME OF THE REGION";N$
30 INPUT "WHAT IS THE STARTING POPULATION";P
40 INPUT "ENTER THE YEAR OF THAT POPULATION";Y1
50 INPUT "FOR WHAT YEAR DO YOU WANT TO KNOW THE POPULATION";Y2
60 INPUT "ENTER THE GROWTH RATE (E.G.TYPE 5 FOR 5%)";G
70 G=G/100
80 FOR Y=Y1+1 TO Y2
90    P=P+P*G
100 NEXT Y
110 PRINT "IN ";Y2;" THE POPULATION OF ";N$;" WILL BE";P
120 PRINT "DO YOU WANT MORE CALCULATIONS";
130 INPUT X$
140 IF X$="YES" THEN 20
150 PRINT "GOOD DAY."
160 END
```

PPP 6   In this program the user supplies information for the BANK program initially written for PPP 5.

```
4 REM----------------------------------------------------------
6 REM                          BANKS2
8 REM----------------------------------------------------------
10 PRINT "THIS IS THE LAST INTERNATIONAL BANK."
20 PRINT "WHAT IS YOUR NAME PLEASE";
30 INPUT N$
40 PRINT
50 PRINT "WELL ";N$;" WE AIM TO PLEASE. WHAT INTEREST RATE"
```

(continued)

```
60 PRINT "WOULD YOU LIKE? (INPUT AN ANNUAL %- E.G. 5 FOR 5%)";
70 INPUT R
80 PRINT "HOW MUCH ARE YOU GOING TO DEPOSIT";
90 INPUT A
100 PRINT "FOR HOW MANY YEARS WILL YOU LEAVE THE MONEY WITH ME";
110 INPUT Y
120 PRINT
130 PRINT "PLEASE STAND BY WHILE I CALCULATE YOUR BALANCE."
140 FOR I=1 TO 500: LET X=X+I: NEXT I
150 LET R=R/100
160 LET B=A
170 LET C=0
180 LET C=C+1
190 LET B=B+INT(B*R*100)/100
200 IF C<Y THEN 180
210 PRINT
220 PRINT "THANK YOU FOR WAITING ";N$
230 PRINT "YOU WILL BE HAPPY TO KNOW THAT YOUR BALANCE"
240 PRINT "WILL BE $";B
250 PRINT
260 PRINT "YOU WILL BE SORRY TO HEAR THAT WE WILL HAVE TO"
270 PRINT "REPORT THAT YOU HAVE HAD A CAPITAL GAINS OF"
280 PRINT "$";B-A;".  YOU WILL OWE THE IRS $";
290 PRINT INT((B-A)*.2*100+.5)/100
300 END
```

PPP 8   This program allows deposits and withdrawals to savings.

```
6 REM------------SAVINGS------------
10 PRINT "WELCOME TO THE BIG CITY FIRST NATIONAL BANK"
20 PRINT "WE HAVE A SPECIAL 'DAY IN TO DAY OUT' SAVINGS ACCOUNT"
30 INPUT "HOW MUCH DO YOU WISH TO DEPOSIT";B
40 INPUT "WHAT INTEREST RATE WOULD YOU LIKE. (E.G. FOR 5% TYPE 5)";R
50 INPUT "ENTER THE YEAR";Y1
60 INPUT "WHAT DAY OF THE YEAR IS IT";D1
70 R=R/100/365
80 PRINT "YOU MAY MAKE DEPOSITS AND WITHDRAWALS."
90 PRINT "DO YOU WANT TO DEPOSIT (TYPE 'D') OR WITHDRAW (TYPE 'W')"
100 INPUT "MONEY TODAY";T$
110 INPUT "ENTER THE YEAR";Y2
115 IF Y2<Y1 THEN PRINT "YEAR MUST BE ";Y1;" OR LATER":GOTO 110
120 INPUT "ENTER THE DAY OF THE YEAR";D2
125 IF Y2=Y1 AND D2<D1 THEN PRINT "DAY MUST BE MORE THAN";D1:GOTO 120
130 D3=D2+(Y2-Y1)*365+365-D1
140 FOR I=1 TO D3
150    B=B+B*R
160 NEXT I
170 IF T$="W" THEN 230
180    IF T$="D" THEN 200
190       GOTO 280
200    INPUT "ENTER YOUR DEPOSIT";B1
210    B=B+B1
```

(continued)

```
220    GOTO 280
230 INPUT "ENTER AMOUNT OF WITHDRAWAL";B2
240 IF B-B2<0 THEN 270
250    B=B-B2
260    GOTO 280
270 PRINT "YOU DON'T HAVE THAT MUCH MONEY-TRANSACTION CANCELLED"
280 PRINT "YOU NOW HAVE ";B;" DOLLARS."
290 PRINT "DO YOU HAVE ANY MORE TRANSACTIONS (TYPE 'Y' FOR YES).";
300 INPUT A$
310 Y1=Y2
320 D1=D2
330 IF A$="Y" THEN 90
340 PRINT "THANK YOU FOR BANKING AT BCFNB."
350 END
```

PPP 10   CHANGE100 calculates change when $100 is offered to pay for a purchase.

```
6 REM------------CHANGE100------------
10 PRINT "THIS PROGRAM WILL CALCULATE THE LEAST NUMBER OF BILLS"
20 PRINT "WHICH MUST BE GIVEN WHEN A PURCHASE IS MADE AND A $100"
30 PRINT "BILL IS TENDERED TO PAY FOR THE PURCHASE."
40 PRINT "ALL PURCHASES ARE IN WHOLE DOLLAR AMOUNTS."
50 PRINT "PLEASE ENTER THE PURCHASE PRICE."
60 INPUT P
70 C=100-P
80 PRINT "THE CHANGE WILL BE:"
90 IF INT(C/20)<1 THEN 120
100    B1=INT(C/20): IF B1=1 THEN Z$="BILL" ELSE Z$="BILLS"
110    PRINT B1;" $20 ";Z$
120 C=C-20*B1
130 IF INT(C/10)<1 THEN 160
140    B2=INT(C/10)
150    PRINT B2;" $10 BILL"
160 C=C-B2*10
170 IF INT(C/5)<1 THEN 200
180    B3=INT(C/5)
190    PRINT B3;" $5 BILL"
200 C=C-B3*5
210 IF INT(C/2)<1 THEN 240
220    B4=INT(C/2): IF B4=1 THEN Z$="BILL" ELSE Z$="BILLS"
230    PRINT B4;" $2 ";Z$
240 C=C-B4*2
250 IF INT(C+.0001)<1 THEN 280
260    B5=INT(C+.0001)
270    PRINT B5;" $1 BILL"
280 N=B1+B2+B3+B4+B5
290 C1=B1*20+B2*10+B3*5+B4*2+B5
300 PRINT "THAT IS A TOTAL CHANGE OF $";C1;". AND A TOTAL OF ";N;"BILLS"
```

PPP 12   SALES considers local sales tax on five purchases.

```
6 REM------------SALES------------
10 PRINT "WELCOME TO THE PASSTIES DEPARTMENT STORE"
20 PRINT "SALES TAX IN THIS STATE IS 6% OF PURCHASE PRICE"
```

(continued)

```
30 PRINT "PLEASE ENTER STOCK NUMBER OF YOUR ITEMS"
40 PRINT "FOLLOWED BY THE PURCHASE PRICE."
50 PRINT "YOU SHOULD ENTER THE TWO NUMBERS ON THE SAME LINE"
60 PRINT "WITH A COMMA BETWEEN THEM."
70 PRINT "STOCK # AND PRICE FOR ITEM 1";
80 INPUT S1,P1
90 PRINT "STOCK # AND PRICE FOR ITEM 2";
100 INPUT S2,P2
110 PRINT "STOCK # AND PRICE FOR ITEM 3";
120 INPUT S3,P3
130 PRINT "STOCK # AND PRICE FOR ITEM 4";
140 INPUT S4,P4
150 PRINT "STOCK # AND PRICE FOR ITEM 5";
160 INPUT S5,P5
170 PRINT "STOCK #","PRICE","TAX","ITEM COST"
180 T1=P1*.06: C1=P1+T1
190 T2=P2*.06: C2=P2+T2
200 T3=P3*.06: C3=P3+T3
210 T4=P4*.06: C4=P4+T4
220 T5=P5*.06: C5=P5+T5
230 PRINT S1,P1,T1,C1
240 PRINT S2,P2,T2,C2
250 PRINT S3,P3,T3,C3
260 PRINT S4,P4,T4,C4
270 PRINT S5,P5,T5,C5
280 PRINT
290 A1=P1+P2+P3+P4+P5
300 A2=T1+T2+T3+T4+T5
310 A3=C1+C2+C3+C4+C5
320 PRINT "TOTALS",A1,A2,A3
330 END
```

Chapter 4

EX 4.2 Program Output:

```
18
16
10
130
200
130
16
8
10
6.5
54
```

EX 4.4 Program Output:

```
1 1 2 3 5 8 13 21 34 55
```

LAB 4.2   Program Output:

```
TYPE THE DAY IN MARCH REQUESTED AND THE NUMBER OF SEATS.
?4,2
RESERVATION O.K.--ISSUE 2 TICKET(S) FOR MARCH 4 .
STILL 1 EMPTY SEAT(S) ON MARCH 4
NEXT REQUEST PLEASE.

TYPE THE DAY IN MARCH REQUESTED AND THE NUMBER OF SEATS.
?13,5
SORRY, ONLY 3 SEAT(S) AVAILABLE.
  FOR MARCH 13 . MAKE ANOTHER REQUEST.

TYPE THE DAY IN MARCH REQUESTED AND THE NUMBER OF SEATS.
?13,3
RESERVATION O.K.--ISSUE 3 TICKET(S) FOR MARCH 13 .
STILL 0 EMPTY SEAT(S) ON MARCH 13 .
NEXT REQUEST PLEASE.

TYPE THE DAY IN MARCH REQUESTED^C
```

LAB 4.4

```
4 REM----------------------------------------------------------------
6 REM            BUBBLE (SORTS NUMBERS INTO DESCENDING ORDER)
8 REM----------------------------------------------------------------
100 PRINT "PROGRAM TO SORT A LIST OF NUMBERS INTO ASCENDING ORDER"
110 DIM A(100)
120 PRINT
130 PRINT "HOW MANY NUMBERS TO BE SORTED";
140 INPUT N
150 PRINT "TYPE IN THE LIST OF NUMBERS ONE AT A TIME:"
160 FOR I=1 TO N
170   INPUT A(I)
180 NEXT I
190 ITEMS=N
200 REM====================================================
210 REM           ROUTINE TO USE BUBBLE SORT ON A()
220 ITEMS=ITEMS-1
230 IF ITEMS=0 THEN 340
240   FLAG=0
250   K=1
260   IF A(K+1)<=A(K) THEN 310
270     TEMP=A(K+1)
280     A(K+1)=A(K)
290     A(K)=TEMP
300     FLAG=1
310   K=K+1
320   IF K<=ITEMS THEN 260
330   IF FLAG<>0 THEN 220
340 PRINT
400 REM====================================================
410 REM   ROUTINE TO PRINT N ITEMS, 4 ITEMS/LINE, 14 COLS/ITEM
420 K=0
```

(*continued*)

```
430 J=1
440 IF J>4 THEN 500
450   K=K+1
460    IF K>N THEN 520
470     PRINT A(K),
480      J=J+1
490      GOTO 440
500 PRINT
510 GOTO 430
520 PRINT
530 END
```

LAB 4.6
```
4 REM------------------------------------
6 REM                  TREE2
8 REM------------------------------------
10 PRINT TAB(35)"*"
20 FOR I=1 TO 20
30    PRINT TAB(35-I)"*"TAB(35+I)"*"
40 NEXT I
50 PRINT TAB(35-I)"***********************";
55 PRINT "********************"
60 FOR I=1 TO 3
70    PRINT TAB(30)"+"TAB(40)"+"
80 NEXT I
90 PRINT TAB(30)"+++++++++++"
100 END
```

PPP 2 ARRAY moves the largest and smallest numbers in an array to the ends of the list.

```
6 REM------------ARRAY------------
10 PRINT "THIS PROGRAM REQUIRES THAT YOU ENTER 10 NUMBERS"
20 PRINT "THE PROGRAM THEN SELECTS THE LARGEST AND SMALLEST"
30 PRINT "NUMBERS FROM YOUR LIST AND PRINTS THEM."
40 DIM A(20)
50 FOR I=1 TO 10
60    INPUT A(I)
70 NEXT I
80 L=A(1): S=A(1): L1=1: S1=1
90 FOR I=2 TO 10
100    IF A(I)<S THEN LET S=A(I): S1=I
110    IF A(I)>L THEN LET L=A(I): L1=I
120 NEXT I
130 PRINT "THE SMALLEST NUMBER IS";S
140 PRINT "THE LARGEST NUMBER IS";L
150 T=A(1): A(1)=S: A(S1)=T
155 IF L1=1 THEN L1=S1
160 T=A(10): A(10)=L: A(L1)=T
170 PRINT "THE NEW LIST IS :"
180 FOR I=1 TO 10
190    PRINT A(I);
200 NEXT I
210 END
```

PPP 4   GRADES takes information supplied by the user, calculates averages and prints the results in a table.

```
6 REM------------GRADES------------
10 DIM A(5,5)
20 PRINT "THIS PROGRAM ACCEPTS FIVE GRADES FOR EACH OF FIVE STUDENTS"
30 PRINT "IT THEN AVERAGES THE SCORES AND PRINTS A TABLE OF RESULTS."
40 PRINT "PLEASE ENTER THE SCORES FOR THE STUDENTS AS REQUESTED."
50 FOR I=1 TO 5
60   PRINT "ENTER GRADES FOR STUDENT #";I
70   FOR J=1 TO 5
80     INPUT A(I,J)
90     T(I)=T(I)+A(I,J)
100    NEXT J
110    M(I)=T(I)/5: S(I)=I
120 NEXT I
130 PRINT "STUDENT","    TEST GRADES";"           AVERAGE"
140 PRINT ," 1   2   3   4   5"
150 FOR I=1 TO 5
160   PRINT "STUDENT #";S(I),
170   FOR J=1 TO 5
180     PRINT A(I,J);
190   NEXT J
200   PRINT "       ";M(I)
210 NEXT I
220 END
```

PPP 6   This program extends GRADES to produce letter grades.

```
6 REM------------GRADES2------------
10 DIM A(5,5)
20 FOR I=0 TO 5: D$(I)="F": NEXT I
30 D$(6)="D": D$(7)="C": D$(8)="B": D$(9)="A": D$(10)="A"
40 PRINT "THIS PROGRAM ACCEPTS FIVE GRADES FOR EACH OF FIVE STUDENTS"
50 PRINT "IT THEN AVERAGES THE SCORES AND PRINTS A TABLE OF RESULTS."
60 PRINT "PLEASE ENTER THE SCORES FOR THE STUDENTS AS REQUESTED."
70 FOR I=1 TO 5
80   PRINT "ENTER THE MAXIMUM GRADE FOR TEST #";I;: INPUT B(I)
90   B1=B1+B(I)
100 NEXT I
110 FOR I=1 TO 5
120   PRINT "ENTER GRADES FOR STUDENT #";I
130   FOR J=1 TO 5
140     INPUT A(I,J)
150     T(I)=T(I)+A(I,J)
160   NEXT J
170   M(I)=INT(T(I)/5+.5): S(I)=I
180 NEXT I
190 FOR I=1 TO 5: G(I)=T(I)/B1*100: K=INT(G(I)/10): G$(I)=D$(K): NEXT I
200 PRINT "STUDENT","    TEST GRADES";"          AVERAGE";"   GRADE"
210 PRINT ," 1   2   3   4   5"
```

(continued)

```
220 FOR I=1 TO 5
230   PRINT "STUDENT #";S(I),
240   FOR J=1 TO 5
250     PRINT A(I,J);
260   NEXT J
270   PRINT "     ";M(I);"     ";G$(I)
280 NEXT I
290 END
```

PPP 8   The part of the output which is underlined represents the input by the user.

Program Output:

```
PLAYER #   ? 2
WINS       ? 11
LOSES      ? 13

PLAYER #   ? 4
WINS       ? 12
LOSES      ? 9

PLAYER #   ? 1
WINS       ? 16
LOSES      ? 11

PLAYER #   ? 7
WINS       ? 9
LOSES      ? 9

PLAYER #   ? 3
WINS       ? 12
LOSES      ? 13

  TO SORT ON PLAYER #   TYPE 1
          ON WINS       TYPE 2
          ON PERCENTAGE TYPE 3
?3
PLAYER #        WINS        LOSES        PERCENTAGES
2               11          13           .458333
3               12          13           .48
7               9           9            .5
4               12          9            .571429
1               16          11           .592593
```

Chapter 5

EX 5.2   Program Output:

```
1   2   4
2   4   8
3   6   12
4   8   16
5   10  20
```

EX 5.4   Program Output:

    2
    1

EX 5.6
```
10 FOR I=1 TO 10
20   X=INT(16*RND(1))+5
30   PRINT X;
40 NEXT I
50 END
```

EX 5.8
```
10 FOR I=1 TO 10
20   X=INT(3*RND(1))+1
30   PRINT X;
40 NEXT I
50 END
```

EX 5.10
```
10 FOR I=1 TO 10
20   X=INT(101*RND(1))-50
30   PRINT X;
40 NEXT I
50 END
```

LAB 5.2
```
6 REM------------WEATHER2------------
10 PRINT "THIS PROGRAM WILL COMPARE TEMPERATURES FOR 1874 AND 1875"
20 DIM A(12),B(12),C(12)
30 FOR I=1 TO 12
40   READ A(I)
50 NEXT I
60 FOR I=1 TO 12
70   READ B(I)
80   C(I)=A(I)-B(I)
90 NEXT I
100 PRINT
110 PRINT "MONTH","1874","1875","DIFFERENCE","AVERAGE"
120 FOR I=1 TO 12
130   PRINT I,A(I),B(I),C(I),(A(I)+B(I))/2
140 NEXT I
150 PRINT
160 FOR I=1 TO 12
170   IF C(I)>=0 THEN 200
180     PRINT "MONTH #";I;"WAS WARMER IN 1875 BY";-C(I);"DEGREES."
190     PRINT
200 NEXT I
210 DATA 19.0,18.9,23.3,29.6,51.3,58.1,65.3,64.4,60.0,45.7,29.9,21.0
220 DATA 5.9,1.3,19.4,33.3,48.5,56.7,63.0,61.5,52.8,39.9,28.5,25.7
230 END
```

LAB 5.4
```
4 REM----------------------------------------------------------------
6 REM                          SURVEY1
8 REM----------------------------------------------------------------
100 PRINT "DATA GATHERED ON QUESTIONNAIRE"
105 PRINT: PRINT TAB(20)"PERCENTAGE OF VOTERS IN EACH CATAGORY"
110 PRINT: PRINT TAB(30)"AGREE"TAB(40)"DISAGREED"TAB(53)"NO OPINION"
```

(continued)

```
130 READ N: LET K=1000/N
140 FOR I=1 TO 3
150   FOR J=1 TO 3
160     LET X(I,J)=0
170     LET Y(I,J)=0
180     LET Z(I,J)=0
190   NEXT J
200 NEXT I
210 FOR I=1 TO N
220   READ S,A
230   FOR J=1 TO 3
240     READ C
250     IF S=1 THEN 280
260       LET X(J,C)=X(J,C)+1
270       GOTO 290
280     LET Y(J,C)=Y(J,C)+1
290     IF A>=16 THEN 310
300       LET Z(J,C)=Z(J,C)+1
310   NEXT J
320 NEXT I
330 FOR I=1 TO 3
340   PRINT I;TAB(5)"FEMALE VOTE:"TAB(30)INT(X(I,1)*K)/10;
350   PRINT TAB(43)INT(X(I,2)*K)/10 TAB(56)INT(X(I,3)*K)/10
360   PRINT TAB(5)"MALE VOTE:"TAB(30)INT(Y(I,1)*K)/10;
370   PRINT TAB(43)INT(Y(I,2)*K)/10 TAB(56)INT(Y(I,3)*K)/10
380   PRINT TAB(5)"UNDER AGE 16 VOTE:"TAB(30)INT(Z(I,1)*K)/10;
390   PRINT TAB(43)INT(Z(I,2)*K)/10 TAB(56)INT(Z(I,3)*K)/10
400 NEXT I
700 DATA 20
710 DATA 0,15,1,2,1,0,33,2,3,1,1,21,1,1,2,0,22,2,2,3
720 DATA 1,36,3,1,1,1,14,2,2,2,0,13,3,2,2,0,55,3,3,1
730 DATA 1,49,1,3,2,1,32,3,1,1,0,44,2,2,2,1,56,3,2,2
740 DATA 0,32,2,2,1,0,42,3,2,1,1,15,1,1,2,1,22,2,1,1
750 DATA 0,34,3,1,2,1,10,1,3,2,0,28,2,1,2,1,15,1,2,3
990 END
```

LAB 5.6

```
4 REM----------------------------------------------------------------
6 REM                           DIAMETER
8 REM----------------------------------------------------------------
10 INPUT "HOW MANY PEOPLE AT YOUR PARTY";N
20 INPUT "HOW MANY SQUARE-INCH BITES EACH";B
30 LET A=N*B
40 LET D(1)=2*SQR(A/3.14159)
50 LET D(2)=2*SQR(A/(2*3.14159))
60 LET D(3)=2*SQR(A/(3*3.14159))
70 FOR I=1 TO 3
80   PRINT "IF YOU ORDER";I;"PIZZA(S), THE DIAMETER SHOULD BE ";
90   PRINT "AT LEAST";D(I);"INCHES."
100 NEXT I
110 END
```

LAB 5.8

```
4 REM----------------------------
6 REM            COIN
8 REM----------------------------
10 RANDOMIZE
20 FOR I=1 TO 100
30    LET R=RND(1)
40    IF R>.5 THEN 70
50    PRINT "  TAILS";: T=T+1
60    GOTO 90
70      LET H=H+1
80      PRINT " HEADS";
90 NEXT I
95 PRINT: PRINT
100 PRINT "NUMBER OF HEADS =";H
110 PRINT "NUMBER OF TAILS =";T
120 END
```

LAB 5.10

```
4 REM-------------------------------------
6 REM                DICE
8 REM-------------------------------------
10 RANDOMIZE
20 PRINT "FIRST DIE","SECOND DIE","TOTAL"
30 FOR I=1 TO 10
40    LET X=INT(6*RND(1)+1)
50    LET Y=INT(6*RND(1)+1)
60     PRINT "   ";X,"   ";Y," ";X+Y
70 NEXT I
80 END
```

LAB 5.12

```
4 REM----------------------------
6 REM            MELODY
8 REM----------------------------
10 RANDOMIZE
20 PRINT "HERE IS YOUR MELODY!!"
30 PRINT "DO RE MI"
40 FOR I=1 TO 6
50    LET K=INT(3*RND(1)+1)
60    ON K GOTO 70,100,130
70    REM
80    PRINT "RE FA MI"
90    GOTO 150
100    REM
110    PRINT "MI SOL FA"
120    GOTO 150
130    REM
140    PRINT "SOL FA MI"
150 NEXT I
160 PRINT "MI RE DO"
170 END
```

LAB   5.14   Write a quiz program using either SPACE or GOSUB for inspiration as needed.

LAB 5.16

```
4 REM------------------------
6 REM          CARDS
8 REM------------------------
10 RANDOMIZE: DIM C$(13): GOSUB 300
20 FOR I=1 TO 5
30    LET K=INT(4*RND(1)+1)
40    LET L=INT(13*RND(1)+1)
50    ON K GOSUB 100,150,200,250
60    PRINT TAB(20);"THAT IS CARD #";I
70 NEXT I
80 PRINT "THIS IS YOUR HAND!"
90 END
100 REM----SUBROUTINE #1----
110 PRINT C$(L);" OF HEARTS. ";
120 RETURN
150 REM----SUBROUTINE #2----
160 PRINT C$(L);" OF CLUBS. ";
170 RETURN
200 REM----SUBROUTINE #3----
210 PRINT C$(L);" OF DIAMONDS. ";
220 RETURN
250 REM----SUBROUTINE #4----
260 PRINT C$(L);" OF SPADES. ";
270 RETURN
300 FOR I=1 TO 13: READ C$(I): NEXT I: RETURN
400 DATA "ACE","TWO","THREE","FOUR","FIVE","SIX","SEVEN"
410 DATA "EIGHT","NINE","TEN","JACK","QUEEN","KING"
```

PPP 2 A RUN of BATAVG produces the following.

Program Output:

PLAYER #	AT BAT	HITS	BAT.AVG.
1	50	19	.38
2	43	10	.232558
3	51	13	.254902
4	49	17	.346939

OUT OF DATA Line 120

PPP 4 SUGGESTION: Simulate only a little of the output. After you see how it is going you should enter the program and let the computer do the rest of the work for you.

PPP 5 This program generates numbers and places them in subdivisions of the range (1 to 99).

```
6 REM-----------NUMRANGE------------
10 PRINT "THIS PROGRAM GENERATES 300 RANDOM NUMBERS, SORTS THEM INTO"
20 PRINT "THREE SUBDIVISIONS, COUNTS HOW MANY ARE IN EACH SUBDIVISION,"
30 PRINT "AND CALCULATES THE SUM OF EACH SUBDIVISION."
40 N=300
50 R=99
```

(continued)

```
60 S(0)=0: S(1)=33: S(2)=66: S(3)=R
70 A(1)=0: A(2)=0: A(3)=0: T(1)=0: T(2)=0: T(3)=0
80 FOR I=1 TO N
90    X=INT(99*RND(1))+1
100    FOR J=1 TO 3
110       IF X>S(J-1) AND X<S(J)+1 THEN A(J)=A(J)+1: T(J)=T(J)+X
120    NEXT J
130    T=T+X
140 NEXT I
150 PRINT
160 PRINT "RANGE","HOW MANY #S","  SUM"
170 FOR I=1 TO 3
180    PRINT S(I-1)+1;"TO";S(I),A(I),T(I)
190 NEXT I
200 PRINT
210 PRINT "TOTALS",N,T
```

PPP 7   This program calculates the population of a lifeform.

```
6 REM----------LIFEFORM------------
10 PRINT "THIS PROGRAM CALCULATES THE SIZE OF SUCCESSIVE GENERATIONS"
20 PRINT "OF A LIFEFORM WHICH REPRODUCES AT A SPECIFIED RATE"
30 M=10: F=10
40 I=1
50    IF M<F THEN G=2 ELSE G=1
60    ON G GOSUB 500,700
70    F=F1: M=M1: F1=0: M1=0
80    PRINT "THE POPULATION AFTER GENERATION";I;"IS:-"
90    PRINT "        ";M;"MALES  AND  ";F;"FEMALES."
100    IF F=0 THEN 300
110    I=I+1
120 IF I<=25 THEN 50
130 PRINT "AFTER 25 GENERATIONS THE LIFEFORM IS STILL ALIVE."
140 GOTO 330
300    PRINT "THERE ARE NO MORE FEMALES REMAINING."
310    PRINT "THE LIFEFORM IS EXTINCT AFTER";I;"GENERATIONS."
330 END
500 REM------SUBROUTINE FOR EACH FEMALE PRODUCING ONE OFFSPRING
510 FOR J=1 TO F
520    GOSUB 900
530 NEXT J
540 RETURN
700 REM------SUBROUTINE FOR EACH FEMALE PRODUCING THREE OFFSPRING
710 FOR J=1 TO 3*F
720    GOSUB 900
730 NEXT J
740 RETURN
900 REM------SUBROUTINE TO DETERMINE SEX OF OFFSPRING
910 X=INT(2*RND(1))
920 IF X=0 THEN M1=M1+1 ELSE F1=F1+1
930 RETURN
```

PPP 10   PURCHASE calculates change as four items are purchased.

```
6 REM------------PURCHASE------------
10 M(10)=10
20 FOR I=1 TO 9
30   M(I)=0
40   READ A(I)
50 NEXT I
60 READ A(10)
70 FOR I=1 TO 4
80   P(I)=INT(5000*RND(1))/100:T=T+P(I)
90 NEXT I
100 PRINT "THE FIRST PURCHASE COSTS $";P(1)
110 X=INT(P(1)/20)+1: M(10)=M(10)-X
120 PRINT "YOU MUST USE ";X;" $20 BILLS TO PAY FOR THAT"
130 PRINT "AND YOU WILL GET ";20*X-P(1);" IN CHANGE."
140 C=20*X-P(1)
150 GOSUB 1000
160 PRINT "YOU NOW HAVE:-"
170 GOSUB 2000
180 FOR I=2 TO 4
190   PRINT "YOUR NEXT PURCHASE COSTS $";P(I)
200   J=1
210     IF M(J)<=0 THEN 240
220       P(I)=P(1)-A(J): M(J)=M(J)-1
230       IF P(I)<=0 THEN 260 ELSE 210
240     J=J+1
250   IF J<=10 THEN 210
260   C=-P(I)
270   IF C=0 THEN PRINT "THAT IS THE EXACT CHANGE: GOTO 300
280     PRINT "YOUR CHANGE IS $";C
290     GOSUB 1000
300   PRINT "YOU NOW HAVE:-"
310   GOSUB 2000
320 NEXT I
330 FOR I=1 TO 10
340   T1=T1+M(I)*A(I)
350 NEXT I
390 PRINT "YOUR FOUR PURCHASES COST A TOTAL OF $";T
400 PRINT "YOU HAVE A TOTAL OF $";T1;" LEFT."
410 END
1000 REM------SUBROUTINE TO GIVE CHANGE------
1010 IF C>=10 THEN M(9)=M(9)+1: C=C-10
1020 IF C>=5 THEN M(8)=M(8)+1: C=C-5
1030 IF C>=2 THEN M(7)=M(7)+1: C=C-2
1040 IF C>2 THEN 1030
1050 IF C>=1 THEN M(6)=M(6)+INT(C): C=C-INT(C)
1060 IF C>=.5 THEN M(5)=M(5)+1: C=C-.5
1070 IF C>=.25 THEN M(4)=M(4)+1: C=C-.25
1080 IF C>=.1 THEN M(3)=M(3)+1: C=C-.1
1090 IF C>=.05 THEN M(2)=M(2)+1: C=C-.05
1100 IF C>0 THEN M(1)=INT(C/.01+.005)
```

(continued)

```
1110 RETURN
1990 '------SUBROUTINE TO DISPLAY CURRENT MONEY------
2000 FOR K=1 TO 5
2010   IF M(K)>0 THEN PRINT M(K);A(K)*100;" CENT PIECES."
2020 NEXT K
2030 FOR K=6 TO 10
2040   IF M(K)>0 THEN PRINT M(K);A(K);" DOLLAR BILLS."
2050 NEXT K
2060 PRINT "PLEASE TYPE 'RETURN' WHEN READY TO CONTINUE"
2070 INPUT A$
2080 RETURN
5000 DATA 0.01,0.05,0.1,0.25,0.5,1,2,5,10,20
```

Chapter 6

EX 6.1 To produce output on the printer change the PRINT statements to LPRINT statements. Apple users should use PR#1 (see pg. 172).

EX 6.2 As each grade is entered, it is compared to the lowest and highest grade, MIN and MAX. If it is lower than MIN, MIN is assigned the value of that grade. If it is higher than MAX then MAX is assigned the value of that grade. One way to initialize MIN and MAX is to assign the largest and smallest machine values. Another way is to assign both of them the value of GRADE(1) outside the loop.

EX 6.4 Insert a line between 205 and 210

```
207 WHILE N$< >"0"
```

Also change line 275 to end the loop

```
275 WEND
```

EX 6.5 The following program will generate names starting with the letters 'GL', followed by either 2 or 3 letters from the list.

```
4 '----------------------------------------------------
6 '                    SOAP1
8 '----------------------------------------------------
100 PRINT: PRINT
110 PRINT "PROGRAM TO GENERATE NAMES BEGINNING WITH 'GL'"
120 '------GETS 5 VOWELS AND 5 CONSONANTS FROM DATA------
130 FOR I=1 TO 6
140   READ A$(I),B$(I)
150 NEXT I
160 '--GENERATES ALL WORDS STARTING WITH 'GL' THEN A VOWEL--
170 '----------ENDING WITH ONE OF THE 5 CONSONANTS.----------
180 FOR I=1 TO 5
190   FOR J=1 TO 5
200     PRINT "GL";A$(I);B$(J),
210     PRINT "GL";A$(I);B$(J);A$(2),
220     PRINT "GL";A$(I);A$(I+1);B$(J),
230     PRINT "GL";A$(I);B$(J);B$(J+1),
240     PRINT "GL";A$(I);B$(J+1);B$(J),
250   NEXT J
```

(continued)

```
260 NEXT I
270 DATA A,S,E,P,I,T,O,R,U,B,A,Y
280 END
```

EX 6.7 The advantage of using LINE INPUT is that the computer accepts punctuation in the Input.

LAB 6.2 Note differences on your machine between the OUTPUT produced when you RUN "DTDEMO1" and when you RUN "DTDEMO2" so that in future programming you can use whichever method is the more appropriate.

LAB 6.4
```
10 REM      STRLOOP (STORING AND EQUATING STRING VARIABLES)
20 PRINT "WHEN YOU HAVE FINISHED TYPE 'DONE' FOR YOUR NAME."
30 LET A$=">>> "
40 READ B$, C$
50 PRINT "WHAT IS YOUR NAME";
60 INPUT N$
70 IF N$="DONE" THEN 100
80 PRINT A$; B$; C$; N$; C$; "...ETC..."
90 GOTO 50
100 END
200 DATA "GOOD MORNING",", "
```

PPP 2 The information supplied by the user is underlined for a RUN of the program AGE.

Program Output:
```
AGE = ?-5
TOO YOUNG
AGE = ?0
TOO YOUNG
AGE = ?5
TOO YOUNG
AGE = ?20
TOO YOUNG
AGE = ?21
ELIGIBLE FOR INSURANCE
AGE = ?22
ELIGIBLE FOR INSURANCE
AGE = ?64
ELIGIBLE FOR INSURANCE
AGE = ?65
ELIGIBLE FOR INSURANCE
AGE = ?66
TOO OLD
AGE = ?999
TOO OLD
```

PPP 4 AGE is modified to check for zero and 99.
```
6 REM------AGE1 (TEST AGE BRACKET)------
10 PRINT "AGE="; : INPUT A
20 IF A <= 0 THEN PRINT "YOU CAN'T BE THAT YOUNG": GOTO 10
```

(continued)

```
30 IF A > 99 THEN PRINT "CONGRATS.-BUT PREMIUMS EXCEED BENEFITS": GOTO 80
40   IF A < 21 THEN PRINT "TOO YOUNG" : GOTO 80
50     IF A > 65 THEN PRINT "TOO OLD" : GOTO 80
60       PRINT "YOU ARE IN THE AGE RANGE 21 TO 65"
70       PRINT "ELIGIBLE FOR INSURANCE"
80 END
```

PPP 6   Table of taxes on net income

```
6 REM------TAXTAB (ON INCOME $5000 TO $150000)------
10 PRINT "THIS PROGRAM WILL CALCULATE THE FEDERAL TAX"
20 PRINT "ON YOUR INCOME USING TAX TABLES."
30 DIM A(11,3)
40 FOR J=1 TO 3
50   FOR I=1 TO 11
60     READ A(I,J)
70   NEXT I
80 NEXT J
85 PRINT "INCOME","TAX","PERCENT OF INCOME"
90 FOR M=5000 TO 150000! STEP 5000
100   J=1
110     IF M < A(J,1) THEN K=J-1: GOTO 130
120   J=J+1: IF J < 11 THEN 110
130   T = A(K,2)+A(K,3)*(M-A(K,1))
140     PRINT "$";M,"$";T,INT(T/M*10000+.5)/100;"%"
150 NEXT M
5000 DATA 4400,6500,8500,10800,12900,15000
5010 DATA 18200,23500,28800,34100,41500
5020 DATA 272,608,948,1583,1847,2330,3194
5030 DATA 4837,6693,8812,12068
5040 DATA .16,.17,.19,.22,.23,.27,.31,.35,.40,.44,.50
```

PPP 8   GREET produces a form letter for birthday greetings.

```
6 REM------GREET (FORM LETTER FOR BIRTHDAYS)------
10 INPUT "WHAT IS YOUR FRIEND'S NAME"; N$
20 INPUT "IS HE/SHE MALE OR FEMALE (ENTER M OR F)"; S$
30 IF S$="M" THEN S=1 ELSE S=2
35 INPUT "WHAT DAY OF THE WEEK IS HIS/HER BIRTHDAY";D$
40 PRINT "WHAT AGE RANGE DOES YOUR FRIEND FIT"
50 PRINT "       ENTER 1 FOR LESS THAN 21"
60 PRINT "             2 FOR 21 TO 35"
70 PRINT "             3 FOR 35 TO 50"
80 PRINT "             4 FOR OVER 50"
90 INPUT A
100 IF A < 1 OR A >4 THEN 40
110 GOSUB 1000
120 INPUT "HOW ARE YOU FEELING";H$
130 INPUT "WHAT EVENT HAVE YOU BEEN TO LATELY";E$
140 INPUT "WHO DID YOU GO WITH";C$
160 PRINT "WHAT SEASON IS IT (ENTER 1 FOR SPRING, 2 FOR SUMMER"
170 PRINT "3 FOR FALL, OR 4 FOR WINTER)."
180 INPUT S1
```

(continued)

```
190 IF S1 < 1 OR S1 > 4 THEN PRINT "PLEASE ENTER 1, 2, 3, OR 4": GOTO 160
200 GOSUB 2000
210 PRINT: PRINT: PRINT
220 PRINT "DEAR ";N$;","
230 PRINT TAB(5+LEN(N$));"HAPPY BIRTHDAY! SO YOU MADE ANOTHER YEAR"
240 PRINT L$(A)
250 IF M=1 THEN 280
260 PRINT "YOUR SWEETNESS AND WARMTH ARE MATCHED ONLY BY YOUR BEAUTY AND CHARM"
270 GOTO 290
280 PRINT "WHEN THEY MADE YOU IT SEEMS TO ME THEY THREW THE MOLD AWAY"
290 PRINT "AND SO I HOPE THAT YOU ENJOY THIS, AND MANY MORE, BIRTHDAYS."
300 IF M=2 THEN 320
310 PRINT "WITH ANY LUCK WE WILL SURVIVE EVEN WITHOUT THE MOLD."
320 PRINT TAB(5);"WELL ";N$;", WHAT SPECIAL TREAT CAN I WISH YOU?"
330 PRINT W$(S1)
340 PRINT "LAST WEEK ";C$;" AND I WENT TO ";E$
370 PRINT "AND SO MAYBE WE CAN DO THE SAME WITH YOU."
380 PRINT TAB(5);"I HOPE YOU ARE IN GOOD HEALTH FOR THIS SPECIAL DAY"
390 PRINT "I HAVE BEEN FEELING ";H$;" LATELY."
400 PRINT "ONCE AGAIN.  HAPPY BIRTHDAY."
410 PRINT TAB(10);"SEE YOU ON ";D$
420 END
1000 L$(1)="IF YOU KEEP THIS UP WE WILL HAVE TO CELEBRATE 21 SOON."
1010 L$(2)="THEY SAY YOUR AGE IS THE PRIME OF LIFE-WHAT DO YOU THINK?"
1020 L$(3)="LIFE USUALLY BEGINS AT 40 - I THINK YOU STARTED AT 35."
1030 L$(4)="LIKE A FINE WINE YOU IMPROVE WITH AGE - WHOSE CELLAR WERE YOU IN?"
1040 RETURN
2000 W$(1)="SPRING IS IN THE AIR; SO ARE BALLOONS, POLLUTION, AND BIRDS"
2010 W$(2)="OH THESE LAZY DAYS OF SUMMER, RELAX ON THIS SPECIAL DAY"
2020 W$(3)="THERE IS A NIP IN THE AIR, HERE IS SOMETHING TO TAKE THE CHILL OFF"
2030 W$(4)="WINTER WINDS MAY WHINE BUT WE HAVE OUR FRIENDSHIP TO WARM US"
2040 RETURN
```

Chapter 7

EX 7.1

```
6 REM------PUZZLE1------
10 FOR I=1 TO 4
20    READ A$(I)
30    IF I=3 THEN PRINT "YOU "; ELSE X=2
40    IF I=1 THEN PRINT "THIS "; ELSE G=G+X
50    IF G=2 THEN PRINT "WISHES ";
60    FOR X=1 TO 10 STEP 2
70      IF X=10 THEN PRINT "STOP ";
75      IF ((G+3*I)/(G-3*I))>8 AND X>8 THEN PRINT "A ";
80    NEXT X
90    PRINT A$(I);
100   IF (I+X)<13 OR G>14 THEN PRINT "PROGRAM ";
110 NEXT I
500 DATA ,,,"SMART "
```

EX 7.2
```
6 REM------NUMBERS------
10 PRINT "GOOD MORNING": N=1
15 INPUT "TYPE A NUMBER";A
20 FOR I=1 TO 10
30    IF N>3 THEN PRINT "***DONE***": END
40    IF A>0 THEN INPUT "TYPE A NUMBER";A ELSE PRINT "GOOD MORNING": N=1
50    IF A<0 THEN PRINT "AH, THAT'S BETTER": PRINT "ONE MORE TIME": N=N+1
              ELSE IF A>999 THEN PRINT "TOO BIG"
55    A=1
60 NEXT I
```

EX 7.3
```
6 REM------PLANNING------
10 ' DIMENSION ARRAYS
50 ' INITIALIZE VARIABLES
100 ' STATE OPTIONS
200 ' GET USER'S RESERVATION REQUESTS
250 ' CHECK REQUESTS AGAINST AVAILABLE TICKETS
300 ' IF REQUEST EXCEEDS AVAILABLE TICKETS GIVE USER ANOTHER CHOICE
350 ' ISSUE TICKETS
400 ' CHECK FOR NEXT REQUEST
```

LAB 7.2   Changes which have to be made to BUBBLE2 are:
```
110 DIM A(5000)
120 PRINT "HOW MANY NUMBERS TO BE SORTED (MAX=5000)
140 IF N>5000 THEN 120
```

PPP 2   The time required to sort 800 numbers using the BUBBLE SORT is such that it is better to calculate the time by examining the time required for smaller numbers and extrapolating to 800. The numbers in parentheses in PPP 5, below, were calculated in this way.

▶ *Note 1:*   The sorting times shown for exercises in Chapter 7 and Chapter 8 were obtained using a Z-80 microprocessor running at 4 MHz. Your system will produce different times, but the ratios between times should be similar.

▶ *Note 2:*   The SORTX algorithm used here is based on the INSERTION Sort Algorithm shown in page 159 of *A BIT of BASIC* by Dwyer and Critchfield (Addison-Wesley 1980).

PPP 4   SORTX uses the Insertion method for sorting.
```
4 REM--------------------------------------------------------------
6 REM      SORTX    (SORTS RANDOM NUMBERS INTO ASCENDING ORDER)
8 REM--------------------------------------------------------------
100 PRINT "PROGRAM TO SORT A LIST OF NUMBERS INTO ASCENDING ORDER"
110 DIM A(800)
120 PRINT "HOW MANY NUMBERS TO BE SORTED (MAX=800)";
130 INPUT N
140 IF N>800 THEN 120
150 FOR I=1 TO N
160    A(I)=INT(32000-64000!*RND(1))
170 NEXT I
```

(continued)

```
180 PRINT ">>> THE UNSORTED NUMBERS ARE:"
190 GOSUB 430
200 REM=========================================================
210 REM           ROUTINE TO USE INSERTION SORT ON A()
220 LIMIT=N                        'N ITEMS TO BE SORTED
230 FOR I=1 TO LIMIT-1             'START LOOP THROUGH ARRAY
240   J=I                          'SEARCH COUNTER
250   LET T=A(J+1)                 'SWAP, STEP 1
260   IF J<1 THEN 330              'SEARCH COMPLETE
270     COMP=COMP+1                'COUNT COMPARISONS
280     IF T>A(J) THEN 330         'INSERTION PLACE LOCATED
290       SWP=SWP+1                'COUNT SWAPS
300       A(J+1)=A(J)              'SWAP, STEP 2
310       J=J-1                    'DECREMENT COUNTER
320       GOTO 260                 'CHECK POSITION IN SEARCH
330   A(J+1)=T                     'SWAP, STEP 3
340 NEXT I                         'ARRAY IS SORTED
350 PRINT ">>> HERE ARE THE SORTED NUMBERS:"
360 GOSUB 430
370 PRINT COMP;" COMPARISONS AND ";SWP;" SWAPS."
380 END
400 REM=========================================================
410 REM  SUBROUTINE TO PRINT A(), 3 ITEMS/LINE, 13 COLS/ITEM
420 K=0
430 FOR J=1 TO N
440   T=J-3*INT((J-1)/3)
450   PRINT TAB(13*T-12);A(J);
460   IF T>=3 THEN PRINT
470 NEXT J
490 PRINT
500 RETURN
510 GOTO 430
520 END
```

PPP 5   Summary of times for BUBBLE2 (random numbers), BUBBLE3 (numbers in reverse order) BUBBLE4 (numbers in order), and SORTX (Insertion sort with random numbers).

Sample Size #	BUBBLE2 (Random) sec.	BUBBLE3 (Reverse) sec.	BUBBLE4 (In Order) sec.	SORTX (Random) sec.
25	6	9.7	0.4	4.2
50	18	28	0.7	13.2
100	73	113	1.0	49
200	288	449	1.4	198
400	1192	(1796)	3.1	(660)
800	(4768)	(7184)	5.8	(2396)
	swaps and comparisons for 50 numbers			
swaps	596	1225	0	596
comps.	1194	1225	49	640

Chapter 8

EX 8.1   1.   Set GAP=INT(N/2), where N = number of items to be sorted
             2.   While GAP>0, do steps 2.1 through 2.3
             2.1   Set I=GAP as a pointer into the "middle" of the data
             2.2   While I<N, do steps 2.2.1 through 2.2.3
             2.2.1   Set J=I-GAP as a pointer "gap units" to left of I
             2.2.2   While J>=0, do steps 2.2.2.1 through 2.2.2.2
             2.2.2.1 If A(J+GAP)>A(J) swap, else goto 2.2.3
             2.2.2.2 Set J=J-GAP to look further left
             2.2.3   Set I=I+1 to move data pointer right
             2.3   Set GAP=INT(GAP/2) to cut gap in half

EX 8.3   If your computer recognizes the difference between upper- and lower-case characters, STSHELL will not order strings correctly. It will order upper-case letters followed by lower-case letters. For mixed-mode strings the final order will depend on the order of the individual letters. The solution is to define a function like the one in the program in section 5.4, or create a subroutine to convert lower-case characters to upper case before you sort the strings.

EX 8.5

```
4 REM-------------------------------------------------------------
6 REM            RCDSHEL1 (SHELL SORT OF ARRAY BY RECORD)
8 REM-------------------------------------------------------------
100 PRINT "PROGRAM TO SORT AN ARRAY USING AN ITEM FROM THE RECORDS"
110 PRINT "FOR SORTING."
115 PRINT: PRINT
120 INPUT "HOW MANY RECORDS DO YOU HAVE";N
130 INPUT "HOW MANY ELEMENTS IN EACH RECORD";E
140 DIM A$(N,E)
145 PRINT: PRINT
150 FOR I=1 TO E
160    PRINT "WHAT IS TO BE IN ELEMENT #";I;"OF EACH RECORD";
170    INPUT E$(I)
180 NEXT I
185 PRINT: PRINT
190 FOR I=0 TO N-1
200    PRINT "FOR RECORD #";I+1;"ENTER "
210    FOR J=1 TO E
220      PRINT "ELEMENT #";J;: INPUT A$(I,J)
230    NEXT J
235    PRINT
240 NEXT I
245 PRINT: PRINT: GOSUB 2000
250 PRINT "WHICH ELEMENT SHOULD BE USED AS THE KEY FOR SORTING?"
260 FOR I=1 TO E
270    PRINT "FOR ";E$(I);" TYPE....";I
280 NEXT I
290 INPUT K
```

(continued)

```
300 PRINT "THE UNSORTED RECORDS ARE:"
310 GOSUB 1000
370 PRINT: PRINT
380 REM==========================================================
390 REM         ROUTINE TO USE SHELL SORT ON ARRAY A$(N,E)
400 GAP=INT(N/2)
410 IF GAP<=0 THEN 600
420   I=GAP
430   IF I>=N THEN 590
440     J=I-GAP
450     IF J<0 THEN 580
460       IF A$(J,K)<=A$(J+GAP,K) THEN 580
470         FOR L=1 TO E
480           TEMP$=A$(J,L)
490           A$(J,L)=A$(J+GAP,L)
500           A$(J+GAP,L)=TEMP$
510         NEXT L
520         J=J-GAP: GOTO 450
580     I=I+1: GOTO 430
590   GAP=INT(GAP/2): GOTO 410
600 REM                   END OF SORTING ROUTINE
610 REM==========================================================
620 PRINT "THE SORTED RECORDS ARE:"
630 GOSUB 1000
640 END
1000 REM------------------------------------------------------
1010 REM                 ROUTINE TO PRINT THE ARRAY
1020 FOR I=0 TO N-1
1030   FOR J=1 TO E
1040     PRINT USING X$(J);A$(I,J);
1050   NEXT J
1060   PRINT
1070 NEXT I
1080 RETURN
1980 REM------------------------------------------------------
1990 REM         ROUTINE TO ESTABLISH FIELDS FOR PRINTING
2000 FOR I=0 TO N-1
2010   FOR J=1 TO E
2020     L=LEN(A$(I,J))
2030     IF L>L(J) THEN L(J)=L
2040   NEXT J
2050 NEXT I
2060 FOR J=1 TO E
2070   X$(J)="\"+STRING$(L(J)," ")+"\"
2080 NEXT J
2100 RETURN
```

LAB 8.2
```
4 REM-------------------------------------------------------
6 REM     STSHELL (SHELL SORT OF STRING DATA IN ARRAY A$()
8 REM-------------------------------------------------------
100 PRINT "PROGRAM TO SORT STRINGS ENTERED BY USER"
```

(*continued*)

```
110 DIM A$(100)
120 PRINT "HOW MANY STRINGS TO BE SORTED (MAX=100)";
130 INPUT N
140 IF N>100 THEN 120
150 FOR I=0 TO N-1
160   PRINT "STRING #";I;": ";:LINE INPUT A$(I)
170 NEXT I
180 PRINT ">>> THE UNSORTED STRINGS ARE:"
190 GOSUB 430
200 REM============================================================
210 REM           ROUTINE TO USE SHELL SORT ON A$()
220 FOR K=1 TO 10: FOR L=1 TO 600: NEXT L: PRINT CHR$(7);: NEXT K
225 PRINT "START OF THE SORT"
230 GAP=INT(N/2)
240 IF GAP<=0 THEN 355
250   I=GAP                         'INITIALIZE I LOOP
260   IF I>=N THEN 350              'LOOP WHILE I<N
270     J=I-GAP                     'INITIALIZE J LOOP
280     IF J<0 THEN 340             'LOOP WHILE J>=0
290     IF A$(J)<=A$(J+GAP) THEN 340  'ORDER IS OK, DON'T SWAP
300       TEMP$=A$(J)               'SWAP, STEP 1
310       A$(J)=A$(J+GAP)           'SWAP, STEP 2
320       A$(J+GAP)=TEMP$           'SWAP, STEP 3
330       J=J-GAP: GOTO 280         'SHIFT J LEFT, CONT. J LOOP
340     I=I+1: GOTO 260             'INCREMENT I, CONT. I LOOP
350   GAP=INT(GAP/2): GOTO 240      'NEW GAP
355 PRINT "END OF THE SORT"
360 FOR K=1 TO 10: FOR L=1 TO 600: NEXT L: PRINT CHR$(7);: NEXT K
370 PRINT "SORTED STRINGS ARE:"
380 GOSUB 430
390 END
400 REM============================================================
410 REM  SUBROUTINE TO PRINT A$(), 3 STRINGS/LINE, 26 COLS/ITEM
430 FOR J=0 TO N-1
440   T=J-3*INT(J/3)
450   PRINT TAB(26*T+1);A$(J);
460   IF T>=3 THEN PRINT
470 NEXT J
490 PRINT
500 RETURN
```

LAB 8.4
```
4 REM----------------------------------------------------------------
6 REM            RCDBUB (BUBBLE SORT OF ARRAY BY KEY FIELD)
8 REM----------------------------------------------------------------
100 PRINT "PROGRAM TO SORT AN ARRAY USING AN ITEM FROM THE RECORDS"
110 PRINT "FOR SORTING."
120 PRINT: PRINT: INPUT "HOW MANY RECORDS DO YOU HAVE";N
140 PRINT "EACH RECORD NEEDS AN AUTHORS NAME, BOOK TITLE, AND COST"
150 DIM A$(N,3)
160 PRINT: PRINT: B$="                              "
```

(continued)

```
180 FOR I=0 TO N-1
190    PRINT"FOR RECORD #";I+1;"ENTER NAME, TITLE AND COST SEPARATED BY COMMAS"
200    INPUT A$(I,1),A$(I,2),A$(I,3)
210    A$(I,1)=LEFT$(A$(I,1)+B$,10)
220    A$(I,2)=LEFT$(A$(I,2)+B$,20)
230    A$(I,3)=RIGHT$("000"+A$(I,3),5)
240 NEXT I
250 PRINT: PRINT
260 PRINT "WHICH ELEMENT SHOULD BE USED AS THE KEY FOR SORTING?"
270 PRINT "TYPE 1 FOR AUTHOR, TYPE 2 FOR TITLE, TYPE 3 FOR COST"
280 INPUT K
290 PRINT: PRINT
300 PRINT "THE UNSORTED RECORDS ARE:"
310 GOSUB 1000
320 PRINT: PRINT
400 REM=========================================================
410 REM       ROUTINE TO USE BUBBLE SORT ON ARRAY A$(N,E)
420 LIMIT=N-1
430 SPOT=-1
440 FOR I=0 TO LIMIT-1
450    IF A$(I,K)<=A$(I+1,K) THEN 520
460      FOR L=1 TO 3
470        TEMP$=A$(I,L)
480        A$(I,L)=A$(I+1,L)
490        A$(I+1,L)=TEMP$
500      NEXT L
510      SPOT=I
520 NEXT I
530 IF SPOT=-1 THEN 570
540    LIMIT=SPOT
550    GOTO 430
570 REM                    END OF SORTING ROUTINE
600 REM=========================================================
610 PRINT "THE SORTED RECORDS ARE:"
620 GOSUB 1000
630 END
1000 REM----------------------------------------------------------
1010 REM                ROUTINE TO PRINT THE ARRAY
1020 FOR I=0 TO N-1
1030   FOR J=1 TO 3
1040     PRINT A$(I,J);"  ";
1050   NEXT J
1060   PRINT
1070 NEXT I
1080 RETURN
```

PPP 1   To modify SHELL2 to SHELL3 all that has to be done is to change line 160 so that the numbers are created in reverse order.

```
160    A(I)=N+1-I
```

PPP 2   The time to sort 800 numbers using SHELL SORT is not as long as required for BUBBLE SORT, but it is still better to calculate longer times by examining the times required for smaller numbers and extrapolating to 800. Numbers in parentheses in PPP 4, below, were calculated in this way.

PPP 3   To produce SHELL4 from SHELL3 Line 160 again is the only thing which has to be changed.

```
160    A(I)=I
```

PPP 4   Comparison between SHELL2, SHELL3, SHELL4, and SORTX

Sample Size	SHELL2 (Random)	SHELL3 (Reverse)	SHELL4 (In Order)	SORTX (Random)
Size	sec.	sec.	sec.	sec.
25	3.2	2.7	1.2	4.2
50	8.6	6.5	3.7	13.2
100	18.6	16.1	9.2	49.1
200	53.5	38.1	21.8	198
400	190	89	50.5	(660)
800	(570)	(178)	(117)	(2396)

comparisons and swaps for sample size of 50

comps.	353	263	203	640
swaps.	172	105	0	596

PPP 7   This program uses SHELL SORT and swaps the Index array.

```
4 REM------------------------------------------------------------
6 REM     INXSHELL (SHELL SORT OF 2-D ARRAY BY INDEX ARRAY)
8 REM------------------------------------------------------------
100 PRINT "PROGRAM TO SORT AN ARRAY USING AN ITEM FROM THE RECORDS"
110 PRINT "FOR SORTING."
120 PRINT: PRINT
130 INPUT "HOW MANY RECORDS DO YOU HAVE";N
140 PRINT "EACH RECORD NEEDS AN AUTHORS NAME, BOOK TITLE, AND COST"
150 DIM A$(N,3),P(N)
160 PRINT: PRINT
170 B$="                    "
180 FOR I=0 TO N-1
190    PRINT"FOR RECORD #";I+1;"ENTER NAME, TITLE AND COST SEPARATED BY COMMAS"
200    INPUT A$(I,1),A$(I,2),A$(I,3)
210    A$(I,1)=LEFT$(A$(I,1)+B$,10)
220    A$(I,2)=LEFT$(A$(I,2)+B$,20)
230    A$(I,3)=RIGHT$("000"+A$(I,3),5)
240    P(I)=I
250 NEXT I
260 PRINT "WHICH ELEMENT SHOULD BE USED AS THE KEY FOR SORTING?"
270 PRINT "TYPE 1 FOR AUTHOR, TYPE 2 FOR TITLE, TYPE 3 FOR COST"
280 INPUT K
290 PRINT "THE UNSORTED RECORDS ARE:"
300 GOSUB 1000
310 PRINT: PRINT
400 REM========================================================
410 REM       ROUTINE TO USE SHELL SORT ON ARRAY A$(N,E)
```

(continued)

```
420 GAP=INT(N/2)
430 IF GAP<=0 THEN 550
440   I=GAP
450   IF I>=N THEN 540
460     J=I-GAP
470     IF J<0 THEN 530
480       IF A$(P(J),K)<=A$(P(J+GAP),K) THEN 530
490         TEMP=P(J)
500         P(J)=P(J+GAP)
510         P(J+GAP)=TEMP
520       J=J-GAP: GOTO 470
530     I=I+1: GOTO 450
540   GAP=INT(GAP/2): GOTO 430
550 REM                    END OF SORTING ROUTINE
600 REM=========================================================
610 PRINT "THE SORTED RECORDS ARE:"
620 GOSUB 1000
630 END
1000 REM--------------------------------------------------------
1010 REM                   ROUTINE TO PRINT THE ARRAY
1020 FOR I=0 TO N-1
1030   FOR J=1 TO 3
1040     PRINT A$(P(I),J);"   ";
1050   NEXT J
1060   PRINT
1070 NEXT I
1080 RETURN
```

Chapter 9

EX 9.1   For the human it may be easier to read the form:

IF XDIG = X(I) AND YDIG = Y(I) THEN HFLAG = 1

However, the computer may have to do less work with the other form, since if XDIG is not equal to X(I) then it will not check further.

EX 9.2   Using I instead of X in Line 180 produces:

180   PRINT TAB((I-50)*.5+6);I;

PPP 4   To adapt TREAS3 to a video display, you should:

After Line 196, clear the screen.
Position the cursor before printing the grid.
Match code for the grid to your graphics.
Position the cursor in a text area before Line 360.
Indicate the position of a dig on the grid. (Mark hits and misses in different ways.)
Reposition the cursor for comments in Line 520 and 530.
Perhaps clear the screen and have a 'Big Picture' for a winner.

PPP 6   The section in Line 370 to Line 540 must be changed to allow different players to try to find the treasure.
This can be done by changing Lines 470 and 480 and adding Lines 375, 475, and 535.

```
375 FOR I=1 TO 2
470   HIT(I)=HIT(I)+1
475   THIT=HIT(1)+HIT(2)
480   IF THIT<4 THEN 510 ELSE 560

535 NEXT I
```

Chapter 10

PPP 1   Programs from Part I which might be made into menu-driven programs are:
QUIZ, PRINT programs, Branching programs (IF...THEN, GOTO, FOR...NEXT, GOSUB, ON x GOTO), Variable assignment (LET, INPUT, READ-DATA)

PPP 3   KEYCIPH modified to use a 'one-time pad'.

```
100 '****************************************************
110 '*    ONETIME    (DATA ENCRYPTION USING A ONE-TIME PAD)   *
120 '****************************************************
125 DEFINT A-Z
130 KY$="": TX$=""        'STRING VARIABLES TO HOLD KEY & TEXT
140 DIM KC(255), TC(255) 'ARRAYS FOR ASCII CODES, KEY & TEXT
201 '-------------------------------------------------------
202 '                 MENU SELECTION MODULE
203 '-------------------------------------------------------
210 PRINT: PRINT"*****   MAIN MENU   *****": PRINT
220 PRINT" 1 = ENCIPHER TEXT"
230 PRINT" 2 = DECIPHER TEXT"
240 PRINT" 3 = QUIT PROGRAM"
250 PRINT: PRINT"YOUR CHOICE";: INPUT C
260 ON C GOTO 410, 610, 810
270 PRINT"PLEASE TYPE 1,2,OR 3": GOTO 250
400 '-------------------------------------------------------
401 '                 TEXT ENCIPHERING MODULE
402 '-------------------------------------------------------
410 PRINT: PRINT"ENCIPHER MODE"
412 PRINT">>> ENTER KEY STRING (UP TO 255 CHARACTERS):"
414 LINE INPUT KY$: LK=LEN(KY$)
430 PRINT">>> ENTER PLAIN TEXT (UP TO 255 CHARACTERS):"
440 LINE INPUT TX$ :  LT=LEN(TX$)
445 GOSUB 5010          'GENERATE KEY CODES, STORE IN KC()
450 GOSUB 1010          'CHANGE TEXT TO ASCII, PUT IN TC()
460 GOSUB 3010          'ADD KEY CODES TO TEXT CODES
470 GOSUB 2010          'CONVERT ASCII TO TEXT, PUT IN TX$
```

(continued)

```
480 PRINT: PRINT">> ENCIPHERED TEXT IS:"
490 PRINT TX$: PRINT
500 GOTO 210
600 '-----------------------------------------------------------
601 '                   TEXT DECIPHERING MODULE
602 '-----------------------------------------------------------
610 PRINT: PRINT"DECIPHER MODE"
620 PRINT">> ENTER KEY STRING (UP TO 255 CHARACTERS):"
630 LINE INPUT KY$: LK=LEN(KY$)
650 PRINT">> ENTER ENCIPHERED TEXT (UP TO 255 CHARACTERS):"
660 LINE INPUT TX$: LT=LEN(TX$)
665 GOSUB 5010          'GENERATE KEY CODES, STORE IN KC()
670 GOSUB 1010          'CHANGE TEXT TO ASCII, PUT IN TC()
680 GOSUB 4010          'SUBTRACT KEY CODES FROM TEXT CODES
690 GOSUB 2010          'CONVERT ASCII TO TEXT, PUT IN TX$
700 PRINT: PRINT">> DECIPHERED TEXT IS:"
710 PRINT TX$: PRINT
720 GOTO 210
800 '-----------------------------------------------------------
801 '                        QUIT MODULE
802 '-----------------------------------------------------------
810 PRINT"PROGRAM IS TERMINATING WITHOUT SAVING ANY DATA"
820 PRINT"TO USE AGAIN, TYPE 'RUN'"
830 END
997 '=========================================================
998 '             SUBROUTINES FOR PADCIPH
999 '=========================================================
1000 '
1001 '   SUBROUTINE TO CONVERT CHARS IN TX$ TO ASCII IN TC()
1002 '   ASCII CODES KEPT IN RANGE 32-95 TO AVOID LOWER CASE
1003 '
1010 FOR K=1 TO LEN(TX$)
1020    TC(K)=ASC(MID$(TX$,K,1))
1030    IF TC(K)>95 THEN TC(K)=TC(K)-32
1040 NEXT K
1050 RETURN
2000 '.......................................................
2001 '   SUBROUTINE TO CONVERT ASCII IN TC() TO CHARS IN TX$
2002 '
2010 TX$=""
2020 FOR K=1 TO LT
2030    TX$=TX$+CHR$(TC(K))
2040 NEXT K
2050 RETURN
3000 '.......................................................
3001 '   SUBROUTINE TO ADD ENCIPHERING CODES TO TC()
3002 '   RECALL THAT LT IS THE LENGTH OF THE TEXT IN TX$
3003 '
```

(continued)

```
3010 FOR M=1 TO LT
3040    TC(M)=TC(M)+KC(M)
3050    IF TC(M)>95 THEN TC(M)=TC(M)-64
3060 NEXT M
3070 RETURN
4000 '.........................................................
4001 '    SUBROUTINE TO SUBTRACT ENCIPHERING CODES FROM TC()
4002 '    RECALL THAT LT IS THE LENGTH OF THE TEXT IN TX$
4003 '
4010 FOR M=1 TO LT
4040    TC(M)=TC(M)-KC(M)
4050    IF TC(M)<32 THEN TC(M)=TC(M)+64
4060 NEXT M
4070 RETURN
5000 '.........................................................
5001 '    SUBROUTINE TO GENERATE KEY CODES DERIVED FROM KY$
5002 '    CODES ARE KEPT IN RANGE 32-95, SHIFTED LEFT TO 0-63
5003 '
5010 S=0
5020 FOR J=1 TO LK
5030    S=S+J+ASC(MID$(KY$,J,1))
5040 NEXT J
5045 XX=RND(-1)
5050 RANDOMIZE S
5060 FOR J=1 TO LT
5070    KC(J)=64*RND
5080 NEXT J
5090 RETURN
```

PPP 4   Additional commands have been added to LEDIT1.

```
10 '*********************************************************
20 '*              LEDIT2 (LINE EDITOR PROGRAM)             *
30 '*********************************************************
100 ' SOME SYSTEMS WILL NEED TO CLEAR SPACE FOR STRING VARIABLES
110 ' IF YOU NEED IT REPLACE THESE LINES WITH: 100 CLEAR 5000
120 DEFINT A-Z
130 CL=0: HL=0
140 DIM FP(100)                     'LINKED LIST
150 DIM N$(50),B$(50),TM$(50)       'TEMPORARY BUFFER
160 DIM T$(100,50)                  'TEXT BUFFER
170 DIM F(100),SP(100)              'LINE LENGTH AND SPACE COUNTERS
180 X$(0)="": FOR M=1 TO 10: X$(M)=X$(M-1)+" ": NEXT M
200 '-----------------------------------------------------------
210 '              GIVE DIRECTIONS TO THE USER
220 '-----------------------------------------------------------
230 GOSUB 820: PRINT "CURRENT LINE NUMBER NOW = 0.  TO APPEND TEXT"
240 PRINT "AT LINE # 1 RESPOND   CMD? A   AFTER? 0"
250 PRINT "..............................."
```

(continued)

```
300 '----------------------------------------------------------
310 '              INITIALIZE POINTERS FOR THE LINKED LIST
320 '----------------------------------------------------------
330 AV=2: FP(1)=0
340 FOR I=2 TO 99
350   FP(I)=I+1
360 NEXT I
370 FP(100)=0
380 GOTO 1130                        'GET LINE WIDTH
400 '----------------------------------------------------------
410 '                GET A COMMAND FROM THE USER
420 '----------------------------------------------------------
430 PRINT "CMD?";: LINE INPUT;L$
440 L1=CL: L2=CL
500 '----------------------------------------------------------
510 '                INTERPRET THE USER'S COMMAND
520 '----------------------------------------------------------
530 IF L$="E" THEN END
540 IF L$="H" THEN PRINT: GOSUB 830: GOTO 430
550 IF L$="V" THEN 930
560 IF L$="I" THEN 1030
570 IF L$="A" THEN V$="AFTER" ELSE IF L$="G" THEN V$="WHERE" ELSE V$="FROM"
580 PRINT TAB(10); V$;: INPUT; L1: L2=L1
590 IF L$="A" THEN 1230
600 IF L$="G" THEN 2430
610 PRINT TAB(20); "TO";: INPUT L2
620 IF L$="C" THEN 1630
630 IF L$="D" THEN 2030
640 IF L$="L" THEN 2430
650 IF L$="P" THEN 2830
660 IF L$="R" THEN 3230
670 IF L$="T" THEN 3830
680 IF L$="S" THEN 4830
690 PRINT"NO SUCH COMMAND": GOTO 430   'GET NEW COMMAND
800 '----------------------------------------------------------
810 '                H COMMAND (HELP SUBROUTINE)
820 '----------------------------------------------------------
830 PRINT"AFTER 'CMD?' TYPE A(PPEND), C(HANGE), D(ELETE), E(ND)"
840 PRINT"G(OTO), H(ELP), I(NFORMATION), L(IST), P(RINT)"
850 PRINT"R(ESTRUCTURE), S(PACE), T(AB), OR V(ERIFY)."
860 PRINT"RESPOND TO OTHER ? PROMPTS WITH A LINE #.  RESPONDING"
870 PRINT"WITH 'ENTER' GIVES CURRENT LINE #. USE THE 'I' CMD TO"
880 PRINT"FIND THE CURRENT LINE #."
890 RETURN                            'CONTINUE WITH PROGRAM
900 '----------------------------------------------------------
910 '                V COMMAND (VERIFY CURRENT LINE #)
920 '----------------------------------------------------------
930 PRINT
940 PRINT USING "##:";CL;
950 FOR M=1 TO F(CP): PRINT T$(CP,M): NEXT M
```

(continued)

```
960 PRINT: GOTO 430                      'GET NEW COMMAND
1000 '----------------------------------------------------------
1010 '          I COMMAND (GIVES INFORMATION ABOUT LINE #S)
1020 '----------------------------------------------------------
1030 PRINT TAB(5)
1040 PRINT "CURRENT LINE IS #";CL;"   HIGHEST LINE IS #"; HL
1050 PRINT: GOTO 430                     'GET NEW COMMAND
1100 '----------------------------------------------------------
1110 '                 THE USER SETS THE LINE WIDTH
1120 '----------------------------------------------------------
1130 INPUT "ENTER WIDTH OF LINE TO BE USED ('ENTER'=65)";W
1140 IF W=0 THEN W=65
1150 PRINT: GOTO 430                     'GET NEW COMMAND
1200 '----------------------------------------------------------
1210 '                 A COMMAND (APPEND AFTER LINE L1)
1220 '----------------------------------------------------------
1230 PRINT
1240 PRINT USING"##>";L1+1;:GOTO 4400 'TO SIMULATE LINE INPUT
1250 PRINT: L=0
1260 FOR M=1 TO RW: B$(M)=N$(M): L=L+LEN(B$(M)): NEXT M
1270 IF L=0 THEN 1460
1280 IF MID$(B$(1),4,1)="." THEN 1460
1290 IF AV=0 THEN PRINT "BUFFER FULL": GOTO 1460
1300 R=1: LN=1
1310 CL=L1+1
1320 I=1: K=1
1330 IF FP(I)=0 OR K=CL THEN 1360        'I IS LINE POINTER
1340 I=FP(I): K=K+1: GOTO 1330           'K IS LINE COUNTER
1350 '
1360 J=AV: AV=FP(J)                      'RESET PTR TO AVAILABLE SPACE
1370 FP(J)=FP(I)                         'CHANGE OLD LINK
1380 FP(I)=J                             'SET NEW LINK
1390 F(J)=RW
1400 FOR M=1 TO F(J)
1410    T$(J,M)=B$(M)                    'STORE USER'S TEXT IN TEXT BUFFER
1420 NEXT M
1430 CP=J: HL=HL+1                       'CP IS PTR TO CURRENT LINE
1440 IF CL=HL THEN HP=CP
1450 L1=CL: GOTO 1240
1460 PRINT: GOTO 430                     'GET NEW COMMAND
1600 '----------------------------------------------------------
1610 '                 C COMMAND (CHANGE LINES L1 TO L2)
1620 '----------------------------------------------------------
1630 CL=L1
1640 IF L2>HL THEN PRINT "2ND LINE TOO HIGH": GOTO 1790
1650 I=1: K=1
1660 IF FP(I)=0 OR K=CL THEN 1690
1670 I=FP(I): K=K+1: GOTO 1660
1680 '
1690 IF FP(I)=0 THEN PRINT "NO SUCH LINE": GOTO 1790
```

(continued)

```
1700 CP=FP(I)
1710 PRINT USING "##:";CL;
1720 FOR M=1 TO F(CP): PRINT T$(CP,M): NEXT M
1730 PRINT USING "##>";CL;
1740 FOR M=1 TO F(CP): T$(CP,M)="": NEXT M
1750 GOTO 4400                        'SIMULATE LINE INPUT
1760 FOR M=1 TO RW: T$(CP,M)=N$(M): NEXT M
1770 F(CP)=RW
1780 IF CL<L2 THEN CL=CL+1: GOTO 1650
1790 PRINT: GOTO 430                   'GET NEW COMMAND
2000 '-----------------------------------------------------------
2010 '            D COMMAND (DELETE LINES L1 TO L2)
2020 '-----------------------------------------------------------
2030 CL=L1
2040 IF L2>HL THEN L2=HL
2050 FOR C=0 TO L2-L1
2060 I=1: K=1
2070 IF FP(I)=0 OR K=CL THEN 2100
2080 I=FP(I): K=K+1: GOTO 2070
2090 '
2100 IF FP(I)=0 THEN PRINT "NO TEXT TO DELETE": GOTO 2160
2110 J=FP(I): FP(I)=FP(J)
2120 FP(J)=AV: AV=J
2130 HL=HL-1: CP=I
2140 IF HL=CL THEN HP=CP
2150 NEXT C
2160 CL=L1-1: IF CL<0 THEN CL=0
2170 PRINT: GOTO 430                   'GET NEW COMMAND
2400 '-----------------------------------------------------------
2410 '              L COMMAND (LIST LINES L1 TO L2)
2420 '-----------------------------------------------------------
2430 I=FP(1): K=1
2440 IF L2>HL THEN L2=HL
2450 IF I=0 THEN PRINT "BUFFER EMPTY": GOTO 2570
2460 IF K<L1 THEN CP=I: GOTO 2530
2470 CP=I
2480 IF L$="R" THEN 3250              'RETURN TO RESTRUCTURING
2490 IF L$="T" THEN 3860              'RETURN TO TAB ROUTINE
2500 IF L$="S" THEN 4880              'RETURN TO SPACE ROUTINE
2505 IF L$="G" THEN PRINT
2510 PRINT USING "##:";K;
2520 FOR M=1 TO F(I): PRINT TAB(4);T$(I,M): NEXT M
2530 I=FP(I): K=K+1
2540 IF K>L2 THEN 2560
2550 GOTO 2460
2560 CL=K-1
2570 PRINT: GOTO 430                   'GET NEW COMMAND
2800 '-----------------------------------------------------------
2810 '         P COMMAND (PRINTS TEXT ON THE LINE PRINTER)
2820 '-----------------------------------------------------------
```

(continued)

```
2830 I=FP(1): K=1
2840 IF L2>HL THEN L2=HL
2850 IF I=0 THEN PRINT "BUFFER EMPTY": GOTO 2940
2860 PRINT "TURN PRINTER ON --- READY";: INPUT Z$
2870 IF K<L1 THEN 2900
2880 CP=I
2890 FOR M=1 TO F(I): LPRINT T$(I,M): NEXT M
2900 I=FP(I): K=K+1
2910 IF K>L2 THEN 2930
2920 GOTO 2870
2930 CL=K-1
2940 PRINT: GOTO 430                     'GET NEW COMMAND
3200 '----------------------------------------------------------
3210 '              R(ESTRUCTURE FROM LINE L1 TO L2)
3220 '----------------------------------------------------------
3230 S$="    "
3240 GOTO 2430                           'GET VALUE OF I FROM LIST COMMAND
3250 J=1: TN$(1)="": TN$(2)="": M=1
3260 IF T$(I,J)=X$ THEN J=J+1: GOTO 3260
3270 L4=LEN(T$(I,J))
3280 TN$(3)=RIGHT$(T$(I,J),L4)
3290 IF LEFT$(TN$(3),1)<>" " THEN 3320
3300   L4=LEN(TN$(3))-1
3310   TN$(3)=RIGHT$(TN$(3),L4): GOTO 3290
3320 P=1
3330 IF MID$(TN$(3),P,2)<>"  " THEN 3360
3340   TN$(2)=LEFT$(TN$(3),P)+RIGHT$(TN$(3),L4-P-1)
3350   L4=LEN(TN$(2)): TN$(3)=TN$(2): GOTO 3330
3360 P=P+1: IF P>=L4 THEN 3370 ELSE 3330
3370 IF RIGHT$(TN$(3),1)=CHR$(29) THEN TN$(3)=LEFT$(TN$(3),L4-1)
3380 L4=LEN(TN$(3))
3390 IF RIGHT$(TN$(3),1)=CHR$(13) THEN TN$(3)=LEFT$(TN$(3),L4-1)
3395 IF TN$(1)<>"" THEN TN$(1)=TN$(1)+" "
3400 TN$(1)=TN$(1)+TN$(3)
3410 L4=LEN(TN$(1))
3420 IF J<F(I)   THEN 3540
3430   IF L4<W-2 THEN 3510
3440     P=W-2
3450     IF MID$(TN$(1),P,1)=" " THEN 3470
3460     P=P-1: GOTO 3450
3470     T$(I,M)=S$+LEFT$(TN$(1),P)+CHR$(13)+CHR$(29)
3480     PRINT T$(I,M): M=M+1+SP(I)
3490     J=J+1: F(I)=F(I)+1: TN$(1)=RIGHT$(TN$(1),L4-P)
3500     L4=LEN(TN$(1)): IF L4>W-2 THEN 3440
3510   T$(I,M)=S$+TN$(1)+CHR$(13)+CHR$(29): PRINT T$(I,M)
3520   FOR N=M+1+SP(I) TO F(I): T$(I,N)="": NEXT N: F(I)=M+SP(I)
3530   PRINT: GOTO 2530                  'GET NEXT VALUE OF I
3540 IF L4<W-2 THEN J=J+1: GOTO 3260
3550 P=W-2
3560 IF MID$(TN$(1),P,1)=" " THEN 3580
```

(continued)

```
3570 P=P-1: GOTO 3560
3580 T$(I,M)=S$+LEFT$(TN$(1),P)+CHR$(13)+CHR$(29)
3590 TN$(1)=RIGHT$(TN$(1),L4-P): PRINT T$(I,M): M=M+1+SP(I)
3600 J=J+1: GOTO 3260
3800 '--------------------------------------------------------------
3810 '          T COMMAND (SETS TAB FOR LINES L1 TO L2)
3820 '--------------------------------------------------------------
3830 PRINT "INPUT NUMBER OF SPACE TO BE INDENTED";: INPUT S
3840 S$="": FOR C=1 TO S: S$=S$+" ": NEXT C
3850 TN$(2)="": L3=LEN(S$): GOTO 2430 'GET VALUE OF I FROM LIST COMMAND
3860 J=1
3870   IF T$(I,J)=X$ THEN 4180
3880     L4=LEN(T$(I,J))
3890     TN$(3)=RIGHT$(T$(I,J),L4)
3900     IF LEFT$(TN$(3),1)<>" " THEN 3930
3910       L4=LEN(TN$(3))-1
3920       TN$(3)=RIGHT$(TN$(3),L4): GOTO 3900
3930     TN$(1)=TN$(2)+TN$(3): L4=LEN(TN$(1)): TN$(2)=""
3940     IF L3+L4<W+3 THEN LET TN$(3)=S$+TN$(1): GOTO 4080
3950       TN$(3)=S$+TN$(1)
3960       P=W+1: SFLAG=1: L4=LEN(TN$(3))
3970       IF RIGHT$(TN$(3),1)=CHR$(29) THEN TN$(3)=LEFT$(TN$(3),L4-1)
3980       L4=LEN(TN$(3))
3990       IF RIGHT$(TN$(3),1)=CHR$(13) THEN TN$(3)=LEFT$(TN$(3),L4-1)
4000       IF MID$(TN$(3),P,1)=" " THEN 4020
4010         P=P-1: GOTO 4000
4020       TN$(2)=RIGHT$(TN$(3),L4-P)+" "
4030       TN$(1)=LEFT$(TN$(3),P)
4035       IF RIGHT$(TN$(1),1)=" " THEN P=P-1: GOTO 4030
4040       L5=LEN(TN$(2))
4050       IF LEFT$(TN$(2),1)=" " THEN TN$(2)=RIGHT$(TN$(2),L5-1):GOTO 4040
4060       IF J=F(I) THEN TN$(2)=TN$(2)+CHR$(13)+CHR$(29)
4070       TN$(3)=TN$(1)+CHR$(13)+CHR$(29)
4080     L4=LEN(TN$(3)): M=0: IF TN$(2)="" THEN 4160
4090     P=L3+3: M=M+1
4100       IF L4>=W+3 THEN 4160
4110         IF MID$(TN$(3),P,M)<>X$(M) THEN 4150
4120           IF MID$(TN$(3),P,M+1)=X$(M+1) THEN P=P+1: GOTO 4150
4130             TN$(3)=LEFT$(TN$(3),P-1)+" "+RIGHT$(TN$(3),L4-P+1)
4140             L4=L4+1: P=P+M
4150         P=P+1: IF P<W+3 THEN 4100
4155         IF L4<W+3 THEN 4090
4160     T$(I,J)=TN$(3)
4170     PRINT T$(I,J)
4180 IF J<F(I) THEN J=J+1: GOTO 3870
4190 IF T$(I,J)=X$ THEN 4230
4200   IF SP(I)=0 THEN 4230
4210     FOR M=1 TO SP(I): T$(I,J+M)=X$: NEXT M
4220     J=J+SP(I): F(I)=F(I)+SP(I)
```

(continued)

```
4230 IF LEN(TN$(2))<=3 THEN 4260
4240   TN$(1)=TN$(2): L4=LEN(TN$(1)): TN$(2)=""
4250   J=J+1: F(I)=F(I)+1: GOTO 3940
4260 PRINT: GOTO 2530                    'GET THE NEXT VALUE OF I
4400 '-----------------------------------------------------------------
4410 '                ROUTINE TO SIMULATE LINE INPUT
4420 '-----------------------------------------------------------------
4430 FOR M=1 TO 25: N$(M)="   ": NEXT M
4440 C$="": CO=3: RW=1
4450 K$=INKEY$: IF K$="" THEN 4450
4460 PRINT K$;: IF ASC(K$)=8 AND CO=3 THEN 4450
4470 IF ASC(K$)=8 THEN N$(RW)=LEFT$(N$(RW),CO-1): CO=CO-1: GOTO 4450
4480 N$(RW)=N$(RW)+K$
4490 IF ASC(K$)<>13 THEN 4510
4500 IF L$="C" THEN 1750 ELSE 1250     'END OF LINE DETECTED
4510 CO=CO+1: IF CO<W+1 THEN 4450
4520 '
4530 'CHECK IF LAST BYTE IS SPACE
4540 IF K$<>" " THEN 4570
4550 RW=RW+1: CO=3
4560 PRINT TAB(4);: GOTO 4450
4570 CT=0: L=LEN(N$(RW)): C$=""
4580 IF MID$(N$(RW),L,1)=" " THEN 4620
4590 C$=MID$(N$(RW),L,1)+C$
4600 CT=CT+1: MID$(N$(RW),L,1)=""
4610 L=L-1: GOTO 4580
4620 N$(RW)=LEFT$(N$(RW),L)+CHR$(13)+CHR$(29)
4630 P=4:'IF L=W+1 THEN 4670
4640 IF MID$(N$(RW),P,1)<>" " THEN 4660
4650   N$(RW)=LEFT$(N$(RW),P-1)+" "+RIGHT$(N$(RW),L-P+1): P=P+1
4660 P=P+1: L=LEN(N$(RW)): IF L<W+3 AND P<W+3 THEN 4640
4670 PRINT N$(RW)
4680 RW=RW+1: CO=3+CT
4690 N$(RW)=N$(RW)+C$
4700 PRINT TAB(4) C$;: GOTO 4450
4800 '-----------------------------------------------------------------
4810 '   S COMMAND (INSERTS SPACES BETWEEN LINES FROM L1 TO L2)
4820 '-----------------------------------------------------------------
4830 X$="   "+CHR$(13)+CHR$(29)
4840 PRINT "INPUT NUMBER OF SPACES BETWEEN LINES";: INPUT SP
4850 IF SP>3 THEN 4860 ELSE 4870
4860 PRINT "INPUT A NUMBER NOT GREATER THAN 3": GOTO 4840
4870 GOTO 2430                          'GET VALUE OF I FROM LIST COMMAND
4880 P=0: Y=F(I)
4890 FOR M=1 TO F(I)
4900   IF T$(I,M)=X$ THEN 4920
4910     P=P+1: TM$(P)=T$(I,M)
4920 NEXT M
4930 F(I)=P: P=1
```

(continued)

```
4940 FOR M=1 TO F(I)
4950   T$(I,P)=TM$(M)
4960   IF SP=0 THEN 5000
4970     FOR N=1 TO SP
4980       T$(I,P+N)=X$
4990     NEXT N
5000     P=P+SP+1
5010   NEXT M
5020   F(I)=P-1: SP(I)=SP
5030 SFLAG=1
5040 IF F(I)>=Y THEN 5100
5050   FOR M=F(I)+1 TO Y
5060     T$(I,M)=""
5070   NEXT M
5100 GOTO 2530                              'GET NEXT VALUE OF I
9999 END
```

Chapter 11

PPP 2   MORTGAGE is modified to allow the interest rate to be changed each year.

```
100 '*******************************************************
110 '*      ARMTAB (ADJUSTABLE RATE MORTGAGE TABLES)      *
120 '*******************************************************
130 A$=" "
140 PRINT"* AMORTIZATION TABLE *"
150 '----------GET INPUT-----------------------------------
160 PRINT"AMOUNT BORROWED (PRINCIPAL)";: INPUT PR
170 PRINT"NUMBER OF MONTHS TO PAY";: INPUT MO
180 IF MO<= 0 OR INT(MO) <> MO THEN 170
190 PRINT"INTEREST RATE PER YEAR (6.5% = 6.5)";: INPUT R1
200 '----------CALCULATE INITIAL QUANTITIES-----------------
210 R = R1 * .01 / 12: P=PR: M=MO: J=0
220 GOSUB 560
230 '----------CALCULATE & PRINT TABLE--------------------
240 TI = 0: TP = 0: SP = 0
250 PRINT"MONTH    PRINCIPAL    INTEREST  +  PRINCIPAL  =  MONTHLY"
260 PRINT"NUMBER   OWED         PAYMENT      PAYMENT       PAYMENT"
270 FOR K = 1 TO 60: PRINT"-";: NEXT K: PRINT
280 F3$=" ##    $###,###.##    $#,###.##     $#,###.##      $#,###.##"
290 FOR J = 1 TO MO
300   I1 = P * R
310   P1 = E - I1
320   IF J = MO THEN P1 = P: I1 = E - P1
330   PRINT USING F3$; J, P, I1, P1, E
340   TI = TI + I1
350   TP = TP + P1 + I1
360   SP = SP + P1
```

(continued)

```
370    P = P - P1
380    IF J=MO THEN 420
390    IF J/12=INT(J/12) THEN PRINT"MORE (Y/N)";:INPUT D$ ELSE GOTO 410
400      IF D$ = "N" THEN 420 ELSE GOSUB 530
410 NEXT J: J=J-1
420 PRINT"PRESS <RET> TO SEE TOTALS FOR";J;"MONTHS";: INPUT D$
430 '----------SUMMARY------------------------------------
440 PRINT TAB(21);"TOTAL          TOTAL          TOTAL"
450 PRINT TAB(21);"INTEREST       PRINCIPAL       PAYMENTS"
460 FOR K = 1 TO 60: PRINT"-";: NEXT K: PRINT
470 F4$="$##,###.##      $###,###.##      $###,###.##"
480 PRINT TAB(19);: PRINT USING F4$; TI, SP, TP
490 '----------AGAIN?------------------------------------
500 PRINT"AGAIN (Y = YES)";: INPUT A$: IF A$="Y" THEN 130
510 END
520 '======  SUBROUTINE TO ADJUST RATE AND MONTHLY PAYMENT =======
530 PRINT"CURRENT RATE = ";R1
540 INPUT"ENTER RATE FOR NEXT YEAR";R1
550 R=R1*.01/12: M=MO-J
560 E = (P * R * (1 + R)^M) / ((1 + R)^M-1)
570 RETURN
```

PPP 3 SEQDEMO1 allows for adding data to data file 'ORIG'.

```
4 '------------------------------------------------------------
6 '              SEQDEMO1 (PROGRAM TO ADD DATA TO FILE)
8 '------------------------------------------------------------
100 PRINT "THIS PROGRAM WILL ALLOW YOU TO ADD DATA TO AN EXISTING"
110 PRINT "SEQUENTIAL FILE CALLED 'ORIG'."
120 PRINT "HERE IS THE DATA ALREADY ON 'ORIG':": K=0
130 OPEN "I",1,"ORIG"
140 OPEN "O",2,"TEMP"
150 IF EOF(1) THEN 200
160    INPUT #1,M$,Z$,D
170    PRINT #2,M$;",";Z$;",";D
180    PRINT USING "\          \ \                    \ ##.##";M$,Z$,D
190    K=K+1: GOTO 150
200 PRINT "** ";K;" RECORDS ON FILE **"
210 K=K+1
220 PRINT "ENTER THE NEW DATA:"
230 PRINT "RECORD #";K
240 PRINT TAB(12);"PRODUCT CODE >>>";: INPUT C$
250 IF C$="-1" THEN 320
260    PRINT TAB(12);"PRODUCT NAME >>>";: INPUT N$
270    IF N$="-1" THEN 320
280      PRINT TAB(12);"PRICE >>>>>>>>>";: INPUT P
290      IF P<0 THEN 320
300        PRINT #2,C$;",";N$;",";P
310        K=K+1: GOTO 230
320 CLOSE 1: CLOSE 2
330 KILL "ORIG"
```

(continued)

```
340 NAME "TEMP" AS "ORIG"
350 PRINT "HERE IS THE DATA NOW ON 'ORIG':": K=0
360 OPEN "I",1,"ORIG"
370 IF EOF(1) THEN 410
380   INPUT #1,M$,Z$,D
390   PRINT USING "\         \ \                 \ ##.##";M$,Z$,D
400   K=K+1: GOTO 370
410 CLOSE 1
420 PRINT "**** ";K;" RECORDS ON FILE ****"
430 END
```

Index